JUNE 17-1971- FEH.

ON & OFF
SOUNDINGS

Caribee running off before increasing Norther crossing Tongue of the Ocean, Bahamas. Photo by Carleton Mitchell

ON & OFF
SOUNDINGS

EDITED BY

W I L L I A M   H .   T A Y L O R

INTRODUCTION BY

H E R B E R T   L .   S T O N E

D. VAN NOSTRAND COMPANY, Inc.

TORONTO   NEW YORK   LONDON

NEW YORK
D. Van Nostrand Company, Inc., 250 Fourth Avenue, New York 3

TORONTO
D. Van Nostrand Company (Canada), Ltd., 228 Bloor Street, Toronto

LONDON
Macmillan & Company, Ltd. St. Martin's Street, London, W.C. 2

Library of Congress Catalogue Card Number 51—12776

DESIGNED BY EUGENE V. CONNETT

FIRST EDITION

Acknowledgments

THE STORIES *and articles in this book appeared in their original form in* Yachting. *Some of them have also appeared in books and other publications, and the editors wish to express their appreciation of the cooperation of publishers and copyright holders in making it possible for us to use them in "On & Off Soundings." The following stories have appeared in the publications indicated below.*

"Across the Great Bahama Bank," in "The Cruise of Diablesse," publishers, Dodd, Mead & Co.

"An Accomplishment of Sail," in "The Commodore's Story," publishers, Ives Washburn, Inc.; copyright, Vincent Gilpin, co-author of the book with Commodore Munroe.

"Passage Sails," in "Yacht Sails, Care and Handling," publishers, W. W. Norton.

"Pointers on Handling Light Sails," in "Yacht Sails, Care and Handling," publishers, W. W. Norton.

"Handling Square Sail," in "Navigation for the Amateur," publishers, Outing Co.

"Trooping from Dunkirk," in "Yachting World and Power Craft," British magazine.

Contents

PART I

PART II

Introduction

BY HERBERT L. STONE

WHEN THE editors of *Yachting* selected and prepared the material for "Just Cruising" two years ago, we found our task a difficult one for just one reason—an embarrassment of riches in the way of material. In culling over the issues of the magazine for the past 40 years we had selected many times more stories and articles, as worthy of reproduction in book form, than the limitations of practical book publishing made it possible to use.

For that reason the first book was limited to the general subject of cruising, and even in that category we eventually had to shelve several times as many good yarns as we could include in the book. This, and the excellent reception which "Just Cruising" has received from the reading public, seemed to indicate that another book of selected material from the magazine was in order, and "On & Off Soundings" is the result. We hope you will like it at least as well as you did "Just Cruising," perhaps even better.

In "On & Off Soundings" we have widened the scope of the material to include other fields besides cruising. Since yachtsmen are today's heirs to the traditions of the days when most of the world's trade was carried in sailing vessels we have included a few yarns of deep water, coastal and Great Lakes sailing vessels, whalers and fishermen. The part played by yachtsmen in naval and other activities afloat in two wars is recognized by the inclusion of several wartime yarns, ranging from the comedy of "Old Gentlemen's War" and "Two Bells and a Half" to the adventure of "Trooping from Dunkirk" and "Lifeboat Passage."

High adventure, gales and shipwreck always made good

reading, so we have included, perhaps, a disproportionate number of such tales. Some of these, like "My Boat Foundered!" and "Wreck of the *Merlan*," are worth more than casual reading because they combine, along with gripping narrative, observation on the causes of and the ways of avoiding misadventure afloat. To balance the adventure yarns we have included a sprinkling of stories of the more peaceful and characteristic aspects of cruising and sailing, like "Happy Ending," "Crickin'," and "Goodbye Pacific, Hello Maine."

With 44 years of *Yachting* to select from, we have included some of the best of the recent stories and articles along with those of years ago—by pure coincidence the oldest article, "To Each Man His Craft," published in 1915, and the newest in point of writing and publication, "An Error in Navigation," 1951, are by the same author, J. T. Rowland, though the latter yarn deals with an incident of many years ago.

Part II of "On & Off Soundings," as in "Just Cruising," is concerned with the "how to do it" type of article in which yachtsmen, even those of long experience, can usually find something of instruction and interest. Here again the scope has been broadened, with a number of articles on racing technique, on retirement afloat, as well as on navigation, sails, engines, ship handling under sail and power, and the like. An article on handling square rigged vessels may seem decidedly out of the realm of practical advice in these days of high powered engines and ultramodern racing rigs, but we feel that many modern sailors are interested in knowing the technique of handling the old wind ships, as expounded in "Handling Square Rigged Vessels," by the late Captain Edmund I. Morton, who was mate in several vessels in which I sailed in my and his young days.

So we offer you a mixed cargo, and without further introduction, we leave you to take off the hatches and, as Jerry Graham would put it in deepwater diction, "break bulk."

PART I

1

An Error in Navigation

by JOHN T. ROWLAND

[1951]

Daryl was built in Salem, Mass., for Dr. Grenfell's medical mission on the Labrador. Only 30 feet long but a fine little sea boat, she carried a moderate spread of sail and a ponderous oil engine, with fuel capacity for 500 miles. After several years' service in those rugged waters she was replaced by a newer and larger boat. The Doctor sold her to the Hudson's Bay Company for use at a new post in Baffin Land, and since I had sailed a number of boats north to the Mission in previous summers the Doctor gave me first whack at delivering her.

My answer, consisting of the single word "Yes," was on its way back before the wires had cooled from the invitation.

This was the spring of my senior year at Yale (1911) and a long-suffering Faculty gave me special final exams and permitted me to be absent from my own graduation, for we had a long way to go—Bob and I. Bob English, two years my senior, was the best companion and the most unscarable person—with the possible exception of Dr. Grenfell—that I've ever been ship-mates with. He was also an outstanding natural mechanic. The only time I ever saw him look glum was when we made our first inspection of the *Daryl*. I think even the Doctor experienced a qualm over letting us shove off for those lonely sub-Arctic waters in which no boat so small had ever sailed so far north.

This was not because of *Daryl's* diminutive size—we had discounted that in advance—but on account of her truly deplorable condition. She had been for several years attached to the Mission post at Mecatina Island, where the resident physician was no doubt a better doctor than a boatman. She was battered, dirty and dishevelled. Her sails were patched and her rigging hung in bights. Her insides were a mess, and the motor . . .

"I think they've been running this bunch of junk on seal oil!" was all Bob could say. It was plastered with some black, gummy substance and held together with wire and surgeon's tape. Worst of all—and this really gave us pause—the stern bearing had come adrift and was revolving with the propeller under *Daryl's* stern.

"Well, Chief," I told Bob, "if you can get the thing to run I'll help out with the sails and maybe we can jackass her back to St. Anthony for overhaul."

Thus began an outstanding small boat voyage. True, *Daryl* was a decked vessel and not an open boat, but in view of her size and the distance travelled along sub-Arctic shores, I question if it has ever been equalled. One of its episodes involved a navigational mystery that has never been solved, though I have told it to many shipmates and we have pored over charts and current tables by the hour. Perhaps the best explanation was Bob's. "The *Daryl* just has a horseshoe, Skipper. We can't go wrong if we try!" Perhaps—but I was plenty scared.

The Chief made the engine run. We limped down the Strait of Belle Isle with a shaft vibration which, even at slow speed, seemed likely to rip off the keel, and with the booms of our bagging sails topped up to keep them from dragging in the water. It was rather a nerve racking trip. I thought of it years later while crawling across the English Channel in a destroyer that had her bow bent around at an angle of 90 degrees. At least, on this earlier cruise, there were no lurking submarines to dispute our passage, and we made St. Anthony at last. This is a harbor near the north end of Newfoundland, and was headquarters of the Grenfell Mission, with a marine railway on which to haul *Daryl* out for repairs.

The Chief had purchased over $100.00 worth of spare parts from the builders of her engine in New York, and he had a most extraordinary set of tools. The latter he eventually gave to his successor as engineer (a full-bred Eskimo whom he trained in a remarkably short time) but the spare parts, we both felt, should be paid for by the Company. The Factor at our destination offered to give us a reciept for everything else, including stores left on board; but the spare parts, for some reason, stuck in his crop.

"Very well," said the Chief, "if you don't wish to receipt for them I will throw them overboard, *including those I have put into the engine.* Then you may as well take the boat and sink her too!" He would have done it, what's more.

We remained ten days in St. Anthony, Bob, as he expressed it, playing a joke on her antiquated motor while I attended to the hull and rig. When we had finished she travelled twice as fast as she had on the creep down the Strait. That engine was really a museum piece, albeit wholly practical for the job. It burned kerosene and had a pair of immense, spherical bulbs on the cylinder heads that glowed cherry-red when the motor was running. Being smack in the middle of the small cabin, they constituted quite a hazard. We were always afraid of falling upon one in a seaway and being burned fatally before we could get off.

We also acquired a shipmate at St. Anthony in the person of Old George Ford—a kind, gentle and wholly admirable individual of part Eskimo descent. Dr. Grenfell gave us Old George at the last moment as pilot for the northern coast, since I had never been so far north and the charts then existing were remarkable chiefly for what they left out. Probably not one in ten fishing schooners that went "down along" the Labrador every summer even had a chart on board—nor could the skipper have read it. The "Coast Pilot" in common use consisted of a doggerel verse that was handed down from father to son. This gave the compass courses of the "proper schooner runs" and went on interminably, since the coast is long. I once knew quite a bit of it but can now recall only a single verse—and am not too sure of that:

"From Grandy Head steer North by East till Georges Island is
    come by;
Then let her go at East-northeast to where the White Bear
    Islands lie."

The purpose of these "Directions" was to keep a vessel in
known waters where many a keel had ploughed before. I could
save much distance by plotting a straight course on the chart
from cape to cape, but when I first laid her head on the empty
horizon Old George's dismay knew no bounds. The second day
out I had to reprimand him for secretly altering course, and
when we reached northern waters I found that his knowledge
consisted chiefly of dog-sled routes along the shore. Nevertheless, he had one bit of local knowledge which probably saved
our lives. Poor chap, he must have suffered acutely most of the
time, yet he never showed resentment and in all dealings with
the natives he was our interpreter, counsellor and guide. He
loved the Chief and never tired of listening to his rendition of
popular songs on the mouth organ and vocal improvisations on
"Casey Jones." At the end of the voyage he entered the service
of the Hudson's Bay Company at one of the northern posts, and
there, I believe, he died.

For a month we made our way northward through ice and fog
along the island-studded coast to Cape Mugford, where an easterly gale drove us to refuge in a landlocked cove that we might
never have found but for the pilotage of an ancient Eskimo,
whom we took aboard at nightfall—kayak and all—in Mugford
Tickle. Sitting on the forward deck, without benefit of compass,
he guided us through a channel so intricate that I could scarcely
find my way out in broad daylight. The water grew calm and
the wind suddenly ceased. All about us were high hills barely
discernible through a downpour of sleety rain. "Anchor now,"
he said to Old George. We did, and found seven fathoms and
a good sticky bottom. Beyond the nearer hills we could hear
the strife of tide and roar of wind sweeping into Mugford Tickle.

There was shelter here but not much else—and the summer
was passing. After three days in this dreary gunkhole Bob and

I decided to tackle the weather outside. At this period the chart of the Labrador, dating from surveys made by His Majesty's ships in 1870 and earlier, consisted largely of dotted lines to show the probable trend of the coast, interspersed with such legends as "Heavy pack-ice encountered here" and "Numerous islands in this vicinity." I carried, also, a sketch map on which Dr. Grenfell had been working for several seasons and which, while far from accurate or complete, did show more detail than was vouchsafed by the Admiralty's publication. North of Cape Mugford the coast grows high and bold, with cliffs of several thousand feet and deep inlets—old glacial fjords running back into the mountain axis that parallels the coast.

We waited till noon the next day for the wind to moderate, if it would, and then drove *Daryl* out through Mugford Tickle. We had to double the Cape, which rises nearly 2000 feet on its seaward side. A tremendous sea had been kicked up by the solid week's gale. In the troughs one appeared to drop out of the world, and from the crests one could see a thunderous surf crashing against the perpendicular cliffs, with spray flung to incredible heights up the sheer wall.

"That," said the Chief, "would be a swell place to go ashore!" He had hardly spoken when the engine died. Foolishly, I had been skirting the Cape. It lay dead to leeward and less than half a mile away.

Bob dove into the engine room like a prairie dog into his hole. George and I gave each other a startled look and snatched the stops off our furled sails. It was blowing too hard for the mainsail, but we gave her jib and jigger—more to be doing something than because we hoped they would do much good. In the deep troughs of the sea we were practically becalmed but on each crest the canvas would fill with a bang that threatened to blow it away. Each time we topped a sea the cliffs appeared nearer. The Chief, working on his back under the motor, grunted ambiguously when I asked what was wrong. Presently his head emerged, smeared with grease. "How long have I got?" he asked.

"Maybe 20 minutes—with luck."

"One connecting rod bent and the big-end bearing frozen. I'll see what I can do."

Our engine was ponderous and its parts were large, heavy, and more accessible than in the modern marine motor. Yet it seemed impossible that any man could make that repair in less than an hour's time, at the very least. I offered to help but was told to get out of the light.

I climbed back into the cockpit and gave Old George the bad news. He nodded gravely and remarked it was perhaps as well that his wife had died the year before. We sat there saying little—just watching the cliffs approach.

All at once I spied a small, sandy cove in a crevice of the Cape, some distance ahead on our lee bow. It offered no protection, but a vessel might possibly be run ashore there. Old George saw it too, and together we sprang to the main halyards and ran the sail up. As the boat heeled over with this added burden, sulphurous language issued from the cabin; but we were too busy to pay much heed. It was a race against time—the most exciting one in which I have ever taken part. George tended sheet while I jockeyed her over the seas for everything I knew. It might have been one minute or ten when it became clear we should not make it. Higher and steeper the seas were mounting up—with roaring, foaming crests that picked the little boat up and hurled her bodily toward the shore. Old George's face, which had been tense, settled into an expression of resignation that I envied. Then I thought of Bob, trapped like a rat down below. It would be better to face it on deck. . . . I dropped the wheel and slid forward to the hatch.

"Chief!" I was shouting—when there came a muffled bang under our stern.

Silence. Then, BOOM—BOOM—BOOM. Silence again. BOOM—BOOM, BOOM, BOOM, BOOM, BOOM. . . .

Bob stuck his head up, wiping sweat and grease out of his eyes. "She'll run now—after a fashion," he said. "For Jesus' sake, get that sail off her before I fry myself on the hot bulbs!"

In 15 minutes Cape Mugford had disappeared in the welter of mist and spray astern, and *Daryl* was poking her nose hopefully into a sea that became more civil the further we went from land. With the quick forgetfulness that God grants sailors, we were soon joking about the close shave. We ran north with our booms well off and the engine limping frantically to keep up with the boat. I learned now what the Chief had done. He had disconnected the bent connecting rod from the crank shaft and removed the rod and its piston bodily from the motor—a Herculean task for so short a time, particularly under the conditions. This left the motor short one functioning cylinder, but it *ran.* Later on, he replaced the bent rod with a spare one and hooked her up again.

We felt so jubilant that for a time no one paid much attention to the weather. The Chief came up into the cockpit and blew strident chords through his mouth organ, which fitted nicely the temper of the day. At nightfall we crept into a sheltered bight and dropped anchor. Bob labored on the engine while George and I tried to get some rest. At first dawn, which comes early in that latitude, we ran out to sea. Long, shelving points of rock and wicked reefs lay all about us and we marvelled how *Daryl* had ever gotten in there in the dark. A few miles north we came to Hebron, a post and Mission of the Moravian Brethren.

This was a Sunday—August 13—and I find it thus recorded in my journal: "Anchor at Hebron about 10:30 A.M. Wind fresh NE with rain. Glass rising rapidly till noon, then wind hauls ENE and freshens more, and glass starts down again; fog and intermittent rain—very cold and nasty. . . . Well anchored in shoal water off Post. No danger of dragging if anchors are clear. Not sure, because I was at wheel when they went down and George, who was forward, did not notice."

Behind that restrained comment one detects a note of exasperation—the more acute since the Chief had been ordered to his bunk with a high temperature and a touch of flu. I went ashore for medicine and barged in on a Sunday service. Twenty or thirty Eskimos, resplendent in their best koolitahs and beaded sealskin boots, were singing hymns and reading the responses *out of books.* When I complimented Dr. Schmidt on the accomplishment and expressed wonder at hearing the natives speak German, he looked

startled and replied with some asperity that the service had been
conducted *in Eskimo!* Despite this *faux pas* he treated me kindly
and sent me back aboard with aspirin and Epsom salts.

The next day's journal reads: "August 14. Light air South, fog
and rain. Damn this weather! How shall we ever get north before summer is gone? Under way at 11 :30. Wind shifts to NE
and freshens. Glass falling. Weather offshore cloudy and threatening but not thick. Hell of a tumble outside but smashed her on
until 6 :00 P.M., when we made Anchorage Cove in Big Island in
mouth of Saglek Bay. Only 20 miles for eight hours' run! Fog
thick, cold and dreary. So ends."

The Chief insisted on resuming duty. The breakdown off Cape
Mugford had been caused by a stoppage in one of the small
copper tubes through which lubricating oil was supposed to flow
by gravity from an automatic oiler. The Chief had cleared this
when he installed the spare parts but there was no way to tell
if it was functioning properly except by tearing the whole works
down. I urged him to wait, but he would have none of it, and the
engine was ready for a morning start.

The wind meanwhile had drawn into the East and freshened,
with a falling glass. Rain squalls replaced the fog. We were cold
and tired, and the Chief was still sick. Old George reminded
us that the worst part of the coast lay ahead. But there was
still a long way to go, and the wind was fair.

Offshore it freshened until *Daryl* had all she could take, and
along the eastern horizon lay a strange, whitish loom which
George told us was the "blink" of ice. Ahead on our lee bow the
forbidding black coastline rose into snowcapped peaks. When
pressed, *Daryl* would do seven knots. Bob opened his throttle
full and came up to enjoy the ride. At the wheel, I was having
difficulty to jockey her through the stronger gusts. George looked
as though he would have liked to be somewhere else, but the Chief
drew a deep breath and roared out his latest version of "Casey
Jones." It would have been sensible to reef—but the going was
much too good!

As the day wore on the wind moderated somewhat and brought
in rain and vapor. One may have, on the Labrador, a gale of wind

and a dense fog that swirls and eddies like snow. A fine combination that makes with floating ice and uncharted islands and reefs! We lost sight of the coast; but I had taken a bearing on a bold promontory which jutted out far to the north, and steered to clear that by a mile or two. We thought it might be in the neighborhood of Nachvak Bay.

Daryl kept going like a racehorse. Now and then, through a tunnel in the mist, we would catch a glimpse of the high, wild coast of black basalt rock with the seas dashing against its base. Once a small island, or large tidewater rock, rose directly in our path. A big vessel would have butted her brains out before she could be turned, but *Daryl* spun handily and ducked around the island's leeward point, while the seas that broke over it wetted down her deck.

Old George, thrown out of his bunk by the turmoil, crawled up into the cockpit with a white face and crouched against the end of the house. I was beginning to be a little anxious over the prospect of darkness, fog and wind; and even the Chief's face had lost its cheery grin. Suddenly Old George pointed ahead and shouted, "Ice!" We saw nothing, and knew that Old George couldn't either. I wondered if he was going off his chump. Then we heard a deep *"Boom"* like the detonation of a naval gun.

"There she is again!" yelled George. "You hear it? A big berg!"

The seas break against a large iceberg as on a cliff, and where the berg has a scooped-out side (as is often the case) a hollow reverberation results. I had heard it before, but not under conditions quite like this. For precious seconds I sat rooted at the wheel while the sweat seemed to freeze on my neck.

Closer! Much closer the sound rang out again and through the mist I could detect a white loom of breakers all along on our lee side, as well as ahead. This time there was no chance to swing *Daryl* off the wind!

I spun the wheel up and yelled to Bob and George to flatten down the sheets. We jammed her on the wind and held our breath—and prayed.

She rose over a big sea, shivered and stopped dead. Without

a motor that would have been the end. But, burdened as it was, the old oil engine kept her moving. I blessed the Chief's judgment in not having shut it off. *Daryl* staggered to windward against a dozen successive seas. Slowly the warning sound drew aft. When it was off our port quarter I let her head fall off to give the sails a good full. She sprang ahead once more and soon the iceberg was lost in the welter astern.

Bob looked at Old George, huddled in the forward corner of the cockpit, and then at me and shook his head. I knew what he meant. It was still daylight but evening was fast coming on. We couldn't ram on like this through the night. And yet, where to go? I hoped Nachvak Bay might provide a solution, and that *we could find it when we got there.* It would not be quite wholesome to go roaring in blind on such a coast!

By mid-afternoon we had doused the mainsail. This somewhat reduced our speed but *Daryl* went more comfortably so. The Chief managed to boil the kettle, and we had a reviving mug-up all around. Old George advised strongly against trying to make a harbor in Nachvak Bay. He had once been at the H. B. C. post there and told us the place offered no shelter for a small craft and was little better than a trap. He had seen fishing schooners capsized at anchor by the terrific squalls that swept down the funnel-shaped fjord. This did not sound very good, but neither did the coast further north appear too inviting on the chart. It was a succession of mountainous headlands and deep, shelterless fjords. Dr. Grenfell's sketch map, which was on a larger scale than the Admiralty chart, showed a group of small islands off Kamaktorvik Point, some 15 miles to the northward of Nachvak Bay. When I called George's attention to these he almost jumped with joy.

"The very thing, sure! Them's the —— Islands" (an Eskimo name I never did master). "There's good harbors in among them; I've been there many's the time!"

So the next thing was to find them. I knew, of course, what our position *ought* to be, but there are so many sources of error in the kind of sailing we had been doing that I could not be positive of it within a radius of several miles. Currents, lee-

way, the difficulty of steering a straight course under such conditions, all contributed to the uncertainty. Yet, in that low visibility, we had to hit those little islands on the nose.

"Take care you don't run past," George went on, "or we'll
be into the old Arctic pack."

I knew what he had in mind—the heavy floes of pack ice
that drift down out of Davis Strait in the summer. They frequently cover acres—even miles—and may be *anywhere,* and
are a far worse danger than land or even bergs on a black,
stormy night. This was probably the "blink" we had seen.

Old George did not chide me for disregarding his advice,
several hours back, to make harbor while we still could, but I
knew what he must be thinking while Bob and I discussed the
leeway and set. We were still debating this when there came one
of those miracles that sometimes happen at sea. The mist lifted
and gave us a glimpse of the coast. It lasted only a few moments,
but that was enough. Directly abeam, to port, lay the promontory
for which I had been steering, and Old George recognized it as
the White Handkerchief on the north side of Nachvak Bay. Our
relief knew no bounds. True, we still had to make the islands
through the fog, but at least we knew where we were and could
lay a course which, if the chart as right, ought to bring us to
them before dark.

I put Old George to steer while Bob and I went below. It was
the first time since early morning that I had left the wheel. Bob
brewed more coffee on the red-hot ignition bulbs. We had another
mug-up and a smoke while I spread out Grenfell's chart and laid
off the course. It was 4:30 P.M. and we had perhaps three hours
of daylight left.

It struck me that there was something queer about this new
course, but I was in a hurry to take some coffee up to George,
and, once on deck, I grabbed the wheel so that he could swallow
it down. The wind was blowing harder again and, what with
steering and watching my sails, I became too absorbed to question the course any more.

At 5:30 Bob relieved me and I went down to catch a nap,
leaving orders for a sharp look-out and to give me a call at the

first sight of land. The motor was running smoothly and the rhythmic motion of the little boat may have lulled me to sleep. I do not exactly know when, out of my subconscious, came a sudden realization of what it was that had bothered me about the course. In plotting it, *I had made an error of forty-five degrees!*

Understand, in those northern waters the magnetic needle points to northwest instead of true north, due to the proximity of the North magnetic pole. On Dr. Grenfell's chart, this had been taken care of by printing a reference compass that conformed with the local variation. Courses laid off by that required no correction. I knew this perfectly well, but, due possibly to fatigue, I had gone ahead mechanically and applied the local correction as though working on the Admiralty chart. This fantastic error would make *Daryl* miss our longed-for island by more than ten miles, out to sea!

With a powerful vessel, it would have been a simple matter to lay off upon the chart our erroneous course and the distance travelled, and from that position to plot a new course to our destination; but the case was not quite so easy for us. Ragged storm clouds and scud were streaming in from the east and even through the rain a heavy, black bank shrouded the horizon. With darkness coming on, I had no mind to go hunting for some little islands that lay only a few miles to windward of that wicked, rockbound coast; for if I missed them by ever so little we would not know it until we ran into the cliffs. George lay snoring in his bunk, for which I was grateful; but I made a clean breast of my mistake to the Chief. He laughed!

We had another mug-up and talked things over. Since we must already be well to windward of the islands there seemed nothing for it but to hold our course and keep a sharp look-out for ice.

In half an hour a new storm burst upon us. The Chief and I put *Daryl* under forestaysail and reefed mizzen. Then I took the wheel while he went below and slowed the motor. When he got back on deck darkness was coming on. We decided to let her jog through the night and keep all hands on deck, with one man steering and the other two watching for ice. But since Bob had

had no rest at all, I roused out Old George to take the wheel for a bit.

The Chief turned in but could not sleep—not, as he quite emphatically told me, through any anxiety, but because the sloweddown motor offended his soul. She was apt to "gum up" when running slow. So he came on deck and I went down and went to sleep. It probably was not a deep sleep, because I was both worried and guilty over my stupid mistake, but for which we should long since have been peacefully lying in a sheltered cove.

A heavy roll threw me out of my bunk, but there was still a little daylight, so I climbed back, determined to get what rest I could. To copy one of George Washington's famous remarks, I lay down to think and not to sleep. We had been under way some four hours since leaving Nachvak. Assuming an average speed of five knots, we had come at least 20 miles, which would put us well north of the islands even had we been on the correct course. The wicked coast under our lee was a menace, but the greatest danger was *ice*. This might be lessened by heaving-to, but in that event we would drift toward shore, and in storm and darkness might find ourselves, before morning, in a worse predicament still. We were in a mess, and a real one. Nothing for it but to keep on slowly as we were going, and trust to . . .

A great shout from the cockpit brought me up all standing. My head caromed off a deck-beam and I fell against the engine, but got off with a scorched sweater and a burnt thumb. The shouting kept up, and there was a quality in it I could not understand. I tried to get on deck. Miraculously, the vessel's motion had ceased, but she was still heeled over and the cabin floor was slippery with oil. It was like trying to run in a dream.

The Chief's head and shoulders were framed in the open hatch. "Land in sight, Skipper, all around us!"

Then George's gleeful voice: "That's them, all right. That's the islands! Who'd have believed—we come straight as a die!"

In the gathering darkness I could see the Chief's quizzical grin, which seemed to say—"Now, how do you account for *that?*" I grabbed the throttle and brought the engine to "stop."

Through sheer humanity, we had not taken Old George into

our confidence, but that a little boat should make a perfect land-fall in such weather, was a matter for congratulation *even if the course were correct*. Old George said he "had never seen the like, nor had never sailed with such a fine navigator before. How much did you allow, sor, for leeway and set?"

"Oh, just enough," I answered weakly, while the Chief grinned discreetly behind Old George's back.

The storm blew itself out overnight, and the next day dawned bright and clear. We loitered long enough to take some sights and establish the position of the islands—which were correctly plotted on Dr. Grenfell's chart. Off to the westward the high peaks of Labrador lifted their snowy heads over the horizon. We could see the crest of Mr. Razorback and our compass gave the correct magnetic bearing. We had come, as Old George said, "straight as a die." But how?

There must, of course, have been some compensating error, but it was too great to be ascribed to current, bad steering or lee-way. Indeed, current would have acted the other way. What, then, could it have been? My own theory, which may have interest in the light of recent discoveries, is that it could only have been due to a local ore body which disturbed the compass.

Magnetite, the magnetic ore of iron, does exist on that coast. I do not know that it has ever been discovered in that precise locality, but even today the northern Labrador is seldom traversed and little known. Magnetite sometimes occurs in large masses, in association with Archaean gneisses and schists. These last form the very backbone of the Labrador and a large mass of magnetite would cause a local disturbance of the compass, so this theory seems the most logical that can be produced.

Our compass showed no aberration within the islands them-selves. Still, if such an ore body existed in the vicinity of Nachvak Bay, it might have deflected our course for a time, and we might have run past its influence before the islands were reached.

Whatever the mysterious cause that bent our course, there was another even greater. That was the force or circumstance—call it what you will—which led me to make a stupid error that precisely compensated. So precisely, indeed, that we entered the islands by the proper channel and were in their midst before we saw land at all! Had I not erred we would certainly have missed them and might easily have lost our lives, for only a few miles north we did encounter, in broad light of day, the old Arctic pack.

I don't know the answer—but it makes a person think. If you choose to call it a miracle I won't complain.

2

Old Gentlemen's War

by WESTON MARTYR

[1948]

I HAVE A LARGE NUMBER of old friends and ex-shipmates among American ocean-racing men. I hesitate, therefore, to spin this yarn, because I know the dastards will not believe it. I don't blame them. They know me as a sour old sailor with white whiskers, who likes his own way and refuses to be ordered about by anybody. They tell me I wear terrible clothes and use worse language, so when I tell them I commanded one of His Majesty's Ships during the recent Trouble . . . Well, I can hear them: "Wot! Old Wes a Captain in the Navy! Haw, *haw,* HAW."

I will admit that the last thing on earth I ever expected myself to be was skipper of a vessel flying the White Ensign. But the war created some remarkable effects.

I did my best to get myself into the Navy as soon as war broke out. It seemed to me I was just exactly the kind of man the Navy needed and I called in person at the Admiralty to tell them so. Unfortunately, I did not manage to see any Admirals. The only man I did see was the Petty Officer at the front door. He took one look at me and said "Beat it." Naturally that led to trouble. I . . . Well, never mind. But I didn't join the Navy that time.

After that I judged the best method of approach would be to write to the First Lord of the Admiralty. I told him the sort of man I thought I was and that I was ready to take on anything, from his job down. But his secretary must have lost my letter, or

something, for I got no reply. So I wrote to the First Sea Lord.
I wrote four times. I did not even get an acknowledgment. So I
said to hell with the Royal Navy and joined the Royal Observer
Corps out of spite. I knew the Navy had made a bad mistake and
I knew the Navy would be sorry for it, sooner or later. I was
right. Less than five years later, early in '44, I heard an Admiral
on the radio saying the Navy was in urgent need of men who
could handle small ships. He called out loudly for volunteers.

Well, I know Admirals don't sing out for help unless they are
in a real mess; and I knew the country couldn't afford a mess
then, with the Normandy invasion just ahead of us. So I judged
I'd better help. I sent in my name. And I got a prompt, affirmative
reply *this* time. My telegram told me to stand by for orders, so
I packed by sea bag in a hurry and stood by. At the end of four
months I was still standing by, so I decided to let the Navy get on
with its war by itself. I put my curse on that Admiral and un-
packed my sea bag.

That same night I got a telegram, ordering me to report immediately to something called the S.V.P., Royal Naval Dockyard, Portsmouth. I got to Portsmouth next morning and found,
by golly! it was D-Day, so I hurried to the Dockyard in case
they tried to start the Invasion without me. I was charging
through the Dockyard gate when a petty officer said "Halt!"
He had two guns in his belt, so I halted. He looked at my white
hair and beard and said, "Well, sonny, what do *you* want?" I'd
been standing up all night in a crowded train, so I said, "All I
want from you is civility. And gardamned little o' that." And he
said, "Pass, friend. You'll be for the Small Vessels Pool. Past
the flagstaff and second on the right."

In the S.V.P. Office I found a fierce-looking commander and a
good-looking WREN. The commander gazed at me and said
"What's *your* age?" I said, "Twenty-six. And I'm not arguing—
I'm telling you." He said, "Ho! How many years have you been
handling ships?" I said, "About fifty. You give me command of
a ship and I'll guarantee I'll handle her."

He turned to the WREN. Says he, "Gladys, what's the next
job on the list?" Gladys said, "Deckhand in M.F.V. *555.*" I said,

"Deckhand! Wot, me? And what *is* an M.F.V. anyway?" The commander said, "Sort of a bumboat. Sign here!" And that's how *I* joined the Navy.

I found H.M.S. *555* at Gosport victualing pier. She was a 100-foot motor vessel and a very horrible sight. She flew the White Ensign, but she was filthy. Her stempiece was broken and all her bulwarks for'ard were stove in. She mounted four machine guns and an Orlikon but she smelled to heaven of rotten cabbage and fuel oil. What hurt me most though, was a sort of hoarding erected on top of her wheelhouse on which was painted, in great white letters, this noble and inspiring legend: "MEAT:BREAD:SPUDS."

Not even "Potatoes." I sat down on that pier and wept.

An elderly gentleman, with a white cavalry mustache, looked out from the wheelhouse window. He said, "Good afternoon. Can I assist you?" I said, "Thanks. But I'm past all help. The Navy's got me. I volunteered, in a weak moment. I hoped to command a landing craft, at least, but they've made me a deckhand aboard this—er—bumboat."

The old gentleman said, "You're lucky. That's nothing to what the Navy's done to me. That commander chap in the office asked me if I'd ever held a command and I said I'd commanded a Brigade of Cavalry in 1914 and my own little motor yacht since. Then Gladys said the next job on the list was command of this thing. So here I am. And I'm scared to death. I don't know how to handle a ship of this size. She's much too big for me. I told the commander so, but he just laughed and told me to carry on and obey orders.

"The *orders* are simple enough. We load up here with meat and bread and stuff and then steam out to the Invasion Fleet and supply any ship wearing the White Ensign or the Stars and Stripes that signals us. The trouble is, it's blowing hard out there, with a big sea, and this is a brute of a ship to handle and I'm clumsy with her and I admit it. The consequence is we've nearly sunk half a dozen destroyers and a couple of cruisers already, and what we'll hit next heaven knows. I don't.

"The crew consists mainly of retired Army officers like me. There's a sporting old baronet who's done a bit of yachting and a B.B.C. announcer chap who's done a bit more. Our engineer is 75 years old. He's the proprietor of a garage in Blackpool and he's never been afloat before. But he's all right so long as he's not seasick. Our star turn is the chef. He was a major in a Commando Regiment before his heart packed up, but he cooks like a cock angel. You'd better come aboard, for here come our cabbages. We've been waiting for this 200 bags to fill us up. Come aboard! Get the baronet and a couple of colonels and stow the greens on deck, while we get under weigh."

Sir George and the colonels were perfectly charming men, but totally unused to manual labor. By the time we had stowed those bags of vegetables, 555 was well out in the Channel. I looked around. With the Invasion in progress I had expected to see hundreds of ships. What I did see was thousands. An absolutely amazing sight. Sir George said, "An awe-inspiring spectacle, sir, what? The power and might of Britain and America, moving in for the kill. The Hun'll never stop this, sir. Nothing could stop it."

I said, "It looks as if we couldn't even stop it ourselves, now." Indeed it looked and felt just like that. Very heartening and impressive. It made me begin to think at last of Victory and Peace. But the skipper brought things down to earth just then by roaring, "Destroyer on the port bow, flying the Bread flag. Stand by to go alongside."

Thanks to the wind and the tide, and one or two other factors I will not mention, we berthed alongside that destroyer in rather too dashing a manner. In fact we carried away her boat-boom, a couple of fathoms of her rail and her companion ladder. I was horrified. In the Merchant Service, if you damage another ship, you have to pay for it and then some. I had yet to learn that in the Royal Navy they don't fuss and haggle about such things. When that destroyer's commander strolled along from aft to to gaze at the damage, I ducked. He said, "Well, well. I ask you for bread and you give me beans." Our skipper said, "I'm sorry, sir. All my fault. She got away from me." And the Commander

said, "Oh! That's all right, Skipper. Won't you come aboard and
try our pink gin?"

I said, "Well, I'll be damned." Sir George said, "Yes, God bless
the Royal Navy."

Our next victim was a cruiser. Armored, thank heavens, or we'd
have sunk her. For our diesel went full ahead instead of full astern
at just the wrong moment, and we hit her right amidships and
bounced off. A bearded face popped out of the porthole we had
dented. It said, "Now then! You can't come in here. This isn't a
public right-of-way. Nor yet a public lavatory. This is one of
H.M.'s ships, this is. It's *you* I'm talking to. You in that wheelhouse, with that horrible face. You're dead. You've been dead for
years and years. Go home—if you've got a home. Go back to your
mother—if you ever had a mother. Tell her you aren't fit to push
a baby's pram, let alone handle that *thing* you've got there. Now
you go away, you silly old basket. Go away. Go right away. And
don't come back or we'll torpedo you."

So we went away. Sir George said, "Skipper, I think we'd be
wise to ignore cruisers in the future and confine our attentions
to destroyers. They seem much more friendly."

We put in the next hours feeding a convoy of ships that had
just come back from Normandy. They were hungry and cleaned
us out, so we returned to Gosport for more supplies. The dockyard people loaded us up with beef and spuds. They did the loading and we said, "Thank heavens for that," and fell asleep where
we stood.

We worked 22 hours that day. The next day we only worked
20. But the average age of our crew was 62 and on the third day
the strain began to tell. One hundred tons weighs only 100 tons.
I know that. But I also know, now, that 100 tons of sides of beef
and sacks of potatoes weigh a thousand tons by the time you
have lifted them up from your deck and dumped them aboard a
score or so of destroyers. And if you are over 60 years old that
thousand tons weighs well over a million. At the end of the third
day, therefore, we had to get an ambulance and send two colonels
to the hospital. The rest of us then sank into a coma. All except
the skipper.

He said, "Look here, chaps, I'm done. Wes is the only sailor
aboard the ship and I think he ought to be skipper and not me.
Anyway I want a rest. I tell you what I'll do. I'll go up to the
office and see Gladys about it. She'll fix things up." So he saw
Gladys and she did fix things up. And that's how I became a skipper in the Royal Navy.

I went ashore and told the Port Captain we could not carry
on at the pace we were going. The Captain said, "If you men
don't feed the Fleet, the Fleet will starve. If it starves it can't
fight. If it doesn't fight the Invasion's a washout and we've lost
the war. So your chaps must keep going till they drop."

I said, "They *have* dropped. But I tell you what. I think if you
give us the grub for four or five good hot meals a day and all
the rum we can drink, it ought to keep us going."

The Captain said he'd see the Admiral. When he came back
he said, "Skipper, the Admiral says you are to be given everything you ask for."

We managed to keep going night and day for some weeks.
We fed the Navy. We also knocked it about a good bit but, so
far, we hadn't actually sunk anything. Things were going well.
The Invasion was succeeding. The pressure on the crew of
H.M.S. 555 eased up a bit. Also, we were getting artful. I made
the epoch-making discovery that, whenever I wanted a drink, all
I had to do was to make a bit of a dent in the Navy and scrape
off a little of its paint. The procedure went something like this:

Me: "There are two destroyers ahead, flying the Bread flag,
ours and a Pole. I'm getting a little bored with the Navy's pink
gins. What do Poles drink, General?"

The Mate: "Schnapps and vodka and all sorts of queer things."

Me: "Right. Stand by to go alongside that Polish destroyer
on the starboard bow. And get things properly organized *this*
time, Mr. Mate. Make a smart job of it, and don't let Sir George
lassoo himself with the heaving line like he did last time. I don't
mind *our* Navy laughing at us, but not these chaps. I see she's got
an ash-shoot on her port side. I'll carry it away and see what
happens."

We sneak up on our victim's starboard quarter and then lay along her port side when she isn't expecting it and before she can get her ash-shoot aboard.

Sir George (preparing to heave his line): "I say, old chap. D'you mind catching this rope? Thanks, so much."

Our flaring bulwarks for'ard catch the ash-shoot nicely and crush it. Outbursts of the Polish language follow. The ship's British liaison officer strolls up and says, "Mornin', Skipper. What's going on here?"

Me: "Your people were a little slow getting their shoot aboard, that's all, Sir. They've scraped my paint a bit, but never mind it. If anyone asks questions I'll say it was my fault."

The Officer: "Ah! That's very nice of you, Skipper. Come aboard and have a drink, won't you?"

It was as easy as that, most times. But there was one occasion when things considerably misfired. The occasion was a destroyer flying the Bread flag and the Stars and Stripes.

I said: "Stand by to go alongside that American destroyer."

The Mate: "Aye, aye, Sir. American ship, what? Rye and mint juleps. You're an artful old man, Skip. I wish you'd let me take her alongside this time. I'd like to sample some of those queer American drinks."

Me (only too well aware of the unnatural drinking habits of the U.S. Navy): "All right, General. You can be skipper for this Act. Come up here and take the wheel."

The General climbs into the wheelhouse and takes over. Says he, "Hang it! She's got nothing sticking outboard anywhere, so I fear I'll be forced to carry away a bit of her rail. D'you mind, Skip?"

Me: "*You* are in charge."

The General: "Right. Stand by to get your bow line aboard her, Colonel, and then make it fast good and solid, because I'm going to go full speed astern and swing alongside her in rather a brutal fashion. My intention being to carry away just one fathom of her rail—no more."

The General endeavors to execute this maneuver, but is foiled by some officious Yanks, wielding fenders.

Destroyer's Number One: "One of our fenders has stove in your bulwark planking aft here, Skipper."

The General: "Oh, that's all right, Commander. Little thing like that won't hurt her."

Commander: "So I see."

The General: "All my fault. I was a bit too brusque with the engines, what? I say, you know, this is the first American ship I've ever been alongside of. Would you mind if I came aboard for a minute or so and had a look round?"

Commander: "Sure. Come aboard and welcome."

The General goes aboard and disappears aft with the commander. Presently he reappears and climbs aboard the *555*, looking pale and shaken.

Me: "Hullo, General! Anything the matter? You look as if you'd had a nasty shock."

The General: (leading me out of sight behind the wheelhouse): "Shock! Why, Skipper, it's incredible! Fantastic!! Inconceivable!!!"

Me: "What is? The rye and juleps?"

The General: "Rye! By gad, sir! You'll never believe it, but it's a horrible, ghastly fact. It's beyond all nature. The awful truth is—*the American Navy is* TEETOTAL!"

Such events as these were merely incidents in a whole lot of hard work. The time came when all we old gentlemen began to get considerably browned off. We had been working too hard for too long. We judged we deserved at least a word of thanks from the Navy. Instead the Navy completely ignored us. We were, in fact, fed up and grousing. A bad sign.

Then, one fine day, we received a signal to proceed alongside the Flagship immediately. Sir George said, "Whatever can the Flagship want *us* for?" I said, "I can guess. We've been knocking the Navy about for weeks and, up to date, we've got away with it. But I knew our luck couldn't last. A Day of Reckoning was bound to come. And this is It. For heaven's sake don't hit *her*."

When I crept aboard, I was led before no less a person than the Admiral himself. I judged I had better get my blow in first, so I said, "I'm sorry, Sir. I know we've done more damage to the Fleet in the last few weeks than the enemy has done since the war started. But we couldn't help it. Our crew is inexperienced and our ship couldn't be more unsuitable for the job. What we really need for this work is a coster's barrow and a nice, quiet little donkey."

The Admiral said, "I have heard rumors of some minor damage, but don't let that worry you. I know, of course, your boats are unsuitable and that you men are old and tired. But the boats and the men were all we had left. And the job *had* to be done. The ships had to be fed. You have fed them. That's why I sent for you. I wish you to tell your people I appreciate what they have done. Tell them they have earned the gratitude of the Royal Navy."

When I gave the crew the Admiral's message there was silence for a while aboard the battered old *555*. Then the General said, "That's very handsome of the Admiral. We all ought to feel very proud. It means, of course, we've got to stop grousing and carry on, now, until it kills us."

I said, "Yes. Why not? Bring out the rum jar."

Sir George stood up, as straight as his lumbago would let him. He raised his glass. "Gentlemen," he said, "another few weeks of this work will kill us. That's certain. The Admiral's as good as sentenced us all to death. But . . . well . . . anway . . . Here's God bless the Royal Navy."

3

Happy Ending

by ALFRED F. LOOMIS

[1932]

I MET TOMMY WILEY for the first time on the French coast, off the shifting entrance to Trouville. The tide was at the top of the flood, all but turned, the wind was slight, and as I didn't want to be locked out of the wet basin, I was entering under power. Ahead of me I saw a lovely cutter—not one of your old-fashioned type, which are beautiful in their ruggedness, but a racing boat, slender, low of hull, tall of rig, gracefully proportioned for speed. She was finished bright, and in the warm sunlight her pine deck and mahogany sides seemed to lend a creamy glow to the rippling whiteness of her sails. Coming to the western edge of the narrow channel she tacked and slowly gathered way on the other board. There I overtook her and was passing with a silent wave when her helmsman called across the almost breathless water.

"Are you a stranger here, *Swastika?*" (*Swastika* being the name of my yawl.)

"Yes," I returned. "Am I standing into danger?"

"You'd better leave the next black buoy to starboard," he replied. "It's fifty yards out of position."

I had idled my motor at his first word, and now had so little headway that the two yachts drew together. "Thanks," said I. "I'd probably have gone aground. Can I return the favor by towing you in?"

Wiley looked aloft at his towering spread of canvas, cast a calculating glance at the lock gates perhaps a quarter-mile away, and gently shook his head. "I think I can make it," he declared. "The element of uncertainty doubles the enjoyment."

"Well," said I, dubiously, for the wind was very light and dead ahead. . . . "See you inside." And I motored in.

I had been moored in the Deauville basin for at least twenty minutes when I stepped to the gates to see how the element of uncertainty was coming on. *Thalassa*—I had read her name in passing and looked up her ownership in Lloyd's—was again on the starboard tack, inside the jetties, but seemingly bound up-channel for Trouville. The current had begun its ebb. The wetted surface of the lock gates which betrayed the falling tide was at least four inches wide and growing fast. The uniformed guards by the gates silently watched the diminishing water, apparently oblivious of the yacht's maneuvers. When the level reached a certain mark they would close the basin whether one or a dozen boats remained outside. They had to, for the safety of those moored within.

As the minutes passed and the water subsided I became unable to curb my impatience. "Are you coming in?" I called. "Shall I tell them to wait for you?"

"They won't," Wiley calmly answered. "I think I'll do the trick."

As he neared the south side of the narrow harbor he came about, heading a hundred yards high of the gates, no more than twenty yards between his fragile bow and the solid masonry of the retaining wall. I saw at once that for each foot he forged ahead the ebb current carried him a yard to the westward, and admired Wiley for the closeness of his calculations. If a sudden puff had caught his sails he might have come to grief. But he discounted that contingency.

Perhaps three minutes had passed when the French guards began to lose their immobility. They exchanged words and motioned with their hands to supplement their conversation. But as yet they made no move toward closing the gates. I stood transfixed, willing *Thalassa* to hurry in; and if mind had true supremacy over matter she would have leaped forward, torpedo-like. Instead she drifted slowly downstream, ever slightly nearer.

The moment came when I, by leaning out, could have placed my hand on *Thalassa's* bow, and I made as if to do so. But Wiley stopped me. "Give her another minute by herself," said he. "That will put her inside. I might get a little puff."

I restrained myself and the seconds dragged on. The puff came. The cutter, heeling slightly, seemed to gather herself like a bay mare before slipping inside.

"Voila," said one guard, unemphatically, as he closed his gate some eight or nine inches astern of *Thalassa*.

"Bravo," rejoined the other, with somewhat more feeling.

When the gates joggled together I ran across and came up alongside the cutter at the west side of the basin.

Wiley was putting the boom rest into place as his two paid hands made fast the mooring lines. "Lower away," said he, and turned toward me. "If they had closed the gates in my face I would have drifted out with the stream and sailed on to Le Havre. It wasn't a matter of life and death."

I stepped aboard to help lower sail, and marked that he worked with extreme deliberation. It was not the deliberation of a lazy man or of one mentally slow. Rather it was the cautious movement of one who has schooled himself to avoid violence of gesture. Later when he asked me below to have a drink and begged me to excuse him from participating, I jumped to a conclusion. "A yachtsman who doesn't drink?" I asked. "It seems hardly proper."

"It's my heart, you know," said he, apologetically. "Got a bit of shrapnel near it during the war, and I have to take things easy."

With the picture of his calm, leisurely entrance vivid in my mind I was ready for the moment to believe that he could always take things easily aboard *Thalassa*. But then I had another image of such a racing boat bouncing in the short Channel sea, and I exclaimed, "Surely, man, you don't think sailing is good for the heart!"

He laughed. "I'm not easily frightened to death, if that's what you mean, and if it comes on to blow I have two excellent hands who do the heavy work. *Thalassa* steers like a witch. At such times I chock myself off in the cockpit, take the helm, and I haven't a thing to worry me. Fortunately, yachting is the only sport for a man with my diaphanous attachment to life. I say 'fortunately,' because all other sports bore me to extinction."

That evening Wiley accompanied me aboard to supper and we revealed our differing cruising philosophies and techniques in mutual tolerance and understanding. My preference is to go on and on to new waters—his, he told me, was to explore each harbor thoroughly, to know the coast under all conditions of wind and tide, to feel as much at home on the sea as his *Thalassa*, which was named for it. I need not add that he was wedded to sail and tiller and entertained complete contempt for anything that was rotary in its movement.

It was the next year, I think, that I saw Tommy Wiley again. Once more I was entering under power—this time at Dieppe—and I own to a twinge of shame when he saw me with my sails furled. He sat in the stern sheets of a mahogany skiff, a uniformed sailor at the oars moving him from place to place as he took soundings with a three-pound lead. Later, when the tide lifted and I passed through the Pollet draw to find mooring in the Duquesne basin, Wiley came in after me and accepted my invitation to step aboard.

As if to set my mind at rest he began by telling me that Dieppe was one haven, what with Channel packets coming and going, at which he always took a tow. And he hoped (somewhat to my surprise) that we might go out together so that if I felt disposed he could be spared a fee. I told him that I would suit my departure to his.

"Now that that's settled," I added, "will you kindly tell me what treasure you expected to pick up with your lead from the polluted floor of Dieppe?"

He seated himself carefully in a chair which I had had brought for him on deck, and humorously shrugged his shoulders. "I was doing that," said he, "to get away from my paying guests. They

wanted me to come to this port, and in a way I had to. But I'm
dashed if I have to caper about with them ashore."

He sat with his chair turned so that he faced *Thalassa*, moored
a hundred yards or so from us, and I noticed that his eyes continually caressed her lovely hull and lofty mast.

"Isn't this a new departure?" I asked. "Guests on *Thalassa?*
I thought you liked going your own gait."

"I do. More now than I did a year ago. These are *paying*
guests." He paused a moment and continued in the best counter-
feit of an offhand manner that he could assume. "The fact is I've
had terrific financial reverses. I can't afford the cutter. I can't
give her up. I would die ashore. So to make both ends meet I
have to take these guests. They're good fellows, you know, but
they don't love the sea as I do, and I have to get away from them
from time to time. By the way, do you think this makes me a
professional?"

"You, a professional!" I hooted. "An amateur is one who
loves something. If you love *Thalassa* enough to share her rather
than give her up altogether—or, looking at it from another
angle, if you're so keen about sailing that you will endure the
embarrassments of paying guests rather than stay ashore, I think
you are doubly an amateur."

Nevertheless, I reflected uncomfortably that in the opinion of
those who really matter, Wiley's amateur status had been impaired.

Our third meeting, a year later, occurred in the Channel south
of the English port of Newhaven. I had noticed a sailing dinghy
scooting along, her helmsman immovable at the tiller, head back
and eyes unwavering on the luff of his sail. Calm overtook us
and I launched my skiff, rowing over for a talk with the intrepid
stranger.

"Wiley!" I exclaimed, grasping his gunwale and fending off.
"Where's *Thalassa?*"

"This is she," he replied gravely. "You hadn't heard that my
other boat was burned at Bembridge just after I had hauled her
out last fall?"

"I heard about the fire," I replied. "But *Thalassa*—that dream of beauty."

Our two small boats lifted leisurely to the heave of the sleeping sea. "Perhaps it was for the best," said Wiley stoically. "I—well, I had been expelled from my club for professionalism—you know, those paying guests—and I doubt if I could have gone on with her. Now I live in a room by the sea at Newhaven and sail this little dream of beauty—again an amateur, I hope. I make no comparisons with my old love, but I feel a more intimate companionship with the sea in this 14-footer than I ever did before."

He said nothing of the shock of his loss or of his expulsion from the fellowship of Corinthians, but, scanning his face, I could see that he had definitely aged. I asked no questions, other than the routine one of, "Have you been caught in anything dirty?"

"Yes, but I've been able to run for it. And you ought to see her off the wind." His grave face brightened vividly. He held out a hand, palm down, and oscillated it slightly from the wrist. "Like that," said he. "A marble on her thwart would hardly roll six inches from side to side. Oh, marvelous!"

"Your heart?" I asked. "Does it give you any trouble?"

"No more than usual. I'm no weakling, you know," he boasted. "I can reef, haul, and steer with the best of you, so long as I take things easily."

I asked Wiley if he intended to lie there becalmed all night, and he elected to think my question facetious. "There will be wind before dark. Plenty of it. Where are you bound?"

"Newhaven," said I, at random. "If the wind is west it will be a close reach in."

"And a close squeak for boats that aren't weatherly."

"As bad as that?" I asked. "Say, wouldn't you like me to bring over the yawl and tow you a bit? Not in, but to weather a mile or so."

He looked toward the distant shore, marked at that moment by the smoke of a steamer leaving Newhaven. "No thanks, I ought to make it."

"Then, how about tying in a reef while I'm here. Wouldn't that help?"

"No. I'll need whole sail for the first hour or so, and perhaps I shan't have to reef at all."

The first darkening of the water to westward now became apparent. Expressing a final wish that I could do something to assist Wiley, I rowed back to my *Swastika* and boarded her as the wind came in. The meeting had been a pleasant one, for, rising above his personal misfortunes, Wiley had suffused me afresh with his love of sailing. I found myself thinking fatalistically that if (or rather, when) he did overtax his heart in some such exigency as this approaching westerly he would die happy.

As I gathered way, *Thalassa* glided past me and I noticed how much at union with his boat this sailor was—stretched at ease, one arm thrown carelessly along the tiller, head just showing above the gunwale, and face uplifted so that his eyes commanded the luff of his sail. After nodding to me he looked to westward and nodded his head more emphatically, as if to say, "I told you so."

A moment later he looked back and called, "Better get your skiff aboard. This will be quick."

I thought him unduly anxious—as well he might be in an open boat—and left my skiff towing. Because of my neglect I was unable to watch some two hours later when the time came for him to reef. In the interval the wind had shot up to gale force and the slumbering sea had leaped to tumultuous, vicious life. What with heaving to to lower my mainsail, and inexcusably sagging down and overriding my skiff, my men and I had the busiest half hour of our experience. When they had righted the skiff and manhandled it aboard I had time to look around and see how Wiley had managed. He, too, was shortened down, and although his boat seemed to skip bodily from crest to crest he told me afterward that she made remarkably easy weather of it.

Swastika reached port first, and I was in readiness to receive him as he came careening up the narrow harbor. Though he made an eggshell landing alongside my yawl, he depended on us

to secure him and lower his wildly slatting sail. And one of my
men and I had to lift him bodily to my deck and below to a bunk.

"I did it that time," was all he would say of his experience
at sea. I inferred that he spoke of his heart rather than of his
feat of seamanship, for he added, "Looks like a spell with the
doctor."

The next day we got him ashore and to his own room, where
a doctor stethoscoped him and made other tests. His verdict—
bed, and no more sailing—brought a look of profoundest gloom
to Wiley's face. I stayed in port several days, visiting the sick
man frequently. When, finally, I left, it was with his assurance
that he was well cared for and that he would obey the doctor's
orders and do nothing rash.

"The fact is," he told me, "I *feel* weak for the first time since
I left the base hospital. This damned heart of mine, you know,
has what they call a pericardial adhesion and has to turn itself
upside down every time it pumps. It may knock off work any
minute."

I returned after two weeks, blithely expecting, as a well man
does, to find Wiley recovered. But there was a wasted look to
his face that took my breath away. Out of bed, but confined to
his room, almost his first words expressed his repugnance to life
ashore.

"I feel like a sick bear in a cage," said he, "padding about,
wall to wall, bed to eating tray. If I could have a little sail on a
calm day it would give me new life. But I haven't had quite the
gumption to slip out against the doctor's orders."

"That's right," I counseled him. "Obey orders and build up
slowly."

He turned savagely upon me. "But what's the use?" he asked.
"If I stay in this hole I'll die. Sailing always does me good. If
this wind would only let up!"

Although the vagaries of Channel weather are unpredictable
by me, there seemed little chance of that. In the last week the
wind had blown half a gale for five days and a whole gale for
the other two. The sea pounded on the shore until it rattled the

windows of the sick man's room. The wind howled down his chimney and puffed wisps of dead ashes out of the black grate.

"As for me," said I, "I'm quite content to be in port."

But that night the wind died. I awoke in the morning full of the joy of sunshine. In the leftover swell finding its way into the harbor the moored boats still rolled reminiscently, but the surface of the water was flecked by the gentlest of winds from the northeast. I looked out of the main hatch to see who had come and gone. Early though it was, *Thalassa's* mooring was empty.

I jumped into my skiff, and ashore, and ran full tilt to the lighthouse on the west pier, still damp from its bath of spray. Far to sea I saw a leg-of-mutton sail, slowly dwindling.

Full of misgivings, I returned aboard for breakfast and by an effort of will resisted the temptation to put after the afflicted man. Though his heart was weak his weather sense was still strong and I convinced myself that he would not get caught out a second time. All that lovely summer day I loitered at the harbor mouth, watching the shipping and ever turning an anxious glance to sea. At last I saw him coming from the west, sailing on an easy reach. As he drew near I could distinguish him in his familiar pose, arm thrown carelessly along the tiller, head showing above the gunwale, eyes on the luff of the sail. When he came nearer still I saw that the luff shook slightly and that *Thalassa's* course was not arrow-straight.

Before I had time to digest the significance of this, a deep-throated whistle blistered my ear drums and I looked around to see the Dieppe steamer charging out from her wharf. At full speed almost before she reached the entrance, she was giving all lesser craft the signal to keep clear. I looked again at *Thalassa*. What was she going to do, skim across the steamer's bow, or luff up and pass astern? A careful seaman would, of course, have passed astern, but I remembered Wiley's delight in his calculation of clearances when first I saw him at Trouville. *Thalassa* held to her course, clearing the packet's knife-like bow by a distance measurable in feet rather than in yards. I saw her stern rise to the bow wave, and just before the black hull of the steamer intervened I thought I saw Wiley put her about for the entrance.

It was my next thought that he had cut his distance so close that the steamer had run him down. But in a few seconds *Thalassa* reappeared, almost shaving the steamer's stern, and bobbing in her wake. She straightened up and on the starboard tack entered the harbor, the tide under her. A thrill of admiration tingled me as I saw that Wiley's nonchalance remained superb. He did not once look astern at the black death that had so narrowly escaped him.

The wind by now was almost gone (getting ready for another week of southwesterlies, I thought) and it was more by the indulgence of tide than air that *Thalassa* drifted slowly to her mooring. But Wiley, sailor that he was, still kept his glance riveted to the luff of his sail.

Running ahead to my skiff I jumped in and shoved off. *Thalassa* sailed serenely on until her bow actually kissed her mooring buoy. Then, though she seemed to hesitate an instant, she kept on.

Speechless, I rowed alongside and touched Wiley's arm where it lay carelessly along the tiller. Its coldness was communicated through the coat sleeve to my fingers. I looked at the lifeless face and saw that though the eyes were open the mouth was closed, the corners of the lips just lifting to a smile.

"God!" I whispered. "If we could all go out as happily as that."

4

Fighting Sperm Whales

by CAPT. JAMES A. M. EARLE

Formerly Master of the Whaleship "Charles W. Morgan"
as told to GEORGE M. SHEAHAN, M.D.

[1927]

I HAVE BEEN ASKED many times concerning the perils of whaling and its fierce excitement, oftentimes by admirers of the man who has become (and deservedly), a sort of patron saint of whaling, namely Herman Melville. Have such scenes as he describes ever happened? Does the whale turn upon his human enemies with the malice, spirit and savage temper of an infuriated bulldog, or is he merely a great stupid victim whose revenge, when it does occur, is wholly accidental?

It will be remembered that the cetacean hero of Melville's story is a sperm whale, and therein lies the answer. The sperm is an athletic leviathan, a powerful, heavily-muscled, tightly-strung and well-knit fellow going directly, solidly and with determination about his business; a heavyweight athlete as it were. His lower jaw is long, strong and practical; his temper, sometimes, is highly irritable.

The right whale, on the contrary, though perhaps as large, is distinguished more by what can best be described as suppleness. So flexible is his great tail on his body that when plunging he appears to whirl it in the air with a flourish, or wriggle and turn it on its axis. In a lateral plane he can, with wonderful rapidity, sweep the flukes literally from ear to ear. His mouth, of course,

is without value in offense; his fins he uses against the killer
whale, but he never shows fight to boats in the manner of an
angry sperm. It is true that many men have been done to death
in the right whale fishery, but the causes have been accidental,
like the blind, wild plunge of the harpooned whale, the lightning-
like flow of the line, or a threshing tail. Once he is struck by the
harpoon no one can tell what a whale will do.

It was my fortune (good or bad as you choose to view it)
more than once to meet a fighting sperm. Two such encounters
remain vivid in my memory, and in the telling I live them over
again. The first occurred in the early '70s while I was harpooner
of the third mate's boat of the *Rainbow*, off French Rock, and
the second (which cost the life of my chief officer) while I was
in command of the bark *Charles W. Morgan,* off the coast of
Japan.

French Rock, southernmost of the Kermadec Isles, is a barren pinnacle three or four hundred feet high and perhaps two
acres in extent, lying about 300 miles north of New Zealand,
in 31° South latitude, on the 180th meridian. French Rock whaling grounds were famous in those days and will be found indicated by the classic drawing of a pair of flukes on many of the
old charts.

We had lowered for a school of whales—it was moderate
weather with a good breeze—and running free in the whaleboat at about six knots we came down from behind, and to starboard, of a husky 70-barrel bull. I planted two harpoons in his
side, threw my box warp over as the mate shoved the tiller down,
and we shot away. I then turned to my sail and let go the halyards. The boat's crew caught the sail and tied it up; they did
this while seated, it being a bad breach of discipline to stand up
at this critical juncture. The bow oarsman meanwhile had cast
off the backstays and I wound them speedily around the 18-foot
mast, then lifted the mast, let it come down aft where the officer
caught it, and, with the crew, pulled and passed it aft, letting it
rest on the gunwale, top overside and heel under the tub thwart.
All this in a much shorter time than it takes in the telling. Boat-
steerer and officer then changed ends. As the officer went forward

to his station the men took their places at their oars—the boat-steerer's oar was almost always carried shipped—making three oars on the starboard side and two on the port. This was the invariable custom, the starboard being the "three oar side" and the port the "two oar side." We were then ready for further action.

When struck, the whale had dropped his jaw and had rolled over, bringing the under part of his body and his huge mouth and bristling teeth directly towards us. But the momentum of the boat had carried us by, and now he lay aft and to leeward, kicking and threshing.

"Pull three, stern two. Lay me on there, Earle!" came the swift order, bringing boat and fish head and head. Most whalemen prefer to lance at about the center of the broadside (bomb also, for that matter, but lower down), so the next order followed rapidly. "Pull ahead all," and as the three oar side ranged along the officer flung first one lance and then another. A lance is made somewhat different from a harpoon—much the same difference in fact as between the war and hunting arrowheads of the Indians.

The mate seized his lance warp, hauled strongly, succeeded in pulling it out of the monstrous coat, but before he could lay a hand on the lance itself, the whale grabbed it in his mouth and snapped it in two, the two-inch oak pole breaking like a piece of matchwood. In so doing he had turned and we were again parallel and headed in the same direction.

"Pull hard, pull hard there, bullies," and we circled away from him, the line, of course, still fast but with slack to handle the boat and one turn around the loggerhead for emergency. We intended to come in from behind again, allowing room for a natural sweep of the tail—for we did not like his handling of his tail or of his jaw—but as we advanced he turned with us, always facing us.

"Stern all, stern all, and slew the boat around," came the next order. But the whale still turned and faced us. The midship oarsman—I can see him now, and I knew then what he was going to do, too, but I hadn't time to stop him—took his 18-foot oar, the longest in the boat, pulled it back a little distance and gave him a fierce jab in the side. Quick as an angry dog the whale turned, seized that oar and snapped it off well above the blade! He was brave, no doubt at all about that, and considering his huge bulk, a mighty lively fish.

Harpoon and lance had now failed, moreover it was clear that he was more than a match for us. The only remaining chance for capture seemed to be another attempt to "take him head and head" and bomb him as we passed by. The gun was ready—it was an old muzzle loader and handled in much the same way as we handle a shotgun today—the order came "Spring hard, spring hard, bullies" and the men again bent to their oars. Whether the whale fathomed our plan or not I do not know, but before we could reach him he rolled again, mouth wide open, and rushed toward us. The officer fired, the bomb passing directly down the huge throat and causing a quick snap together of the jaws. We circled again, for the situation was critical, but the next spout was thick blood, and we closed in. The officer selected his point of attack with care, the lance was thrust in, time and again, feeling and seeking for the "life"—the process known as "pumping him"—until the flurry, when we followed on the outside of the circle, towed about at 20-fathoms length, until the inevitable end.

.   .   .   .

The middle of the fair weather season nearly 30 years ago—the second week of July to be exact—found the American whaleship *Charles W. Morgan,* then under my command, taking on supplies at Hakodate in the island of Yezzo, one of the few ports of the Island Empire open to foreigners. The scant 48 hours' shore leave was a welcome break for officers and men between the successful seven months' cruise we had accomplished and an even longer one in prospect. Much had to be done. In addition to the essential supply of wood already aboard, fresh vegetables (against the scurvy) and water must be loaded in quantity. But it was all finally attended to; the crew, after the usual excitement and disturbance, was rounded up, anchor was weighed and, with topsails, topgallant sails, courses and all fore-and-aft sails sheeted home, the old bark once again began to walk the water like a thing of life.

We were bound through the Suva Straits to the east coast of Japan, where a departure would be taken for the Southern Pacific grounds, the old New Zealand right whale grounds hundreds of leagues to the south and southeast, whose exact center can be indicated as at the intersection of the 37th degree South latitude and the 170th meridian. Our officers and crew were typical and consisted of captain, first, second, third and fourth mates, four boatsteerers, a cook, a steward, two boys, the carpenter, the cooper, engineer (for the donkey engine) and twenty-two men before the mast, each bound to certain duties and occupying the curious and exact position in the social scale of the ship determined by the age-old, ironclad custom of the industry. I call it an industry, for an industry it was, and one whose high positions were reached by no short or easy apprenticeship. Some detail of these men and their duties will appear in the course of the story.

The first hours of the voyage passed swiftly, all hands busily occupied with the countless tasks of a deep-water ship. Watches were chosen and set, and the first morning dawned much like the beginning of a clear June day off the New England coast. As the day grew brighter two men ascended the ratlines to the hoops of the fore royalmast, where, scanning the watery fields, they swung with the gentle motion of the ship. Though our destination was far away, no opportunity for the taking of a whale must be missed.

A steady breeze from the land filled the sails; to leeward, miles away, a broad belt of dark blue and drift showed the presence of the Japan current, rolling on its eternal journey from the burning Bay of Bengal to the frozen Aleutian Islands. A few months previous it had been teeming with fur seals on their spring migration, but now it was deserted. Westward rose the mountainous coast of Japan where the tide rolled, then as now, into deep indentations between the heavily wooded hills.

Suddenly, from the masthead, came a long-drawn cry startlingly familiar, but never failing to stir its hearers to wild excitement. Who that has heard that cry can ever forget it? It is like the call of fate itself.

Lookout: "Blows, Blows!"

Officer of the deck: "What do you see, there?"

Lookout: "Sperm whale I think, sir." (Note the language of politeness, caution and deference to authority. None must pass final judgment but the autocrat of the ship, nor must the officer of the deck report without getting all possible information.)

"Where away?"

"Off the lee beam, sir."

"How far off?"

"About two miles, sir."

Officer of the deck going to skylight and reporting to captain: "Whale off the lee beam, sir; he calls it a sperm whale!"

I took my long spyglass in hand—it was a trusted companion of many voyages—and ran aloft to have a look at him, my mind the while active with conjectures and details of the coming hunt. From the crosstrees there was no doubt. About two miles to leeward lay a large sperm whale, his broad, gray, glistening back rounding up from the surface, leisurely swimming to the north and spouting his single feathery jet with the amazing clock-like regularity characteristic of these enormous creatures.

"Call all hands, Mr. Mate, and get your boats ready; there is a hundred barrels of good sperm in his overcoat and he wishes it cared for in the *Morgan's* lower hold!"

Followed a pounding and thumping on the forecastle door; a loud shout of "Roll out and go in the boats—sperm whale;" a hustling on of jackets and sea boots; a rush up the steps; a swift trampling of feet on the deck and a seeming confusion that was in reality expedition born of long practice and many drills. In an instant the men were at their stations, the tub oarsman with his canvas hardtack bag and the after oarsman with his cask of water. The boatsteerer and the officer of each boat took their places aboard, the former at the bow falls and the latter aft.

"All ready, sir!" sang out the mate.

"Hoist and swing!" came the reply. A swift short pull lifted the boats a trifle, clearing the heavy wooden cranes which were thereupon swung in and hooked behind the bulwarks.

"Lower away!" There was a swift roll and clucking of blocks and cordage; down dropped the boats, striking the water at almost the same instant. The remaining members of the crews clambered down the sides on the slideboards and took their places, tackles were unhooked, and the chase was on.

Sometime, before you die, you must go to New Bedford and there see whaleboats and gear, not pictures nor yet models, but the real, old, sweet-lined, long, double-enders, fitted with sweeps of a length and toughness suited to the arms of strong men, and then you will understand.

Whaleboats, when possible, sail until the harpoon is flung. Once clear of the hull of the *Morgan,* our boats, their crews animated by keen rivalry, excitement and the almost universal human desire for gain, set sail with all speed. With started sheets, a fair wind and a good rap full they swept down upon their prey, the mate's boat leading, followed, as on a towline, by the third's, and at a little distance by the two remaining boats foaming along much like yachts in a race. Yachts, though, never raced for such a prize.

From the crowsnest I watched them, the *Morgan* lying still with main yards braced up on the starboard tack, fore yards square, and wheel half way down (a maneuver essential to the checking of headway before the boats were lowered), drifting slowly along, and the lookout's regular cry of "Blows-Ah-Blows" signaling the spouts. When about a mile away the whale curved his gigantic back well out of the water, something like a man making two tries for a handspring—"rousing" we call it. Then from aloft, "There go flukes," and he disappeared almost perpendicularly in a smother of foam.

No concern was felt, for it is almost a certainty that his reappearance will be on the same course he was traveling when he sounded. It is even possible to foretell with accuracy the length of his absence. This fellow took about an hour—we timed him by watch on his first submersion, knowing well he would come up to the minute the next time. So, on his second rising his great head and back appeared in an almost straight line fore and aft between Swain's, the chief mate's boat, and Peckham's, the third's. They were men between whom a strong rivalry existed, not an uncommon thing, especially when the younger is crowding the older.

Above, the sun shone from a clear, blue sky on a rushing and breezy ocean. The leading boats with their silent crews were at an equal distance from the quarry, on whose great gray sides the waves lapped, then rolled away in foaming bubbles. He was nearly 90 feet long and in the full pride of strength and vitality. Mr. Swain's boatsteerer, a thoroughly practical, keen-eyed, cool-headed young fellow (with an eye to the main chance for profit of all concerned), was the first to speak, calling to his officer, "We are right ahead of him, sir; this is Mr. Peckham's chance; he is right behind him where he can't be seen and he surely will see us before we get there." (A whale's eyes are set above the angle of the jaw and a slight turn of the head and body brings his vision, which, at close range, is strictly lateral, to bear forward.) But you cannot keep a man from his fate.

"I don't care a damn," roared the mate. "I am going to take him," and suiting his action to the words he first signaled the third, who took in his sail, standing by with his oars, then faced the monster. They approached rapidly, the whale's head and the sharp stem of the on-rushing whaleboat meeting and sliding by, then, side to side, and almost touching. Farther yet forged the stem, the mate hoping to deal the blow in the "life mark."

"Give it to him," came the hoarse command, and at that close range two harpoons were driven below the hump with all the willing power of a strong and practised arm.

The agony of the stabs galvanized the monster into action; and his action was worthy of his power and size. From the *Morgan* I could see only those terrible, ponderous flukes towering, the central point of a seething circle of white water. In an instant the boat shot clear of the commotion, sail down and a waif up.

"A stoven boat," I thought. Then a second waif appeared. "An injured man." I swung the ship off, squared the main yard, set the foresail, and we bore down to leeward to render aid. It was clear that we had met a foeman worthy of our steel, for, when high spirited and a fighter, the hunted sperm whale presents a peril as great as the sum of his size and speed and strength.

We rounded to about 100 yards from the stoven boat with fore yard aback. Meanwhile, the second's boat advanced—for there was need of attracting the brute's attention away from the disabled crew. Two more irons were flung and again the scene became a maelstrom of seething, swirling, circling white water, that terrible tail with its broad spreading flukes threshing and flailing with savage ferocity. Again came a lull in the combat, and on the edge of the whirlpool, lifting and falling, could be seen a sail and its spars spread out on the water, a sweep or two, and here and there a black spot, the head or shoulders of one of the crew—nothing more.

I was now drawing closer to them. The whale remained at the scene of the second encounter lying almost level with the water through which his bulk could be plainly seen, watching and waiting—and full of fight. Occasionally when the irons pricked deeper in his side with the motion and pull of the trailing lines he rolled and threshed.

I signaled the return, for our first care must be the injured. One by one the boats came alongside. Peckham had saved all men from the destroyed boat, but the second mate was unconscious and one man was wounded. The fourth mate reported no mishaps, and all hands stood by anxiously awaiting the return of the first's boat, which approached slowly. One short—still he might be lying hurt—no, there was surely one man missing!

"Anyone injured, Brown?"

"Mr. Swain, sir, he was knocked overboard, the flukes caught him I think; he had hold of the tiller and it's broken off short. Steering oar broken, too, sir. I cut the line and we searched everywhere. We found his hat floating, but no other trace."

So there it was. Poor Swain would never again hear the bells or see the welcome shore of old New Bedford. His was a case where the influence of fate or chance—call it what you will— seems to have been far stronger than any poor human mind could have foreseen. A man of nearly 50 years, married, he had gone whaling in his younger days only to settle down on shore (as he thought) for the rest of his life, as a coach driver between New Bedford and Dartmouth. As commonplace a matter as street railway competition and the lure of high wages had driven him whaling again, only to perish thus tragically in the far reaches of the Pacific!

What was to be done? Attend to the injured at once and then we would see. Willing hands carried them below and we cared for their wounds, rubbed them and wrapped them in blankets. One man was detailed as nurse. On deck, the tangle had been straightened out and once again the boats were ready.

"What now, sir?" said the boatheader. "Shall we try him again?" "Yes," I replied, "use your oars. You take him on his left side and Peckham on his right. Don't try to fasten, but bomb him, both of you at the same time."

Clearing the ship, the crews again set upon the whale, but this time armed with weapons against which all his courage and mighty strength were of no avail. Ranging alongside from behind, and at point blank range, Peckham fired. The bomb entered perhaps a little ahead for the "life mark," but near enough, for immediately following the explosion the great head dropped and the great body rolled, exposing the whole of the left broadside. Into it, just at the round of the belly, with merciless and deadly accuracy, the boatheader in the second boat fired, the bomb bursting almost in the chambers of the heart.

"You will destroy no more boats," sung out the boatheader as the whale sounded, seeking once again the depths of the ocean.

But the awful air hunger had to be satisfied, and again he rose, rushing forward, snapping his jaws, head lifted high, pushing a little wave ahead; he vomited and purged, and the thick dark blood rose rhythmically from his spout. Three times, for so strong burned the flame of life within him, did he complete that circle, game to the core, more and more slowly rolling, and more and more feebly righting himself; then the current of his life blood ceased to flow, the jaw fell, and the poor dry spout hole frenziedly opened and closed with his last gasps, until death was upon him, and he rolled upon his side, "fin out"—for the last time.

5

Why I Like to Cruise

by GRETTA PRINCE

[1940]

IT'S THE LITTLE THINGS I like. Not just the wind and the sails and the sparkling blue alone, but the hundreds of little things everybody remembers. They are the fun—they *are* cruising. I like the start of a cruise. The piles of suitcases and duffel bags, mounds of charts, blankets, mountains of canned goods and food finally disappear; stowed so successfully that some of the more important items are never seen again. I like the way things are stowed so that, when a ship feels a good blow, it's always the oatmeal and the cocktail glasses that get loose!

I like skippers. They change so much on the water! The most courteous friend ashore becomes a swearing fiend in a good blow off Maine. I like navigators, too. They use charts, slide rules and the *Coast Pilot* to tell you how to fetch the red spar that is dead off your port bow. I like the way they never trust each other and always recheck each other's courses. They shoot the sun and the stars tirelessly, rush below like madmen to read the chronometer, figure furiously on paper and chart—and find that we have been cruising in the middle of a Vermont farm!

I like the careful science of sun bathing. The hours spent turning from one side to the other; the changing of clothes with every shift of wind, sail, sun or temperature. I like the slow tanners, the quick burners, the nose peelers, the reckless sufferers and the scientific oilers!

I like the way boats' crews stare at each other through binoculars. I like the way voices carry over the water, all unbeknownst to the owners. I like the beer companies who make beer cans to shoot at!

I like cruising. I like the daily provisioning of a ship. I like the list over the ice box where all things needed are listed: "Bacon; eggs; gasoline; bicarbonate of soda; buttons for Bill's pants." I like the endless wisps of wool and dust that appear on the cabin floor. I like the way brass corrodes right after polishing.

I like the way a crew evolves a complete lingo of its own after a few days out. Names, jokes, bits of song, all completely unintelligible to the hapless relief crew late in arriving.

It's the little things I like. The strange places things are found. The sunburn cream in with the cigarettes and sunglasses. One green sock back of the stove, and the best rum in the Skipper's shore-going shoes. I like the way the first mate spends hours picking pebbles out of his rubber soles. I like the way matches disappear, and opened cigarette packages seem to vanish. I like the way ice picks and beer openers always get lost; the way postage stamps stick together in a soggy lump. I like the way every cook aboard has a new idea for perfect coffee, and later, when the horrid mess of grounds, cooked egg, and shell is finally scraped out of the percolator and dumped overboard, I like the way the glass top always goes with it!

I like to go ashore. I like the way the right kind of shore friends offer you hot baths first and say hello afterwards!

I like the way everyone becomes feverishly busy when it's time to relieve the helmsman in a flat calm. But let it blow a good stiff breeze, and all hands jump for the tiller to feel the pull of the wind and the rush of the waves. I like the way my best nail brush is used for the companion steps and the potatoes!

I like the times and places that the Skipper chooses to fix things. The decks have just been swabbed and we are finally relaxing with cans of cold beer, when he decides to take the head apart up on deck! I like the way the pressure stove never works perfectly, and I like the look on the Skipper's face after trying to fix it.

I like breakfasts—particularly when it's my turn to get them.

There is the "no-juice-before-teeth-brush-school," and the "give-me-my-juice-before-I-smoke" school. There is the hot cereal crowd and the cold cereal bunch—but I like the way they always agree on one thing: the coffee is always foul!

I like Maine natives. They row out in dinghies to watch you bump a poorly marked reef—and then call, "Thought you'd clip that one!"

I like hot bouillon and pilot biscuit sent on deck in a foggy stretch. I like the "children's hour" after the hook is dropped in some lovely new harbor. I like the smell of wet wool drying over a Shipmate stove. I like the pails of garbage to be dodged on deck until after we are out in the open sea. I like no telephones, no set hours, little odd cat naps, duties to be done, singing in the dark. I like to cruise.

I like the night. The way I tumble exhaustedly below to go to bed—I and all the rest of the crew simultaneously. I find one small corner and cower there, amidst cries of "Hey, don't look now, I'm undressing." I keep a frantic eye on the wash room door—and then lose my chance because I can't find my pajamas. And then miss again when some cur beats me to it. At last the door opens, I dash, I scrape a shin, but I reach my wet goal!

I like the towels in the head—always damp, ownership always uncertain. I like the row on row of private cures—the headache cure on every shelf, the sure cure cold remedies, the whole gamut of laxatives! I like the way my still unsuccessful compatriots in the cabin pound on the door and shout: "Don't pump so hard! Slow and easy does it." At last I emerge, smelling of soap. I am ready for sleep. Good God, look at my berth! In my absence, every extra suitcase, the binnacle, the spinnaker and the crew's wet oilskins have been piled in it. I like to cruise!

I like the way order finally comes out of chaos. The last tooth is brushed, the last paper handkerchief is tucked under the last pillow. The Skipper puts up the porthole screens, turns out the last light, stumbles over the extra mattress on the floor . . . and peace descends with the lap of Maine waters against the hull. Peace . . . until an unmistakable buzz announces that the screens were put up too late! I like to cruise.

6

The Wreck of *Merlan*

by KEITH DOUGLAS YOUNG

[1950]

THE UNLUCKIEST YACHT in the Sydney-Hobart yacht race of 1948 was undoubtedly the 43-foot Bermudian sloop, *Merlan,* built, owned and sailed by W. L. Curtis, of Geelong, Victoria. Not only was possible victory in the race snatched from her grasp a few hours before the finish, but the boat herself was destined to meet her end a few weeks later on the merciless, rocky reefs off Point Lonsdale, at Port Phillip Heads, near Melbourne.

But if *Merlan* was the unluckiest of boats, her crew of four can lay fair claim to being among the luckiest people alive today. I should know. I was one of them.

There were just three of us left to return the *Merlan* to Geelong, after the Sydney-Hobart Race, as the other members of our racing crew of nine had to hurry back to Melbourne for business reasons. Those remaining were Lance Curtis, vice commodore of the Royal Geelong Yacht Club; Eric Walker, a former yacht owner, with 40 years of sailing experience; and myself, a yachtsman since knickerbocker days. It certainly was a skeleton crew to bring the *Merlan* back to Victoria from Tasmania, so when Brian Shaw, a young Launceston yachtsman, volunteered to make the voyage across Bass Strait with us we accepted with alacrity.

We left Georgetown, at the mouth of the Tamar River, in Northern Tasmania, at about 1:30 P.M. on Friday, January 14 —not, as events proved, a particularly auspicious day on which to

have sailed. The weather forecast promised fine weather with
southerly winds veering to southeast, which would give us an
easy run to the Heads. According to the radio reports all barom-
eters in Tasmania were rising; and with the weather seemingly
assured, we felt no forebodings as we set out under full sail on
what should have been a simple and speedy passage of one and
one-half to two days, for the approximately 250 miles.

Fine weather stayed with us for the first day, and we made
good time with a favorable wind and a gentle swell which set
the reef points jigging against the inward curve of the sail. The
smooth racing hull of the *Merlan* porpoised forward in a
series of powerful lunges while the towering mast described a
pattern of arabesques and circles against the sky. It was perfect
sailing weather.

The log reading after 24 hours showed us to be considerably
more than half-way home. However, during the afternoon of
the second day our barometer began to fall, slowly at first, but
with increasing rapidity as evening approached. At the same time
a dirty black scud began to build up in the sky. The almost hourly
stream of planes which had been in sight as they sped overhead
were lost to view in the rapidly forming cloud-wrack. These
planes, in addition to relieving that sense of mid-ocean loneliness
and isolation, had served as a good check on navigation. It was
comforting, however, to be able to hear them still.

By midnight that night (Saturday) our glass, which had been
steady at 30.05, had dropped to a menacing 29.5 and showed
signs of falling still further. A fresh breeze was blowing, but not
yet strong enough to cause us any real discomfort or worry.
Merlan, still under full sail, was giving a good account of herself,
although solid water and spray were being hurled aboard in some
of the gusts. It was obvious to us that the worst was still to come.

We carried on for a further hour or so, then decided to take
the mainsail off and set the storm trysail. This was accomplished
without much difficulty as the wind lulled temporarily while we
were shifting sails. Hardly had we made everything secure when
it really began to blow. The advance guard of the gale, as forecast by the rapid fall of the barometer, finally menaced our ship.

Shortly after the gale struck we sighted our first light on the Victorian coast. This was identified as the Cape Woolamai Light. Here it became necessary to change course to the west in order to stand up to the Heads. Our position was confirmed some little time later when the unmistakable 22½-second flash of Cape Schank was sighted in the murky distance.

By this time the wind had veered round to the west. We decided to get away from the land and stand in once more in the morning. With the night pitch black and the coastal lights periodically blacked out in driving rain squalls, it was scarcely safe to approach the land too closely.

There was no rest for any of us that night. Those who tried to snatch a little sleep found it almost impossible to wedge into a bunk securely enough to avoid being pitched out as *Merlan* fell heavily off some of the more precipitous seas. In addition, it had become bitterly cold and all our clothing was thoroughly saturated. It was impossible to prepare any sort of a hot meal or drink. The best we could do was to snatch a handful of biscuits, an orange or an apple and perhaps a bit of chewing gum. I had quite a battle keeping my cigarettes and matches dry, but succeeded by wrapping them securely in a spare oilskin.

It was a thoroughly miserable night. Next morning (Sunday) found us under trysail and jib, ploughing through a lumpy gray sea with the wind coming in gusts and sometimes petering out altogether before coming in just as freshly from another quarter. There was a powerful temptation in some of the calmer spells to put the full mainsail back on and make a run for the Heads before the wind came in again. However, the glass was still down round the 29.5 mark and, bad as the previous night had been, we still felt we had not yet received the full weight of the storm indicated by the glass.

Putting about, we stood in once more towards the land, and about midmorning made our second landfall which was identified as the southern end of Phillip Island in Westernport Bay. We were at this time still some considerable distance off shore and making slow progress under reduced sail. Again we changed course to make directly for Port Phillip Heads, whereupon the wind began to build up until in a short time it was blowing half a gale directly out of the west. This was rather disheartening, as it meant we had to drive *Merlan* right into the teeth of the wind under trysail, not a particularly efficient sail at the best of times.

By midday the wind had mounted to full gale—about Force 10 or 11 on the Beaufort scale. Some of the gusts we estimated at from 70 to 75 m.p.h., a figure which was later confirmed by Weather Bureau observations made at the time ashore. This state of affairs prevailed for the next few hours, during which we tried to battle our way to the west under the inefficient trysail. Then the wind helped us by backing to the south'ard so that we eventually found ourselves making heavy going against a full sou'westerly gale along the Victorian coast between Cape Schank and the Heads.

Huge seas rolling up Bass Strait were making it difficult and dangerous for those of us who found it necessary to remain on deck. In spite of efforts to ease her over some of the worst of the seas our decks were being continually swept. There was hardly a moment when the self-bailing cockpit was free of water; for as fast as it could drain the contents of one sea another would pour aboard. Much of this water was finding its way below, where, to add to our troubles, both pumps had gone out of action. Soon the water below reached a level several inches over the floor boards and it became necessary to bail with a bucket, which we continued to do for the ensuing several hours.

In the early afternoon of Sunday it was decided to take in the trysail. Even that small patch of canvas was more than the boat could safely stand. With an almost continuous series of breaking seas hurling themselves feet deep across the decks this was a hell of a job.

Blinded and almost choked by the tumultuous waves, Lance, Brian and I clawed our way forward where, on looking aloft, I was somewhat startled to see the mast trembling and vibrating like a plucked harp string. The red and blue burgee of the Royal Geelong Yacht Club, its nether end frayed and tattered by the wind, still streamed from the truck. After considerable effort we managed to get the sodden trysail off her, leaving only a single lightweight jib which we expected would blow out at any moment.

Then back to the cockpit for a trick at the tiller. At the end of an hour, it was time for another spell at the bucket. To our dismay, the water was gaining on us and was now splashing up over the mattresses on the bunks. It was now a matter of getting into shelter quickly, or having the boat founder under us.

It was too late to turn back and run for shelter at Flinders or anywhere in the lee of the Schank. Heaving to was likewise out of the question, owing to the size and force of the seas. With the deadness of the sloop occasioned by the terrific weight of water in her, there was always the danger that they would overwhelm us.

Merlan had behaved magnificently in all that we had come through, and any boat less honestly built would, I am convinced, have foundered long before. But there is a limit to what even the best craftsmanship in wood can stand, and it was apparent that *Merlan* was tiring. The bailing was by far the worst of all our previous ordeals. Not only did the bucket become progressively heavier as it was handed up full each time, but the crew handling it had to brace themselves against the unpredictable dips, lurches and wrenches of the yacht.

Meanwhile, under the single jib, we had gradually closed the land until *Merlan* was not more than a mile or two off shore. The height of the seas and the flying spray was such that we could catch only brief glimpses of the nearby coastline. By midafternoon we estimated that we could be only a short distance from the Heads. We expected the entrance to be hazardous, but our condition was such by this time that it would have to be attempted in spite of the risks.

At about 4:00 P.M. I wedged myself securely against the boom and strained to catch an identifying glimpse of the shore. At the moment I was about to give up, I caught one brief glimpse of the white shaft of the Lonsdale Lighthouse on the western side of the Heads. This momentary peep was sufficient to give us a bearing, and we discovered we were about a mile due south of the Heads. It was a simple matter then to ease our sheets and run for the

Heads and what we earnestly hoped would be shelter, safety and rest.

As we drew closer to the entrance we could see the tidal signal flying from the yardarm of the Lonsdale Light. It informed us that the tide was adverse—that it was ebbing. There was no turning back. We would have to try and force our way through. The regular steamer channel in the center of the Rip was a churning, boiling maelstrom in which I am convinced no small boat could possibly have lived. Further to the east lay the dreaded Corsair Rock, unseen in the welter of white water that was the Heads, a lurking menace. Our best, in fact our only plan was to carry on as we were—as close as possible to the Lonsdale side.

With gigantic seas sweeping up under our stern as we stormed along on a northerly course, we were picked up and literally hurled ahead at terrific speeds on the crests of some of the waves. A breaking sea would almost certainly have meant our end; but though many times it did look as though we might be overwhelmed by water hurtling up astern, none broke upon us.

The next greatest danger was the possibility of a broach, and this actually happened during our hazardous dash through the Heads. I found myself grabbing for a grip on something as *Merlan* was picked up by a monster sea charging up astern and hurled ahead at a speed we estimated to be in the vicinity of 15 m.p.h. As the yacht began to slide down the almost perpendicular slope of the wave the great bulk of water which had forced its way below all ran to the nose of the boat. This, of course, left the helmsman with no control and we had a ticklish minute before the yacht was brought back on her course. But this single broach, as it turned out later, had been sufficient to bring us within the orbit of Lonsdale reef, quite lost to view beneath the boiling surge.

Next moment we struck the reef! It was a mortal blow for *Merlan*. That much was obvious after the first shock. I was standing at the foot of the hatch with a just-filled bucket which I was about to hand up to Brian. To the accompaniment of a horrible grinding sound I was pitched the full length of the cabin, where I picked myself up, dazed and shaken, with the bucket still in my hand. The dreadful, tearing, rending, crunching sound as the yacht drove on the rocks is something quite impossible to convey.

Picking myself up I began to fight my way to the hatch and escape—through an indescribable confusion of sodden sails and clothing, charts and navigation instruments, mattresses and tins of food which had been flung out of burst lockers. My one thought, I suppose naturally enough, was to get on deck.

Just as I reached the foot of the hatch (about five seconds after the initial shock) *Merlan* struck again. Once more I was hurled the length of the cabin, to end up even more bruised and battered at the foot of the mast. A second time I clawed my way through the hatch just in time to see and feel a really terrific sea lift *Merlan* bodily and hurl her forward on to the reef. Brian, who had apparently secured a firm grip on something substantial, seemed to be all right. Eric, tightly lashed in the cockpit, had likewise emerged unscathed though the heavy bronze fitting at the rudder head had snapped completely off, leaving him with the now useless tiller in his hands.

At the moment of impact, Lance had been flung violently against the doghouse at the after end of the cabin and his face was a mass of blood which poured from a nasty gash near the bridge of his nose. The effect was pretty ghastly. Apart from the shaking up and a few bruises and scratches, I seemed to be in working order.

The jib had blown itself out at the moment we struck. After a moment Brian and Lance went forward to lower it, but they found the halyard in such a tangled mess that they were forced to abandon the attempt. In the meantime I had returned below, where I managed to retrieve four life jackets. We put them on. Beyond doubt, those life jackets saved our lives in the struggle which was to come.

Within minutes, a large crowd of holidaymakers had begun to gather on the shore about half a mile away. There was, of course, absolutely nothing they could do, but we must have provided them with an interesting spectacle. The keeper of the

Lonsdale Light had witnessed the entire happening and had telephoned at once for the lifeboat stationed at Queenscliff.

Before long the lifeboat appeared, but because of the tremendous sea running, the adverse tide and the treacherous currents
and tide-rips, it could not be brought close to the wreck. Things
never looked more hopeless. We held a bit of a conference to
decide what our best course of action might be and whether we
might, by our own efforts, save ourselves. It was clear to us that
so long as the gale prevailed there was absolutely no hope of a
boat approaching us. It seemed, therefore, that we would have to
take to the water and try to make for the lifeboat cruising up and
down about a quarter of a mile away in the lee of the reef.

It was now about 5:00 P.M., and since the tide appeared to be
at low water slack we determined to make our effort before darkness set in.

On the cabin top was a small plywood dinghy. Though none
too optimistic about its chances of supporting the four of us in the
waters swirling and boiling over the reef, we did hope that it
might perhaps carry us some of the way. It did—about six feet.
We had barely left the stricken *Merlan* when our cockleshell
dinghy was swamped and we were left struggling in the powerful,
sucking tide-rip.

Within seconds the seas had taken complete control and we
had been swept dozens of yards apart. The same gigantic wave
which had engulfed our tiny dinghy seemed, once it had us
firmly in its grasp, to sweep each one of us in a totally different
direction. Then began a nightmare struggle before the eyes of
some hundreds of people.

We had swamped in one of the labyrinthine channels of the
reef, a channel through which a vast volume of water was swirling at a terrific pace. I began swimming desperately but, like the
others, was entirely at the mercy of the currents.

The most fortunate of the four, I managed to crawl through a
mass of slimy kelp on to a more solid portion of the reef. Actually I crawled part way onto the reef three times only to be
washed off. But on the fourth attempt I contrived to hang on.
Clinging grimly to the reef for a few minutes to catch my breath,

I recovered some strength. Then began a staggering walk to the leeward side, where I knew I would once more have to take to the sea for a swim to the lifeboat. Before doing so I turned to see how my shipmates might be faring.

I was elated to see Brian dragging himself on to the reef, but was quite alarmed to see Eric and Lance, supported solely by their life jackets, being swept out past the wreck into a position which seemed fatal. Then, as I watched, Eric was swept by a wave into a favorable current and began to approach the reef. He began to struggle once more and by dint of furious efforts was at last able to clamber on to the water-swept rocks. Somewhat later, Lance, nearly spent, made it also.

By this time a group of Queenscliff fishermen had succeeded in launching a dinghy and by a marvelous combination of seamanship and courage had brought the boat right up to the reef from which we had expected to have to make another swim to the waiting lifeboat. One error in judgment, one unpredictable sea sweeping aboard their dinghy, and they too, would have been struggling for their lives.

It was a comparatively simple matter to pile into the dinghy, a solidly-built 15-footer, but there was still the dangerous quarter-mile pull to the waiting lifeboat. The seas had not abated, and with eight men aboard even a 15-foot dinghy is somewhat crowded. But our rescuers displayed faultless seamanship; we got a line to the lifeboat and were hauled alongside. In a matter of moments we were wrapped in coats and blankets and a man-sized pannikin of rum was thrust upon each of us. First aid was applied to our cuts and scratches received on the boat and more especially from the jagged rocks on the reef. And so we were rescued.

The next morning, refreshed and invigorated by some substantial meals and the first decent rest in about 60 hours, we returned to the scene of the wreck. *Merlan* had shifted off the reef on the rising tide the preceding night and now was lying wedged between two shoulders of rock in about 15 feet of water. The only parts of her showing were the mast and a portion of the boom. Whether anything could be saved was extremely doubtful.

After this experience one would think that we had had enough of the sea. But Lance has declared his intention of building *Merlan II.* Eric is still sailing on Sydney Harbor. Brian has his own boat in Launceston and has no intention of retiring from yachting. I have just completed arrangements to sail in the square-rigger *Passat,* on the voyage from Port Victoria in South Australia around the Horn to the United Kingdom.

7

Crickin'

by WILLIAM H. TAYLOR

[1949]

WE WERE SAILING up one of Maine's great tidal rivers, in no hurry, with no particular destination and no desire for company or bright lights that night, when we saw this place on the chart. It was a little river that meandered down to the bigger river, and somehow it looked intriguing—the more so since none of us had ever heard its name mentioned. Even the omniscient "Cruising Guide to the New England Coast" failed to throw any light on it, and that clinched matters. We *had* to take a look at any place that skippers Duncan and Blanchard hadn't heard about.

The chart showed a sounding or two just inside the mouth, and from there on just a thin, winding black line. But the tide was down and the worst we could do was to stick a while in the mud— if there weren't any blind boulders. There was a buoy at the narrow entrance from the main river, and inside a widish bay opened up—a solitary enough spot itself, with one saltwater farm just inside of the gut and a couple of summer camps in the spruces along the far shore. The whole bay looked shoal, but the chart vaguely indicated a fathom-and-a-half channel, unmarked, winding through it, so with a good eye for distances-off and an occasional cast of the lead we eased across, wondering what made the chart-makers so sure there was a further opening to the eastward.

We were almost across when it began to open up. Some great

convulsion of the earth, geological ages ago, had split a huge granite ridge clear through, as though with a mighty ax. The Indians must have ascribed it to the work of whatever local god got credit for tearing up those parts. Straight as a string, roughly east and west, an eighth of a mile long and with vertical granite walls maybe 60 feet apart rising to spruce-topped heights well above our masthead. Here was no place for sailing, for not a breath of air could get to the bottom of that canyon unless the wind happened to be blowing fresh and due east or west; we gave her the engine, dead slow, and poked into it.

With the exhaust echoing off the granite walls we eased through, three fathoms of water under us and not much more on either side. We had hit it at low water slack—coming out next morning we bucked a four-knot flood current. Inside it widened out again, a pretty little river ambling down among wide flats on which a dozen men were digging clams, working at top pace against the return of the tide which soon drove them ashore. Back of the flats were rolling evergreen hills, an old farm and, up the river—up the river now being southward—a launch or two moored off a little wharf, and a shanty. We poked up as far as we deemed wise and anchored with half a fathom under the keel in millpond-smooth water. The water was a bit muddy but, thanks to lying under a hot sun all through the afternoon ebb, it was warm enough to let us really enjoy swimming—the only time I ever did in Maine.

The place? I've given you the clews—go find it! I've run across a cruising man or two since who'd been in there, and it must be known to quite a few. But if too many find it, it won't be fun any more.

It was one of the most enjoyable incidents of a delightful cruise. Next time we go to Maine, I think we'll spend less time running the offshore courses and visiting the better known ports, and try to find another lovely gunkhole or two up some other river.

Long offshore passages have their fascination, and there are those cruisers who like to hop from yacht club to yacht club with lots of bright lights and conviviality between runs. But if you're gaited for it, there's nothing like "crickin'," or "gunkholing," or "eel-rutting." Call it what you like, but it's the game of finding the little, hide-away harbors where few yachtsmen go; the kind of anchorage that you sort of crawl into and wrap yourself up in, and that becomes crowded if more than three boats anchor there at the same time; the sort of chimney corner which the 1200-series charts rarely even hint at and to which even the detailed small-area charts offer little more than a hint, because there's no sensible reason for the government to survey them in detail.

Crickin' is not limited to any special locality, though of course there are few usable eel ruts on open, seaswept coasts. There are a wealth of nice little gunkholes along the New England coast, from Long Island Sound to Eastport, Me., and beyond. The Chesapeake, with its many rivers running 10, 20, even 50 miles back among the woods and farmlands, is a gunkholer's paradise. From what they tell me, the North Channel and some other Great Lakes sections, and the Northwest coast from the head of Puget Sound on up, were made to order for the cricker, and so, in entirely different surroundings, are the Louisiana bayous and marshes of which Irving Johnson wrote so entertainingly in "Bayou Boating." (See "Just Cruising.") The Florida Keys are full of eel ruts, and the Bahamas, surprisingly enough, are ideal for this kind of cruising, though it takes a little getting used to, to recognize a snug harbor when it is wide open on one side, as to visible above-water protection, as far as the eye can reach across the shoal banks. Not all gunkholes are the work of nature. Some, like the various "sandholes" along the north shore of Long Island, are by-products of industry and some, like Hatchet Bay, on Eleuthera, in the Bahamas, have been opened up artificially.

The ruination of the gunkhole is popularity. Some thirty years ago I remember seeing deer come down out of the woods and stroll along the shore of Hadley Harbor, on Naushon Island, in Massachusetts. But one of the last weekends I was in there some kind of motorboat convention was in progress and they were setting up an unholy din that must have put any deer, not stone deaf, into a gallop for the far end of the island. The "sandholes" at Lloyd's Point, Eaton's Neck and Mt. Sinai, on Long Island, were peaceful places once, but on a summer weekend now you couldn't find swinging room there if you wanted to and, if you like peace and solitude, wouldn't want to.

A friend of mine used to live on a cove in a Long Island bay. He and a couple of neighbors moored their boats in front of their homes, in a deep hole behind a shallow mud bar which effectively discouraged weekend cruisers from using the cove. But one day one of the residents set up a couple of very inconspicuous range poles ashore as a leading mark for the one four-foot channel across the bar. That weekend three strange boats spotted the range and came in. The next weekend there were a dozen, and though the range was promptly removed, the days of seclusion, peace and clean beaches were over in that cove.

So the pressure of a swelling boating population around the big cities has transformed many a one-time quiet gunkhole into a place to be avoided on summer weekends. For hunting good gunkholes, as for other kinds of hunting, you have to get away from the centers of population. Once out of weekending distance of the cities, however, you can start picking out likely-looking eel ruts on the chart, and if you find other cruisers in them it's a pretty safe bet that they'll be the kind of sailors you'll be glad to meet. Many a solid friendship has begun over a noggin of rum in a secluded gunkhole that two congenial crews happened to pick the same night to visit. Such local people as you're likely to meet up the eel ruts are usually friendly folks, too; local fishermen, mostly, and a few summer cottagers and campers of the simpler sort. Not having been over-exposed to too many of the wrong kind of yachtsmen, they probably retain some faith in human nature, and they may even scull off in the dory to bid you welcome, and offer lobsters and blueberries at the local prices, and of the real flavor.

The previously mentioned "Cruising Guide" will lead you into many—but by no means all—of the eel ruts east of New York, but in most places, as in New England prior to the GUIDE's publication, the word passes from mouth to mouth, and only if you seem the right sort will you hear of the choicest spots—the ones each cricker particularly prizes. For the true cricker collects pet gunkholes just as other men collect paintings or Indian relics, and he's damned careful whom he shares them with. Some skipper you meet far up a Chesapeake Bay creek may say, "Sure, this is a nice little anchorage. But you ought to go into So-and-So, now. Here, I'll show you where 'tis on your chart. No buoys, but there's water enough if you keep the big tree on this point lined up with a white barn just about there—and when you get in past the marshy island follow real close along the starboard-hand shore. Now just here there's a little crick opens up to starboard and you go up the middle of her and anchor right in among the woods. Better run a stern line ashore—there isn't much swinging room." If he tells you something like that, don't miss it.

Even if you're a stranger in a strange land, you can pick your gunkholes off the chart, by following your hunches and the lay of the land, and find some mighty nice cricks.

You can go crickin' in most any kind of a boat, if she isn't too big or too long-legged. Obviously, it's simpler in a powerboat than under sail, though the man who does his crickin' under sail is apt to look down his nose at the powerboat skipper, much as the fly fisherman looks at the man who uses worms. If you choose a powerboat, be sure she has a good solid skeg to protect her wheel and rudder, because sooner or later you'll put her on the ground. If you're the type of pilot who travels only in the steamer channels, leaving all buoys on the proper hand like it says in the book, crickin's isn't for you. The cricker goes where there are no buoys, and going aground, lightly, is all in the day's sport to him. Room for a fat flounder under his keel is all he asks, and if he bumps across a bar to get into an eel rut, or lies with his keel well set in the mud at low water, it's all right with him. His keel, if it isn't metal, has a good husky worm-shoe on it for just such contingencies'

He doesn't require any special equipment, though a sounding pole, in addition to his lead, is quick and handy for shoal water; he likes to keep a kedge anchor made up with a good long, light rode, for rectifying his more serious errors; and a tall mast with spreaders, or a long bowsprit, make good places to conn the ship from where the water's clear enough to see a few feet under. Ample capacity for fuel, ice and supplies is desirable, because you can't obtain them in the better gunkholes.

There are times for crickin', and times when it's the better part of valor to stand on for the next well-buoyed harbor, unless you know your crick well enough to bowl right in regardless. It isn't, for instance, healthy to explore the entrance of an unfamiliar gunkhole when the wind's blowing fresh onshore, even in a powerboat, or when there is a swell breaking across the entrance—though a swell may help you find the shoal spots by cockling up or breaking on them. The best time for smelling your way into most strange gunkholes is on the first half of the flood tide. A lot of the shoals and boulders will still be bare, giving some idea of the trend of the channel, and if you *do* put her on the tide will soon lift you off.

On the other hand, there are some swell gunkholes that can be entered and left only with the tide well up. For instance, in eastern Maine, with its big tidal range, you can sail into places (with deep water inside) whose entrances are blocked by bare ledges at low tide. Even those should be attempted with the tide still making. Exploration in thin waters on a falling tide is always risky, especially so if there's a big range of tide or if there are boulders and steep-to ledges. Grounding on mud or sand flats, in protected waters, is no more than a nuisance, but around the rocky coasts of Maine and Fundy, for instance, grounding on the ebb could cost you your ship. There are other places, like the reversing falls of the St. John's River, in New Brunswick, that can be safely navigated only during a period of a few minutes at high water slack—such places are especially prevalent in the Northwest.

What the fresh water sailors do, without any tide, I don't know. It certainly makes gunkholing sound risky to one used to depending on a rising tide to help rectify his mistakes. On the other hand, there's no danger there of an ebb dropping out from under the ship and letting her fall off the edge of a jagged ledge.

But let's suppose things are just right for a try at that little harbor you've heard about, but never been into, just up ahead.

The wind's light and offshore, tide just starting to flood, no surge along the shore, indications of a fair day tomorrow, and you've a couple of dependable hands aboard. So hold her up inshore and get out the chart. It doesn't show much—just a creek coming down into the head of a cove—no soundings, no indications of anything more than a shallow drain. But George Brinker said he'd been in there and it was a honey of a hole—deep water inside but a shallow bar across the mouth. George got in and his boat draws three inches more than yours, so let her come up for it.

But is it this cove, or around the next point? The shore is pretty much all alike along here, no conspicuous landmarks. A couple of quick bearings on distant objects make you sure this is the right bight, and you hold up while half of your crew insists it must be around the next point. The chart shows some boulders and a half-tide ledge in the cove. Well, there's the ledge—come in to leeward of it and then haul up on the bearing for the mouth of the creek—if this is the right cove, she'll show soon enough. And, meanwhile, Mac better skin up aloft and keep an eye out. In a few minutes the bare ledge is abeam and, Mac, from the spreaders, thinks he sees the entrance dead ahead.

So you stand in. Now what was it George said—favor the starboard hand and watch out for a ledge to port? Or was it the other way, and didn't he say something about coming in with the opening bearing west nor'west?

"Shoalin' up," hails Mac, and you slack the main sheet to slow her a bit. "Looks better now! Ease her along in." The shore's getting close, but that little river mouth sure looks inviting.

"Hard alee," sings out Mac from the spreaders in a tone that means "And damn quick, too." Round she comes, and you look over the side and see bottom. "Sand bar in there," comes down from aloft, as you pay off, "work over more to the nor'ard and try it again."

You do, but this time Mac reports a ledge of rock ahead, and as she comes through stays you think maybe you feel her heel touch ever so lightly. Run offshore a little way, let the boys jog her around while you jump into the dink with your sounding

pole and go take a poke at it. Sure enough, there's the ledge Mac
saw. No channel here. Sound back along the bar to the southward. Ah, there she deepens a bit. Four feet of water here now,
and you're drawing four and a half. Oh, well, the tide's coming.
Now for a range—the point of the northerly beach right under
the clump of trees on the hill back there. Follow that line in.
Good enough; now she deepens. Good water inside, like George
said. So back aboard, and get the mainsail off her. She'll work
in under jib and mizzen—a handy ship's what you want for this
kind of stuff, and let somebody else win the races. And just make
a note of that range in the log in case you come here again.

Well, the tide should have made enough by now. Let her go
in on the range. "Shoaling fast," calls Mac from aloft, and takes
a good grip on the rigging, just in case she stubs her toe. But
she doesn't. The tide's made and she must have all of two inches
clear water under her—full and plenty for a hardened cricker.
Pinch her up past the point of beach, then wipe off again as the
channel winds, with Mac calling down directions for the best
looking water.

You haul up around another point—no open water in sight
now. You might be 100 miles inland. The trees are closing in
around you now, the yawl is barely moving, and Mac slides down
from aloft with a suggestion that the best anchorage looks to be
up there off that little cob-wharf with the fisherman's launch tied
up to it. The fisherman himself pauses in the door of his shanty to
look you over—the only sign of life in sight, though a road runs
back from his dock into the woods. Surprised, no doubt, to see a
stranger in this place, though he doesn't show it.

The anchor chain rattles out—not much of it, for there's only
two fathom of water and you won't need much scope here—you
could ride out a hurricane in this landlocked pool. Pretty good
for a bunch of strangers, getting in here so easy, with no buoys
or anything to help. Old Captain John Smith must have piloted
himself into places that way when he first explored this coast—
maybe into this very pocket. You feel a little like explorers,
illogically enough considering the boat and dock there and the

fact that George was in last month and lots more cruisers probably know the place. How about a swim and a drink before you light the stove?

That's crickin'. If you like it, there are a hundred little pockets waiting to be explored. And if you don't, then stick to your buoyed channels and blue water.

8

Lifeboat Passage

by GEORGE G. BREED

[1943]

"KEEP AWAY FROM THE SHIP," warned the submarine captain as his buff-colored monster pushed her ugly nose into the choppy sea and drew away from our lifeboat. "I intend to use *artilléry*."

We had suspected he was up to no good when he surfaced a hundred yards or so from us as we lay alongside our ship, rolling about in the Atlantic swells and abandoned after her bow had been blown off by a torpedo. So we took his advice, and proceeded to widen the gap of water between ourselves and the ship as much as possible. We were aware that just one round of his "artillery" might produce a chemical reaction in that cargo of ours that would be as violent as it was sudden. He didn't have to plant many salvoes in that cargo and, soon after he opened fire, her stern disappeared beneath the waves.

So that was that. It was up to us to "smell our way to Gloucester"—or rather to the nearest land, which was the Azores, the submarine captain had told us in reply to our question. We had been torpedoed at night, and it was now the next day. The sky was overcast and the wind light from the southwest—fair for a course to the Azores. The sea was sufficiently choppy to preclude any beautifully rhythmic performance at the oars, but not heavy enough to cause discomfort. The air was mild and the water by no means numbing.

Luckily, we had been able to go back aboard the derelict ship some hours before she finally went down, and had supplemented the equipment of our lifeboat with a sextant, a chronometer, navigation books and the ship's standard compass. The latter was particularly valuable in a steel lifeboat, for its 7½-inch card was obviously less subject to deviation than the 3-inch model provided for the boat.

The submarine having made off, we set about taking advantage of the fair breeze. But the boat's sail was not to be found. The boat had been swamped on lowering and had lain awash alongside the ship for half an hour or so before we boarded her from the raft in which we had left the ship. Although it was in a bag of fairly heavy canvas, I suppose the bundled-up sail had enough air trapped in it to give it buoyancy. So it was somewhere to leeward, drifting into limbo along with the rudder, which (among other things) was also gone when we boarded the boat. Fortunately all of the oars—one steering sweep and eight standard oars—were still there. Also, we had the mast. We stepped it and rigged the shrouds and forestay, and then looked over the possible substitutes for a sail. The obvious one was a tan-colored weather screen of fairly heavy canvas.

The standard rig for these lifeboats is a jib and mainsail, the latter being gaff-rigged with no boom. We laced our jury sail to the gaff. Being somewhat longer than the gaff, the outboard corner hung and flapped loosely, like a bloodhound's ears. This was accentuated by the fact that the "leach" of our sail—which had, after all, been cut for a different use—had an angle in it which ran out to second base and back to third. So we had two clews. For the benefit of those who like to experiment in sail design, let me say that two clews are as necessary and useful in a sailboat as two rudders.

In general, our ersatz sail reminded me of a suit which a friend of mine bought in Liverpool during the last war, after being torpedoed. It fitted him swell, all but the coat and pants. But, combined with the oars, the sail gave us steerage way and a little steadier motion.

There were two other lifeboats in sight. Both these had set their sails and borne off to the northward, but one—Number 3, in charge of the boatswain—hove to, to "gam" with us as we lumbered after her. I took five men out of her, bringing the number in our boat to 14. Before leaving the ship, I had determined with fair accuracy the course and distance to the center of the Azores, and gave this to the deck cadet who was to be the navigator for No. 3. We passed over to them some of the cigarettes we had collected on the ship and then stood off for the Azores. We had agreed to keep together, which obliged No. 3 to heave to at frequent intervals. She gradually drew ahead, was a red blotch on the horizon at dawn, and disappeared later that morning.

Hoping to add a tenth of a knot to our speed, we took another rectangular screen—about the proportions of these long, useless pieces of lace they put on a dining table—and rove it on the forestay, as a jib, but it was quite useless. We were considerably handicapped in adapting the canvas to our needs. Apparently while the boat lay awash alongside the ship a sea had smashed the locker containing emergency equipment and strewn its contents in the bilges and on the surface of the water. Among these was the sailmaker's kit, which was not to be found.

The following morning I took some sights. After my experience as a navigator on ocean races, I thought celestial observations in a small boat would be as easy as a ride uptown in the Fifth Avenue Coach. But even a yacht is a far steadier platform than that lifeboat was, and I had to work at it a long while before I could catch the sun as it danced about the horizon. I finally got a fairly consistent sequence of sights that gave a longitude. This I later crossed with a latitude sight which was only fair, as it had commenced to blow late that morning and the boat was already bobbing about "like a cork," as one of my companions put it.

The fix showed us a few miles northeast of the ship's last position. As I knew that our last fix on the ship was a good one and that we had not travelled far since then, these sights served chiefly to reassure me that sextant, chronometer and technique were probably adequate.

We had spent the previous afternoon in inventory. In most

respects we were exceptionally well provided for a long voyage. We had supplemented the uninteresting standard rations with two and a half crates of delicious Florida oranges and a crate of the tastiest, juiciest apples I have ever had. These, especially the apples, were wonderful thirst-quenchers.

The water situation was also reassuring. Beside the two metal tanks built into the boat, we had picked up on the ship two wooden water breakers. Also comforting was a complete outfit of blankets. Beside the six which were part of the boat's equipment, practically every man had brought along at least one blanket in our second abandon-ship. In fact, we sat upon great mounds of blankets, a part of which I had been obliged to give the Deep Six, as they seriously interfered with the management of the boat. Later on, they were followed by the bulky suitcase containing the portable transmitter. I was loath to do this, but it occupied a space into which a man could squeeze himself for a few hours' sleep. Besides, the ship's radio operator, whom I had taken from No. 3, declared emphatically that it "wasn't no damn good anyway."

Despite the boat's initial mishap, most of the other emergency equipment was there, if a trifle wet: lantern and kerosene, distress signals, bilge pump and bailer, flashlights, signal lamps and mirror, a chart in a watertight container and fishing tackle. But we lacked two important accessories; the sea anchor and storm oil. We set about to improvise an anchor out of a piece of canvas and some metal canisters, but without a palm and needle we weren't able to do much.

The next morning gave early indications that we should soon have what a Swedish friend of mine would describe as "planty o' vind." We did! By noon the seas were slopping over the gunwale fairly frequently, which kept us quite busy with the pump and a couple of buckets. There was no way of shortening sail, so early in the afternoon we doused it and hove to, keeping her into the sea with the oars. She fell off continually; we got some unpleasant slaps from breakers and it was constant "pully-hauly" at the oars to keep her into it. The watch-in-three that I had set up the day before was changed to watch-and-watch, but it was

obvious that the men couldn't keep that up long. So we turned
her stern into the sea, and found it a lot easier to swing her into
an oncoming roller with a "Give way starboard, hold water port,"
or vice versa.

We had put my not very ingenious sea anchor over the bow,
but I think it only irritated an approaching wave. I soon replaced
it with a bucket on a bridle, using our sea painter, and this was
better, especially when we swung stern to. Later on—during that
awful night—I can remember looking back on that tumbling
waste of water and foam. Just astern of us was the one cheering
sight in that whole grim panorama: the phosphorescent glow
about that bucket as it seemed to dig its heels in and pull back
on the bridle.

By nightfall, it was blowing a fresh gale from the southwest,
with the wind still rising. So far, we had been all right, for in the
daylight both the helmsman and the men at the oars could spot
a big one coming, and get the stern swinging toward it. Even
so, we'd had a couple of unpleasant jolts when a wave broke
against our metal hide with the "pong" of some grisly jackpot.
With the darkness coming on, it would be difficult, if not impossible, to see a roller far enough off to get set for it. To say that
I considered our situation grave would be a gross understate-
ment. As the gathering gloom announced that the sun was, as
the Portuguese say, "going to bed," I no more expected to see
him return than if I had just stepped off Bunker Hill monument.

This was probably an unnecessarily dismal estimate of the
situation. But as I listened to the roar of those seas grow louder
and more ominous—thinking "Now would I give a thousand
furlongs of sea for an acre of barren ground, brown furze, anything"—I didn't see how we could possibly keep from being
capsized. The seas were already coming from a wide angle. All
we had to do was to fall off so that one of those horizontal
cataracts could catch us broad on the quarter, and we'd be rolling
over and over like a piece of driftwood on the beach at East-
hampton. However, we lashed everything and prepared for the
worst.

Early in the evening, casualties began. The bushings that held the rowlocks were of brittle iron, and one by one they fell apart under the strain when a wave caught the blade of an oar "full and by." Before the night was over, every one of them was broken and we had been obliged to lash the rowlock to the gun-wale. This was not efficient but it enabled the man to work the oar. No. 2 port was the last one to go and, in that dark welter of men and gear and water, there was nothing to be found in the way of a lashing except a short length of wire. So, for two hours thereafter, a pint-sized engineer squeezed himself into a pretzel shape between the men at the oars and held that rowlock in place with the wire.

Around 3:00 A.M. the gale reached its full fury. Peering anx-iously into the blackness astern, I saw seas converging upon us from either side, baring their teeth with a menacing roar, like the wolves pursuing the Russian nobleman's flying sleigh, in which there were no babies to be thrown overboard. Which of these ravening crests would reach us first? Often my first guess was wrong and I had a few seconds to get the boat swinging in the right direction. Half a dozen times the boat heeled at a fear-ful angle as one of those white-fanged wolves crashed against our side, and time and again the oarsmen were up to their waists in foam as a breaking wave savagely swept the boat from stern to stem. It was no longer watch-and-watch, for all hands were continuously at the oars or bailing, with a chance for one or two at a time to drop out for a few minutes "blow." A couple were actively sick.

To the ominous snap of ruptured bushings was soon added the noise of rending oars. Picking the boat up bodily, a sea would slide it sidewise. Perhaps one of the men had his oar too deep. The next instant, the blade was buried vertically, the handle flew upward and, before he could boat it, the oar was snapped. Be-fore the night was over, we had three oars left.

When daylight broke the next day it was blowing from the northwest, a very chill wind, but it was obviously moderating. After 13 hours at the helm, I practically fell asleep in the middle of a command to the oarsmen. I awakened that evening to find my hand badly swollen and painful. During the gale I had been

aware of a pain in my thumb, on which there had been a small
burn. It was now obvious that this was a virulent infection. That
was the end of my left hand as far as any useful function was
concerned, as it had swelled to three times its natural size. This
was inconvenient, to say the least, as I am left-handed.

Sometime around noon the next day my temperature, which
had risen with the infection, fell enough for me to think and talk
lucidly, which must have been a tremendous relief to my companions. I found that the wind had dropped to a light breeze
and, while the boat continued to bounce around, we shipped no
more seas—except when a bucketful or two slopped over from
one of those bastards bred of every gale that suddenly leap at
you from any direction. We therefore stepped our mast and set
the sail. It scarcely gave her steerage way and didn't steady her
appreciably. And it was a pain in the neck to have to use a steering oar under those conditions; about like using snowshoes on an
inch of wet snow. But fortunately the wind was fair for the
Azores and the weather promised to be good for some time.
Pending results from celestial observations, I assumed that the
gale had pushed us 25 or 30 miles to the east, and accordingly
set a new course to the left of our original one.

About this time we ate our last oranges and I can tell you we
were sorry to see them go. They and the apples had been nectar
for, although the temperature was around 70°, you would be
surprised how thirsty you get on only a few ounces of water a
day. Furthermore, emergency rations, though bursting with vita-
mins, tend to produce a savage thirst. These rations are carefully
checked, renewed each time the ship returns to port, and sealed
in two watertight metal boxes. They are sufficient for a minimum
of 30 days for a full boat's crew.

We did not start on ours until we had been out three days, the
crew subsisting for two days on the fruit—which obviously
couldn't last—and a great quantity of peanut bars, which two
of the men obtained by breaking into the slop chest upon their
return to the ship. We decided to have three meals a day, at each
of which each man would receive three ounces of water. Breakfast was at 7:30 and consisted of two malted milk tablets and a

biscuit or cracker known as the "C-type ration." Malted milk tablets are tasty in a glass of hot milk but they are exceedingly dry by themselves. The C-type ration, in shape and size like a graham cracker, is somewhat harder than a dog biscuit and nowhere near as toothsome.

Lunch, at noon, comprised two more milk tablets and a square of milk chocolate. It was good chocolate, but have you ever tried to get real tough clay off the anchor and the deck? It takes a hell of a lot of water.

Supper offered two more tablets and the one appetizing viand in our larder, pemmican. Though many of you may have eaten it, I'll venture to describe it. It is made of raisins and meat and other concentrated and highly nutritious foods, and it's greasy and wet, which makes it go down easily. It tastes like some sort of plum pudding with hard sauce.

Two days later, we bent a critical eye upon our sail and became extremely dissatisfied with it. Everybody was encouraged to suggest improvements and we began a series of experiments in which we hung up that amorphous polygon in half a dozen different ways. The winning design was by a seaman who made a yard of the gaff and spread it as a lug sail. This was a great improvement, and we immediately began to foot faster.

In the morning, I undertook to find out where the gale had taken us. The navigational accessories were a limp and soggy lot. Although I had lashed them under the thwarts, they were all, in the police reporter's phrase, "suffering from immersion." The chronometer was still ticking but the face was half full of water, and the navigation books were soaking wet.

As I could not use my left hand, I instructed a signalman in the use of the sextant. It was no easy trick in that choppy sea. I can only compare it to taking a sight some Saturday night in one of the denser parts of Times Square, constantly thrust about, with one's elbows jostled by the surging throng. And the evening and the morning were the fifth day.

During the early hours of the next morning I devoted some time to determining the bearing of Polaris. I think it was in about these same waters that Columbus was alarmed to discover an unsuspected deflection of the compass. I can understand his consternation at finding, after several days at sea, that he'd put his faith in a treacherous set of corrupt and fickle magnets. The cause of error in our case was that that confounded iron bath-tub of ours had pulled the needle 15° or 20° to the westward.

The following noon we got a latitude sight which looked quite reliable. For the first time, the sun had been unobscured for a good half hour on either side of the meridian so we could be almost sure we'd caught her at top center. This showed us in the latitude of the Azores. Combined with a debatable longitude, this put us northwest of San Miguel Island. I swung around to a course of 140°.

I think that navigation was, for me, the worst ordeal of our entire boat ride. With my "Almanac" and Ageton soaking wet, the pages were stuck together as if they had been glued. It was a temper-searing task to find your place in the tables. However carefully you pried the pages apart, half of a page would often come up in your hand. Not infrequently, the entry you sought was illegible, and you'd start over, with another sight. But, bless that galaxy of learned gray heads at the Naval Observatory, they print the "Air Almanac" on non-coated stock which stands up well under a wetting and is nowhere near as sticky as the coated paper of the "Nautical Almanac" and the Ageton tables.

Observations during the next two days consistently put us east of San Miguel. I was now faced with the most unpleasant choice I ever hope to make. Should we turn back and hunt for these islands, wretched little fly specks on that chart of ours? We might easily wander about for weeks. Or should we launch out upon a 1000-mile journey to the continent (which we couldn't *possibly* miss) with all its hazards of starvation and storm? I was fairly sure we were in the latitude of the islands; I wasn't sure that we were east of them. If we *were* west of them, a course for Gibraltar might bring us within sight of one of the islands.

We inventoried the rations and found we had more than 30 days of everything but pemmican, of which we had 15. Of water we had about 25 days at our established rate of consumption, which could probably be cut in two—with no allowance made for what just one heavy rain might do for us. I consulted the crew. Should we put her on the course for Gibraltar? I must confess, I felt it was as big a piece of hypocrisy as a Nazi election, for they hadn't any idea whether our navigation was good or bad. But the Fuehrer got a unanimous vote, and we swung over to a course of 97°. It proved a fortunate decision.

During the next two days the clouds prevented any satisfactory observation. Then, about 9 o'clock at night, eleven days after leaving our ship, we picked up a flashing light a little to starboard. We stood toward it, and after two hours I caught a rhythm to it, proving it to be a navigational light. Not wishing to raise hopes unduly, I pointed out that, while it was probably a lighthouse, it might be an offshore buoy.

At the height of the discussion we picked up another light, on the port bow. They were loath to quit that first one, but this was a steady light, and the other (which we later learned was the lighthouse on the northwest corner of San Miguel) was still a long, long way off. So I swung her over. During the next hour that light assumed some fantastic shapes, but at last we realized that it was a ship. We set off a parachute flare and I sent the signalman forward with a flashlight. What he sent I don't remember, but they came back with: "What do you want?"

The light of another flare must have given them their answer, and a few minutes later we were basking in the glow of a great rectangle of lights surrounding the legend "RED CROSS—INTERNATIONAL."

She was a Red Cross ship, carrying food and clothing to prisoners of war. As my crew scrambled up a sea ladder, I patted her steel plates—to show my affection and to be sure they were real. Then the boatswain, a bronzed, lean and kindly Portuguese who had once lived in Brooklyn, came down and took me on his back, for it was a job for two good hands going up that ladder. Near the rail, other hands grabbed me and pulled me over the bulwark and onto the deck. I stood erect to find a steward standing deferentially before me with a bottle of cognac poised above a goblet. "Would you like a drink, sir?" he asked.

Such an account should end, "That's all I remember."

9

Harbors Can Be So Nice

by CARLETON MITCHELL

[1948]

MAN HAS SPENT several thousand years figuring out ways to make himself comfortable. Civilization, basically, is a process of insulating man from nature, an insidious affair involving ice cubes, inner spring mattresses, fleece-lined overcoats, and ear muffs.

Strangely, there are individuals who wear leaky oilskins after the rest of mankind has developed the intelligence necessary to come in out of the rain, an atavistic minority who find enjoyment in being wet and cold. These are the yachtsmen. Some may think their point of view sadistic, but perhaps their appreciation of comfort is sharpened by previous discomfort. How could a button-pushing apartment dweller properly evaluate the joy of something so simple as dry socks, a bowl of hot stew and a warm bunk?

Sometimes I think that sailing is like hitting yourself over the head with a hammer because it is so much fun to stop.

I must admit that I love harbors. I am a connoisseur of harbors. In fact, I am so fond of them I often wonder why I ever leave one. The time between is just a lot of damned water messed up by wind, menaces to navigation and indigestion from cold beans.

Don't think that I am alone in my love. Just get in a session with any yachtsman and ask him about his pet cruising area:

you'll find it consists of water of great treachery and turbulence, squalls of disastrous force, but—ah me!—harbors of the purest ray serene, snug, landlocked little nooks beyond compare. And there is always the one just too perfect for alien eyes, the ultimate sanctuary, whose location can only be coyly hinted.

In my cruising there have been many harbors, each part of the memories that go with small boating. Good harbors, bad harbors, indifferent harbors. Places where you squatted over a bar-taut chain and waited for the dawn; places where even the most timid skipper would never awaken to push back the companion slide for a quick look around; the gamut from insecure holds on sunken coral ledges to just a-settin' and a-drinkin' and a-watchin' the afternoon sun burnish the dull water of secluded gunk holes, full of peace and content, and not a-hatin' nobody.

But somehow I recollect two with especial clarity, perhaps because of the nature of the hammering on the softest part of the skull that preceded my introduction to them.

The first was when my wife and I started out from Cheboygan, Mich., on what was supposed to be a "health" cruise. After a series of disasters that were the result of the long wartime layup of our borrowed boat we eventually reached a lovely hidden nook called Pilot Cove, a last pause before beginning the North Channel run.

I had lost some of my earlier faith in the invincibility of the internal combustion engine, and of the watertight integrity of a hull that had been cradled for nearly a third of its 15 years. I was also acutely conscious that the crucial section of our tiller cable consisted of a length of ⅜" cotton line pieced into the parted ⅜" bronze cable. Bright in my memory was the maneuver of steering her with the engines performed three days earlier when the cable had failed. It was a maneuver I did not care to repeat.

But as I swam in the cold, clear water and rowed Zib as she fished with her usual unrewarded zest, I was content. The boat that morning had eaten up the miles and seemed hungry for more. The barometer, whose pessimism I was finally reconciling to the altitude, was up to a point where on the ocean a mere gale might be expected.

To prove to ourselves the ease with which a power boat can be handled by two persons, we had put in at Pilot Cove just for lunch, a swim, and a bit of fishing. "Take it easy," the doctor had said. "Don't exert yourself. Get away from a sea-level climate; go some place with a little altitude and some piney woods." And I was following the doctor's orders. I was certainly away from salt water, as I had diluted my pre-lunch nip with a dipper from over the side, and there were enough pines on Drummond Island to satisfy all the doctors in New York.

Around one o'clock we started cheerfully enough on a course which I supposed was somewhere around east, the compass card being too discolored to read. Soon we crossed False Detour Channel and the U. S.-Canadian Boundary Line and were off Cockburn Island in the Province of Ontario. A remarkably short time later we were abeam of Monk Point, and I was made aware that the wind was beginning to come in from the west. When we had first left Pilot Cove, our bow flag was blowing back straight. A little later, crossing the channel, I noticed that it hung limp on the staff, so that the wind had picked up to our speed, which was approximately 15 knots. Now the flag began to blow out ahead like a bowsprit and I could feel the wind ruffle the hair on the back of my neck.

We crossed Mississagi Strait and came abreast of the western end of Manitoulin Island, the largest fresh water island in the world—a fact that at the moment concerned me less than that the old *Kate* was becoming somewhat hard to steer. As the strain increased on the cotton line it stretched in the immemorial manner of cotton line, so that quite a bit of wheel was necessary to get a little bit of rudder. We continued despite the sanctuary of Meldrum Bay a few miles to starboard. Soon, however, steering arrangements began to demand attention. As a sea passed, the boat would settle and appreciably slow; as the next rolled under she would lift her stern, pick up speed, and sheer badly. It became necessary to grind the wheel hard over to get any response at all.

At a call Zib came on deck to take over. As soon as we slowed down, *Kate* swung into the trough and began to wallow. I finally got at the tiller cable in the after cockpit by moving the dinghy, poking the upper part of my body through a hatch and standing on my head. The cotton line had increased in length by several inches, but somehow I managed to take up the slack and make secure.

Off again, things were better, and about three the lighthouse on Cape Robert lay abeam. Suddenly over the other noises I became aware of a strange thudding sound from the engine compartment. A peek through the hatch revealed water being churned by the propeller shafts, the flooring around the engines covered, and water sloshing high on the batteries to either side. The engines were drenched by their own splatter. It was not a happy moment. I yelled for Zib to come on deck, slowed the engines and put the boat on a course which would take us into smoother water behind the cape.

With the sea nearly abeam, *Kate* tried to show us how far she could roll each way without actually going all the way 'round. I dived down the companion to get the pump in the cabin. After four back-breaking heaves, I realized I was lifting against something more solid than water. By removing the companion ladder, peeling back a carpet, and prying up floor boards, I came to the intake of the pump. It was cunningly placed to defy any attempts at cleaning. My probing fingers encountered a fine mesh screen solidly matted with lint from the carpet, and nothing short of dynamite in the bilge could have gotten the pipe elbow off. Water began to cover the cabin floor. I knew there was a spare hand pump in the locker aft, but had not tested it. I found the plunger so dry that it would not get suction.

Shouting profanely unflattering remarks at myself for arriving in the present situation, I took the deck bucket to the cabin. It would not go down into the bilge. The two parts of a double boiler would fit between the frames, however, so I bailed with both hands into the bucket, then dumped the bucket into the sink. After what seemed an endless period, we rolled our way into the lee of the point, the sea began to moderate, and I could stop bailing long enough to look at chart and pilot book.

The Canadian "Great Lakes Pilot" describes an anchorage about a mile beyond the lighthouse on the east shore of Cape Robert, but the phrase "a vessel will find excellent shelter from westerly gales" was not entirely reassuring. The wind had begun from the west but, by the time we stood in for the cape, it had hauled around to the northwest. The books say that because most low pressure areas pass through latitudes above Georgian Bay, the heaviest blows come from the west, but there was no reason why this one should not continue on around the compass. A shift beyond north would make the shelter a lee shore.

On the other hand it was nearly 15 miles to Gore Bay, the first place that looked snug. In describing it the "Pilot" noted cheerily: "The harbor is small but well sheltered from all weather, so is much used as a harbor of refuge." And "refuge" was exactly what was craved!

I popped up on deck to point out a distant headland which looked like the entrance to Gore Bay and immediately ducked back to my double boiler. After a few minutes, we were away from the shore and into the full sweep of the Channel. The sea had got up some more. Before making the cruise, the distances had seemed so short and the water so sheltered that I had been careless about checking gear. But the sea running outside the cabin windows and confronting me each time I straightened to pour a bucket into the sink was something to behold. It was big, it was short, and it was damned steep. I didn't like to think what might happen if we lost control.

Just as I began to take consolation from appreciable headway against the leak, Zib, who has sailed more miles of open ocean than most men, said that she was frightened and wanted me to take over. Coming topside, I took one look and would much rather have been down bailing where I couldn't see what was going on. It was blowing hard and the seas were showing a tendency to crest. Steering was really difficult. The effect of squatting and stopping after a wave passed under was much more pronounced; in fact, for long moments *Kate* seemed to lie dead in the water, only to have the next wave come up under her and shoot her forward like an arrow from a bow. On some she would run straight and true but on others the tendency to sheer was like coming to a curve on a roller-coaster.

And then, so help me, I saw a log ahead. It was about 200 feet in front and lay pale brown on the black water. I began trying to ease *Kate* away, when suddenly it became apparent that logs dotted the water like a handful of matches tossed in a basin! In the distance I could make out the squat form of a tug and immediately guessed the logs had broken away from a pulp raft. Even now I get cold chills thinking of threading through the maze with the tiller cable again stretched so that a full turn of the wheel meant almost no swing to the rudder, and not daring to put on any sudden pressure which might result in its parting. Finally, the logs began to thin out and I thought we were clear.

Not quite! Several seas ahead I saw one rise and disappear and rise again. I tried to ease off to starboard but *Kate* sheered back to port; I tried to ease off to port and she slithered back to starboard. The log came closer. We continued to head for it. It was like a magnet. I yelled down to Zib that there was a log ahead we couldn't avoid. It came closer and closer until I finally took the chance of putting one engine into reverse. It had no appreciable effect. Then, with the log only a boat-length away, and me mentally reviewing the stowage of the life preservers, old *Kate* took a sudden lunge and sheered off as clean as you please. The log lay astern. Janet Head and the wide easy entrance to Gore Bay lay to starboard.

Anything further would be anticlimatic. We powered on up the gradually narrowing harbor, the seas decreasing at every yard. We made fast to a dock so sheltered that the nearby water looked like a pond on a sleepy summer afternoon.

I went below and carefully chipped a hunk of ice to just fit the biggest glass aboard, uncapped a bottle of soda and located the bottle of Scotch stowed away for an emergency. This was it. . . . Considerably later I went on deck and watched the pines on a nearby hilltop writhe and sway. There was not a ripple around us. During the night the wind went around to north and to the east of north and blew just as hard. We still lay with slack lines.

The second harbor I recall with particular clarity is Mosquito Cove, on the north shore of Jamaica. My appreciation of it is based on what might have been, rather than what was. We were lucky—and it certainly could not be said that our luck came as a reward for living right. Not at Montego Bay!

We had arrived in *Carib* after several weeks of cruising the Gonave Gulf of Haiti, a downhill slide to Kingston and the south shore of Jamaica to Negril Point, then a beat back along the north coast. Unfortunately, although favored in many other ways, Montego Bay is a harbor only in the sense that a projecting shoulder of land offers protection from the prevailing Trade Winds. So long as the wind remains steady out of the east and the diurnal variations of the barometer remain constant you can begin your noon drinking with a clear conscience.

However, the Bay is wide open anywhere west of north. As Jamaica is well within the range of the more violent northers which come lashing down into the West Indian area after having rolled a blizzard across winter-bound United States, it is just like looking down the muzzle of a large cannon without knowing at what moment somebody will set it off. The first mariner to be caught was Columbus, who on his second voyage was so charmed by his discovery that he called it *El Golfo de Bien Tiempo,* the Fair Weather Gulf, only to later have reason to repent his optimism.

Leslie Fletcher, a local yachtsman, piloted us into an inner harbor off the Montego Bay Yacht Club. From the shore no division from the roadstead was visible, the harbor consisting of a submerged reef to the west and the remains of a sunken breakwater to the north. At the elbow was a gap of sufficient width and depth to accommodate *Carib,* provided an outlying clump of coral was dodged and a turn made to bring the entrance into proper bearing. During an easterly the inner harbor was perfectly calm, whereas there was considerable roll in the outer roadstead.

A few yards ahead of us swung Leslie Fletcher's own little ketch, *Ranger*, a marine skeleton at the feast. She was gradually being put back into commission after having been sunk at her mooring by a blow some months earlier. That norther began as a hard squall from the northwest, the body of the gale following without pause. Within a matter of minutes there was white water over the sunken breakwater and reef; soon huge seas were toppling across the entrance and continuing to break across the whole inner harbor. It built up so rapidly that Leslie was unable to move *Ranger* behind some cays a couple of miles away. He had to watch helplessly while his boat was overwhelmed by the creaming rollers until finally only the tip of her mast showed through the smother. Every boat in the area either sank or dragged ashore.

Just a nice sheltered harbor! Practically landlocked! A sweep of 300 feet to the east and 300 miles to the west!

Despite all the delights of Montego Bay, a certain measure of apprehension was always present. The slightest alteration in the track of the baragraph, any change in the morning easterly or in the making up of the afternoon squalls in the mountains behind the town, or even a calm when the breeze should be blowing, would set off a train of weather conversation.

From the first, Leslie told us of Mosquito Cove, a few miles down the coast, a harbor snug in any wind but with a narrow entrance flanked by reefs and hard to make out at a distance. It would be no place to approach for the first time with a big wind and sea on the stern. Leslie was willing to show it to us, but it was late in the season for a norther and each day seemed too full of other things. (I hope the reader will be charitable enough to allow he knows how 'tis!) And day after day the weather remained perfect. Nearly calm at dawn, a light easterly setting in around eight freshening to be fairly strong by ten and reaching its maximum strength around four. The clouds which had been gradually gathering and thickening on the mountain tops would then creep down the valleys toward the sea. They would invariably pass to the west of Montego Bay but near enough for us to see rain spilling down. The wind would die and another quiet star-studded night would commence.

The morning of Monday, March 18, was as beautiful as it is possible for a tropical morning to be; never was the sky bluer, the mountains greener, or the water a more vivid pattern of both. But that afternoon the breeze was lighter than usual. There were no white caps off the beach and fewer squall clouds over the land. On Tuesday it was calmer than it had been during our experience. The barometer was slightly down, and in the afternoon a faint zephyr flicked in from the northwest. Our bow swung to the open sea.

Time to get out, say you, and right, say I. But the land has ties—people, things, and the slow unwinding of red tape—especially where a clearance for Cuba is involved.

On Wednesday after the morning calm a light breeze came in from the northwest. Carrying my papers from building to building I cast unhappy glances at the harbor. Meeting Leslie, I found that his barometer stood at the lowest reading he had ever seen outside the hurricane season. But the officials could not be hurried. It was dark before the final paper was stamped.

We turned in ready for an early start. At two I came fully awake with the feeling that all was not well. On sitting up I found rain streaming across the deckhouse windows. We were rolling slightly. Pushing back the companion slide I discovered a jet black arch off to windward—and windward was northwest.

Squalls came down in regular procession, each bringing a lot of rain but little wind, periods of flat calm between. At four o'clock the pen of the barograph made a little deeper dip. At five, the wind freshened slightly and the sea began to build—a long swell impelled by a strength of wind which had not yet arrived In the first soupy light neighboring small boats could be seen plunging heavily. Breakers commenced to curl on the reef a couple of hundred feet to port. Leslie had told me that this was the danger signal which meant getting out—and fast! I could see lights in the windows of his house overlooking the harbor, and wished for his counsel. Abruptly we began to surge against our chain and the growl of wind in the rigging became loud below.

Suddenly through the rain I made out a small boat struggling toward us and almost immediately recognized it as the narrow dugout canoe that had been drawn up on the sand by Leslie Fletcher's house. It was barely making headway. As it came closer I saw that Leslie was prone on the bottom to reduce windage. The boat was diving and scooping into the seas. Leslie was lying in water and cupping it over the side with both hands. His son was paddling. As they came under the stern I hooked the bow line, and for the first time noticed Leslie's expression: I have never seen a man so upset. He was repeating: "You've got to get out of here at once!"

We were ready and in a few seconds had the engine going and the windlass manned. As we worked Leslie shouted instructions to his son for saving the lighters belonging to the Fletcher Company.

"What about *Ranger?*" I asked.

"Nothing I can do about her," he answered. "She isn't rigged and there isn't a motorboat in Montego Bay to tow her behind the cays."

So *Carib* got underway and nosed out through the little cut, the gray water bursting into white a few feet to either hand. In the roadstead the seas were big, but not cresting, and we got on the forestaysail and mizzen and began to work offshore, burrowing in the lazarette for the storm trysail as we went. Slowly we forged ahead until we could see breakers far along the coast.

Then, so help me, the wind began to moderate—in fact, it dropped quickly, so that inside an hour we had only a moderate breeze. It then conveniently hauled into the north, allowing us to lay westward parallel to the shore. But the long rolling swells continued to march in endless ranks from the northwest. Someone somewhere was catching hell—but this time it wouldn't be us!

Below, *Carib* was in the worst scramble of the entire winter. We had forgotten to close the ports. Magazines, books, clothes and everything loose had gone down to be soaked into a sodden mass. And aloft we had our only rigging casualty in months of cruising, the springstay parted where it went over a roller fitting at the head of the mizzenmast.

Our spirit of thanksgiving was not diminished by minor troubles. Sitting in the cockpit we were able to appreciate the beauty of Jamaica's coast, green and rolling foothills lifting beyond a strip of white sand beach to become blue-shadowed mountains disappearing into clouds. At around nine o'clock Leslie pointed to a section of shore that looked like every other section and said, "There is the entrance."

I saw nothing but headed in. As we neared, a narrow cut appeared just to the west of long, sloping, green fields. Hills lifted abruptly below the lower end. We came closer, rising and falling on the long swells, and suddenly looked into a channel, blue between foaming ledges of coral. We entered, following by color the line of deepest water. Suddenly *Carib* popped out into a most perfect circular harbor ringed to the water with mangrove trees. The transition was so sudden as to be startling—a gunk hole just a few yards from the ocean! Here, as Leslie had promised, "You could lie through a hurricane with a bent pin on a piece of thread."

We quickly responded to the comforts of Mosquito Cove. Before we had finished a second cup of coffee made more authoritative and aromatic by the addition of another of the products of the isle of Jamaica, a huge breakfast made its appearance. Zib and Vicki had staged a complete recovery. The sun shone from a cloudless sky. Wet gear festooned the lifelines. Our flags hung limp, and lazily I made a mental note to row ashore later and climb the hill to find out what the wind was doing. A fishing expedition was organized. I sat on the wheelbox and let that old sensation of peace—that "harbors can be so nice" feeling— take me over. The hammer had been swung threateningly enough, but only applied gently; still, I was happy to be where I was. The Cayman Islands and Havana could wait for another day.

But, most of all, I shall always remember Mosquito Cove

because of having entered and shared it briefly with Leslie Fletcher—a man whose sailor's creed was so true that his first thought had been to help another. While I won't forget the Cove, I won't forget that canoe struggling up to our stern, or the shivering, dripping figure scrambling aboard to share our chance.

10

A Cruise That Failed

by ROBERT FRENCH

[1944]

"Robert French brought the venerable 56-foot schooner 'Babboon' home to San Pedro late in June from Hawaii, 'farthest west' of the intended world cruise on which the former Burgess 'Forty' started last January. French was the only member of the 'Babboon's' original crew to stay with the ship."—from "West Coast Bubbles" by Waldo Drake, YACHTING, June, 1936.

THIS IS A BELATED ANALYSIS of why a cruise failed, with some suggestions as to how a similar situation might be avoided in some of the long ocean voyages that are being planned. Perhaps the time that has elapsed since the sailing will allow a less emotional approach. The elements that make for the success of a long cruise may be divided into three main heads; suitable boat, suitable crew, and suitable finances. These factors are variable within wide limits but, it was an improper balance of these factors that caused the untimely end of the cruise of which I write.

One afternoon in November of 1935, four young fellows went to see the motion picture "Mutiny on the Bounty," which had just come out. While still in that escapist fog which surrounds one fresh out of a movie, somebody said:

"Boy! Would I like to go to the South Seas!"

"Let's do it! Gee, those native girls!"

"Yeah, and rum—we'll live on fish!"

"I know a guy who knows all about boats, how to run 'em and everything!"

So they came over to my office and asked me if I'd be interested in going along as skipper. None of them knew a thing about boats. I didn't know them well, but business was rotten and the rum and fish idea sounded pretty good; and, anyway, who would pass up a chance like this? My own offshore experience was not extensive, but was supplemented by a passionate interest, over a long period, in every phase of yachting from design to navigation. A trip to the Orient as able seaman in a tramp freighter, which included getting tamely shipwrecked; a season on the Great Lakes, including the Chicago-Mackinac Race; on the Pacific Coast, five years in the Six-Meters and two years in the Eights. On top of this, a lot of miscellaneous cruising, which, in Southern California, is essentially open sea work.

They were the most enthusiastic kids I ever saw. We sat around till midnight telling each other about all the places we'd go and all the hell we'd raise, and wound up with the plan of a 'round-the-world cruise to last about three years. They must have consulted their parents that night, because the next morning we started out to look for a suitable boat.

Within a week we had bought the *Babboon*, a 56' by 48' by 14' by 8' 10" schooner, designed by Edward Burgess and built by Lawley in 1888. Two brothers put up the purchase price and took title to the boat; the rest of us made such contributions toward expenses and supplies as were commensurate with our current resources. More about the boat later; but she was as sound and able a craft as might be desired for real offshore work. A slight modification of rig, a little yard work, fitting out, and a couple of shakedown cruises occupied about a month. Then we were off on the first leg—to Honolulu.

Six days out found us about 90 miles from home, due to calms. Then followed about 1000 miles of sailing in variable winds, mostly to windward, before we picked up what little of the NE trades prevail in January. The passage was uneventful and was made in 24 days—not remarkable time, but pleasant enough sailing. It was, of course, beset with all the standard annoyances of life in a small boat and, in addition, had the special disadvantage of a green crew which seemed to have neither the desire nor aptitude to learn even the first principles of seamanship. The trip also had all the pleasures inherent in handling a smart sailer over a long distance and the ineffable satisfaction of making a perfect landfall.

In Honolulu, a cottage was rented and the boat virtually abandoned. Once ashore, arguments that had been held under control at sea broke into the open. As a result, one of the crew returned home. Seeking to bolster the efficiency of the crew, I obtained the services of a young friend who had little sea experience but was naturally adapted to the life and could learn quickly. He came by steamer from Los Angeles to replace the man we had lost.

After about two months in Honolulu, we sailed for Hilo, a passage of about 200 miles which took four days. We planned to stay there a week but actually stayed a month. During that time, the tendency of the original crew members to disperse became more pronounced. One of the crew flew back to Honolulu and got married. Another was requested by his family to come home. That left the *Babboon* with a crew of three—one of the initial party, my friend, and myself.

We had decided by then to omit the South Seas and go directly to the Philippines by way of Wake and Guam. We sailed from Hilo for Wake Island at noon, made a few miles offshore and were becalmed. I don't know where the Trades were but there we sat for three days in sight of Hilo. During this time, the remaining member of the original crew lost his interest in the venture and declared his intention to discontinue the cruise. He was, by that time, the nominal owner of the boat. With the coming of the wind we proceeded to Honolulu, whence he returned home by steamer. I recruited two inexperienced but willing boys, and took *Babboon* back to Los Angeles.

This passage took 25 days and included some spirited sailing weather, plenty of wind and plenty of calm. The boat was turned over to the two owners, who sold her almost immediately. How different the end of this story might have been had there been a breeze the day we left Hilo!

So ended the "world cruise" of *Babboon,* less than six months after the start. Of this time, only some 58 days were spent at sea. A total of eight men, comprising five different crew lists, served the ship.

Now, looking backward at the cruise to its beginning, the chances for success appeared good. First, there was an excellent vessel; second, an enthusiastic crew; third, there was sufficient money. Why, then, did the cruise fail?

Let us start with the first element: a suitable vessel. I do not wish to enter into the never-ending controversy as to what is the ideal world cruiser. However, the experienced yachtsman looks for certain things in a boat for this purpose. She must have seaworthiness, comfort, safety, sail-carrying ability and a number of other equally important qualities, all of which should be conservatively appraised. Assuming that one cannot afford to have such a vessel designed and built to suit his particular requirements, he will be fortunate indeed to find a suitable boat for sale at a price he can afford. It is unlikely that the ideal boat will be found; therefore the final choice resolves itself into weighing one available boat against another, neither of which may be the buyer's idea of perfection. Some alterations will have to be made to the rig and accommodations, expenses for which should be reckoned in with the purchase price.

We were lucky in our search in finding the *Babboon* almost immediately. While old, she was admirably adapted to offshore work, and was in top-notch condition. She had a large gaff main and a 16-foot bowsprit. With the aid of Nick Potter, the rig was redesigned for strenuous offshore work by using a jib-headed main and cutting eight feet off the bowsprit.

When built in 1888, for Charles Francis Adams and Arthur Adams, she was a cutter, carrying about 3100 feet of sail. Subsequently, she was converted to a schooner. After our alterations, she had only about 1100 square feet, but she was still an excellent performer. Returning from Honolulu, she did 198 nautical miles in a noon-to-noon (23½-hour) run. She often turned in runs of over 150 miles in 24 hours in moderate weather. The only time that she was reefed it was blowing so hard that the fore boom showed signs of giving way. Then she was strapped down flat and made over 600 miles to windward in four days. She was flush decked with a clipper bow, moderate freeboard, a sharp entry, slack bilges, a fine run, and too much draft (8' 10"). Her tremendous lateral plane helped her to windward and yet she would move remarkably fast in light airs.

Probably all schooners with a deep forefoot require a good deal of steering when running before a strong breeze. *Babboon* was no exception, yet she never was out of control. Her low center of gravity made her rather uneasy in a calm but gave her plenty of sail-carrying power. Seldom were oilskins necessary because of spray, and she never pounded.

Life in a small yacht is usually made miserable not by one outstanding defect but rather by the sum of a number of small annoyances. Chief among these on *Babboon* was a leaking deck. The leaks were persistent and seemed to move about and no amount of fixing would eliminate them. There is hardly a more delicious feeling than crawling into a warm, dry bunk after a trick at the wheel in bad weather, but in *Babboon* during a blow, a really dry bunk was rare.

In this cruise, it was not the defects of the ship that caused the failure. A summation of her good points and bad shows a large credit balance. She was well suited to the work at hand. Her cost and operating expenses were well within the financial limits of the party. She was not, however, properly suited to the crew. Each member of the original party, except myself, had come from a rather luxurious home life, with little outdoor experience—and no experience with living in cramped quarters with others. *Babboon* would have been a dream ship to many a world cruiser but, for this particular group, she wasn't nearly big enough or refined enough.

My advice to prospective world cruisers about the type of boat is simple: if you can't get the boat you want, get the best you can but in any case let her have a tight deck. *Get a boat that suits the crew.* If they're all ex-Six-Meter men, better find something that will get to windward. If they are inexperienced, comfort is a vital factor. If they are all experienced yachtsmen—well, at least you'll have something to argue about.

Now for the second factor: the crew. A crew is composed of individuals, who must somehow be welded together into a congenial group. Perhaps tolerance is the outstanding virtue of the individual crew member for a long cruise. Other virtues might be: a willingness to do his share, a lively interest in many subjects and, above all, a love of boats and the sea that is not a passing infatuation.

I would not care to enter into a detailed character analysis of each member of our crew. In the first place, I do not feel qualified to do so. Secondly, this would reveal my own foibles! Let it be said, merely, that the original group was lacking in tolerance and, to a greater or lesser extent, the other virtues aforementioned. To most of them, *Babboon* was a means of transportation rather than a ship; her passages a means to an end rather than an end in themselves. Politically, the ship functioned as a democracy, each member having a vote on policy. As the skipper, I had in addition full authority in technical matters. I believe that this is a good way to operate but aboard *Babboon* peace and good will were not always present—nor were they ever unreservedly absent.

To myself, who rather dislike firearms, the intense preoccupation of the boys with guns seemed out of place and dangerous in a yacht and took away attention from the proper upkeep of the ship. The extent of the armament that got aboard was almost unbelievable—five service revolvers, five army rifles, three other rifles, three shotguns, two air pistols and 12,000 rounds of ammunition. These occupied the best locker in the ship and seemed to require constant attention—and a lot of oil on the cabin floor.

The next best locker was crammed with camera equipment but the only pictures I have of *Babboon* on this cruise were presented to me by a Chinese boy in Honolulu. Now I'm not decrying hobbies or divertissement when cruising, but the equipment can certainly become a nuisance. When I think of the times I had to dig the sextant case from under a pile of guns, or found it shoved into a corner somewhere, I think maybe I should have foreseen then the early failure of the cruise.

Another point that seemed of little interest was learning seamanship. A good deal of the course to Hawaii is off the wind, often running wing-and-wing, and learning to steer calls for close attention. I don't know what the world's record for jibing is, but sight unseen I'll bet my bottom dollar on our performance. Inch-and-a-quarter boom guys, made fast to the anchor bitts, boom tackles to the rail and slacking peak halliards couldn't make up for the inattention of some of the hands that held *Babboon's* wheel. We jibed in all possible ways and in a few that looked impossible, such as jibing both the main and the fore while wing-and-wing. Fortunately the foresail had vertical cloths and a bolt rope up the leech; otherwise it would have been split a dozen times. It wasn't a bad sail, either. Once she was brought up into the wind with the preventers set, she sailed backwards fairly well, although a little hard to steer.

Arriving in Honolulu harbor, we drank up the one bottle of hooch aboard and were filled with brotherly love for a while. I think everyone had a fine time in the Islands, so fine that perhaps the joys of life afloat began to look a little dim. When the last man flunked out and the world cruise was definitely ended, I was mightily discouraged but agreed to sail the boat back to Los Angeles. My young friend was still with the ship and enthusiastic about sailing anywhere. We cast about for some good sailors but ended up with two totally green hands who impressed us at least with their adaptability. One was a Korean about 20 years old, born in Hawaii. He was one of the darndest liars I have ever known and one of the most interesting.

Out of a number of prospects, we picked the two we did mostly because we liked them. This group functioned together beautifully and the trip home was in a happy ship. The new boys were willing workers and eager to learn. After a week at sea, they could reef, hand and steer and made up for their inexperience with enthusiasm for sailing and seamanship. Each of them had knocked around a bit and had learned how to entertain himself, and all their amusement hadn't been store-bought or ready made.

Now, there had been crews aboard *Babboon* that didn't click, and here was a crew that did. How come? Frankly, I'm not exactly sure. The last crew aboard, the one that clicked, was *selected*. All the other groups aboard were assembled arbitrarily. Politically we were a limited monarchy on the homeward leg— there was only one boss. Looking back over the history of seafaring, that system has been proved successful. I guess every ship should have a skipper whose word is final in all things.

So, in choosing your crew for a long voyage, if you can't get the people you want, get the best you can but, in any case, let them be tolerant. Get experienced sailors if possible, for they will know in advance the grief to be encountered in a small yacht, and how to make the best of it. Avoid the nervous type, the man who is always in a hurry, or the man with a supersensitive nature. Beware of the green hand who may be temporarily overcome by the romance of the sea and far places. Have a skipper; let him have full authority in all things, and let him be tolerant. Get people who suit the boat—all of us can stand a good deal of luxury but not all can live happily for long in a boat that offers scant comfort. Get practical people if you can; I know people whose impracticality is a large part of their charm but the charm is shortlived in a small yacht. For instance, one man in *Babboon* traded three of our five sheepskin coats for a brass cannon. It was an excellent little cannon, and made a brave noise, but it wasn't much comfort on a cool night at sea.

Element three, finances, was the only item that was satisfactory in *Babboon*. I don't mean by this that unlimited capital was available or that it was evenly distributed among the original crew members. But the financial condition was workable and did not have much bearing on the failure of the cruise.

Possibly the element of available money is variable within wider limits than the other two factors discussed. The deficiencies are more easily overcome—not so much by getting more money as by doing without. A capable crew can do much of the maintenance of a boat. People in the out of the way places are hospitable and do not expect lavish entertainment in return.

I have talked with many who think they can start out on a

world cruise with little or no credit balance and earn their expenses en route. Those who have had actual experience say that earning money is practically out of the question when once out of the U. S., unless one wants to compete with labor at about 40 cents a day. Writing professionally may net some income but is not a readily negotiable commodity.

Te Rapunga arrived in Honolulu while we were there. She had been 87 days at sea from Australia and had had an extremely hard trip. The crew was worn out, depressed and broke; but they all grabbed typewriters and started to write like mad. At best, it must have been several weeks before they could have obtained any cash from their effort. An old gentleman came into Honolulu alone from Los Angeles in a 36-foot Block Island boat. He, too, was tired, discouraged and broke; and he found he couldn't write well enough to sell. He wanted to go around the world—a lifelong dream—but he returned home instead. There were several yachts for sale in Honolulu at sacrifice prices as a result of intended long trips with quick endings due to one reason or another; lack of money was one of the common reasons.

Profitable trading with natives is a common delusion. Trading may net a little in the way of souvenirs and perishable foods but not much else. A poor trader myself, I have usually come out second best in any deals of this sort, as the average Polynesian is a pretty sharp operator in a trade. He will *give* you almost anything he's got but feels obligated to win in a swap of any kind— and somehow always seems to hold the trump cards. The glass-beads-for-an-island days seem to be about over.

Not that I am advocating world cruises only for those in the upper brackets! But a cash balance large enough to take care of emergencies would be a nice thing to take along. If you can't get all the money you want (and who can?) get what you can; but, in any case, let it suit the ship and the crew. A yacht requiring a lot of upkeep expense and a crew that has little capital are incompatible. Conversely, a bunch of boys with a lot of money will not live happily for long in a cramped little tub, however seaworthy she may be. If the crew members have a lot of guts and enthusiasm and cooperative ability, they can make up for a lot of things that money will buy. Remember that the purchase price of the boat doesn't represent the entire outlay: supplies and gear can run up into a surprising figure. And don't expect any income from the trip itself—if some should turn up, good; but don't bank on it.

11

Trooping from Dunkirk

by T. NORMAN HINTON

[1940]

DUNKIRK! IN ALL the tragedy, all the glory, all the heroism of it there sometimes intruded something out of place; something almost comic. One looked at the heterogeneous assortment of odd-looking craft that sailed there and thought what a fantastic menagerie class they would make; what a nightmare for any handicapper!

Motor cruisers from the Thames and from the Broads, ships' lifeboats, converted and otherwise, barges with brailed sails, river launches, pinnaces and picket boats, drifters and dinghies, beach boats and bawleys, tenders and tugs. A thousand of them or more; I do not know how many. Dutch *schouts* from Amsterdam, now proudly flying the White Ensign; Belgian boats from Ostend; French smacks. Fast launches that made no bow wave but sent fountains of spray spewing from somewhere about amidships as they planed; fire floats, still with their monitors; yachts and R.N.L.I. unsinkables.

But why should I try to paint the picture when I scarce know the texture of the canvas? Let me, rather, try to tell my own tiny part in the great composite whole.

When I say tiny part I mean just that, without any affectation of modesty. The whole episode of Dunkirk was composed of tiny parts, but there were such a lot of them that they amounted, in the total, to a gigantic factor. That observation really tells the story; a tale of a horde of unimportant people sailing a vast collection of ludicrous little boats across the Channel, thereby cheating the German bombers of chances of hitting big targets.

From my own point of view the affair started when I received a telephone call, just before midnight on a certain day, asking me if I would take a motor cruiser from Maidenhead to Sheerness or some such place, and there hand her over to the naval authorities, by whom she had been commandeered. I said yes, of course, and first thing next morning I was giving the men from the local boatyard a hand in getting the vessel launched.

She was the *Curlew,* 37 feet o.a., 10 feet beam, and powered by a pair of Morris Commodores. She was a handsome, healthy sort of craft, built originally by Vosper and reconditioned (with some alterations to the accommodation) by one of the Thames yards. She had a spacious two-berth cabin forward, a comfortable steering shelter, a roomy central cockpit over the engine room, and aft, a galley, a toilet compartment and another two-berth cabin.

She was laid up in her shed when I first clapped eyes on her, but within two hours she was sliding down the slipway and by lunch time the ballast had been shipped. She trimmed nicely with five pigs in the tiller-flat, 25 under the after cabin, and 21 under the fore cabin. I was glad to see this weight securely stowed so that nothing short of a capsize could shift it.

The propeller shafts had, of course, been uncoupled when she was laid up, and I understand that the engines had received no attention for a couple of years or more. Two fitters got busy at once, however, and by late afternoon she was ready to start. By 6:00 P.M. she was at my own landing stage.

I wonder how many other people have sailed off to war from their own front gardens? My youngster was having a birthday party and the guests lined up to wave adieu.

We steamed downstream until a quarter of an hour before closing time and then tied up at Laleham for the night, getting under way again with the dawn. This early start meant that we had to work most of the locks ourselves, and we were not sorry when we arrived at Teddington. Below Richmond we found that we could open up the throttles without causing a nuisance by our wash, and later we arrived at a pilot station.

There we reported to a naval patrol launch and received instructions to fill up our fuel tanks and lay in a supply of provisions for ourselves—that is, the engineer and myself. So he promptly went ashore to buy food, but no sooner had he gone than a naval officer came alongside and handed me a chit to obtain the rations without payment. So we had a double supply, but neither of us was the sort of man to grouse about a little matter like that. Anyhow, we were given another parcel of food when we arrived at Southend, to which port we were instructed to proceed.

Our average speed over the ground was roughly ten knots. They kept us alongside the pier overnight but roused us out before dawn to give us routing instructions. We got orders to take fuel for at least a further 130 miles' cruising. As there had been no real opportunity to check our consumption, we decided to play for safety and, after filling our tanks, we stowed a couple of five-gallon drums of petrol under the engine room hatches, lashing them securely and uttering a prayer that no spirit would splash out of the bungs and on to the exhaust pipes.

Unfortunately, we could not get hold of a funnel for filling purposes, but my resourceful engineer managed to scrounge a fathom of hosepipe, and when the filler of the Primus was tucked into the end of this we had an appliance that enabled us to top-up the wing tanks while holding the drum outboard, thus avoiding the risk of petrol spilling into the bilges. We were mighty glad of that length of hosepipe, later.

We also filled our fresh water tank and, as we were not certain of the cleanliness of this, the cruiser having been laid up for so long, we supplemented the supply by another 20 gallons in two-gallon cans. We wanted to be able to offer the troops a drink and we were not allowed ashore to buy anything with more of a kick in it. We had plenty of good grub for them, anyhow, as well as medical stores for any in need of such. And this reminds me, here and now, to give full marks to the organization behind all this. Not only had the naval authorities rounded up all the boats; they had all the stores ready for us. And they were not niggardly about them, either—real butter for the troops, lots of good, sound, fresh eggs, dozens of white loaves, jars of jam, tins of milk, herrings and canned foods. (Good well-known brands, too, not like the dogs' dinners of 1914–1918.)

Yes, and they gave us a Bren gun to mount on our little foredeck, and a couple of sacks of ammunition. Oh, yes, and they lent us a couple of ratings to man the Bren gun. Good chaps they were, too. Young, but very willing. We had left port some hours before I learned that neither of them had ever been to sea before.

We left in company with a rather larger and faster yacht, the *Cairngorm*. She soon drew ahead of us as I was keeping a knot in hand (for the owner), but suddenly a fast naval launch appeared from nowhere and a rear admiral who was aboard her hailed me and asked if that was the best I could do.

"No quite, sir!" I called back. "I was saving the engines for later."

"Then *don't!*" he replied. "Make full speed for Dunkirk!"

"Very good, sir," I answered, opening the throttles as far as they would go.

He steamed alongside us while he gave us further instructions.

"When you arrive at Dunkirk," he said, "go on past the Mole and put in to a beach about two miles to the east of it. Troops are waiting for you there. Load as many as you can, and if possible put them aboard a bigger vessel and go back for more. If there are no big boats about, bring your men straight back to England." Then he sheered off and left us to it.

We fairly made the *Curlew* tremble. At 1600 revs. there was a good deal of vibration and noise, for the motors had been neglected and were in poor fettle. The needle of the thermometer moved hard around and seemed to be trying to make another circuit of the dial. My engineer opened the hatches to let the cool air in, and I was glad to see the needle ease back to 98 degrees.

There was naught amiss with the oil pressure, thank goodness, and we kept at full throttle all the way across.

As the gull flies, the distance to Dunkirk is about 41 sea miles, but we could not, of course, lay our course as the gull flies. The entrance channel runs practically due east and west, that is to say, more or less parallel with the beach, and the local chart is not a pretty sight.

Nor was the seascape. When still some five miles from the channel entrance, we sighted a great column of smoke coming from a vessel which we could not identify. She was lying on her side and appeared to be about to take the final plunge.

She was too far to port to warrant our changing course and, anyhow, there was shipping quite near her, so we judged that the survivors had been taken off long ago. Two miles further on, however, we sighted another blaze, this time a couple of degrees to starboard of our course. We veered over towards it and found that it was the remnants of a ships's lifeboat, burning so furiously that it was impossible that there could be anybody alive aboard. So we resumed our course and donned our tin hats.

Our full throttle gait had brought us up to the *Cairngorm* by this time, and we tucked ourselves into line astern with her and only a few yards clear. And so we steamed for some time, keeping our station until—and I shall always aver that it was by the intervention of Providence—the engineer reported to me that it was absolutely imperative that I should ease the engines for a spell. I can see now the worried look on his sweat-grimed, steel-hat-crowned visage as he peered up at me through the open hatches.

"Drop the revs, sir! Ease her down a bit—there's one valve sticking and everything's hot!"

I eased her down—promptly—to 1200 revs. And simultaneously, for a reason then quite unknown to me, the *Cairngorm* used her last fractional knot to jump still farther ahead of us.

And in that moment a bomb fell between us!

Had we not slowed down, we must certainly have been hit; so would the *Cairngorm* if she had not speeded up! We learned afterwards that the *Cairngorm's* captain, a Lt.-Commander, R.N.R., had spotted the German plane diving towards us from right astern and he called for full speed just as he saw the bomb released. My reason for slowing was, as I have said, to cool the engines; I had no idea that a plane was near.

Anyhow, the bomb exploded a few feet ahead of our stem and a few feet astern of *Cairngorm's* transom, and the first thing I knew about it was when I was hurled bodily off my perch and against the two large reversing levers. Fortunately, I hung on to the wheel, and I was able to turn her head into a huge column of water that swept towards us. She rose to it, but the lashings on the port leg of the Bren gun's tripod burst asunder and we nearly lost the weapon overboard. The rating who was manning the gun hung on for dear life.

I could not see for a moment, because the sea was still piling up from the bomb explosion and our head was pointing skywards. Then we lurched again and plunged downwards, downwards, over a great wave crest. I looked for the *Cairngorm* and could not see her. "She got it!" I shouted.

And then I saw her. Still afloat and still forging ahead. Somebody aboard her held up both thumbs to us; so she was all right.

I learned later that the explosion had blown her compass right out of its gimbals but, although she took a few splinters aboard, she received no serious damage. (She was not so lucky next day, when a tug bashed into her and sent her to the bottom of a home port harbor like a stone—but that is another story.)

The German plane zoomed away out of sight ahead of us, but scarcely had the unshipped Bren gun been secured when we sighted her returning to the attack from right ahead. This time, however, she dropped no bombs. Instead, she machine-gunned us, and we saw a ploughshare line of splashes as the bullets hit the water a few feet from our side. The Bren guns from the *Curlew* and *Cairngorm* spat out bursts together and the plane made off.

At the entrance to the channel, two drifters lay at anchor, a mine-sweeping cable slung between them. I saw no sign of life aboard either. A little way to port, two raking masts, with ratlines, stuck up through the oily waves. To starboard was the shore and just beyond the dunes was the artillery defending it. Brave chaps, these men, but whether of Gaul or Albion we did not know.

A dinghy, rough-built, black-varnished, empty, came lolloping down on the ebb to meet us. We dodged 'round her and sped on. Cork lifebelts there were in plenty—untenanted but floating abjectly.

Ahead on our starboard bow, a dark grey cloud hung in the sky and blackened as we drew nearer. It was the pall that hung over the doomed city of Dunkirk.

On the shore, the guns roared. Heavy thuds, hollow booming sounds and crisp crackles. High overhead the dreadful drone of a bomber. A flashing, hawk-like shape, darting like a projectile through the sky, gave us the answer. The bomber was German; the fighter British. And the fighter seemed to be moving two feet to the German's one. We did not see the end of the chase— neither did we see the bomber any more.

Wrecks dotted the roadstead. Smallish vessels they appeared to be, judging from their top-hamper, which was all that remained above the waves. And on the beach, hard aground, a drifter, or it may have been a tug, showing us her stern as she sat upon the strand.

And a destroyer, which somehow did not look like a British destroyer and perhaps was not, standing stark upon the beach, broken, where a bomb had hit her, and stained all over with the same hue—rust red. But not the rust of weathering. No, the scar marks of flames that must have swept her from jackstaff to ensign.

The Mole!

Alongside it another destroyer, made fast by springs, warps and breastline, putting up a noisy barrage and sending her shells inshore, over and beyond the stricken city to where (we guessed) the enemy lay. Yet not so absorbed were those aboard her that they forgot to keep an eye to seaward and another one cocked aloft—as we can bear witness, who saw her frighten away another German plane that came into view.

The *Cairngorm* was ahead of us still; perhaps a mile or more ahead of us by now. But we were gaining on her as we passed the Mole because she had slowed down to half speed and was already sounding her way close inshore. That helped us; we could leave our lead line coiled and follow, confident, in her wake. Nor did we slow down, for we yearned (at least I did) for the comfort of her companionship—the companionship of the only other vessel under way in Dunkirk roads that afternoon.

Two spritty barges sat on the beach, "buttoned" together. *Cairngorm* made for them and so did we. Both of us arrived together. They could make good landing stages, we thought, but we dared not tie up; the tide was ebbing and no more than a foot of water remained beneath our keels. So we kept our engines running and held our craft with their forefeet just clear of the sand.

"Both astern! Neutral! Port ahead! Starboard ahead! Check her with both astern! Neutral! Starboard ahead! Port astern! Neutral!"

The beach was thick with troops. Troops sitting down on the drying sand, troops standing up, more troops arriving on the beach. And horses, naked without their harness, galloping forlornly over the shore, aimlessly, senselessly, fruitlessly, trying to get away from the bangs. Motor ambulances, abandoned when they had carried their last sad loads to the water's edge and left to be covered by the sea, which now, receding, disclosed them in all their pathos.

The *Cairngorm* had sent her dinghy ashore, a leading seaman sculling. In shoal water, he turned her and backed her in, so that men could climb over her little transom. They waded into the water and got aboard, two or three of them.

What hour-long minutes! What age-long hours! We had one dinghy between the two of us, *Cairngorm* and *Curlew,* and her gunwales were awash with four aboard. They came to the *Curlew* first and clambered on with their baggage, mountains of it.

Frenchmen they were, but if Frenchmen are excitable, these were not. They were cool, calm, brave, and much at their ease. And as each came aboard, he thrust out his hand in greeting and said: *"Bon jour, m'sieu!"* It struck me as being laughable—yet heroically laughable. Men who can remain gentlemen in such conditions are men indeed. I felt proud when they stepped aboard. They did our little ship honor.

It had been 4:40 P.M. when we arrived at the beach; it was

5:31 by the time we got our passengers aboard—yes, I kept my
log!—and after loading we had to wait until 6:25 P.M. ere
Cairngorm had her complement aboard. She, being larger, took
a few more than we but how many I cannot say. I do know, however, that poor *Curlew* was sadly overcrowded with 24 souls
aboard. No doubt her peacetime owner had considered six a
pleasant party on the Thames at Maidenhead. . . .

Yes, 24, with the cabin roof piled high with baggage under a
lashed-down tarpaulin, was a fair load for the Channel. Fortunately, the Channel was as calm as it ever is. But the Channel is
never calm to a small boat. It was not too bad until dusk fell.
Then we met three transports, Dunkirk-bound, and travelling
fast. In peace time, they had been crack ships on the Dover-
Calais service but now they were showing that their previous best
passage had only been a dawdle; they were travelling—and sending up a wash.

I shouted, *"Prenez garde!"* and the soldiers hung on to anything as I turned her nose to meet the wash. The tinkling sound
that came from the galley gave us a foretaste of what we were to
suffer when, later on the voyage, we met destroyers moving at top
speed. That was worse, much worse.

And it happened after dark. Clouds hung low and blotted out
the stars. Everybody was steaming without lights. And we were
in the path of a far-flung, fast-moving convoy going to pick up
the troops we had left on the beach. I had posted the two naval
ratings as lookouts while the engineer kept his eyes peeled from
amidships. Yet barely had we espied the dark shapes of the
destroyers then they were abreast of us. And a moment later
we met their wash!

I spun the wheel round and turned into it, and I had already
taken the precaution of crowding as many men into the central
cockpit as the space would hold—to lighten the ends, of course.
But even so her bows failed to rise to the crest, and she took most
of it green—or, rather, black. Then she shuddered, shook herself,
and emerged—momentarily triumphant but dreading the next.

What a night that was! Every ship in the world seemed to be
heading towards us and not a light among the lot of us. If the

clouds had lifted, things might have been much better but the lookouts' task was like searching for black cats in coal mines. And it was no comfort to think that, if we could not see the big ships, the big ships certainly could not see us! I felt tempted to turn to the northward and dodge out of the lane into quieter waters but somewhere ahead of us *Caingorm* was going through similar hell and I reflected that if we escaped into the solitude we might be jumping from a frying pan into the fire; some patrolling vessel might mistake us for a U-boat's conning tower.

Anyhow, we pushed on, dodging when we had a chance to dodge, and all the time trying to make port as soon as possible for the sake of our brave but half-drenched and exhausted, passengers.

And then, with still some ten sea miles to go, our starboard engine failed us. We limped on with one.

When at last we made our landfall, we found we were a little off our course, three or four miles "round the corner," so to speak, and not more than a tiny error on a course from Dunkirk. In any case, the mistake did not delay us unduly and with one engine silent we eventually got into our port, landing our troops at 4:00 A.M. Since leaving Southend 24 hours previously, we had had a crowded day. It seemed like a week.

But we were ready for more after a sleep and a feed. And it was worth it.

NOTE: For this first eyewitness account by one who took part in the rescue of the B.E.F. from Dunkirk, *Yachting* is indebted to *Yachting World and Power Craft,* London.

12

Across the Great Bahama Bank in *Diablesse*

by FREDERIC A. FENGER

[1925]

IT WAS A LOVELY DAY toward the end of March—such as would have passed for June up north—when the mate and the skipper found themselves alone on *Diablesse*. What had passed since we had run into Provincetown on that wild night in October seemed so curiously remote that it was hard to believe we were not back in our fitting-out days, with a huge, unknown craft under us to prepare for sea. Only she seemed not so large now, the familiarity of vagrant months of cruising and living had shrunk her, or expanded us, or perhaps done a little of both.

There had been some small adventures in the canals and rivers and sounds of the inside passage, and the taste of half a gale in January, off Cape Fear. That had washed the morale out of Nathaniel, who subsequently had managed to get himself fired in Miami, so that he might resume his passage home to Grenada in less "chancy" ships. For a time there had been one Willie T., a working guest, but he had been called home by an urgent telegram. Fate, and perhaps some wild stories ashore on the part of our ex-cook-and-deck-hand, had rendered us crewless, for in all Miami there seemed not a soul willing to venture the run across the maligned Gulf Stream with us to Nassau. So we had made up our minds to go it alone—the two of us. The northers were about through for the season, and if it did come on to blow we'd just reef in plenty of time instead of sailing into the breeze and having a smell of it first, as the skipper usually does. For we were pretty well shaken down with the little old schooner and each knew the other's ways.

We were loafing in the cockpit—smoking and darning socks— and the balmy afternoon was trying to mock us when a scrubby little motor skiff, with a small white man and a large mulatto in it, circled around us contemplatively and then drifted alongside. The small man, not at all seagoing in appearance, had been giving *Diablesse* a real sailor's once over. Now he introduced himself over the rail and asked if we wished to sell.

No, we did not wish to sell.

He was so plainly disappointed that the skipper asked him aboard for a drink. And that must have been very like having some one say she'll be a sister to you, when you've proposed at first sight. He had a contract, it seemed, to supply some real estate boomer with ten thousand baby coco-palms, which he was going to pick up along the Bahama cays, "—and that would mean many trips and spoil a little ship like this, with all the litter," he added resignedly. Would we like to have some grapefruit? All right, he'd send us a couple of hundred in the morning. Then his keen eyes spotted the skipper's mute fiddle hung between the carlins. "Now if you-all'd like, I'll take you home for supper. I've got a fiddle that was made in 1736 and used to belong to Adelina Patti."

Extraneous matter, perhaps, but that is how things befall one in cruising life, and many of our contacts we could lay directly to *Diablesse* herself. We had our "gam" ashore, and when our friend learned that we were without crew he volunteered to see us as far as Cat Cay and to send his mulatto with us the rest of the way to Nassau.

Another afternoon and we were dropping down the bay, where we anchored for the night inside of Cape Florida. Our friend not only had kept his word as to the grapefruit, but also had brought aboard chickens, a ham, and no end of small provender till our transom lockers and ice chest were filled to bulging. His big mulatto was doing the graces in the galley and all was very well aboard *Diablesse*. She was going foreign for the first time.

Early in the morning we were off, in a light wind from the north, and as we sailed out past the Cape a tiny black and yellow warbler flew on board and hopped about as though making a Sunday morning inspection. Then it flew off and we slipped away upon the almost calm bossom of the bugaboo Stream. Evening found us still in the Stream, drifting to the nor'ard as fast as we were crawling ahead. Night came on, warm and portentous, and we lazed on deck with half an eye to a great thunderstorm gathering to the south'ard. The mulatto grew restless and went below, and the mate slept while our friend and the skipper yarned to all hours—lover and husband of *Diablesse*, one might say, quite content in being at sea with her. For one can share a boat, if not a wife.

First we saw the cloud blink from Great Isaac reflected under the low night set, and then—after a few boat lengths—its flash popped up from the horizon, a bit to loo'ard of our course. The Stream had been kind to us, after all, for here we were only sixteen miles off our course and the thunder squall had melted away astern. We stood on for a bit to gain slacker water and then came about just as "rosy fingered dawn" was spreading out over the east. Where had been the roving eye of Great Isaac, stood its white-and-red banded tower, a lone monument in a wide expanse of sparkling wind-lipped sea. The rattle of blocks on travelers caused a stir below decks. The big mulatto poked his sleepy head up from the crew's hatch, cocked it for a moment at the light tower on our quarter, and drew it down again through its mahogany shell. A thin wheft of blue smoke began to drift to loo'ard from the battered head of our galley pipe. The mate sat up, yawning, and asked, "Where are we?"

The skipper nodded toward the end of the bowsprit. Nothing at first but bare horizon. Then presently, as though they had been waiting till she rubbed her eyes, the tops of palms came up, like so many little balloons, while under them a low island slowly rose from the sea. Great Isaac had retired astern, like a discreet butler.

"That'll be Bimini," said the skipper, "and I'm a-thinkin' she's waving her hands to us." And the skipper began to sing,

> "Hoo-rah! and up she rises,
> Hoo-rah! and up she rises,
> Hoo-rah! and up she rises
> Early in the morn-ing."

Only it was our first tropical island, instead of the anchor, that was rising, and the mate went on,

> "What shall we do with our crazy skipper,
> What shall we do with our crazy skipper,
> What shall we do with our crazy skipper
> Early in the morn-ing."

And *he* answered,

> "Fetch his chow and that damn lively,
> Fetch his chow and that damn lively,
> Fetch his chow and that damn lively
> Early in the morn-ing."

And then the mulatto laid out the breakfast in the cabin and relieved the skipper, who, with a light heart and an empty stomach, went below to join the others.

As we drew near—well along in the forenoon in a lisping breeze—a flotilla of small boats came out, sculled by sturdy negroes and lean whites with gaunt faces that peered up at us from under great broad-brimmed grass hats, and made insistent clamor for us to buy all manner of reef fish, huge sea lobsters and sponges. We dropped anchor off the creaming beach and ran up our "Q." In due time the harbormaster, colored and pleasant-spoken, came out; we bartered for a pilot and stood in.

The water shoaled till the sand ridges of Bimini's door sill fondled our keel, and then deepened hospitably as we swung around the point to enter the almost landlocked harbor. The mate cried out for joy. Here was the isle of palms she had been dreaming over all winter while we had been bumming our way down the coast. For Bimini—it is really North Bimini—lies around an oval lagoon in almost atoll formation—a fitting introduction to our tropic cruising. The south cay closes up the foot of the harbor and meets her sister with drying reefs to the east'ard. Beyond the reefs our first glimpse of the mottled waters of the Bahama Bank.

We hold well up. White sand beaches all around us, sloping up from the clear, almost invisible margin of the turquoise lagoon to the encircling land behind, where tall-columned coco-palms dropped their fan-like fronds lazily above picturesque huts, most of them with thatched roofs. A broad cement walk, built by the village criminals, led up to the tidy customs and the harbormaster's house. And beyond, a neat, white-paled cemetery clung on the back of the ridge, a sobering reminder that even here, after taxes, came death. A fathom and a half of greening tepid water under us, through which we could see every clump of bottom grass for an acre around, as clearly as the castle and washed pebbles in a new goldfish bowl. Our anchor sat down, rested lazily on its elbow for a moment, and then slowly dug in its fluke as it turned over on its back and stared up contentedly from its shackled ring, totally oblivious of a promenading family of small crabs who scuttled away—sank mysteriously into the fluid sand—and came up again to count noses and investigate the rude intruder.

It was a kindly place. The harbormaster sent out a boatload of jelly coconuts, and when we came ashore his jolly black wife cut the lone rose from a treasured bush and gave it to the mate. Then, followed by half the population, we explored the cay, and at the southeast end were shown a well dug by the Spaniards, where the original fountain of youth is supposed to have been. The mate waded and the skipper swam, and when we were thirsty a native would walk up a tree, like a monkey, and knock down a few nuts, which were then pointed and lopped open for us with deft strokes of a cutlass. There is no industry except the gathering of coconuts—which raise themselves—some sisal growing, and some small traffic with wreckers who come in for shelter from the northers. The people fish a little, just to keep from starving. And that was the Bimini of the simple days, before American prohibition turned it into a rum hole.

Three days later we ran down the reefs to Gun Cay, where we stood in and dropped down to an anchorage behind North Cat. The element of time was now gone out of our lives. When we should become bored with sitting in one place, we would hoist our jib and make for another. We'd be fetching down to Grenada for the hurricane season.

So we loafed for a day at Cat Cay, bought a couple of broilers for a shilling, saw our first shark, a big dark fellow, cruising up current along the bottom like a pointer sniffing up field, and had our first essay at conch salad. The next morning we put our friend ashore and got under way.

If one can picture a small continent largely submerged under two fathoms of the clearest water, in which the navigator explores his way through a maze of coral heads, sand bores, shoals and ridges, even by moonlight, its circumference fringed with reefs and mangrove swamps, islands and cays and cuts of intriguing name—Double Headed Shot, Blue Hole, Deadman, Gingerbread, Shroud, Galiot, Washerwoman, Loggerhead, Flamingo—as though they had been taken right out of a boy's book of adventure; and bitten into by two great arms of deep blue ocean, where suddenly the bottom drops away to a thousand fathoms and more, where the shallow sea is mother to all manner of curious marine life, yours for just the seeing—that would be the Great Bahama Bank, extending southerly and easterly from Great Isaac for more than three hundred miles and having a width of over two hundred.

Our way lay across a neck in the northern end of the Bank, sixty-two miles to the Northwest Channel, where we hoped to pick up a pilot from some wandering sponger to take us out to the Tongue of the Ocean, whence there would be blue water to Nassau. From Nassau we would again cross the bank to Ship Channel and then run down Exuma Sound and follow the eastern cays on our way to St. Thomas.

The wind came light and southerly and there was a slight drop in the barometer, indicating a shift around through west, sooner or later. We might get a touch of a norther out of it, in which case we planned to ride it out somewhere under Mackie Shoal—about half way across.

From Gun Cay light we ran ESE for eight miles, where we altered our course to E by S for twenty miles to 25° 27′ north latitude, along which at six o'clock we headed due east for the Northwest Channel. It was a lazy drift, but why use the engine, for at best we should have to spend a night on the bank. One after another the cays behind us melted away into the frail horizon and left us quite to ourselves on the watery overlay of the bank. At times we could make out the keel marks of the mail schooner, which draws two feet more than we.

Diablesse almost sailed herself and for the greater part of the day the helmsman conned his ship as well, picking up the coral heads from the weather run and spoking the wheel from time to time with his foot. It was bizarre voyaging for us, for we were not used to sailing mile after mile over visible bottom. Curious little obsessions presented themselves—that the bottom would rise ponderously and leave us stranded, like Noah's Ark, ere we could sail off into deep water, and there would be many miles to walk among coral hummocks and flopping fishes before we could get back to Bimini; or that the bottom suddenly might drop away and we should be engulfed in a Gargantuan inrush of boiling sea. And if the bottom should shimmy!

Tea in the cockpit, while the sun went down in the flat water and gave place to the moon. We continued on—the skipper or the big mulatto conning from the bowsprit end—until ten o'clock, when clouds began to obscure and we anchored in two fathoms, where the sand ridges begin just under the tail of Mackie Bank. The mate and the skipper slept on deck through the rest of the night, while thunder squalls circled around us and an occasional shower tickled our faces with its swishy edge. But it was warm and we did not mind the rain.

At five in the morning we made sail in a bare whisper o' breeze that strengthened after breakfast till we were threading our way between the ridges at something better than four knots. We seemed to be traveling much faster. By ten o'clock the wind was hardening and hauling into the northwest, with a rising barometer, and the skipper was becoming a bit anxious, as we were sailing into a nasty little pocket for riding out a norther in case we could not pick up a pilot soon enough to take us out through the channel.

Dark clouds were mounting in the north and it had come to the point of making a quick decision as to whether we had not better run back for Mackie Bank, when towards noon we picked up the unmistakable rig of a sponger dead ahead. A pretty race now, to get into blue water before the squall broke. On with the ballooner and the large fisherman's stays'l, and at one o'clock we spoke the sponger, just inside the barrier reefs. One of her crew was already in the crosstrees, but we were taking no chances on following her through. There was some sharp bartering from rail to rail while we took in our light sails.

Three pounds, they wanted.

The skipper'd see 'em in hell first. Somehow he was not so worried now—with the light sails in and *Diablesse* so handy under her lowers we *might* follow the cusses, after all.

"W'at yoo gibe, Yonkee?"

"Three dollars!"

And even while the skipper was regretting that he hadn't said thirty cents, two of the "conchs" jumped into a skiff and were coming alongside.

But the job was well worth the three dollars—and handsomely earned. Narrow-hipped, rangy devils they were, in deep copper, satiny skins, and they sprang aboard with an alacrity that was good even for northern eyes to see. If only we could take on such a fellow in Nassau! One walked right up the fore rigging, his big toes clutching the stays like a monkey's, and set in the crosstrees, while the other made a quick hitch with the painter end and took charge at the wheel. No excitement—no jabbering—just a motion of the hand, perhaps a word now and then, from the one in the crosstrees, who looked out over the water as though he were some urchin surveying his own familiar back yard from up a tree, while we twisted and dodged and worked our sheets through the intricate passage. Even the sponger following close astern did not attempt to nose our wake, but kept one of her own men aloft.

The clouds, now purple-black, had gone around into the northeast and were coming down for us in rising folds. Under them a narrow ribbon of deep blue ocean met the pale emerald of the outer bank water, which was ever shortening, first on one bow and then on the other. All around us lay the varying shades of browns and yellows from the "heads" and sand ridges, and as the widening ribbon of ocean crept up, there came streaks and spots of blue, showing deeper water. Over towards Blackwood Bush a small white boat was silhouetted, cameo-like, against the angry sky. To the southeast a couple of spongers, Nassau-bound, were already shortening sail.

We were still in pale water when the conch aloft called out, "She aal clear now," unlimbered himself from the crosstrees, and came down the shrouds on the run. That had been a bully job o' work, and how those fellows grinned as the mate handed them their money and took over the wheel! With a "Swif' passage, Mistress," they were off in their skiff. The skipper and the mulatto were lowering the fores'l.

The last stop was passed and it had just gone four bells by the clock below, when we shot into the deep blue of the Tongue of the Ocean—and the squall was on us.

Whoosh! And our preventers hummed as we nosed into the first of it, just to gauge its heft. Then slowly we eased away till we were on our course again, with the wind just for'ard of our beam. As our lee rail said good-bye in a roach of foam, the big mulatto scrambled up the canting deck and found refuge in the weather rigging. It was plain that he was a bit nervous.

"Better not stay there," shouted the skipper. "If those shrouds let go you'll fly with them. Clear to Cuba." So he shifted aft a bit and hooked his arms through the life line. "Like as not, that'll go too," persisted the skipper, who was in one of his wild moods. And the mulatto crouched down along the rail—all through the worst of it. Then the rain came, whipping in slanting curtains that shut everything from view but the immediate sea around us, which was making rapidly.

For two hours we tore through it—and that was one of those times when the skipper swore that some day he'd have a boat with boiler iron sails and Hell's own straps to hold her rudder, and *then* he'd whistle for more wind. A time to die happy, if one could but appoint the very hour of one's demise.

When at last we popped out from the tail of the squall, there was one of our spongers, only a mile ahead, with the fores'l off her and her main reefed down to a handkerchief. Soon we passed her, "head up and tail over the dashboard," and as the clouds began to break we picked up the other. The wind had now eased to a fresh breeze, as in the clear end of a summer gale at home, and the seas were longer. It was good ocean sailing. Our lee rail began to dry and the chalk faded away from the mulatto's face as he took more comfort in things. Soon after sighting us, the second schooner ran up her fores'l, but still we gained, and then they shook out the reefs from her main. She was holding us now —not that we were trying to race, for our idea merely was to catch up and follow her in.

It was now well along in the afternoon and New Providence was showing ahead. *Diablesse* straightened up in the softening breeze, like an old lady who has been hurrying unsedately and preened herself in her furbelows of light sails. But our sponger was still some distance ahead and toward sundown she inconsiderately scuttled off to loo'ard, where, in the evening set, we dared not follow through the short cut under the cays. We ordered tea in the cockpit and held on for the light on the end of Hog Island. As the moon came up from the rolling sea we crossed the bar, and at seven-thirty dropped our anchor in the channel off the wharves of Nassau. *Diablesse* had averaged 8.67 knots from the Northwest Channel.

13

Two Bells and a Half

by PHILBROOK PAINE

[1947]

THE STORIES which I have read of the Pacific war usually get around sooner or later to a first of something. First to drop the atomic bomb; first ashore at Buna; first to get back to the Philippines. Heroic stuff from which legends are made, all right; but I maintain that, in my own unheroic way, I also can claim a first in the Pacific—possibly a first and only. I will go even further than that and stake out a claim for being the first and possibly the last man since Fulton to send an order down to the engine room of a ship for two bells and a half. And while it undoubtedly created something of a sensation aboard our Army Transport ship, it never had the publicity which it deserved.

The *TP 243* was a West Coast purse seiner, 74 feet long, converted by the Navy in the early days of the war to a grim, gray dog of war with one proud 20-millimeter on her after deck and an extraordinary ability to roll 60° and come back. But before the Navy ever had a chance to find out how much further she would go over and still come up, it sensibly sold her to the Army. The Army tried her out and promptly gave her to the Army Transport Service with orders to proceed to Brisbane, Australia. And, except for this one time, her career in the war was pretty much routine and unspectacular, being confined to carrying food up and down the New Guinea coast long after the war had swept past that island; though she did eventually get up to the Philippines. The last time I saw her she was lying at the wharf at Tacloban, dirty, tired and unloved; a nonentity in a sea of ships, her past forgotten except for this one remarkable thing. Even as I bade her good-bye, a curious group of ATS men were gathered on the pier, reverently peering up at the pilot-house.

"In there," said a hard-bitten skipper of a tugboat in awed, hushed tones, "a man actually sent down an order to the engine room for two bells and a half."

"It should be preserved as a monument to the ATS," said another. "How did it happen?"

I could have told him, but instead I melted quietly into the crowd and made off. I wanted to be alone with my memories.

The *TP 243* had arrived at Honolulu on the first leg of her voyage out to Australia in a state of considerable disrepair and turmoil, the run from 'Frisco having served as a kind of shakedown, so the Army gave us two weeks to mend our ship and our ways before sending us down to Pago Pago. Except for Sparks and the gunner, who were Army corporals, *TP 243* was manned exclusively by civilian personnel in the Army Transport Service. We had an old merchant marine skipper who for some reason or other unknown to us had joined the ATS instead of going back into the merchant service. Speculation about this included every crime in the book, from scuttling a ship sometime in his past to ordinary incompetence, but I suspect that his age had something to do with it. He claimed he was 65, but he was probably 10 years older. His freely given opinion about the modern sailor was not high and, as events proved, entirely warranted. "Not a seaman in the bunch," he growled over and over again.

I held a rating of second officer, but was on board *243* as a deckhand for the voyage to Australia. The Army had reasonably assumed that this was a good way to get its ATS personnel out to war, and that if a man would make a good second officer he should make an even better deckhand. This was a fallacy.

Our orders eventually came down to sail on New Year's Day, 1943, in convoy with six other purse seiners, escorted by a mother ship called an FP which was almost 100 feet long. We were to rendezvous in the harbor just off the Aloha Tower at 1400 and proceed to Pago Pago.

I was assigned to the mid watch with the second mate so, a few minutes before sailing time, we went up to the pilothouse to stand by. It was an assignment that all of us dreaded because, contrary to supposition, a man who has handled a big ship inevitably has trouble docking and undocking a small one. The skipper could be counted upon to make a mess of it and his nervousness and irritability always got the rest of the crew nervous and unhappy. If anybody was standing on the dock watching, we could count on hitting something on our way out.

At five minutes of two, the skipper came out of his little room that was just abaft the pilothouse, stepped out on the bridge and spoke to the chief engineer. "Wind the bitch up, Chief," he said. He came back in. "Stand by the bells, Paine. Joe," he said, indicating the second mate, "you take the wheel." My heart sank.

Now there are several different methods of indicating to the engineers down in the engine room what maneuver is required, but the system under which we were supposed to operate was two bells for ahead; one to bring her to a stop; three to go astern, and one to bring her back to stop. The next two bells put her ahead again, etc. A jingle calls for more speed. I knew this but, after our first few maneuvers that afternoon, I was ready to believe that something more was called for.

After taking in the lines, the skipper, who was standing on the port bridge wing, yelled in for go ahead. "Two bells," he said. "Two bells, sir," I repeated back and tugged the cord twice. The TP moved slowly ahead, then fetched up short and bumped against the dock. It was discovered that one stern line was still made fast. The skipper roared his opinion of the seaman from the bridge wing and, after the offending line was taken in, decided to back her out. "Three bells," he shouted. "Three bells, sir," I said and pulled three times. We went astern for a short distance and came up all standing against the bow of a tanker that was lying innocently just astern of us. "One bell," cried the skipper, a little too late. "One bell, sir."

Then the skipper suddenly decided on a new attack. He waited to see if the wind would blow us away from the dock. It didn't, because it was coming from our starboard side. We snuggled up against the piling. The skipper blamed the crew, the engineers and God. "Hard left," he cried quickly. The second officer repeated his command and threw the wheel hard over. "Two bells," he said. "Two bells, sir," I echoed. The stern swung out momentarily and the bow nosed along the dock until it plowed gently but firmly into the rudder of a Liberty ship ahead. "One bell, for Chrisake!" shouted the skipper. "One bell, for . . . sir." The TP eased ahead under the counter of the Liberty and we could reach out and touch her sides from the wheelhouse.

An admiring crowd began to gather on the dock and from the after rail of the Liberty, as well as from the bow of the tanker, certain ribald suggestions were made. The skipper had turned a fiery red and was almost beyond coherent speech. "Three bells!" he roared. "Three bells, sir," I repeated dutifully and yanked the cord. We didn't fetch up on the main street of Honolulu but that was because the tanker was there to stop us. "One bell," the skipper sobbed through his foamy lips. "One bell, sir."

The mate of the tanker leaned over the rail of his ship far above us and scrutinized the situation. "Hey, you goddam Japs! quit bumpin' us, will you?" The crew told him what he could do. The second mate at the wheel had worked up a fine sweat trying to follow the skipper's orders. As each maneuver ended with a crash, he put his hands over his ears and said: "Bang!" From the size of the crowd which now lined the dock and watched entranced, it was plainly a time that called for extraordinary measures. No recognized method of undocking was going to get us out of there. The skipper paced hopelessly around the four-by-four bridge, stared belligerently at the gallery on the dock and then gave his order.

Now it has never been fully explained what he did say exactly, but in my eagerness to help in some way to get the ship away from the dock I was ready for anything. I was sure that the extraordinary measure had come. He may have said, "Two bells in a hurry!" The wind was blowing against him.

"Two bells AND A HALF!" I shouted back. What it meant, I

didn't know, but constant nagging on the part of the skipper had weakened my confidence in my maritime knowledge. I suspected that it was an order for a crabwise maneuver. How to give the signal was another problem, stemming directly from the known fact that if you hit a bell once it rings once. For an instant I was hurt to think that nobody had ever told me how to do it. Even the puzzled look on the second mate's face did not deter me. I seized the bell cord and gave it two vicious pulls. Deep from the engine room, I heard the bells ring. Then I gave it the half bell. It started out like an ordinary pull, but just at the last moment, I eased up on the rope. It worked! Sounded altogether, the signal could have been interpreted as "dong, dong . . . ding!"

Elated, I waited to see what happened, and the reaction was not long coming. The second mate took his hands off the wheel and stood gaping at me, unable to speak. "Well, what was the matter with that?" I demanded sharply. Before he could answer, the skipper tottered slowly into the wheelhouse and regarded me in unbelief. I thought that maybe his age had finally caught up with him. He stuttered a few times before he got his question out. "W-w-what did you say?"

"Two bells and a half, sir!" I murmured. The skipper looked as though I had hit him in the face. "Oh!" he said weakly. "Two bells and a half." Without a word he turned and went out on the port wing. He rested his head on the bridge rail a moment before looking up at the crowd. His voice trembled. "Did you hear that?" he cried to the men on the dock. "I've been sailing in ships for 65 years. I was going around the Horn before most of you were born. I've seen many a nincompoop in my time, gentlemen, but this day, New Year's Day nineteen hundred and forty-three in the harbor of Honolulu, is the first time that I ever heard a sailor send down a signal like that. It's history, that's what it is, history. Two bells and a half!"

The reaction on the wharf was instantaneous, and to me rather rude. Men fell down where they were and chewed the planks and pounded the feet of those still able to stand up. In the ship, the full import of the moment had not yet come to the men on deck, but in the engine room, the occasion was marked by the sudden shutting off of the engine. The chief engineer and his assistant climbed wearily up the ladder and perched on the deck below the wing. The skipper glared over the side at them.

It was then that a tradition as deep and as constant as the sea itself came to my aid. The historic contempt with which the deck department generally regards the engineers broke to the surface.

"What the hell's the matter with you?" the skipper demanded suddenly. The deck was sticking together. "When I call for two bells, I want two bells. When I want one bell, I'll yell for it. And, by God, when I want two bells and a half, I want you to goddam well give it to me. Get me? Now get down that ladder and start that engine rollin'!"

The chief shook his head and backed slowly down the ladder. "What the hell do you make of that?" he asked his assistant sadly.

But the triumph over the engineers did something for the skipper, for he bounced into the pilothouse and slapped the chart table. "Okay, Columbus, let's get this crate out of here. You just stand by those bells, Paine, and by God, maybe we can make this crate fly." He went back to the bridge and had the crew break out a spring line. When it was made fast he yelled for hard left rudder and two bells. "Two bells, sir," I answered and tugged on the cord. The stern swung out into the stream. "One bell, Columbus." "One bell, sir." *TP 243* backed smartly away from the wharf, and the skipper gave the orders which set us going slow ahead. The men on the Liberty followed us along their deck, shouting and waving, until we were out of sight around the bend.

Except for the reputation which it gained for us among the ATS fleet, that was practically the end of the incident. However, all the way down to Pago Pago, during the mid watch, we heard the skipper shouting in his sleep: "Two bells. One bell. Three bells, Two bells AND A HALF, Chief, and be goddam quick about it, too!"

14

The Sky Readers

by GERSHOM BRADFORD

[1927]

A HARBOR TUG was boldly cruising far out at sea. Her skipper had sighted a sail, still hull down, and the little boat, in hope of a tow, was making full speed in her direction. It was mid-day and, dinner over, the deckhand was sitting on the bitts forward, the engineer on the rail abreast the engine room, and the captain leaning in the open window of the wheelhouse. All were smoking contentedly in the mild sunshine. It was Nov. 26, 1898.

It was calm, with the characteristic misty-smoky atmosphere of late fall days. The barometer was normal, perhaps a bit high; there was a little swell from the eastward, just a little, but there was no anxiety as to weather aboard the low-freeboarded tug-boat.

It was the custom back in the '90s for these boats to go far to the eastward of Boston Light, especially in calms and light airs, seeking the big schooners from the south with coal and lumber, or a square-rigger from distant ports, that they might give them a lift to a harbor. And the shipmaster whose vessel was rolling helplessly in a calm could hardly resist the offer of a tow, unless for some special reason, such as Sunday. Ships in port of a Sunday are a dead loss. And, too, the weather figured greatly in the decision of the master during the fall and winter months.

There was no radio in those days, and the Weather Bureau was of little use to vessels coming on the coast. The masters of such craft were on their own. All their lives they had trained their faculties to judge the sky signs; it meant success or failure—even life or death. Every part of the sea and sky was under their constant scrutiny, alert for a hint of a shift of wind.

The sail proved to be a four-masted schooner named the— Well, never mind her name, it would hardly be fair.

The wind was so light it failed to fill her sails. There was barely steerageway, and the helmsman lolled on the wheel. The canvas and all slack gear slatted with vigorous thuds as she rolled on the easy swell. Otherwise there was an air of settled tranquility—an air of patient waiting for a breeze.

"Want a tow, Cap'n?"

The master took the offer passively. He seemed perfectly satisfied with the situation.

"No, Jack. Tomorrow's Sunday and I've plenty of time. I'm bound into the Mystic (river)."

He stood easily, with a foot on the low quarter rail, as he exchanged news with the tugboat skipper. He was a handsome, finely built, middle-aged man, with all that commanding assurance of a shipmaster. He, perhaps, lacked some of the graces of the deep-waterman; but coasters had little time for graces.

The deckhand threw a bundle of newspapers to the schooner's deck—observing that traditional courtesy of the sea. The tug swung off. The hope of a Sunday ashore was disappearing from the faces of the crew along the rail, but the master raised his hand pleasantly in parting salute, with a perfect confidence in his plans. There was not a whisper in his mind that he was breathing the air of the most subtle weather-breeder that had ever beguiled the New England coast.

A half-mile to the southward lay a three-master, which immediately became the tug's objective. Arriving close off her quarter, there was here a contrasting scene. All was activity. The crew was getting a big hawser from below; the master, a Portuguese, was nervously pacing the deck.

"Want a tow, Cap'n?"

"Yes. Get me quick out of here," was the surprising answer.

Yet the weather betrayed at least no obvious sign; only the keenest instinct saw some veiled forerunner of a great disturbance. What the Portuguese saw he did not tell.

So this was the situation out at sea beyond the range of communication. It was of no avail that the wires ashore were jammed with warnings. It was being made known that two storms, one from the south and one from the west, had united away to the southward of Block Island, and now, with tremendous intensity, a great blizzard was moving at an extraordinary rate for Cape Cod, close on the heels of all precursory signs.

The tug straightened out on the long hawser at about 2 P.M. and for five hours her propeller churned a rising sea, her smoke was blown by a rapidly making gale against a thickening sky. At 7 P.M. they arrived off the narrow, iron-bound entrance to Boston Harbor with a northeast snow storm at their backs. The steamer *Portland* passed them close aboard heading defiantly to her destruction.

The tug's apparently easy contract was becoming a heavy one. It was nearly midnight when, with the schooner nearly beyond her control, she got her "between the ferries," a snug berth used in those days. Here, with two anchors down, the three-master rode it out, while fifty vessels were being driven ashore outside.

From midnight on through that memorable night the Massachusetts coast was swept by the most violent blizzard ever recorded in those parts. The destruction was tremendous. At one point on the coast where there was a row of cottages one day, the next there was a channel leading inland with six feet at low water.

Weatherwise fishermen, coasters and pilots listened to the song of the sirens, luring them to keep the sea that drowsy November day. After the "world had turned over with a sigh" and the skies had cleared, searchers among the great piles of snow and ice found their bodies tangled with the wreckage of their vessels. But the Portuguese—at least, it paid to sail with genius.

The graceful, able four-master was never seen again. She was literally torn to pieces on the outer ledges in that riot of wind and water. Among the high piles of spars, sails, and timbers of many craft cast up on the beaches, a quarter-board was found bearing her name. That was all to be identified.

Her master's words, of only a few hours before, carry a haunting ring: "No, Jack. Tomorrow's Sunday and I've plenty of time. I'm bound into the Mystic."

15

A Pacific Voyage in 1400 A.D.

by WESTON MARTYR

[1930]

TAHITI LIES in Lat. 17° 30′ S, Long. 149° 30′ W and Hawaii in Lat. 19° 30′ N, Long. 156° W. The distance between the two islands is about 2400 miles—a long passage. If we had to make that voyage in a small yacht we should take care that our boat was seaworthy and well provided with ample food and drink and a navigator who knew his job. Personally, I should refuse to make the voyage at all unless I were shipmates with a really good navigator, a properly adjusted compass, and two or three chronometers with rates I could rely on. It came as a surprise to me, therefore, when I learned that, long before the Pacific was discovered by white men, the Tahitians frequently used to sail to Hawaii and back again in dugout canoes, without any help, of course, from chronometers, compasses or canned food. Consider it! A dugout and no compass and a passage as long as that from Halifax, N. S., to Plymouth, England, and the prospect before you, if you missed your island landfall, of— Well, look at the chart!

With knowledge of the ethnological evidence available and of the surviving native tradition on the subject, it is possible to reconstruct one of these early canoe voyages from Tahiti to Hawaii and return with, I think, fair accuracy.

The canoes used were from 80 to 90 feet long, hollowed out from hardwood logs of three to four feet diameter. Two of these dugout logs, scarphed end to end, were required to make a 90-foot canoe, the joint being sewn with sennit made of coconut fibre. When digging out the logs, a strong flange was left all along the inside top edge, or gunwale. Upon this dugout base topsides were built up (or rather, sewn on) to give a good freeboard. The fashioning of these planks must have been a tremendous job, as metal was unknown to the Polynesians, and all they had to work with were tools of stone and shell and, perhaps, sharks' teeth. Two broad planks about two inches thick were all they obtained from each tree, the logs being divided into two pieces longitudinally, the round parts outside being cut away. The top and bottom edges of each plank were cut to leave stout flanges projecting, as in the case of the gunwale of the dugout. Innumerable holes were bored in these flanges through which the sennit was passed when sewing the planks and the dugout base together.

This form of construction seems fairly strong; indeed, some of the canoes are reported to have remained in use for 100 years, being of course resewn when necessary. Deck beams were lashed on and decks laid in the bow and stern, the midship third being left open. Ocean voyages were invariably made in double canoes; two canoes, one generally larger than the other, being lashed together side by side, but kept apart by a system of strong beams. A floor was laid on the beams amidships, and upon this a roofed shelter was erected.

The sail was an immense affair of woven coconut fibre, spread on light spars and set on a mast stepped amidships in the larger and leeward canoe. The sail was reefed by rolling up the lower spar or boom. The mast raked well forward and at its top was a wide fork over which ran the halyard. The canoes could be paddled and were steered by a long, heavy oar lashed over the stern. I have seen the actual oar used to steer an historical Fijian war canoe named the *Silatolu* and reputed to have carried a crew of 300 men. This oar is about 25 feet long, with a blade eight feet long and two feet wide.

A crew for this voyage from Tahiti to Hawaii which we are reconstructing numbered about 60. They were all picked men and each was an expert at some particular job, such as sailmaking, carpentry, fishing, catching sea birds, cooking, etc. The men went into training for months before the start of the voyage. They were then tested, having to swim immense distances or paddle a canoe for a day or two without food or water, and if a man failed to pass these tests he lost his place in the crew. The skipper was generally a chief noted for his skill in handling canoes, his ability to read the weather signs correctly and his knowledge of the "sailing directions" for the passage. The Polynesians had no system of writing and the courses, landfalls and the strength and direction of the winds and currents likely to be encountered on the voyage were handed down from generation to generation by word of mouth, so that it was advisable for the skipper to have a good memory. The navigator was a medicine man or priest, who made a great mystery of his job and took pains to keep its inner workings secret. He embarked with a basket full of charms, images and other instruments of navigation, including a hollow, carved gourd or coconut shell, of which more later.

The principal items on the provision list were sundried fish and *poi* or breadfruit paste which, if properly looked after, will keep good for months. The drinking water was carried in calabashes; but rain, flying fish, bonito, birds, squid and sharks caught en route were mainly relied on to keep the crew alive. A large number of wooden scoops for bailing were always carried, because the canoes leaked badly at the seams in rough weather.

The canoe would set out from Tahiti at that season of the year which had been found by experience to be most propitious; probably in July when the Trade Winds are fairly constant in strength and direction, and gales are rare. It is as well to look at a chart here to see the sort of job this canoe-load of brown men had before them. Remember that they had no chart or compass and that they must sail 2400 miles, across the SE Trade Wind belt, through the Doldrums, and then across the NE Trades. During the passage the North and the South Equatorial Currents would be setting them to the westward and the Counter Current setting them to the eastward an unknown number of miles per day. At the end of their long passage they must either sight the Hawaiian Islands—or die.

I do not wish to exaggerate their difficulties. They probably knew as much, if not more, about the weather conditions of their part of the ocean as we do today. They also had a fair knowledge of astronomy. They had names for the brighter stars and the most conspicuous constellations. They called the planets "wanderers" and knew the North Star was approximately fixed. It seems certain that they could sail a rough course by the stars and by the sun, making allowances for changes in azimuth. It seems to me, however, that theirs must have been a very rough course indeed. I do not know how far out my dead reckoning would be after sailing 2400 miles without a compass or a log. It would be far enough out, however, for me to miss Hawaii altogether, I'll be bound!

According to native tradition the first "sailing direction" ran something like this: "After leaving Tahiti and the Submissive Isles (the Paumotu Archipelago?) sail with the wind broad on the right hand. When you lose sight of Neve (a star in the southern hemisphere; we do not know which) then Apato'a Feti'a (Polaris) will stand as a guide to you." These directions are clear and take our canoe safely north as far as the equator. I say the equator, because, sailing from southern latitudes, the North Star is not visible until the line is crossed. I also take it that the canoe would then be in about Long. 142° W, because, since leaving the Paumotus, she has been sailing with the wind abeam, and the Trade generally shifts from SE towards E, as one approaches the northern limits of the SE Trade.

The sailing directions for the next portion of the passage seem to imply that one must "Steer for Apato'a Feti'a" (due north) until "the wind dies" and you come to "a region of calms and squalls with much rain and thunder." This is obviously the Doldrums, through which they would paddle, still holding a course north true and steering by Polaris. I judge, therefore, that when they reached the southern limit of the NE Trade in, say, Lat. 8° N, their longitude was about 143° W.

From here on they were told to steer what amounts to a good

clean full and by on the starboard tack through the NE Trades. There is usually more east than north in the wind in the southern portion of the NE Trade belt, the wind coming gradually more and more out of the north as one sails northward. Taking this into account, if we plot on the chart the probable course made good by the canoe, we find, by the time she reached the latitude of Hawaii, that she would be 500 miles or more to windward and eastward of her destination. If she continued to steer full and by she would sail on north and west, into the blue, and that would be the end of her. However, the amazing fact is that, when the canoe reached the latitude of Hawaii *she was turned due west and sailed down her latitude until she made her landfall from the eastward.*

Here you will ask, "But how did they know when they had reached the latitude of Hawaii?" If you had asked the canoe's medicine man or navigator this question I expect he would have told you what I feel sure he told the rest of the crew. He would say "Thanks to my great cleverness and my power of working magic, I am able to ask the stars the way and *they* tell me." I feel certain he said something like that. And then he would take out his charms and images and that hollow gourd or coconut I mentioned before, and perform his magic rites and "talk with the stars," asking them the way to Hawaii. But it is hard to get away with that sort of thing nowadays. The rest of the crew knows too much.

We know, for instance, that in the museum at Honolulu there is a thing called the "Sacred Calabash." It is a large hollow gourd, with its top cut off and there are four small holes bored through it an inch or so below its rim and spaced 90° apart. Until about 1905 nobody knew much about this Sacred Calabash, except that the natives firmly believed it to possess magical properties and affirmed that it, or others like it, had always been used in the old days to guide the canoes in safety from Tahiti to Hawaii. Then Lieut. Hugh Rodman, U.S.N., came along and looked at the Sacred Calabash with an enquiring eye. He filled it with water up to the holes and measured the angle made by the surface of the water and a line drawn from any one hole across the bowl to the top of the opposite rim. He found this angle to be about 19°. Now the latitude of Hawaii is about 19° N and the altitude of Polaris, measured from sea level at Hawaii, is also about 19°. These coincidences caused the Lieutenant to take the Sacred Calabash down to the beach, where he took a sight of Polaris with it. The water in the bowl kept the calabash level and on looking through one of the holes at Polaris he saw the star tangent to the opposite upper rim of the bowl.

It thus becomes clear how the nagivator of our canoe knew when he had reached the latitude of Hawaii. The Sacred Calabash is nothing more or less than an instrument of navigation, crude perhaps, but based upon scientific principles. A sextant, set to measure 19°, could be used in precisely the same manner. It is clear also that Lieut. Rodman was a man with plenty of brains and a suggestive imagination, and this no doubt accounts for the fact that he later became an admiral. Admiral Hugh Rodman eventually commanded the squadron of American battleships which fought in the North Sea during the Great War, and if you wish to know more about him I strongly recommend you to buy his book *Yarns of a Kentucky Admiral,* in which he deals with this matter of the Sacred Calabash in detail.

The return voyage from Hawaii to Tahiti was a simple matter for our canoe; simple as far as the navigation was concerned, at any rate. The canoe merely sailed on a close reach on the port tack through the NE and SE Trades, until she encountered the Paumotus, which archipelago, stretching as it does for over a thousand miles right athwart the course, it would be impossible to miss. Once arrived at the Paumotus, our crew of brown sailors would merely have to ask their way to Tahiti. I wish I could hear some of those yarns they told when they got safely home again. They certainly were proper sailormen, and as such I expect they stretched those yarns a bit. And I think after what they had accomplished that they had certainly earned the right to blow as hard and lie as much as they wished.

16

My Boat Foundered!

by ROBERT UHL

[1950]

MY BOAT foundered. She was a 34-foot cruiser, double planked, twin motored, just out of the shipyard after a thorough overhaul. She didn't hit anything. She was overwhelmed by a heavy sea, and foundered in just three minutes. The four people aboard all got ashore, though for several hours we had little hope of surviving. We made all the papers. I had dozens of phone calls from yachtsmen friends, asking how it happened. For weeks afterward I repeated the story while fellow boat owners shook their heads and told me what I should have done, or shouldn't have done, or what they would have done, or why a similar accident couldn't happen to *their* boats. My friends' reaction to the story was incredulity. My reaction to their comments was alarm that they should be so cocksure, and at what some of them said they would have done.

Suppose I tell you the story, and see what *you* think. I'll admit that there's not much chance of such an accident happening to *you*. Your boat is seaworthy. Her hull is sound. You've got more than the legally required safety equipment. You're a competent boatman and never take chances. In fact, you're more careful than most yachtsmen, and you're not ashamed of it. And if it *did* happen to you, you'd probably make the correct decisions and get your passengers and yourself off in good shape. But just to keep the argument going (and salve my own pride) I'll bet you wouldn't do *everything* just right, or have *all* the right equipment in the right places.

Sachem was a comfortable boat, a bit wet in rough going, but with plenty of freeboard and beam. She had self-bailing cockpits forward and aft, a trunk cabin and a large deckhouse. With two new 92 hp. engines, she cruised at 11 knots. I'd owned her for four years and had no complaints. There were four of us aboard; Jack Carney, his wife Beth, my wife Lucy, and myself. Jack had owned several boats, both sail and power. I'd been around the water for 30 years, racing, cruising and day sailing. Beth was a bride, and had been in a boat only a couple of times before. Lucy had done some weekend cruising, but was never really at home on the water.

We were anchored at Montauk, L. I. We decided to grill some steaks on the beach at Orient Harbor, then go through Plum Gut and up Long Island Sound to Port Jefferson for the night. The day was clear but unseasonably cold. A strong westerly wind and a choppy sea slowed our trip from Montauk to Orient, and we were a couple of hours behind schedule when we finally started for Port Jefferson.

That was mistake number one! There was no reason why we *had* to spend that night in Port Jefferson. It was late, chilly and rough. There were plenty of pretty, comfortable harbors where we could hole up for the night. But because we had said "Port Jefferson" in the morning and no one had the sense to say, "Let's stay in Peconic Bay," off we went. There were few boats out as we headed for the Gut. Passing the lighthouse, we spotted a powerboat about the same size as *Sachem* in apparent distress near Plum Island. A couple of men were dropping an anchor to keep her off the beach, while several people in the cockpit beckoned to us. We had started to her assistance when we saw a Coast Guard patrol boat headed in her direction.

Mistake number two! We said some nice things about the Coast Guard, speculated on what had gone wrong on the other cruiser, watched the Coast Guardsmen get a line aboard her, and continued on our course without a thought of possible trouble ourselves. It was rough, but *Sachem* was an able boat. She could take it. No one thought, "Suppose it gets rougher?" After all, it was no storm—just a 20-mile westerly and a middling rough sea. As we settled on our course, almost due west, *Sachem* seemed to be doing very well, although the spray made it impossible to see anything through the windshield. *Sachem's* windshield wiper, we discovered, was broken. We licked the cold by closing all the deckhouse windows, and the heat of the two engines soon made it fairly comfortable. From time to time, Jack or I would take a look around the horizon from the after cockpit, to be sure no other boats were near and to check on the dinghy.

We decided to lay a straight course for Old Field Point, which took us a long way off shore. The seas seemed to be getting a little heavier and steeper, so I throttled back on the engines and Jack clawed his way up to the bow to stow the burgee and check on things forward. Everything seemed all right. *Sachem* was taking heavy spray aboard, but no solid water. The scuppers in the forward cockpit were clear. As the sun got lower we talked of stopping at Mattituck, the only harbor on the Long Island shore between Orient and Port Jefferson. Lucy wanted to turn in, but we explained that it was a holiday weekend; there'd be a lot of visiting boats at Mattituck; there would be no anchorage. Mistake number three! We kept going for Port Jefferson, which was neither considerate nor wise.

Insulated as we were in the closed-in, warm deckhouse, it was hard to tell just what was happening outside. I was at the wheel, just about sunset. We were navigating by compass, expecting to pick up Old Field Light at dark. Spray was beginning to crash against the windshield with increasing force, and it became harder to hold *Sachem* on her course. Jack was below, and I was about to suggest that he check the bilges to see if we were taking any water when Lucy touched my arm. "Should there be water trickling down like that?" she asked, pointing to a bulkhead (non-watertight) which separated the chain locker from the cabin.

Jack lifted the hatch and found water right up to the floor boards. "This pounding must be loosening her up," he said, as he began to connect the small electric pump which *Sachem* carried in addition to her big Navy bilge pump. Then Jack called up:

"Turn the wheel over to Lucy a minute, will you, and give me a hand."

As I stepped down the companionway, I saw water ankle deep above the floorboards. *Sachem* buried her nose in a sea, and she was mighty slow about coming up. As Jack started for the big bilge pump and I jumped for the wheel, the bow went down again and there was a heavy crash forward. The companionway door leading to the forward cockpit disintegrated into splinters, and solid water poured into the cabin.

It was still light outside, and through the broken door I could see *Sachem's* bows under water. A huge sea swept at her. She hardly rose at all, and a deluge poured into the cabin, washing loose gear before it. The wind swept through the cabin, too, and it was stronger than we had dreamed. There was no panic, then or later. We hardly spoke to one another. I put the wheel hard over, at the same time sending the girls as far aft as they could go, with the hope of lifting *Sachem's* bow.

They went quickly and quietly. Lucy pulled in the dinghy, so we wouldn't foul the painter, and I reversed one engine. Jack grabbed the distress signal packet. As he passed me on his way aft to help the girls put on their life jackets, he said, "It's chest deep in the head. Can you turn her?" But *Sachem* wouldn't answer her helm. With all way lost, her bow under like a sea anchor, green water coming aboard, and wind and wave pressing on her high topsides and bridge, she wouldn't turn even when I opened one engine full astern and the other full ahead. Her screws must have been almost out of water. Then one engine sputtered and stopped.

Sachem was doomed, and we'd better get off. I switched off the remaining engine, lest the propeller foul the dinghy's painter when we cast off. Jack and the two girls already had on life jackets and Jack was holding a smoke signal, but there was too much wind for the smoke to rise. It whipped in a thin stream downwind, invisible more than a few yards away. Seeing its uselessness, Jack stuck the signal in the empty flag socket. I grabbed a life jacket. I had plenty of preservers, all new and neatly stowed under the transom seat. Then I pulled up the hatch in the cockpit deck, where I kept the dinghy's bailing scoop. Even this far aft, water was high in the bilge. I groped in a jumble of mops, fenders, line, canvas and tools for the bailing scoop, but couldn't find it. *Sachem's* whole forward deck was under water now—she might go any moment. On a sudden inspiration, I grabbed a 30-foot coil of one-inch mooring line, made it fast to the end of the dinghy's painter, and took a single turn around a bitt.

The two girls scrambled into the bouncing dinghy without apparent trouble. Jack and I followed. Even at that moment, I remember thinking with inappropriate amusement how difficult it had seemed for us to get into the dink back in Orient Harbor, two at a time, and how quickly and easily all four of us accomplished it now, with the swells towering over our heads and *Sachem* sinking under our feet. The two girls sat on the middle thwart, Jack in the bow, facing aft, and I took the stern seat, facing forward. That way I could row in a normal manner, but with the dinghy moving stern-first and the bow to the seas.

Before leaving *Sachem,* both Jack and I had searched the horizon for signs of another boat. There was nothing to see but the sun, just dipping under the horizon. Jack took off a sneaker to bail out the water which was already splashing over the side of the dink. I warned everyone not to move for any reason, except for bailing, which only Jack was to do. Then we took stock of the situation.

Sachem was almost awash. Would she sink, or was there enough buoyancy in her big, half-empty gas and water tanks to keep her awash? Should we keep the dink in the slight lee she made in the seas, ready to cast off if she went under? Should we board her again and crawl up on her deck house? *Sachem's* deck house was only slightly out of water now, and occasional seas washed right over her.

We decided she'd probably sink, and that we might have trouble casting off in time if she went suddenly. None of us had a knife to cut the painter, and it might foul on the bitt and overturn the dink. Besides, we wanted that line to act as a drag or sea anchor. We couldn't stand the cold for long, either. Jack let go the end of the line; it snaked past the bitt on *Sachem* without snagging, and we were adrift. I began to row, and Jack to bail. About three minutes had elapsed since Lucy first noticed the trickle of water down the bulkhead!

We began immediately to discuss the disaster, but in the midst of the conversation a big sea broke into the dink. Then, and later, I found that if I tried to take part in the conversation, or relaxed my attention even for a few seconds from the big seas sweeping on us, we would take water aboard. I told the girls that I was working the dink gradually in toward shore, which was eight or nine miles away. Of course, I couldn't. It was all we could do to keep afloat. Jack grinned at my explanation, and the girls weren't fooled either.

Lucy was facing forward on the middle thwart. Beth was on the weather side of the thwart, facing me. Both girls trembled violently with the cold, but otherwise sat absolutely still. Even when a big icy wave would slop over the side onto Beth's lap, she took it without a move or a word. Jack tried a couple of distress flares. They were bright enough, but they would have been invisible when we dropped into the trough. If anyone saw them, we never knew. Lucy asked Jack to hold the flares further away from her; as small particles were dripping on her and burning her. Since she did not move, neither Jack nor I thought she had been badly burned. We discovered later that her clothes were dotted with small burned spots and that there were deep, ugly burns across her forearm and leg.

For two hours we rowed and bailed and shivered. I didn't think we'd make shore, and I don't believe the others thought so, either. I was rowing straight down the Sound. Every time I tried to edge in toward shore, the dinghy would nearly swamp, and Jack would bail desperately with his soggy sneaker. I tried not to think of anything but the seas and my rowing. Two or three heavy seas would splash water into the dink. Then there'd be half a dozen or so lesser swells, and if I were careful I could keep them from breaking aboard. The wind blew at around 40 miles, and in the gusts, at 50 or more.

We were thoroughly wet and chilled, and horribly cramped. Try fitting four persons, weighing some 635 pounds, into eight feet of dinghy! My rowing kept me a little warmer than the others, and they got most of the spray. Though it seemed incredible that we could make shore, I wouldn't let myself worry about that; though in the back of my mind all the time was the thought of Lucy, and of our children at home. Instead, I fretted about immediate things. It seemed to me that the leeward oarlock socket was a little loose. Would it loosen further? I had a horror of losing an oar, and clutched the oar handles so tightly my hands began to cramp. Suppose I caught a crab? I learned that if I could keep way on the dink, I could keep my oars out of the water as the big breakers passed under us. The drag of the long painter and mooring line kept the bow up.

I worried about getting lost, too. For a short time I could see, when we lifted to the top of the seas, a distant light which I thought was Old Field. Then we lost that. We picked up and lost several other lights. I steered mostly by the stars and the direction of wind and sea. But there was a light scud of swift clouds overhead. If it clouded over completely and the wind shifted, without a compass, I wouldn't know which way I was headed. After a couple of hours the wind began to moderate. I passed the good word on to the others, who at first didn't believe me. Jack and Beth, facing me, couldn't see the oncoming swells. The seas were as big as ever, and the wind was still blowing hard, but fewer seas were breaking heavily, and Jack had less prolonged bouts of bailing. This was the most dangerous part of our trip, for now I began to work the dink in toward shore. Several times she almost went under, but the others stayed faithfully motionless, and I managed to catch her.

In books, people in lifeboats sing hymns, or pray, or are determinedly gay. We bowed briefly to all the conventions. Beth remarked that she wished she hadn't skipped church that Sunday. I think we each prayed a little, but not aloud—perhaps not even in words. We sang a couple of songs, but it was a feeble effort. There were several wry wisecracks, and I think they were natural and unforced. We were all scared, but no one was panicky. And nothing could really take our minds off our obvious danger. As the hours passed, we were silent for the most part.

Almost imperceptibly, the wind eased and the seas moderated. I was able to make more progress now. We saw a glow in the sky in the direction of shore, apparently from Riverhead or Mattituck. Lucy said nothing, but we all remembered her suggestion that we spend the night at Mattituck. Gradually the shore came closer. We saw a few lights, but as it got later they winked out. Jack tried a couple more flares, with no result except to frighten us, for the seas looked huge in the amber glow. Eventually, the dark shadow of land appeared. Gradually we won our way in. It was after midnight. We'd been in the dinghy between five and a half and six hours.

We scrambled awkwardly ashore, cramped from long immobility. I almost fell when I first tried to use my legs, and my hands were so cupped from the oar handles I couldn't straighten them. Stumbling about in the darkness, we gathered driftwood and ignited it with a flare. Then we carried the dink to the fire and propped it up to reflect the heat and to serve as a windbreak. During the long hours till dawn we huddled together and tried to get warm. We were wet and cold, but not miserable. We'd lost boat, clothes, money, papers, cameras, and fishing tackle. But we were safe!

The *Sachem* didn't go to the bottom, after all. She was found, awash, 26 hours later. When we pulled her out of the water, we were able to study the probable cause of the accident with the insurance adjuster and the builder. This is the way we reconstructed it.

Sachem had been taking the seas as well as anyone could ask. Just before sundown, a violent squall hit us. *And we didn't know it until it was too late!* We couldn't see through the windshield. The bridge deck was closed for warmth. We might soon have felt the difference in the action of the boat, but we didn't have a chance. (Another boat came to grief in the same squall, we learned later.) The seas at once became very steep. If we had been less insulated against the weather we'd have slackened speed at once to avoid burying the bow. Perhaps we were just lulled by the hum of the engines and the warmth of the bridge.

Sachem buried her bow as soon as the squall hit, and that started an unlucky chain of circumstances.

There was a long hatch in the seat of the forward cockpit, not battened down nor secured in any way. Under this hatch was a large cooking gas cylinder, fitted so tightly that the under side of the hatch cover was hollowed out to provide room for the valve. The cylinder was securely fastened against movement in any direction except upwards. We don't know if the heavy sea which filled the forward cockpit floated off the hatch cover, or whether enough water got into the forepeak or chain locker to float the cylinder, pushing up the hatch. Neither hatch cover nor cylinder were in the boat when she was found. In any case, with water coming aboard far faster than the scuppers could handle it, and the hatch missing, *Sachem* had a hole five feet by two feet in her bow. The entire bow filled with water and sank so low that solid water flowed in with each sea, making it impossible to pump her out unless we could run her off. By this time, her propellers and rudder were so high she couldn't be turned.

Sachem has a trunk cabin. A sliding vertical door closed off the forward cockpit from the cabin. When this panel was smashed by the sea, the top of the companionway was only an inch or two above the level of the seat, and at least two feet lower than the forward deck. Naturally, the water in the cockpit flowed down into the cabin.

Many yachtsmen have suggested that we should not have abandoned *Sachem* so quickly. I doubt it. It was apparent that she would be full of water, whether or not she sank. Suppose we had stayed with her, and she sank too suddenly for all four of us to clamber into the dinghy? She might have upset the dink. We could never have gotten into the dink from the water, and with the heavy spume it would have been difficult to breathe in the water. If we had stayed with *Sachem, where* would we have stayed? In the deckhouse? We might not all have gotten out if she took a sudden plunge. We wouldn't have been able to sit on the seats. Only about 2½ feet of the deckhouse was out of water when she was found. I doubt if we could have stood in the deckhouse with life jackets on . . . they'd have floated us off our feet. We might have climbed to the top of the deckhouse and lashed ourselves there. But could we have cast off the lashings if *Sachem* suddenly went under? She had two big engines and no flotation chambers. (It was the unusually large gas tanks and water tank, more than half empty, which kept her afloat.

We might all have gotten into the dinghy but left a turn of the painter on the bitts, ready to cast loose if *Sachem* sank. We considered this at the time, and we're glad we cast off. Even discounting the catastrophe if the painter snagged when we tried to cast off, we might have become inattentive in the hours of waiting in the cold and wet and been dragged down if she sank. There was 30 fathoms of water under her. In any case, I don't think we could have endured 26 hours in the dinghy, cold, wet and motionless, before *Sachem* was sighted. We were all but done in from six hours of it.

Sachem is back in commission today. Here are the major structural changes which have been made:

1. It was finally decided *not* to deck over the forward cockpit entirely, as we first planned to do. That cockpit is mighty handy when you're dealing with ground tackle, and it's a pleasant place in mild weather. But there is now a solid coaming which raises the after portion of the cockpit to the height of the deck. The companionway door is much smaller and heavier. It makes it a bit harder to use the companionway, but we don't mind.

2. The forward cockpit scuppers have been greatly enlarged.

3. The forward bulkhead has been strengthened and made watertight, except for a ⅜″ limber hole.

4. The hatch under the forward cockpit seat is smaller and heavier, and securely battened down.

5. The cooking gas cylinder has been removed from the forepeak and installed in the after cockpit.

What have I learned from our experience that might keep me from repeating it? Jack and I put our heads together, and came up with the following list.

1. A boat can come to disaster with disconcerting swiftness. In most cases you might have time to weigh what course of action to take, to find and put to use your emergency equipment. But

not always. We had just three minutes. Rehearse in your mind what you would do if your boat got into trouble, what equipment you'd want, where it's stowed. In short, give yourself an "abandon ship" drill.

2. It should take a mighty good reason to send a boat out in open, rough water when other boats are staying at anchor. It may get rougher.

3. If you spot another boat in trouble, render what assistance you can. Then, before you sail on, take thought of the fix you may be in if you develop similar trouble.

4. Jack and I have become somewhat prejudiced about forward cockpits. They're wonderful things for handling ground tackle, but the scuppers should be big enough to handle a lot of water quickly, not just rain and light spray. And so that no water can flow down into the cabin, close up the companionway door permanently and climb in and out through a hatch in the cabin top.

5. When seas get so heavy you have to slacken speed, head for shelter, especially if the seas are close together and steep. We were going too fast—I know that now—but I had throttled back as far as I could and still make headway, or so I thought. If *Sachem* had survived that sickening moment when she plunged her bow under water, I might have been able to turn her. But there was no second chance. That first comber finished her.

6. Maybe powerboats are too comfortable nowadays. Don't seal yourself up in an enclosed bridge in bad weather. Boating isn't supposed to be an indoor sport. Get out where you can *feel* the weather! (This is myself, not you, I'm scolding!)

7. Don't exaggerate the seaworthiness of your boat or your own saltiness, or underrate the power of the sea. Most of us, if we examine our "years of experience" honestly, must acknowledge that the greater part has been fair weather sailing. Fishing boats come to grief every year—boats larger, usually, than most pleasure boats, built to take it and manned by the best seamen on earth.

8. Never pass a safe anchorage late in the day.

9. Make sure all hatches are securely fastened.

10. It's idiotic not to have a good working windshield wiper on any enclosed bridge. We couldn't even see our bows clearly.

11. Every boat should have an effective distress signal packet. Our suggestion is a self-igniting floating flare that will burn for a long time, plus a Very pistol and parachute flares, or several rockets or Roman candles, in addition to small hand flares. You can't have too many. In a hard blow, no hand-held smoke signal can be seen very far, but a rocket or parachute flare means "distress" day or night.

12. Be sure you can open your signal packet easily. Jack had a hard time opening ours. I tried to open the kit on a friend's boat recently, and it took several minutes and a large screw driver.

13. It's normal procedure to keep equipment which is frequently used in a convenient spot. Equipment that is used infrequently (such as safety equipment) is too often stowed in out-of-the-way nooks where you may not be able to get it out quickly. Where, for example, do you carry your sea anchor? In the chain locker, under miscellaneous coils of line? I've seen boats in which the life jackets were stored *under* the spare anchor. Keep emergency equipment in a handy spot, even if you don't expect to need it!

14. A good dinghy is a wonderful thing when you need it, and it's nice to have it already in the water, not lashed on top of the cabin. Lightness is a convenient quality in a dink, especially when you must haul it aboard. But lightness may not be the most important quality under such circumstances as we ran into.

15. A loose oarlock or socket may be a nuisance in a harbor. It is a great deal worse in rough water! Make sure the screws are tight, and that the oarlocks fit, and are lashed to the boat.

16. Oars that are too long or too short are a headache. Get oars you can use when the dink is crowded. Lash them in the dink when towing, so they can't be lost.

17. If your boat has bulkheads, are they watertight? Are you sure?

18. If you make expensive improvements in your boat, like new engines, increase your insurance proportionately. (I hadn't

got around to it!) It might be wise, too, to insure miscellaneous equipment and personal belongings, both your own and your guests'.

19. If you have an accident on the water, and the newspapers call you, give them a straight, complete story. Otherwise the printed story may be embarrassing. One paper headlined our story "Four drift ashore in oarless dinghy."

20. Last, but far from least, if you've *got* to be shipwrecked, pick shipmates like those I had!

A Suggested "Lifeboat" Packet

To be waterproof-wrapped and stowed where it can be grabbed instantly, or lashed in the dinghy on long offshore trips. This kit to be kept intact and in addition to any duplicate gear you may have loose on board.

a. Bailing scoop with safety thong.

b. A sharp knife. (We had agreed to hang on to the dink if it swamped or overturned, and to try to lash ourselves to each other with the painter. Lacking a knife and extra line, we might not have been able to do a good lashing job.)

c. A small compass.

d. A flashlight with fresh batteries.

e. Some iodine, bandage, adhesive tape, and burn ointment. We all had cuts and bruises, and one of our party had deep burns.

f. Two or three packets of Army "D" ration or similar rations in a waterproof case.

g. Matches in a waterproof case.

h. A flask of brandy, or something equally warming.

i. A length of strong, light line.

j. Cigarettes in waterproof envelope. Cigarettes help morale.

k. A canteen or jug of water.

l. A canvas bucket would hold the above items, and serve as a sea anchor.

You'll think of other things, of course.

17

The Escape of the *E. A. Horton*

by CAPT. JOHN W. MARR

[1930]

IN THE EARLY DAYS, Gloucester sent a large fleet of vessels to the Bay of St. Lawrence, where they caught trips of mackerel with hook and line during the summer season. This one of her earliest industries was very prosperous and helped to build that old New England town. The first disaster to those American vessels came in 1852, when a howling gale swept the Atlantic Ocean from east to west. So heavy was it that the seas carried away Minot's Light in Boston Bay. Eight of those vessels, with many members of their crews, were lost. Because of this great loss to the North Bay mackerel fleet, the storm came to be designated as the "Yankee Gale."

The Eastern Provinces of Nova Scotia welcomed these American fishing vessels. The merchants located in the Strait of Canso, where the skippers trans-shipped their first trips to their home ports, acted as brokers, and the refitting of the vessels left many thousand greenbacks in the hands of the Canadians. The merchants who had small stores soon built large ones and also many fine wharves, where the Americans purchased barrels, salt and groceries and shipped men. A near view of McNair's Cove and Ship Harbor in those days would remind one of Gloucester and Rocky Neck.

In 1867 the provinces of Nova Scotia came under Confederation, and the Dominion Government sent out armed cutters to protect the inshore fisheries of these localities. The cutters were particularly active along the shores of Prince Edward's Island and Cape Breton, and any American vessel caught fishing within three miles of the shore was liable to seizure by the Dominion Government.

It was in 1871 that the seizure of the well-known fishing schooner *E. A. Horton,* of Gloucester, occurred. The *Horton,* with her trip of mackerel on board, lay to an anchor in British waters, outside a harbor. Her skipper was ashore, wiring the *Horton's* owners for instruction in regard to trans-shipping his catch. In the absence of the skipper, the cook was fishing for cod when Capt. James Torrey, who had command of the Canadian cutter *Sweepstakes,* came sailing by. For this trivial offense Torrey seized the *Horton* and, putting on board a well-armed crew, sailed her into Guysboro Harbor, Torrey's home town. This is a landlocked harbor near the eastern extremity of Nova Scotia; it shelters a small fleet of coasting schooners and fishing smacks. Making the *Horton* fast to a wharf, they stripped her of sails and running gear and put them in a storehouse under lock and key. Capt. Torrey was a strong Conservative, and, as that party was in power, he openly boasted that he would bridge Guysboro Harbor with American fishing craft, a threat which he did his best to fulfill.

The seizure of American vessels created very unpleasant feeling, as the majority of the young men in that part of Nova Scotia earned their livelihood on them, and some were masters. But at the same time it pleased the hard-heads who favored the Tory government.

The *E. A. Horton* was owned by Harvey Knowlton, of Gloucester, and her capture by a Canadian cutter was like the kidnapping of one of his children. Knowlton was a man of iron determination and dauntless courage and when he heard of his vessel's plight he at once resolved to recapture her and bring her back to Gloucester, no matter what the cost. Knowlton did not intend to shoot his way out, but he made his plans to trick the Canadian Government, which had seized not only his vessel but also her summer's catch of mackerel which was stowed in barrels in the vessel's hold.

The boys of the village, including the writer, were much excited over the capture of the fine American schooner lying stripped at Torrey's wharf. We proceeded in a body to get a nearer view of the vessel, but were met by a watchman who curtly informed us that anyone found loitering in the vicinity of the vessel would be promptly jailed. We returned home, a discouraged and disappointed lot of boys.

The *Horton* still had her trip of mackerel on board, and some of her crew who had made the catch (incidentally, natives of Guysboro County) were not far away. The crew depended on getting greenbacks for their work, for Dominion bills were as scarce as black fox skins.

In his younger days Harvey Knowlton had been one of the pioneers in the California gold rush; he knew the mining game thoroughly. While the furore aroused by the seizure was at its height, a stalwart stranger, impressive in appearance, arrived in town. The gentleman claimed to represent big mining interests in the West. At that time, there were in operation several mines within a radius of 30 miles of Guysboro, and this man's breezy personality, coupled with his exhaustive knowledge of mining, created a very favorable impression on the business men of the village, including Capt. Torrey. In fact, the latter labored under a delusion that his own farm was a prospective El Dorado. The stranger displayed some very fine specimens of gold quartz which he claimed to have found in the neighborhood, and everybody was highly excited over the expected development of some well paying mines.

So the gold prospector had a fine chance to get in touch with some of the men who had caught that trip of mackerel, and, as the miner had never seen an American fishing vessel, Capt. Torrey was pleased to show him one of the best of the Gloucester fleet that he had recently captured. The miner looked the vessel over and naturally asked some questions before thanking Capt. Torrey for his courtesy.

The eighth day of October, 1871, fell on Sunday. The wind

changed from southeast to north that evening, bringing heavy rain squalls, and by midnight there was a howling gale of wind blowing out of Chedabucto Bay. And next morning there was no *Horton.* The watchman ran to Torrey's house and reported that the *Horton* had parted her lines and drifted out of the harbor. They both ran, neck and neck, to the wharf, where they found that her lines had been *cut* and that her sails, blocks and rigging were missing out of the storehouse. Capt. Torrey displayed temper as he declared: "It's a bold Yankee trick," and gave orders to wake up the Canadian Navy and bring the *Horton* back. "We'll hang that Yankee crew," said he. He hurried to the telegraph office, but to his consternation discovered that the wires had been cut.

It was now about 8:30 A.M. The *Horton's* lines had been cut about 12:30 that morning, and with eight hours of howling fair wind to her credit, there was little chance of recapturing the American schooner, with Capt. Harvey Knowlton at the wheel. To be sure, the "gold miner" was the only American on board; but her crew, with their summer's earnings in the hold, were as anxious to make their escape as the owner of the vessel.

Naturally, excitement ran high in that old town. Capt. Torrey did not know there had been a crew of Bluenoses waiting five days and nights in a barn for a fair wind to blow out of Guysboro Harbor. He did not know that four came alongside that stormy night with a boat load of groceries and a compass and helped to get the American vessel's sails and rigging out of the old red storehouse.

Day after day wore anxiously away in Guysboro while awaiting the recapture of the American vessel and the old Yankee miner who had played the bold trick on the government of the Dominion. James Torrey and his party fully realized that some Bluenose had betrayed them, for they well know that few men could have piloted a vessel out of the harbor that night. The pilot, if captured, would have suffered the penalty of treason, according to British laws. In some quarters the opinion was that even hanging was too good for the old Yankee prospector who came to their town and stole his vessel away from the government. Tories, more leniently inclined, were in favor of life imprisonment. The majority of the people in the Lower Provinces were opposed to this unfair treatment of the American fishermen, and feeling ran high between the supporters of the Conservative government and the Liberals.

While Capt. Torrey was awaiting the recapture of the *Horton,* she was plowing her way through a mist of whitecaps and sea. The following is part of a ballad composed by some local bard to commemorate the event.

> "Like a great seabird on an ocean flight,
>   Her wings spread to the gale,
>   Her Bluenose crew so brave and true
>   Had released her from the jail.

> "She carved each sea with her white-oak bow,
>   For her native land did sail;
>   She plowed her way both night and day
>   With cutters on her trail."

Capt. Knowlton had his plans well in mind, and with his strong determination he was bound to see them through. Once at sea, none but he and his crew knew whether he was steering for Jacksonville, Florida, or Portland, Maine. He told me several years afterwards, in Gloucester, that he stood at the head of the wharf that stormy Sunday night with his gun, while his men were bending the *Horton's* sails and getting her ready for sea. It would have been lead fever for the man who interfered. He was determined to take his vessel back, and once at sea he would go down with her before he would surrender.

After passing old Cape Canso Light he shaped his course for the western end of Sable Island. If he had met a Canadian cutter she would have had to find a new channel across the northwest bar to capture the *Horton.* As it happened, there was nothing in sight, so he changed course for Georges Banks. He was making a southern passage, and when he arrived in the southwestern part of Western Bank the gale of fair wind had moderated to a light sailing breeze. The man on the masthead sang out: "Sail O, on the lee bow! By her riding sail, she is a vessel laying at anchor."

"We will speak her," said Capt. Knowlton. "She is fishing on Peek-o'-Pike, and I will bet it is the Iron Man in the *David Crockett;* he knows this place well and always gets good trips here this time of the year."

As Capt. Knowlton came within hailing distance a thunderous voice roared: "Where in hell did you get the *Horton?*"

"We took her away from the Canadian Government last Sunday night after church," was the reply.

"But they are awake now," bellowed the Iron Man, who was standing on the quarterdeck of his vessel. "They are on your trail. Watch your step, Knowlton. Keep an eye to windward. The new Halifax cutter, *Sambro Light,* went by here this morning, heading to the westward with every stitch of canvas set."

One of the *Crockett's* dories, loaded with fish, now came alongside the *Horton.* One of the men in the boat drove his gaff-hook into a big halibut and passed it to Knowlton, remarking, "I would like to pass you the captain of that cutter in the same way. Last fall he drove us out of Mallpick in a living gale of wind and we were lucky to escape shipwreck."

"Well, boys," said Knowlton, "I'm glad it is that brave Canadian Frenchman, Lowry. They all seem to fear him, but I have met braver men than he ever dared to be. He will need all his courage if he monkeys with the *Horton* 'round Georges Shoals."

When Knowlton arrived on Georges Banks he sighted the Gloucester handline fleet to the eastward of the shoals; also a large schooner, with all canvas set, approaching from a northerly direction and flying the Canadian pennant at her main truck. With a strong easterly wind blowing and a heavy sea running, Knowlton swung his vessel WNW for the North Shoal. Both vessels were now staggering along with decks awash and all the sail they could safely carry.

Above the roar of the wind a voice rang out from the mast-head of the *Horton:* "Breakers ahead on the port bow!"

The two vessels had now converged and were sailing on parallel courses, the cutter bearing about three miles on the *Horton's* starboard beam. To the utter astonishment of the Canadian captain, the *Horton* headed for what seemed certain destruction. Knowlton previously had several times threaded that tortuous channel between the North Shoal and the Great South Shoal, and knew it well. When he entered the channel, it was breaking masthead high on either side of him. The Canadian dared not follow. He hauled to, in order to go to the northward of the shoal. But when he put his wheel down he carried away his foretopmast and a ballooner. He now had to clear away the wreckage and get as far from that shoal water as he could. In the meantime, the *Horton,* with a quartering wind, was heading for the nearest shore line of the United States, which in this case happened to be Chatham, Mass.

Arriving off Chatham, Knowlton felt safe from capture. Keeping well inshore, he proceeded to hug the beach for 20 miles down to the tip of Cape Cod. Off the Cape, he sighted the cutter, which had made a direct passage. She lay hoveto off Peaked Hill Bar Buoy, three miles off the Cape. That buoy had ordinarily to be rounded to get into Massachusetts Bay.

The *Horton* could have remained inside of the three-mile limit in safety, but Capt. Knowlton was bound to his home port; and since he knew a channel between the Highland and the bar he sailed his vessel through. Once in the bay, a light breeze from the south gave the American the advantage of being to wind-ward. Knowlton headed across for Plymouth, pursued by the Canadian cutter under his lee, not more than a mile away. Before the *Horton* was safe inside three miles of the Plymouth shore, the wind died away entirely, leaving both vessels flat be-calmed.

From this point Knowlton could discern the cutter's guns shining in the sun on her port and starboard bows. The Canadian captain lowered his longboat, manned her with a well-armed crew, and ordered them to board and capture the *Horton*. He did not know that aboard the American vessel was one of the best marksmen of the West in the golden days.

Knowlton gave orders to every man to lie flat on deck. Selecting a place where he was safe from rifle shots, he let the Canadian boat approach within a reasonable distance. Finding that the crew of the longboat paid no attention to a shot he fired across the bow, Knowlton broke off the flag pole with a bullet, sending the flag into the water. The Canadians stopped to pick up their flag, but concluded that their lives were in danger, and returned to the cutter. After a few hours the wind came from the westward. The Canadian skipper shaped his course for Nova Scotia and Knowlton headed the *Horton* for old Cape Ann. Ten days out of Guysboro, the Yankee schooner came around Eastern Point and sailed up Gloucester Harbor, where Capt. Knowlton made her fast to his own wharf. He lost no time in wiring Torrey of his safe arrival, adding that the cutter was returning to Nova Scotia without loss of life. Knowlton did not have to whistle for Johnny Bull; the band played for him and they sang:

"Johnny, there's a bully time in Gloucester tonight,
    With heavy guns afiring and torches burning bright,
    The drums play 'Yankee Doodle' and make the welkin ring
    While the Americans are shouting, 'The *Horton* has got in!'"

The old *Cape Ann Advertiser* reached Guysboro with big headlines: "THE *E. A. HORTON* ARRIVES IN GLOUCESTER." Supporters of the Liberal party were pleased, while the Tories were wishful of revenge. The most important part of it for us lads was the song, and our time had come to get even with Capt. Torrey and his watchman. Mustering a band of village youths, we laid our plans to march to town and serenade Capt. Torrey and his Tory friends, who now swore that they would capture any American vessel caught drawing a pail of water inside the three-mile limit. With a good supply of old cans and torches, we marched through the streets and stopped at the corner of Dog Lane and Front Street, and it is questionable if there was any more excitement in Gloucester when the *Horton*

arrived than there was in Guysboro that night, when we sang
the following:

"While Johnny's sons were sleeping with red ruin on their brain
The friends of Uncle Sam took their vessel back again.
At eight o'clock next morning when they came to look about
They found the gold prospector and the *Horton* had gone out.
While the news of her recapture was circulating round
Those jolly sons of freedom to their native home were bound."

Some of the old Tory hard-heads made strong threats as to
what they would do with us lads, and in reply, we sang:

"Fire away, old England, but Torrey mind your eye;
We will stick by one another like brothers brave and true,
And show those sleepy British what Yankee boys can do.
You new Dominion Government, I warn you to beware;
You better sign a treaty and settle this affair.
Do to one another as you'd like to do by you
And not abuse your neighbor as Torrey likes to do."

This song was repeated so often for the benefit of Torrey
and his watchman that they wished they never had seen the
Horton; and when I shipped on an American vessel and went
away Torrey seemed pleased.

A few years passed by and I came back again, master of the
American schooner *Aberdeen.* Going to the Customs House, I
found a white-haired man seated at his desk. I passed him the
vessel's papers. He looked at them and then at me, then arose
and reached out his hand, saying: "I am pleased to enter and
clear your vessel. It doesn't look as though you had spent all
your time up there singing Yankee songs. It's the same old saying,
'A bad boy often makes a smart man.'" It was my old enemy,
Capt. Torrey.

I never asked him whether he knew the identity of the boy
who had carried meals every night to those men in the barn while
they waited to recapture the *Horton.*

18

Deep Water Diction

by JERRY GRAHAM

[1948]

PERIODICALLY IT BEHOOVES the yachtsman to overhaul his deep water diction for, like his boat and gear, it is subject to deterioration with the passage of time. The corrosive influences, in this instance, have their origin in the steady influx of newcomers to our way of life, with their pseudo-seafaring expressions learned from novels, comic strips and the devil only knows where. Their tongues, when exposed to salt air, are wont to broadcast a virulent type of barnyard contagion that taints the sea atmosphere and tends, in time, to work its way into the vocal cords of all but the hardiest of mariners.

To counteract this influence, we strongly urge that every true yachtsman first check on the purity of his own methods of nautical expression—and we shall do our best to assist him herein—and thereafter insist that his shipmates exercise their tongues, when necessary, in the same seamanlike manner. We have often thought that if our yacht clubs would impose a small penalty for breaches of King Neptune's English committed on the premises, this problem would be quickly solved. If effective steps of some kind are not taken, the inevitable alternative is to find our youngsters, some day, obeying orders to "Go up on the prow, please, and cast anchor" and—shiver our timbers—liking it!

When such fits of despondency seize upon us, we are prone

to turn for solace to Dana's "Two Years Before the Mast," which was written more than 100 years ago when ships were ships, with no "aft decks" or "windward sides" for poor sailors to ponder over. As an example of the brand of seafaring English that was current in those days, and to illustrate the discussion that follows, we shall quote a selected passage therefrom (the italics being ours).

"The *after* yards are then braced up and belayed, the main sheet hauled *aft,* the spanker eased over *to leeward,* and the men from the braces stand by the head yards. 'Let go and haul!' says the captain; the second mate lets go the *weather* fore braces and the men *haul* in to *leeward.* . . . Then the starboard watch board the main tack, and the larboard watch *lay forward* and board the *fore* tack and *haul* down the jib sheet, *clapping* a tackle on it if it blows fresh. The *after* yards are then trimmed, the captain personally looking out for them himself. '*Well* the cross-jack yard! *Small pull* the main topgallant yard! *Well* that! *Well* the mizzen topsail yard! Cross-jack yards all *well! Well* all aft! *Haul taut to windward!*' . . . and the order is given, 'Go below the watch!'"

The above illustrates a number of things, but one of the most impressive of them all, to us, is that seafaring terms have really changed little in the last and otherwise revolutionary hundred years. With a few possible exceptions, which we shall deal with later, every nautical term used above will be readily recognized by the seaman of today as belonging to his own vocabulary. Whether or not he uses them *correctly,* however, is another matter, which concerns us here.

First, let us take the windward-leeward, weather-lee combinations. These are misused by the uninitiated oftener, perhaps, than any other seafaring terms. We speak of a vessel beating "to windward" or running "to loo'ard," and that is correct. But we do *not* speak of a "windward (or leeward) *side*" of anything. "*Weather* side" and "*lee* side" are the correct terms. The distinction is that "windward" and "leeward" refer to *directions* (almost always preceded by the preposition "to") while "weather" and "lee" refer to *tangible objects.* Thus, we walk over "to windward" (direction) to reach the "weather rail" (tangible object), etc. A reference to the quotation above will show these terms correctly used in each instance.

For the benefit of the technical minded, windward and leeward are really adverbs; weather and lee adjectives. The nouns which the latter modify are not *always* tangible objects (*e.g.,* "weather gauge") but the exceptions are so rare that we prefer the simpler, though slightly less accurate, explanation above. Also, apparent exceptions like "Leeward Islands" and "windward work" (wherein windward and leeward are adjectives) are really corruptions of "the islands to leeward," "work to windward," etc.

The forward-aft, fore-after combinations may be similarly described. "Forward" and "aft" refer to *directions* (though the preposition "to" is never used with them) while "fore" and "after" refer to *tangible objects.* You walk *forward* or *aft* (directions) to reach the *fore* peak, *after* peak, *fore*mast, *after* rigging, *after* deck, etc. (all of them tangible objects). There is no such thing as an "aft deck" (so frequently seen in print these days), as any real sailor can testify.

"Aft" and "after" run true to form in all instances; but when we go forward we encounter a few difficulties. This is because "fore" is indistinguishable, phonetically, from "four." Suppose the captain on a small passenger liner orders the "fore" lifeboats lowered and finds the mate lowering all *four!* To avoid such confusion, "fore" usually gives way to "forward" in the plural (*e.g.,* fore hatch, but forward hatches). There are instances when it does so in the singular, also (*e.g.,* forward locker instead of fore locker) and we can only add that just what these instances are is a matter that experience alone can teach.

It must be understood that the nautical tongue is largely idiomatic, and that only a few expressions are subject to rules of usage such as we have attempted above. Eventually we learn to use seafaring terms correctly simply because they *sound* right; and we can offer no better solution to the problem. There is no textbook to follow but, as an aid to beginner and veteran alike, we do highly recommend "Two Years Before the Mast" as a

treasure house of nautical terms properly expressed. Any yachtsman who has not read it should do so for his pleasure and profit,
and any California yachtsman who has not done so can find a
real treat in store for him at the nearest public library. Among
contemporary writers, there are men of wide experience like
Irving Johnson and Alan Villiers who speak and write the seafaring tongue to the manner born. As regards the staff writers
of the various yachting publications, we can only say, "Yes, and
no," and leave it to the regular reader to rate them himself.
There are some excellent and some rather spurious exponents of
the gospel we are attempting to preach here among them.

Closely allied to "forward" and "aft," are "ahead" and
"astern." The latter terms are used when referring to directions
beyond the confines of a vessel. A sailor goes *forward;* but his
ship goes *ahead.* Or he looks *aft* (for some article on deck, say)
but he looks *astern* when his gaze goes beyond the confines of
his ship.

"Haul" and "heave" (often misused) are easily explained.
You *haul* on a line by *hand;* you *heave* on it by *machinery.* Thus,
when you lead the "hauling part" of a tackle (or any line, for
that matter) to a winch, capstan, or windlass, you *heave* on it
thereafter; and that is true whether the machinery in question be
power or hand operated.

"Hoist" refers to something comparatively heavy that is
lifted by a tackle, as a sail, small boat, slingload of cargo, etc.
An anchor, however, is never hoisted, even by hand. It is "hove
up" (by machinery) or "picked up" or "weighed" (by any
means).

"Pull" (with reference to a line) is not used as a verb; but it
is used as a noun as, for example, "one more pull," "give a
small pull on that sheet," etc. Dana gives an example of it in our
quotation. In other words, it refers to a line that is already
fairly taut but needs "a pull" or two to complete the job. It is
never used when *heaving* on a line. "One more *heave,*" or "*heave*
and bust her" are the terms commonly heard then.

The expression "well," repeated so often by Dana's captain,
was in common use in both sail and steam only a few years ago,

but is rarely heard today. Its present equivalent is "that's good," or "okay," both of which sound rather juvenile as compared with the assertive: *"Well* that!" of earlier days. Another obsolescent term is "lay." Dana explains it as follows: "This word 'lay,' which is in such general use aboard ship, . . . (is) used in giving orders instead of 'go,' as 'Lay forward!,' 'Lay aft!,' 'Lay aloft!,' " etc.

We should like to see both of these fine old deep water expressions brought back into the working vocabulary of our present day seamen; and we think it is within the power of our yachting fraternity to do so. We say this because we believe that it is every true yachtsman's policy (and we quote from Skipper Herb Stone) "to reflect the spirit of the sea and preserve its traditions." It is the yachtsman who is saving the art of sailing from threatened oblivion; and it is to him that we must turn to preserve our traditional tongue intact.

There are some old terms, of course, that are quite properly obsolete. Dana speaks of a vessel heading "athwart our hawse." Today (with the adoption of the Rules of the Road) we would say she was "on a crossing course," or "crossing ahead of us," or the like. Another term, "larboard," has long been superseded by "port." During a recent reading of this century-old book, however, we failed to note any other terms that we would regard as unfit for use today.

A sailor goes "below" but he never goes "above." Instead, he goes "on deck" (from below) or he may go "aloft" (from on deck). And when he is aloft he never sings out: "Hey, there," or "Hey, Bill," to attract the attention of someone on deck. He sings out: "On deck!" and the reply to that is simply "Hello!" The man aloft may then express his wants, such as: "Slack the jib halyard a bit" (and no "please," please!). This order is repeated word for word by the man on deck and then executed. "That's well!" or "Make fast!" (from aloft) and "All fast!" (from on deck) complete this picture, all of it according to salt water Hoyle. And what a pleasure it is go aboard a vessel where tradition is so maintained. We wonder how many of them there are these days? Captain Johnson's *Yankee,* we have no

doubt, is one of them; and his young men will act as a healthy
influence on all of us as they scatter, in time, among the yacht
fleets of the country. But this is not enough; and we hope that
every skipper will cooperate in maintaining proper standards of
nautical expression on his own command, be she large or small.
It will pay off well in terms of pride and satisfaction.

"Front" and "back" are not sea expressions: nor are "wall,"
"roof," or "ceiling" (used in their shoreside sense). There is no
"front side" of a bulkhead or cabin or anything aboard ship.
It is the "fore part" of a bulkhead; "after part" of the house,
etc. It is proper to speak of a "ship's side," "cabin side," etc.,
but then it is truly a *side*—port or starboard. What is called a
"ceiling" ashore becomes a "deck head" aboard ship; a shore
"wall" becomes a "bulkhead," "cabin side," "skin," or other
structural detail; and we have a "cabin top," or "top of the
house," but no "roof" at sea.

Incidentally, when ashore we should not forget that shore
people are also entitled to have *their* nomenclature respected,
though the last time we brought this matter up it boomeranged
on us. We had just completed a winter wartime passage from
Liverpool and were heading for the Port Director's Office in the
Whitehall Building to turn in our routing instructions. Entering
the elevator (in civilian clothes), we found a Wave at the controls who announced each floor as a "deck." We chided her about
this, in a genial manner, but without any noticeable effect till
we reached our floor. Then, with scorn dripping from every
syllable, she responded, "Four-teenth DECK—and fooey to you,
Landlubber!"

Nevertheless (and with due apologies to the Navy's indoctri-
nation program) we think it is a bit sophomoric to carry our
saltiness ashore with us. Among friends and in fun such usage is
proper, of course; but it is not in the best tradition of the sea
to go beyond that.

Speaking of the Navy recalls to mind that the term "head" is
of naval origin; and we suggest caution in accepting into our
vocabulary any terms from this source. We have the highest
regard for our Navy but its duties are highly specialized and it

has, of necessity, developed a brand of sea language peculiarly its own, which is widely divergent in many respects from the traditional tongue of our forefathers. The latter called a spade a spade, a toilet a toilet, and gave the matter no further thought. In naval parlance we find it has become (whether more delicately or not we cannot decide) a "head," we find a windlass rather adequately described as an "anchor windlass," and—holy mackerel—a "handy billy" turns out to be a portable *fire pump!* That alone should teach us to stick to our own terminology, quaint and unimpressive though it may be at times.

Whence comes the term anchor "rode," so widely used in yachting circles? On merchant vessels we have always heard it called a "cable," whether of rope, wire or chain (though the terms "anchor rope," "anchor wire," or "anchor chain" are also commonly used). Also, how about the word "doused" as applied to a sail? Personally, we prefer such terms as "take in," "haul down," and the like, as having a more seamanlike ring to them. Are these strictly yachting terms? Are they naval terms? Did they originate with the Banks fishermen?

Returning to more familiar ground: Flags are "run up" or "set," but never "hoisted." Thereafter they are "hauled down."

Sails are "hoisted," or "set," as a rule, though other terms, such as "get the topsail on her," are commonly used. They are never "hauled *up*" though they may be "hauled *down*" or "taken in."

Anchors are *always* "let go," not "dropped" or "heaved over" or (gr-r-r) "cast!" The term "drop the pick," however, is sometimes used in a bantering way in the best of seafaring circles, but only in narration—not in giving orders.

A change of wind direction is correctly expressed as "veering" (if the change is clockwise) or "backing" (if counter-clockwise). With relation to the ship's head, it "shifts" more ahead or "hauls" more fair. The term "veering" is also used to denote "paying out" more cable.

We could go on and on without adding much to this discussion, for the language of the sea cannot be learned from one (or a score) of printed articles. It is acquired piecemeal, a word or a phrase at a time, through contact with seamen at work, just as seamanship is—and the two of them go hand in hand.

Our purpose here has been merely to "break bulk," as it were, by holding a brief survey on a few samples of the rich cargo of salt water idioms that go to make up our language. Properly handled, it is a masterpiece of nautical expression, as well as one of the most picturesque of all living tongues. Let us keep it alive and hand it on to our youth in the same good order and condition as it was handed down to us.

19

An Accomplishment of Sail

by RALPH M. MUNROE

[1927]

THE INCIDENT HEREIN RELATED occurred during the pioneer days of Biscayne Bay, when motorboats were unknown. It shows forcefully the simple, "likable" conditions of life there, when nearly all the interests of the community were mutual. The spirit of helpfulness and quick response to emergencies, so common among seafaring communities, flourished, and the desire for financial compensation for services rendered was scarcely known. Such was Coconut Grove before any other Bay settlement was in being. To us New Yorkers it was a paradise, and a few of us had even then become real settlers, identified with the community. Almost of necessity we owned a boat, which we had sailed down the coast the year before. Built expressly for these waters, at Brown's Yard, Tottenville, Staten Island, a better model could hardly have been conceived, as was proven by her long record of service from Cape Cod to the Rio Grande, until she came to an end in a memorable hurricane at New Orleans many years later.

Presto was 41 ft. 6 in. over all, 9 ft. 4 in. beam at the waterline, and 28 in. draft, just abaft midships, with flat rocker keel 12 x 4 in., having 1½ inches projecting below the garboards. A fin skeg ran from nothing amidships to within three feet of the rudder, which was of the ordinary sharpie balanced type. This skeg was, however, an addition put on after five years of use without it, its purpose being to provide a longer base for beaching or docking, and also to relieve my anxiety regarding the crew forward; for, if not continually cautioned in a fresh breeze, they were in danger of being picked up astern in a moist condition if they did not heed my "Ready about!" I failed to mention that she had round bilges, a centerboard 11 feet long, and carried approximately four tons of iron ballast, cast to fit and fastened down in her lowest spaces. Now this description, in view of *Presto's* many accomplishments, will, we think, be welcomed by many, and pardoned by the rest of our readers.

It was early summer and we were having our usual touch of an extra fresh east-northeast trade wind, bringing boats down to generous working reefs and kicking up a sea worth noticing along the coast. The weekly mail schooner from Key West to Miami was several days overdue and the settlement had begun to tire of watching the southerly skyline for the heads of *Dellie's* sails above the horizon. "Guess she's into a wreck," was finally the verdict and of course there was no use in looking for her longer. That business always preceded mail bags, unless the dinghy could manage inside the Keys with them. Suddenly someone sang out, "There she is coming in the Cape Channel," and after she had headed towards us, "Told you so! After more men; wreck must be close to Fowey."

As *Dellie* rounded up there was a rush for the dinghies and excited men were aboard before the mail could be handed on deck. A hush ensued, for the schooner's captain was telling a far different tale than was expected—one of driving the *Dellie* day and night up the Hawk Channel in order to take the keeper, Captain Larner, off Fowey Rocks Lighthouse and back to Key West before his wife died. He had reached the light that morning and found it impossible to make a landing—far less to have attempted taking the old captain off. This all hands conceded, for they knew well what that reef was like in a "rage." The captain had decided to go up the bay, deliver and take on the Miami mail, get back by dark, and go out to Fowey first thing in the morning, hoping that the weather might moderate in the meantime.

Dick Carney and I, sole crew of *Presto,* went on board, prepared a hasty dinner and decided that we would like to see Fowey Rocks in a rage. The mooring was cast off about noon, after the *Dellie* had sailed for Miami. Soon we were at the Cape, making things snug for a washing crossing the bar. A few minutes later, under reefed sails and eased sheets, we were plunging into the first line of breakers and doing well. Breakers were just pie for *Presto* but, without warning, the familiar sound of a parting rope, a look aft—and there was our dory just turning a backhanded somersault clear of the water and scattering her favors of oars, bailers, and sponge as if she were the horn of plenty.

Away went our hopes of bringing Larner back with us that day. Without that dory and oars there was little chance for our well-laid plans. There were the essentials tossing about, visible only at intervals amid many acres of broken water. By the time we could have salvaged even part of that mess it would be getting late, and we had no spare oars. Yet, while all this was passing through my mind, I had instinctively, and without further thought of possibly being boarded abeam by the sea, hauled that tiller hard up and before our friend Jack Robinson's name could have been mentioned, *Presto,* with sheets still flattened, had jibed over and was going down wind in her old wake, easy and moderate as could be wished for.

Dick had already spotted the flotsam strung out in line about right. He had the end of the mizzen sheet laid at his feet, also the boathook and landing net snatched from off the house top. Now if the next sea would only break just right—and it did. We came first to the dory, with bow in right direction, but capsized. With a turn of his hand, Dick had a loop in the end of the parted painter and with the other hand he completed the bend; another move and he had a turn with the slack sheet over the quarter bitt. Rendering it handsomely, he had the water-filled boat following like a lamb—and by this time we were up with the oars and other fittings. Now if the sea would only behave again! It did, and Dick had an oar in each hand, the wooden scoop bailer next and then the sponge, just visible. The landing net did the trick.

Dickey turned to me and said, "Any more things you want, Skipper? Say the word."

"You take those painter turns off the bitt and play that fish by hand until I get *Presto* out of this pickle."

"Aye, aye," said Dick, and I put the tiller slowly to port. Round she came into the wind and onto the port tack, from whence we had started our former course in quest of flotsam. We hadn't touched a sheet or been boarded by a sea. How did she manage to "stay" so sweetly, with that waterlogged boat in tow and so little way on, while still in the breakers, I'm asked? Well, you don't know *Presto* and I haven't time just now to tell you, but I will say that we hadn't even hauled the mizzen a-weather, which would certainly have hastened matters if we had had any doubts as to her staying.

Another half hour and we were in the Hawk Channel, all clear. Bailing the dory was an easy job after a new piece of line was fast to her. A few slack-ups on the painter and sudden tautening, after she was righted, got most of the water out, and Dick got the rest. About an hour later we were to leeward of the Fowey Light, some 75 yards, and hove to.

The keepers, from their morning's experience with *Dellie,* knew about what we wanted and sent a new heaving line on a buoy which was easily picked up, and we soon had a heavy line aboard and made fast around our mainmast, which was well parcelled. (I say mainmast because she was a ketch.) Then we took in the two forward sails and stopped them, but left the mizzen standing with the boom well guyed to starboard.

There were some broken iron rods on the north side of the light, with none too much water over them, and our head line might part and let her head cant the wrong way, but we needn't have worried. The keepers began taking in the slack of this line as *Presto* surged ahead between the seas. Soon she was entirely within the breakers, her nosepole about 30 feet from the piling, and nothing had happened. A good strong man could have held that line after we reached this position. We didn't stop then to find out why, but accepted the situation. Afterwards we reached a solution which seemed sensible. There was a back draft from the superstructure of the light tower as well as from the piling and its braces below. Being so broken up by this more or less open structure, the wind pressure apparently became more equalized than if the obstruction had been monolithic.

However, there will be no fuss about this; *Presto* lay behind that tower just as comfortable as could be, pitching at times to some extent and doing some rolling, but at no time excessively. Of course there was enough sea round the piling to be very dangerous at times, and spray was flying over the lighthouse platform from the weather side, but so different was it from what it seemed at a distance that Dick and I really felt sort of foolish. Still, every precaution had to be taken that no one would get hurt or the boat damaged.

By my standing in *Presto's* cockpit, and Captain Larner getting down close to the center of the lower platform, each could hear very well what was said above the roar of the wind and breakers, and there we arranged further action, which was successfully carried out. The new heaving line was made fast to the bow of the dory, her long painter carried to *Presto's* main port shrouds with its slack in the cockpit beside me. Two of the keepers tended the dory bow line and kept an eye on the whole situation. Captain Larner stood on the rungs of the iron ladder as far down as the sea would let him.

Dick slipped off his coat and shoes and sat facing the bow in the bottom of the dory with a pair of oars handy. All set, we waited for a smooth. It seemed ages, but when it came I gave the word by hand and mouth, as I could see below the platform. The dory was quickly hauled alongside the ladder, Larner jumped, landing fair, and went down into the bottom. Dick steadied her as the two keepers slacked her back. Abreast of *Presto,* I hauled her nearly alongside with the painter. Another wait for a smooth and a port roll of *Presto.* It, also, came just right and the boats were together. I reached over and grabbed an arm and a collar, while Dick parbuckled his other end and jumped aboard at the same time, cut the heaving line, passed the painter astern and let go our head line.

"Not a bruise or a chafe. How's that, Skipper?" asked Dick.

Nowadays I might have said, "Fine and dandy," but I just shook hands with him. Sail on her again, we waved our hats to Fowey and with a quartering wind were "a-b'iling" along on our way to the Grove. As we again crossed the sand bores Dickey shook his fist at them.

"Don't," said I. "They treated us decent, didn't they?"

"Yes, but that was *Presto*."

Dellie was waiting, anchor short. They had surmised what we had been up to and could see from away off that we had Larner aboard. Before sundown they were well on their way towards Key West and that stricken wife, 18 hours sooner than if *Presto* had not been able and willing.

20

Getting There—and Back

by HERBERT L. STONE

[1935]

PERHAPS THE MOST TRYING EXPERIENCE I can recall in a long
yachting career that covers every kind of cruising, from short
coastwise runs to long offshore voyages, occurred a few years
ago, not through stress of weather, "act of God or the public
enemy," collision, or the various hazards usually connected with
seafaring, but right here on our coast, within a few miles of port
and on a summer day's run that should have been completed
between dawn and darkness. And it was all due to inadequate
and faulty navigating equipment that left us running blind in a
sudden fog that blew in over sea and ship on the wings of a dying
sou'wester and blotted out the coast.

It happened in this way. I had taken a cruise in an auxiliary
sloop from the western end of Long Island Sound down to
Nantucket. In spite of the short distance, less than 200 nautical
miles, it had taken us six days to make the run, due to the persistence of light head winds, the lure of several ports on the way,
and the desire to snug down each night for rest and recreation.
After all, we were in no hurry to push on in order to reach our
objective any earlier, and the 35 or 40 miles a day we could do
between breakfast and supper were enough. But soon after our
arrival at hospitable Nantucket my time was up and, with a shift
of wind from the persistent easterlies of the passage out to
equally persistent airs from the western quadrant, I had to figure

on some quicker means of getting back to the worries of an office desk than a sailing yacht offered.

This was the situation when a friend blew into port with his 38-foot Matthews sport cruiser and asked me if I wanted to go back with him the next day. Eighteen statute miles (about 15 nautical) an hour she'd make, and he planned to get out early in the morning and promised to land me in Greenwich, Conn., by dinner time—12 hours, against the six days we'd spent coming down. It was too good a chance to lose and I jumped at it. As it turned out, it didn't prove quite as easy as we had figured, but that wasn't the fault of the boat—she would have done it if we'd been able to let her.

About seven the next morning my friend was alongside our sloop with his stepper. I transferred my dunnage to her, and a few minutes later we were off. Once clear of the breakwater, we set a course for Cross Rip Lightship and stepped her up to her cruising speed of 15 knots. She settled into her stride easily, the engine purring rhythmically without a skip or break under its cockpit hatch, and I took over the wheel while the skipper rustled some breakfast, as all good skippers should—course NNW to Tuckernuck Shoal bell buoy.

An early summer morning's haze covered the sea and we soon dropped the land, some fitful catspaws from the northward dotting the glaze of sea here and there with darker spots.

After getting her nicely settled on the course, so that a fraction of an inch of wheel would keep her there, my gaze left the compass card for a moment as I took a look around the horizon. When it came back to the card I gave a jump; instead of the NNW point cutting the lubber line, we were heading E x N. Surely we hadn't had time to swing through such an arc in the moment my eyes had been off the compass, and a hasty glance aft showed the wake pointing out straight astern where Nantucket harbor entrance was lost in the haze.

"What's wrong with this damned compass?" I yelled below to the skipper, out of sight in the tiny galley.

"Oh, I forgot to tell you," he said. "It jumped all about coming up here, and I couldn't make any landfalls accurately. In fact, if the weather hadn't been clear all the way I'd never have found the place. Never acted like that before. I put it down to the vibration."

I whistled. Looking at the catspaws on the water, I could see that we were still heading into the wind, and off to starboard I could just make out the loom of Great Point. We were evidently heading about right. Besides, the haze seemed to be burning away, and I let her go as she was, hoping the compass would come back to magnetic north before we had to change course at the bell buoy, which must now be only a mile or so ahead. Intent on keeping a straight wake streaming astern, I soon heard the clang of the bell and veered over to pass it close aboard. The swing started the compass card, but this time it swung as far the other way and finally settled on W. This was getting on my nerves, and I looked about for some iron or steel that might be affecting it, but could find nothing that could account for its behavior. It was well above the plane of the engine.

With the buoy abeam, I hauled her to what I thought was a couple of points to the left and started on the five-mile run to Cross Rip Lightship, which I figured we would see or hear in some 15 minutes. The swing was answered by the compass card, but it kept on going until the N point cut the lubber's line. By this time I realized that the compass needle had lost its directive force, and I knew of nothing we could do to it on board that would help.

Luckily, the haze blew away as the wind freshened a little from the nor'west, the lightship loomed up where it should be, and when we changed course to WNW for the run to the entrance to Vineyard Sound we could see the land on Cape Poge and the shore at Oak Bluffs, on the Vineyard, just off our port bow. The day gave promise of being fair.

Breakfast over, I turned the wheel over to the skipper and taking the compass in its box up forward, away from any possible mass of metal, I had the ship's head swung through an arc to note the effect. The result was just as bad as before; the magnet seemed to have lost nearly all of its directive force. Sometimes it would come to rest with the NNW point on the line, sometimes with the SSW diamond pointing to the ship's head. With no spare compass on board, not even a small one, we were out of luck.

Talking it over, we decided that since the day was now clear, and we would have land in sight all the way down to the Race, and from there in through the Sound, that we would take a chance and keep on. If it showed signs of thickening up we would duck into the nearest port. Right there is where we made our mistake.

Past Nobska and down Vineyard Sound, with land on both sides of us, the little cruiser stepped along at her best and the shores slipped by almost as the countryside does in a car. The lack of a compass did not bother us here and it was easy to fall into the habit of not running on compass courses when in sight of the shore. Vineyard Lightship lifted ahead, and about eleven o'clock came abeam, and we headed boldly across for Point Jude. The sun shone brightly and the shore was a dark blue line receding farther away to the northward all the time. But just the same there was a feeling of uneasiness, of uncertainty, that I had never felt in a boat whose compass I could rely upon.

Early in the afternoon, with Block Island just forward of the port beam, the wind began to back southwest and lighten. We had been steering by it, as much as by the distant land, on the run across from the Vineyard. Now we found it taking us away from the land, instead of parallel with it. For some reason the horizon was not clearly defined ahead, or to the southward, but we didn't sense or feel the reason for this.

We were looking anxiously for Watch Hill as a guide to steer by, but it didn't show, and then, before either of us knew it, there was no horizon anywhere; the wind faded to almost nothing, although our speed had made its dying hardly noticeable, and the first damp smell and feel of fog chilled us. Blind as we were, with nothing but our hearing to give us sense of direction, my first thought was to turn tail for Newport, in the hope of reaching there before the fog bank rolled in. Swinging a circle until we recrossed our outward wake, we straightened on it in a reverse direction and stepped the speed up a peg, while we watched our new wake streaming straight astern until lost in the fog some two to three hundred feet behind us. We must keep it straight at all cost.

Five minutes passed, then ten, and still there was no sign of thinning in the fog, no sight of the sun or blue sky. We swore softly. The fog had already enveloped the coast. We were surely in a jam. Should we keep on as we were going and try to pick up Point Jude fog signal and run for Newport, or swing around once more and try to make the Race in the hope that the fog would lift; or should we stop and anchor while the water was shoal enough to let our none-too-long cable reach bottom?

Neither of the first alternatives was alluring, with a rocky coast and narrow entrances shrouded in fog to run for it if it didn't clear when we arrived. Nor did the inactivity of anchoring in the open appeal to us. First, we must find out what the tide was doing. But my friend evidently didn't figure much on tides with a 15-knot boat, and there was no tide book on board. Also, when I asked him to get a cast of the lead, I discovered there was none on board. Now, the skipper knew better than this. He could do coastwise piloting and knew the value of good equipment. But he had become so accustomed to running in Long Island Sound in daylight, where none of his runs were over a few hours in length, that he hadn't realized the necessity of providing real navigating equipment. So, with the wind now completely gone and not even a ripple showing on the water to give us any sense of direction, we decided to anchor. There was just enough cable to give a fair scope in the ten fathoms of water the chart showed. It would do—unless it breezed up. If it did, it might blow the fog away. If it didn't! So we let go and looked at the time—ten minutes to three. Then we both laughed.

For a while we strained our ears in the hope of picking up a fog signal, either siren or bell, from some lighthouse or buoy. But there was no sound save the lap of the water under the stern as she rolled easily in the long swell. Besides, I discovered there was no light book on board and the only way of identifying such a sound, should we hear one, was from the meager information on the coast chart.

After some two hours without a sound breaking the stillness, we heard the faint blast of a steamer's whistle, one long and two short, signifying a tow. For some minutes afterward we failed to hear it; then it sounded again, nearer by now, but not much. Gradually the sound became louder. She was coming our way, but which way was she headed? We had been slightly to the north of the steamer lane when the fog had shut in. This sound should, therefore, be to the south of us. I looked at the compass, but it gave no help for it showed the sound to be to the NE. It must be wrong. To get the hook and follow the tow meant that we might get afoul of her string of barges, and, anyway, we wouldn't know whether she was bound east or west. We were better off where we were. The towboat passed not far from us, but invisible in the murk, and we had other dreary hours of waiting without a sound.

Night came on, black, murky; the drip of fog from the standing roof was a dismal sound. Shortly after nine o'clock we heard a whistle from what we supposed was one of the Sound steamers bound from Narragansett Bay to New York. We must have been right in the fairway, for she passed us too close for comfort. For an instant we thought of getting our hook and following blindly, guided by her whistle. But then we realized that many of these steamers made from 18 to 20 knots, and that our speed of 15 knots would soon drop us behind, out of earshot. No, better stay where we were, as there was yet no indication of wind. We stayed.

About three in the morning a puff of air blew from some direction, we knew not which. Suddenly we looked aloft and saw stars. The fog was thinning. Then a flash of light stabbed the night and was gone. It came again and this time remained steady. A little later, as the fog blew away before the offshore breeze, a red flash punctured the steady white. I grabbed the chart and studied it carefully. Watch Hill! Counting the seconds, there could be no mistake. Now other shore lights were coming out here and there. The breeze was northerly—the fog would soon be gone. In the east the sky was beginning to lighten. In another hour it would be daylight. We had been inactive long enough. Time to get the hook and be on our way. That damned compass had caused us delay enough.

As the sun came up we were sliding through The Race and Long Island Sound was opening up ahead. No need for a compass in these conditions—but then one could never tell.

Too many powerboat skippers, particularly if they own fast boats, neglect their navigating equipment, and do not use it as they should. The constant use of the compass on this boat, and the steering of set courses on all runs would have shown up its sluggishness and told the observant skipper that something was wrong. Also, a spare compass should always be carried. It will often come in handy. Even if the standard doesn't go bad, someone may put his foot through it. And a compass is no good unless it is correct. So its deviation must be ascertained. It is not hard to find your compass error and make a deviation card. But this story is not the place to tell how to do it. There are plenty of books on the subject, and a compass adjuster will take the kinks out if you can't do it yourself. But by all means know your error.

Oh, yes—and don't forget a light list, and a lead line, and a barometer, and other aids to accurate navigation. There's no telling when you may need them.

21

The *Wanderer*—Slaver Under the N.Y.Y.C. Burgee

by CHARLES H. HALL

[1920]

A HUNDRED YEARS AGO—on May 15, 1820, to be exact—an Act
of the Congress of the United States declared that any citizen
of the United States who landed from any ship's company on
any foreign shore and seized or decoyed or forcibly brought
away any negro or mulatto with intent to make such person a
slave was a pirate and, on conviction, should suffer death. At
that time there were no less than 300 vessels on the African
coast, all protected with two or three sets of false papers, and
all busily engaged in the traffic. The usual course was to sail from
the Congo with a cargo of "black ivory," discharge it in the
West Indies and load sugar and molasses, transport these to
New England to be made into rum and to sail again for the
African coast with plenty of good strong Medford and some
trade goods, there to secure another load of negroes from one
of the barracoons ashore.

On Aug. 9, 1842, the Webster-Ashburton treaty between the
United States and Great Britain was concluded, the eighth article
of which provided that "The parties mutually stipulate that each
shall prepare, equip, and maintain in service on the coast of
Africa a sufficient and adequate squadron or naval force of
vessels of suitable numbers and descriptions, to carry in all not

less than 80 guns, to enforce the laws, rights, and obligations of each of the two countries for the suppression of the slave trade . . ." and so on.

This article was commonly known as "The Cruising Convention." Great Britain lived up to it in letter and spirit; the United States was so touchy upon the right of search, and the slave power was so strong, that our enforcement of the terms of the treaty was rather farcical. True, we usually had the requisite number of ships attached to the squadron, but so much time was lost going and returning, and such long periods were spent in the Azores and at Madeira, that sometimes a ship that was 15 months in the squadron spent a scant 15 days actually on the coast! Judging by the orders issued to our commanders, the Government was more concerned in preventing the unlawful search of a vessel wearing our colors than in the suppression of the slave trade. Indeed, there were people in the South who advocated the revival of that pernicious traffic.

In June, 1857, there was launched at Port Jefferson, Long Island, the *Wanderer,* a schooner yacht built by the well-known shipwright James G. Baylis for M. D. Johnson, a wealthy member of the New York Yacht Club. She was 104 feet over all, 95 feet on the keel, 26½ feet beam and 10½ feet draught. Her tonnage was about 250, and she carried a lofty rig. Her mainmast was 84 feet long, topmast 35 feet, main boom 65 feet, gaff 35 feet and the bowsprit 23 feet outboard. To judge by the boasts of the old shellback who superintended her construction, she was a world beater; even her builder modestly admitted that she would be very fast. She was commissioned and apparently entered upon the peaceful career of a yacht, with nothing more exciting to look forward to than an occasional gruelling race with some of her fleet sisters.

But in less than a year her owner sold her to W. C. Corrie, who was elected a member of the New York Yacht Club on May 29, 1858. A day or two later he took his new plaything and sailed for the South.

She reached Charleston on June 25, and stayed there ten days. It is possible that at this time she was fitted out for her adventurous career, for she was filled up with tanks below her berth deck and could carry over 12,000 gallons of water. Her sailing master is said to have been a brother of that Raphael Semmes who was later to prove such a thorn in the sides of all Yankee shipowners as commander of the Confederate cruiser *Alabama,* and her supercargo was Captain Egbert Farnham, later one of Walker's filibusters. She cleared for "Trinidad and other ports in the West Indies" and sailed, under the burgee of the New York Yacht Club, from Charleston early in July. From Trinidad she stretched away across the Atlantic, calling at St. Helena, and thence to the mouth of the Congo. Here she fell in with H.B.M.S. *Medusa,* cruising for slavers, and Corrie still kept up the pose of a wealthy yachtsman seeking his pleasure afloat. He endeavored to make friends of the *Medusa's* officers and for several days there were dinners on yacht and man-o'-war. On one occasion, when a party of the British cruiser's officers were in the *Wanderer's* cabin and the wine had circulated freely, Corrie suggested that the schooner be searched to be sure she was not a slaver. This new sample of Yankee humor was greeted with roars of laughter. So let us leave the *Wanderer* on the African coast and return for a moment to the United States.

Enter Charles A. L. Lamar, of Savannah. He had a one-third interest in Lamar's Cotton Press there, in addition to other affairs. He is described as about five feet eight inches tall, inclined to stoutness, with a heavy red moustache. The *Wanderer's* cook called him "coarse-spoken." His letters, published some years ago, reveal the daring and impudence of the man. He was a successful slave trader, or rather slave smuggler, the last of that breed. In 1857, he wrote to the Secretary of the Treasury, complaining that his schooner, the *E. A. Rawlins,* had been detained "by your damned saphead of a collector," and he sent in a bill of $1320 for eight days' delay—and very likely the United States paid him the bill. He does not deny that the *Rawlins* is bound on a "blackbirding" expedition, but bullyrags the Secretary for this unwarranted interference with his affairs. Later, he writes to an associate that this voyage was a failure owing to the stupidity of the captain and says: "Discharge him, pay him

nothing and hope with me that he will speedily land in Hell."
He added the *Richard Cobden*—what a name for a slaver!—
and the yacht *Wanderer* to his fleet and suggested the formation
of a stock company to go into the business of importing a "cargo
of African apprentices to be bound for the term of their natural
lives." He had a fast steamer all picked for the venture and
suggested arming her with six shell guns and shipping a fighting
crew, all of whom were to be stockholders in the company. He
declared he could get a first lieutenant in the Navy to command
her! This ship was to carry 2000 negroes to be sold for $650
each.

But turn again to the mouth of the Congo. After a few days
of interchanging courtesies with the officers of the *Medusa,* the
yacht *Wanderer* slipped away to the river, still quite unsuspected,
and packed a cargo of "black ivory" under hatches. How many
she carried we do not know, though one account says 750 young
negroes, from 13 to 18 years of age! Away she went across the
Atlantic, anchoring off the coast of Georgia about Dec. 2, 1858.
Corrie communicated with Lamar, the negroes were landed on
Jekyl Island, now a well-known club preserve, and then taken up
the Savannah River and scattered through the state.

There was a fearless United States District Attorney at Savannah who immediately caused the yacht to be seized and
Lamar, Corrie and such members of the crew as could be found
to be arrested and brought to trial. But, as happened in a long
and shameful series of such cases, no one was punished, though
the schooner was forfeited and ordered sold. Lamar was apparently little affected by his arrest, and appeared at the auction.
He said that the *Wanderer* was his property and that she had
been wrongfully taken from him and asked those present not to
bid on her. The only man who disregarded this request was the
keeper of the jail, and Lamar, after getting the schooner knocked
down to him for $4000, proceeded to punch the luckless warden's
head.

The negroes that formed the *Wanderer's* cargo were scattered
through the state, some of them being taken up the Savannah
River on a steamboat whose pilot was indicted at the same time

as the *Wanderer's* captain. Though a few luckless blacks were found by the marshal they were taken from him at night and spirited away "to parts unknown." Indeed, the whole history of the slave trade is filled with accounts of such trials—and no punishments. It was not until 1861 that a slaver was executed as a pirate, and he hailed from the State of Maine and was hanged in New York.

So Lamar had his yacht again and proceeded to fit her out for another venture to the Congo, whence she returned with 600 blacks. She was chased off the African coast but had the legs of any man-o'-war and made a fast trip to this country. She got ashore in a gale of wind, grounding between Jekyl and Cumberland Islands, Georgia, and a number of the negroes were washed (or jumped) overboard and were drowned. Most of the survivors were shipped to New Orleans and sold there.

She was now too notorious a vessel to avoid suspicion and Lamar planned to send her to China for a load of coolies, at the same time pretending to have sold her. Meantime, at the regular quarterly meeting of the New York Yacht Club, on Feb. 3, 1859, Corrie was expelled and the *Wanderer's* name expunged from the list of Club yachts.

The new captain and ostensible owner was variously known as James F. Potter or Martin or Dresser or Walker. The schooner lay off Lamar's Cotton Press, slowly fitting out, and shipped part of her crew for a voyage to Matanzas as a fruiter. One day in October, 1859, Lamar sought the Collector of the Port and urged him to send a revenue cutter to seize the schooner. He had sold a large interest in her to Martin, he said, had not received a cent, and feared that Martin intended to run away with her. "He had just about made up his mind that he had to deal with a damned rascal," he said. So the next day the Collector and Lamar went to look for her and found that the bird had flown the night before.

Martin had rushed a few loads of stores aboard, shanghaied the men who helped him load, announcing that "Not a man puts his foot over the rail to-night," and gone to sea. When some of the seamen growled at such treatment, he went forward with a horse pistol, a cutlass and a revolver and, inserting the latter in each man's ear, asked sweetly: "Do you want to go ashore?" Then he drove them all down into the cabin and sat there with a pistol in each hand while they signed articles for the voyage to St. Helena. Then he opened several bottles of champagne for the crew. Outside of Tybee, he put the shipping master and his runner in their boat, announced that he was off to Africa for a load of "niggers" and headed away for the Congo, with a derisive message for "all the good people of Savannah."

Apparently the *Wanderer* went to sea short of provisions and without either charts or chronometer, for Martin chased every vessel he met and exchanged longitudes and tried to buy provisions. He was seldom very drunk, but never quite sober, and he drove the schooner hard in all weather. One night he got drunker than usual and sat up in the cockpit with the steward passing up whiskey until the men at the wheel were as drunk as the captain, while he shouted: "This is just the breeze for us! No man-o'-war could catch us to-night!"

"It was a wonder," said the mate, "that he didn't run her under that night."

She made a fast passage to the Azores, doing 340 miles in one day's run, and found two men-o'-war there, so headed for Funchal. There they lost the carpenter, through desertion, and left at a moment's notice to avoid seizure. A few days later Martin boarded a French bark to get provisions and while he was aboard of her, Weston, the mate, who had quarrelled with him continually, made sail and bore up for home. She put in at Tarpaulin Cove and then went to Boston, where Weston delivered the schooner to the U. S. Marshal.

Again the *Wanderer* figured in the United States District Court, and again the United States District Attorney recited that: "At a time past, to wit, on the nineteenth day of October, in the year aforesaid, certain persons, whose names are to the said Attorney as yet unknown, did at a port of the United States, to wit, the Port of Savannah, in the State of Georgia, fit out, equip, and otherwise prepare a certain schooner or vessel called the *Wanderer,* for the purpose of procuring certain negroes and persons of color from a foreign country, to the said Attorney as yet unknown, to be transported in and upon the said schooner or vessel to a certain place to the said Attorney as yet unknown, then and there to be held and otherwise disposed of as slaves." Shortly thereafter appeared one Charles A. L. Lamar, of Savannah, as claimant for the vessel, asserting that she was his and had been stolen from him by Martin. She was appraised at $5940. Lamar gave bond for this amount and for an additional thousand to cover costs, and sold her to Gazaway B. Lamar, his father. She was condemned and Lamar lost his money but got his precious schooner again. He took her South, repaired her and sent her to Havana to be sold. She was there when the Civil War broke out, but Lamar was busy raising a regiment for the Confederacy, and had no time to think of the slave trade. He was later killed in action.

The United States Navy was feverishly building and buying ships when the *Wanderer* comes on the scene again. She sailed into Key West, with her papers apparently good though with slight irregularities, in May, 1861, and was promptly seized by Lieutenant Tunis A. M. Craven—the same Craven who went down in the ill-fated *Tecumseh* with "After you, pilot," on his lips. He discovered that she was to be sold to "certain parties in New Orleans at a high price, to be fitted out as a privateer. I have therefor detained her as a vessel which can be used for no valuable purpose except as a cruiser or dispatch vessel. As a privateer she would be most formidable. . . . She has the reputation of being a remarkably fast sailor, and is ready for sea. Armed with one long 24-pounder, and with a crew of 25 men, this vessel may be disastrously destructive to our shipping in the West Indies, and there was a general feeling of relief expressed among shipmasters in Havana when it was learned that I had seized the *Wanderer*."

Apparently the Navy Department approved of the seizure, for we find the *Wanderer* on the Navy List as a cruiser, patrolling in the Gulf. Through her seizure of the British schooner *Telegraph* she again got into the limelight, this time evoking a letter of protest from Lord Lyons, the British ambassador.

But hard driving had been too much for her, and in 1863 she became a hospital ship at Key West and later the guard vessel there. At the close of the war she is described as "unseaworthy" and sold out of the service. She was put into the cocoanut trade, running to the islands on the northern coast of Honduras, and was finally lost on Cape Henry in a gale.

But what a life she had!

22

North Channel Recco

by CARLETON MITCHELL

[1947]

THIS IS ABOUT a part of the world where you can dip drinking water from over the side, reserving your tank aboard for more important beverage; where, every few miles, snuggles another harbor of such beauty and perfection that it would be famous in a less favored locality; where all the virtues of cruising are combined with those of camping. It is a country at once near and remote, wild and civilized. It offers an almost unparalleled combination of deep water and magnificent scenery, blended by a beneficent providence for the delight and edification of the small boat cruiser.

It is with humility that I write of the North Channel of Lake Huron and the islands fringing the upper shore of Georgian Bay. There are so many who know it so much better! But I prefer to think of my trip in the nature of a reconnaissance mission. Some day I'll go back, and spend days in harbors we entered just to look over against that future day.

I think the difficulties of cruising the North Channel country have been greatly exaggerated, and I say that despite the fact that I did a carom off a certain rock in Whitefish Bay to the great detriment and eventual demise of my rudder. Before leaving Cheboygan, Mich., I was filled with stories that made me expect successive labyrinths of boulders; of islands appearing where the chart showed good water; of sudden squalls and water level fluctuations and even periods of bad visibility. My informants were particularly vehement on the subject of Canadian charts; most unfairly so, I think now.

It is true that some charts are incomplete in the sense that they do not cover certain remote areas that the small boat putterer may want to visit, but these places have no commercial or military significance to justify the expensive business of governmental charting. When you go into such areas you are literally going "off soundings"—although in a sense new to the salt water man. Even here, the stranger has assistance; in Little Current are available land survey maps on which courses through various Bays—McGregor, Finn, Whitefish—have been drawn, with some piloting comments of great help. These maps won't show you where the rocks *are,* but they show you one way to go where they *ain't.* So long as you follow them with reasonable care, you aren't likely to get into difficulty. On our reconnaissance cruise we never steered a compass course, rarely took a bearing, never sounded, never had a lookout forward, and never got into any trouble except once, which I will alibi—I mean explain—in due course.

In addition to its charts, the Canadian Government publishes *The Canadian Great Lakes Pilot,* which is helpful once its simple form is understood. However, no article on the North Channel would be complete without mention of the superb job done by the Great Lakes Cruising Club in its *Port Pilot and Log Book.* The pilotage information given is so thorough as to enable the total stranger to proceed as with an old hand in the bow. Were it not for this volume, cruising these waters would be much more difficult, and my only criticism of the *Port Pilot* is that it is pessimistic in tone even as it makes navigation perfectly simple. No cruiser should set forth without it. Information may be had from the Great Lakes Cruising Club, 30 North Michigan Ave., Chicago 2, Ill.

The foregoing is not to imply that the Sunday afternoon sailor can't get into trouble in North Channel waters. He can, and will—but doesn't it happen to him everywhere? I'm only trying to get across that any decent boat can get around the area without more than proper handling. There is almost no fog in summer; there are no strong currents; there is always a harbor close ahead and close astern; the squalls encountered during six weeks in the general area were not savage. A nasty sea does get up fast if a fresh breeze sets in but, again, a harbor is always handy. All in all, it's a cruiser's paradise, and I'm going into all this at the outset because I am afraid that many with limited experience might hesitate to give it a try if they get the same advance dope that I got.

My wife, Žib—who will *not* hereinafter be referred to as the mate—and I actually made two trips to the North Channel, separated by my flying to Chicago for the Mackinac Race. The first was so beset with mechanical difficulties that it was a nightmare rather than a cruise, through no fault of boat, engines or workmen. After illness had forced a drastic revision of our summer's plans, we asked to borrow Zib's mother's boat for a North Channel cruise; poor Steve Majestic, in Cheboygan, was given five days to make ready a boat which had been laid up for five years! We expected trouble, and had considerably more than anticipated.

From the headaches of that first cruise we derived one positive benefit: we discovered a spot which we will refer to only as "Hidden Cove," a spot so perfect and remote that we selfishly want to keep it for ourselves. I can only justify myself by pointing out that there are doubtless thousands of other places just as wonderful and that part of its charm to us was the circumstance under which we visited it: I suppose that trying to keep this secret will constitute a challenge to all experienced North Channellers. I wish them luck in their search—bad luck. The rocks in the entrance are *terrible*.

The early afternoon of Monday, July 29, 1946, found us jockeying for a berth alongside the dock at Little Current, which was being typical of places all over the world by not living up to its name, there being no current whatever at the moment. That did not stop me from having my usual docking difficulties: we charged around gaily, me sawing first on one lever and then another, while, if neglected for a second, the old *Kate* would "creep" ahead at better than *Carib's* full speed. Zib stood on the bow with a line, all ready, so eventually I got the stern to the dock. So—but hell, I've already said that some guys can get into trouble anywhere, haven't I?

Anyway, we tied up and there we were, Zib, the *Kate M.*, and I, right at the beginning of some of the most perfect cruising grounds in the world. The *Kate M.* was a 38-foot *a.c.f.* open bridge cruiser, powered with twin Buda gasoline engines. For two, her layout was perfect, with the entire boat open except for a small but airy cabin forward of the bridge.

We had entered the North Channel through False Detour Passage and had taken the southern route; that is, had followed the Manitoulin Island shore, and had checked off the miles with a celerity wholly unaccustomed to a windjammer. On our previous trip we had hit most of the preliminary places recommended in the G.L.C.C. *Port Pilot:* Harbor Island in Potagannissing Bay, Pilot Cove on Drummond Island, and Gore Bay. This time we had come right through, except for a two-day stop at Hidden Cove. (*Clue!*)

To me, even in advance, Little Current meant Grant Turner, so I immediately crossed the road to introduce myself. We had already corresponded, and he had sent me the charts for the trip. He made me welcome and it soon developed that we had picked a perfect day to arrive: the Turners were having a picnic dinner on their island in McGregor Bay, and would we join them? We certainly would, and shortly the Turners and the Mitchells were roaring east in a skimming dish powered by a huge outboard engine.

In a remarkably short time we were nearing the Turner's island, a perfect hideaway. Anchored off were the matching Alden cutters, *Wind Song* and *Islander,* owned by Clyde Larish and N. L. Telander, respectively. We swam in water invigorating but not numbing and drank a bit of Scotch which was likewise; we stood on a rocky point and watched the waters of McGregor Bay progressively change colors under a magnificent sunset; later Mrs. Turner produced a dinner that was a fitting climax.

At eleven o'clock the four of us got into the skimming dish and headed back for Little Current. Except for a faint glow from the northern lights, the night was as black as a cave, but beyond slowing briefly to pick up a reflecting disk on a stake, we tore along at 20 or better. And this through waters that I had only a few hours earlier considered a maze of hidden dangers! Even conceding that Grant Turner knows his way better at night than almost anyone else does by day, it made my earlier thoughts on hiring a pilot seem ridiculous.

On the following afternoon we got away on our own, armed with Canadian Government chart 86 and a map of the "Vacation Islands" compiled by Mr. H. J. Defoe. Both may be obtained at Grant Turner's store in Little Current, and Mr. Turner, unfailingly helpful to visiting yachtsmen, will add advice and comments.

Past the Current and clear of Strawberry Island, we encountered a little chop, the breeze being northeast and fresh. Giving the rocks off Stony Point, Great Cloche Island, a good clear, we headed the old *Kate* for the channel between "the Marys" and Little Cloche Island—this somewhat more to prove nonchalance than anything else since the channel to the south of the Marys is much more open. Beyond Little Cloche the chart runs out—we went "off soundings." The neat little rows of numbers cease abruptly under the lettering "Frazer Bay." Beyond is blank paper, except for a few scattered "x" marks that denote known rocks; nearby, the shore line remains in firm lines, indicating that its contours are accurate, but beyond, in McGregor Bay, islands are shown as vague dotted outlines.

There is a brief distance here covered by neither chart; according to Grant Turner all dangers along the east coast of Little Cloche will be cleared if McGregor Bay Point is kept lined up with the eastern end of Heywood Island. From what I learned, this part of Frazer Bay is all deep water right up to McGregor Point. On nearing it, we swung east to parallel the shore below Quartz Rock. But this is not intended as a guide; all the information is better obtained locally. Just take my word that this part of a North Channel cruise is easy.

Behind Bay Finn Point opens one of the most magnificent vistas I have ever seen—which includes some familiarity with the Norwegian fjords from Stavanger to the North Cape. On the Defoe map it is labeled Narrow Bay, which is appropriate. Ten miles long, most of it is less than a half mile wide. The sides are steep, the white rock forming a brilliant contrast to the areas of green trees; the water deep blue and usually reflecting the mountains and the clouds above.

We powered ahead, too overwhelmed by beauty to be apprehensive, following by eye and estimation the line laid down on the chart. We were not alone in the bay; many other small cruisers scurried around or swung in sheltered coves, all looking strangely dwarfed by the vast backdrop.

When you think you have gotten to the end of this amazing formation, you weave around a few rocky islets and another ribbon of water opens. This, according to Defoe, is the real Bay Finn. Proceeding around an abrupt turn to starboard, there opens the final pool—the ultimate anchorage: you lie as snug as an egg in a nest, trees to the water line nodding welcome.

Just before sunset we were joined by *Wind Song;* and the Larishes and their guests, Bud and Sis Snite, came over after dinner and we talked of poking into odd places from where we were clear down to Half Moon Bay in the British Virgin Islands.

On the following morning, I enviously watched Clyde and Bud swig a beer while I emptied—by count—95 buckets of Bay Finn water from the old *Kate's* bilges back into Bay Finn. At such times, no man views the world with proper perspective. But finally the job was done and I had a beer myself and suddenly realized that the day was as nearly perfect as possible: the sky a deep blue dotted with freshly washed patches of cloud, the trees looking greener than usual, and just a faint northeast air.

It was after one when we got up the anchor. The passage out was even easier than in, and seemed even more beautiful. We had decided to spend the night somewhere in McGregor Bay, so retraced our course to McGregor Bay Point, there to swing back around the long peninsula whose north side forms the south shore of McGregor Bay and whose south side forms the north shore of Bay Finn.

McGregor Bay is in some ways lovelier than its southern neighbor. The lower part is dotted with little rolling wooded islands and stark rocks, the upper part becoming a narrow channel through rock walls to open finally into woodland at the shore of McGregor Island itself. Snug little anchorages are everywhere. The only difficult spot seems to be the narrow gap between islands 1213 and 1217 (on the Defoe map every island has a number). We proceeded without difficulty, and finally anchored off McGregor Island itself.

As usual, we tried a bit of fishing, but, as usual, had no luck. Regardless of where I go, it is always a "bad year" or a "bad month" or even a "bad day." The season of 1946 was apparently a "bad year" for the north country. Zib was particularly disappointed as she is a hard working fisherwoman and had had a "bad year" throughout our West Indian cruise the previous winter.

The following morning, Thursday, August 1st, we got away at 10:30, the weather remaining ideal. By 11:45, we had rounded McGregor Bay Point and were back in Frazer Bay, where we set a vaguely southerly course to go between Heywood and Partridge Islands, swung eastward and, after passing the lights on the south shore of Badgeley Island, looked out on the shimmering waters of Georgian Bay. I wouldn't care to push the old *Kate* through this channel in one of the fresh westerlies that abound hereabouts, but on this day the water was glassy and a spectacular color as it reflected sky and clouds.

Just after one o'clock, we docked in front of Jackman's Store in Killarney, a picturesque little village whose approaches are well defined in an insert to chart 86. We had heard that good fishing was to be had in Collins Inlet, so had decided in advance to try to get a guide. Luck favored us in the person of Julian Low, a commercial fisherman just out of the Army and free for the afternoon; before two we were again on our way.

Right here I should note that one of the pleasant things about North Channel cruising is the shortness of the distances involved.

Ten, 15, or 20 miles away takes you into a different section with entirely different scenic characteristics. I admit that we covered too much ground in too little time, but we wanted to see as much as possible. Easy should be the motto.

While we ate sandwiches, Julian wheeled *Kate* into the western entrance of Collins Inlet, a lane of water separated from Georgian Bay by Phillip Edward Island. The inlet is like a narrow rock-and-tree-walled river except for a few wide bays, and would be beautiful enough to draw forth superlatives from anyone not recently from Bay Finn. We tried fishing a couple of likely spots, at one place tying to a sheer rock wall, but without success.

After crawling past Skull Point into Beaverstone Bay (shoal and filled with deadheads), we made an intricate passage among many islands to gain the eastern entrance to the inlet. Tied to a rock in the entrance we found a boat full of fishermen: in response to our queries, they answered that there were plenty of bass but that the bass wouldn't bite on anything but worms, and they didn't have any worms. We did, and tossed them a container. In gratitude they bade us follow to a spot where in the morning the bass had shouldered each other in their eagerness to get the few worms they had. You guessed it: the bass were no longer interested. It was a "bad hour!"

That night we anchored in Jehannes Cove, or Covered Portage, off Killarney Bay. It was the most beautiful anchorage we found in the entire cruise, and for some reason its water was much the coldest for swimming. To reach it (on the advice of Julian Low, whose knowledge of local waters was impressive), we disregarded all the material contained in the *Port Pilot* and made an abrupt turn at the first starboard hand marker when leaving Killarney, to head directly for the gap between Sheep Island and the smaller island to the east. The chart shows plenty of water here, and from its color I think there is.

On the following morning, we got away about eleven, went back over our course to the Killarney entrance buoy, and then headed for Lansdowne Channel. Here the *Port Pilot* becomes incomprehensibly pessimistic: there is a perfectly simple buoyed channel but the *Port Pilot* uses nearly a page in describing how to run it. After almost foundering on the pilotage directions, I had a feeling of anticlimax as we circled through Snug Harbor, which, although beautiful and living up to its name in a gratifying fashion, was not as impressive as some others. Without anchoring, we finished the run through Lansdowne and made for Browning Cove on Heywood Island, where we found *Islander*. This harbor could conveniently break a slow boat's passage from Little Current to any of the more distant bays. We cut our engines for a few minutes and drifted, enjoying a chat with the Telanders.

Back in Little Current, we took on gas and stores, lunched, and had a final visit with the Turners and a briefing on the pilotage of Whitefish Bay. Shortly before five we cast off. The Wabuno Channel is wide open and we made good time to the turn around Great Cloche Island. The first part of Whitefish Bay—which the Canadian Government renamed the Bay of Islands, and so shows on the charts but is never called so hereabouts—is easy. But fairly soon the appropriateness of the new name becomes apparent: there may have been a question of its whitefish population in the bygone days but no one could quibble about the islands!

Beyond Wells Island we bogged down. We were using the Plan of Islands in Whitefish Bay from the *Port Pilot* and flunked out on navigation on arriving at the island which carries the notation on the chart: "Green house with red roof." We stopped and took bearings and mentally retraced our course, but couldn't reconcile the look of things ahead with the shapes on the chart. It was undoubtedly foolish for me to want to continue, as we had less information on Whitefish than on the other bays, but we had gotten to the ends of the others and wanted to do the same with this. It looked intriguing: a maze of islands of all shapes and sizes, some wooded, some rocky. Still, we would probably have turned off to a nearer anchorage except that I discovered an outboard powered skiff coming up astern.

We hailed them and the boat came alongside: a guide and a couple—and they had a string of bass to prove they were really fishermen. They were headed for the town of Whitefish Falls and would be glad to show us the way. Bob, the guide, pointed out the channel around the "Green house with red roof" and we proceeded. No trouble at all, and I wondered why I hadn't seen it for myself.

On the way it was decided that we would join forces to try our luck at fishing in the morning. We hated to leave without one "good day" so plans were made for an early rendezvous and we dropped them off the town, and continued on to the last pool in Whitefish Bay, where, ironically enough, we had to anchor near a bridge and listen to the horns of passing automobiles. Except for this, the anchorage was ideal.

At 8:15, we picked up two skiffs off the town, took aboard two guides and two couples, and proceeded. Inside of fifteen minutes, near island 2974 where Bob had shown considerable uncertainty the previous afternoon, we hit a rock. It was another demonstration of the peril of divided responsibility afloat: Bob and the other guide, Ernie, were standing beside me at the wheel giving advice. I was half watching the chart but altered course on Bob's recommendation a matter of seconds before the bump. It wasn't his fault—he only knew where rocks weren't for an outboard craft, and was a fishing guide, not a pilot. It was the old story of depending on unqualified local knowledge. I write this in a vein of "Learn ye from the mistakes of the foolish, brothers!"

We bounced and continued without losing way. I could detect nothing wrong, but remembering the naked condition of rudder and wheels, felt vaguely uneasy. There was no trouble during the run of several miles to Hunt Point, where we anchored while Zib joined the fishermen and I went over the side to feel for damage. Beyond a slight crimp of the edges on two blades of the starboard wheel, I could detect nothing; the rudder didn't carry a discernible blemish, nor did the port wheel. With a sense of vast relief I launched the dinghy to see if I could do better as a fisherman than as a pilot.

While it wasn't a really "good day," neither was it a wholly "bad day"—we caught enough bass and pike for lunch ashore. Never did fish taste better: Ernie simply dipped them in flour

and dropped them into a blackened frying pan and the result
would have put any chef to shame.

We finally got up anchor and started for McBean Channel
just after two. The afternoon westerly had set in about noon
and steadily freshened. Beyond Bedford Island, the sea was quite
steep and it was necessary to reduce speed sharply. Just as I
began to hope for some shelter from Amedroz Island, there was
a terrific bang under the stern—about three times as violent as
that of the morning. My first reaction was to swear at rocks
appearing where the chart showed 20 fathoms, but then the bow
swung off and I realized that the wheel was having no effect.

For a few moments, *Kate* wallowed horribly in the trough
while I verified and loudly lamented the passing of the rudder.
Getting her off before it and keeping her there was no fun. Fortunately, Bedford Harbor was close. I had noted it as we steamed
by earlier and also noted that a large yacht was well inside.

We anchored near *Eleanor,* of Lafayette, and her captain
gave me a ride to Little Current in his launch. Grant Turner was
surprised to see me back so soon—and did a gentlemanly good
job of hiding his amusement. While his son Barney readied the
boat he found a machinist who would work the following day,
which happened to be Sunday, and we got away for Bedford
Harbor in *Northerner.* By the time we came alongside *Kate,* the
night was black enough to swallow an ebon squall cloud that at
sunset was building to the northwest but which continued to
assert its threat by spitting purple fire.

It was agreed that I would follow a flashlight tied on *Northerner's* stern, only turning on my lights in case of breakdown.
Grant headed out and we swung into his wake. Have you ever
tried to follow a feeble little flashlight on an utterly dark night,
especially through occasional spatters of rain? To follow a boat
making probably six knots when your boat, rudderless, could
hardly be controlled at less than twelve; when, after every few
yards of straight running, your boat would take so violent a
sheer that full ahead-full astern would be necessary to correct it,
while that light would get dimmer and dimmer—and as soon as
you got straightened out with sufficient way, you would be about

to climb right over the other fellow's transom? I have often heard powerboat men speak casually of "steering her with the engines," but personally I'll take a hammock slung between two trees 67 miles from the nearest water, fresh or salt.

Anyway, we got there, despite the port throttle control coming loose in my hand when we were nearly off the docks in Little Current. After Grant's job in shepherding us, it would have been rather sad to pile up on the rocks in the middle of the harbor, but we didn't miss them by far.

The next morning found *Kate's* stern hauled clear by a two horse power (on the hoof) engine on the end of a tackle. Our bronze rudder post had sheered off at an old weld, up inside the hull. The machinist fashioned a discarded automobile axle and a scrap of boiler plate into a serviceable steering unit. It was nearly midnight when we had a drink to a finished job.

The following noon found us in Wabuno Channel. A fresh westerly was blowing and again we faced a steep chop beyond Bedford Island. There the unfortunate resemblance ceased; at reduced speed, *Kate* slogged ahead finally to gain the lee of Fox Island.

Here begins yet another cruising ground of great beauty and interest. The tangle of islands that fringe the northern shore of the North Channel forms narrow lanes known as the Whalesback and McBean Channels, which together constitute a sheltered passage of some 20 miles. Elsewhere it would be renowned; here it is just one more thing that should not be missed.

Around two, we entered McBean Harbor, a fine, picturesque anchorage at the foot of the mountain by the same name whose bulk is a landmark for the entire area. After a swim and some lunch we had a nap, getting under way again shortly after five.

There is nothing difficult about the pilotage through the channel with the proviso that all islands and rocks are identified and accounted for. One interesting formation is called Little Detroit; it is an extremely narrow cut through rock and is the point where the channel changes names from McBean to Whalesback. During this run the weather was overcast and a strong breeze was blowing from a little south of west. Outside we would have been unable to continue but inside the water was smooth.

The Whalesback Channel takes its name from a prominent rock of that name and, as usual, it was difficult to discover the resemblance that had inspired the voyager of long ago. Still, it forms a good mark and is easy to spot. John Island lies a short distance beyond. Its harbor is rather large but furnishes a good protection. The *Port Pilot* notes that the shores abound with blueberries but it was too late to try for any. There were also some intriguing little islands along the south shore which invited exploration, and Zib was sure that there would be lots of bass in the channels between. We decided that we'd have to come back. . . .

But we want to go back to every one of the harbors we visited—go back and swing around a hook until the snows come. Some day we'll do it.

23

Pacific Capsize

by GERALD SMITH

[1948]

THIS COULD BE CONSIDERED the narrative of a series of errors. It has always been my contention that nothing adventuresome or worth writing about ever happens to a good sailor. I have always tried to be reasonably careful and never thought anything out of the ordinary would happen. However, something did happen, something that will never happen again, I hope.

We left Grays Harbor, Wash., about August 30th and crossed the bar outward bound for tuna about 7:00 P.M. We had six and one half or seven tons of ice, 900 gallons of fuel, 200 gallons of water, and plenty of grub for a month, if necessary. The course was SW; everything was O.K. and the goose hung high. By daylight we were about 70 miles offshore and well into the blue water, so we put the poles out and threw the gear over, altered the course to about SSE and continued running full speed, since we were not getting enough fish to warrant slowing down.

I tuned the radio in on 2638 and 2738 several times during the afternoon, and it seemed that they were getting a good showing of fish down off Cape Blanco. We continued on our course until dark and kept hearing boats talking about heading south until it seemed that all the boats on the Pacific Coast were heading for Cape Blanco. Don and I decided to go more or less NW as it seemed there were going to be plenty of boats for what fish there were down south. We kept zigzagging up the coast, about 60 to 110 miles offshore, until we were approximately 70 miles SW of Vancouver Island and set a course approximately parallel to the Canadian Coast to a point about 70 miles south of Cape Cook. I think we had been out six days and had only six fish up until dark September 4th.

The engine had been getting harder and harder to start and I suspected burnt valves. We were a good many days full speed running from any known school of tuna, so Don and I decided to run inshore the next day and try to pick up a trip of salmon off the Canadian Coast, as salmon trolling speeds would not burn the valves any worse.

I tuned in 1630 at 8:30 P.M. for the Canadian weather report and also to take a radio bearing on Esteban. While I was at it, I got a bearing on Quatsino and Cape Flattery, which gave us a pretty good fix and established our position as 65 miles SW of Esperanza. The weather report was for 35 miles SE wind during the night, including September 5th. Anyway, nothing to worry about or make any special preparation for since a southeaster that time of the year seldom blows for more than 24 or 36 hours. We always unbend our chain and anchor as soon as we get offshore and lash them alongside the pilot house. It is only a few minutes' work to shackle the sea anchor into the end of the cable and just a matter of throwing the sea anchor overboard and using the brake on the windlass until you have the scope desired. We couldn't see any necessity for running at night as a 35-mile southeast wind would make it unfishable for salmon for two days, anyway. If it should really blow, it was only a matter of minutes to have the sea anchor out and be riding like a duck.

The wind started to blow about midnight. I took a look at it about two o'clock and, as we were not doing any unusual gymnastics, I went back to sleep. Don got up about six o'clock and made coffee. He started the engine and ran our course while I was still in the bunk about half awake and half asleep. We were running in a beam sea to make our course and making fair weather out of it as we still were carrying our riding sail, which does a lot to steady the boat and take the roll out of her. However, it got to a point where we were rolling the main poles under and Don hove-to to take the poles in.

A word of explanation as to the way the poles are rigged. There are two poles 45 feet long, about 4½ inches in diameter at the butt and 1½ inches at the tips, rigged port and starboard and hinged on top of the bulwarks about parallel with the mast. They are raised just forward of the shrouds and rest in a spreader notched to hold them about three feet above the hounds. The spreader is about six feet wide so that, when raised, the poles lay in a bit and the two tips just about touch. Ordinarily, it is no chore to take them in as they have permanent fore and aft stays and double lifts for hoisting. However, in bad weather you have to be careful as it is possible to break the mast off above the hounds, if, after you have let the hold-down loose and are raising the pole at the same time, the boat should take a fast roll and the pole slam into the spreader. I have found only one successful way to take the poles in when the weather is really bad. It is to let the boat drift in the trough and leave the sail up to give her a good list, take in the lee pole, turn the vessel to give the other side a list and then take that pole in.

It was about eight o'clock in the morning when Don stopped and suggested we take the poles in. I got up and took a look but suggested we wait until it quit raining as it was blowing at least 50 miles an hour in puffs and blowing a solid sheet of rain and water. I lay back in the bunk to finish my smoke and wait for it to quit raining while Don had another cup of coffee. The rain soon slacked off so my partner took a quick dive out of the galley door to get his oilskins and hat; then back into the galley to put them on. He just about had his boots and oilskins on when I heard a sea break on the starboard side of the house and the boat took a little more heel than usual. Don was standing by the after galley door when she evidently got another breaker that filled her sail, as he said water was pouring off the sail. The boat had a definite port list and did not appear to have her usual buoyancy.

I remember Don saying that he thought the boat was going to turn over. I half rolled and half fell out of my bunk to get to a pilot house window and watch as I just couldn't believe that she wouldn't right herself.

Don was certainly right. She was not only turning over; she was already on her side. The mast was slightly under water and there was absolutely no indication of righting herself. When you think of it, she didn't have a chance, as she had two bow poles 38 feet long, two 45-foot main poles, and a heavy mast overbalancing her as well as the wind and swell.

Things were happening too fast for me to remember what Don was doing as I had been lying in the bunk in my B.V.D.'s. I had to try to rustle up some clothes, as you don't last long in that kind of weather and in the water without anything on. Did you ever try locating your clothes while standing on an oven door and bumping your head on the exhaust stack? It would have been an advantage to be a monkey just about that time. I grabbed what clothes I could that floated out of my locker and jammed them between the steering wheel and clutch lever to keep them from floating away.

In the meantime Don had opened the starboard pilot house door and was standing on the side of the wheelhouse getting lines cut loose to tie on with. It dawned on me that the life preservers were in the foc'sle and we had better be getting them if we were ever going to, as water was pouring down into the engine room and foc'sle through the engine room hatch, which was now completely under water and the hatch cover floating open. I slid out the starboard door and onto the forward deck and managed to get the skylight open and down through it.

I had quite a time locating the life preservers, as everything was upside down, but I managed to find a couple and pass them up to Don, who put his on and lashed mine to the boat so it wouldn't float away. I passed the mattresses and all the blankets I could gather up to my partner but everything was torn away from him before he could get a line on it, except one blanket. By the time all this had happened, the wheelhouse and foc'sle were fit for occupancy only by fish and marine life.

I would reach down through the door in the trough of the swell, and get an article of clothing, and put it on as I could while waiting for a chance to retrieve one more article. I finally managed to end up with the oldest pair of summer trousers I owned, three good shirts, and a pair of worn out squaw socks. Don was in pretty good shape, as he was fully dressed with oil-skins, boots and a southwester over his cap when the boat rolled over. He already had himself tied on and a piece of 18-thread manila about seven fathoms long cleared for me with one end made fast to the pinrail. I wasn't long in getting the free end in a bowline about my middle and the long wait started.

When the vessel capsized, the drag of the mast, sail and poles acted as a rudder and she swung around and put her bottom to leeward, which was certainly a blessing as far as we were concerned. We had our life lines fastened to the chain plates and so could stand on her side at about the copper paint line, facing the weather, hanging onto our lines and bracing ourselves whenever we saw a bad one coming. The wind was still howling and showed no signs of letting up. Brace ourselves as we might and hold on as best we could, we would still be washed off to the length of our lines and buried under tons of water about every five minutes.

The first eight hours were pretty grim. We were wet and cold, no relief was in sight and dark was coming. However, the picture got better about two hours before dark as the sea was moderating and we were not being washed off quite so frequently; also, we were being blown in towards shore. However, we still had probably 50 miles to go and our drift was approximately three-quarters of a mile an hour. We were feeling good at the time, though; just a matter of comparison, I guess.

About ten or eleven o'clock a steamer passed about two miles outside of us, heading east towards Cape Flattery, probably coming from the Orient. Of course we didn't have a flare or any way of making a distress signal so we just stood there and voiced our opinions of any misbegotten so and so that would stand quite so far offshore.

Don and I couldn't find a great deal to talk about as he had been fishing with me the whole season and we were pretty well talked out by this time. Also, we were saving our strength. If the wind should turn and blow from the northwest, we wouldn't have much future to worry about. Time passed much faster than you would expect and daylight was rather a surprise. We were quite leg-weary, since we hadn't had a chance to sit down yet. The sun came out about ten o'clock. The sea was moderating and there was probably only a ten-mile southeast breeze; in fact, it was quite balmy and we had a chance to sit down on the side of the hull and get a little rest. The day passed quite uneventually, as did that night, until daylight of the 7th. The wind came up with the sun but we did not mind too much as it was still holding southeast and our chances were getting better all the time. We were feeling good enough to crack a joke occasionally.

My partner had been mate on Liberty and Victory ships all during the war, and had been to Australia, the South Pacific, the Atlantic coast, and just about everywhere Uncle Sam sent ships. About this time he mentioned that all during the war he hadn't even gotten his feet wet, and then came home to this.

In the afternoon we started to look shoreward as it appeared that we might be seeing mountains above the shore haze. We had been drifting 48 hours by a little after daylight and, as there is a definite easterly set to the Japanese current off that coast and the wind had been holding SE, we were drifting just about NNE. We were still in the Japanese stream as the water temperature was about the same as when we turned over, 60.5°. By afternoon it seemed that the water was getting colder and we started looking longingly towards shore. It cleared up a short time later and we definitely saw shore and some landmarks that we recognized, about 20 miles off, I should judge. The water was not only colder but we had hit the inshore set, which was setting us noticeably westward. Just before dark we saw a small vessel five miles inshore.

Things were beginning to look up and it was about time, as all the salt spray being licked off our lips had started to make us dry. The boat's forward fuel tanks had been filled through the vents. The mast was down in the water at 45°, there was no freeboard aft or forward and only about two feet amidships

on her side. I had always figured the boat would float if
swamped, but now I began to wonder.

The wind started to blow again after dark. It was really
quite nasty as, with all the buoyancy gone and but little freeboard, a swell of any size saturated us. However, the wind was
still SE, which pleased us, in spite of being wet all the time. We
were being drifted up the coast rather fast and not so much towards shore now. The westerly current set along with the SE
wind was not doing us much good and it looked as though we
might hit shore about Cape Scott at this rate.

We were a little better off at night now. The day before, we
managed to rescue my sleeping bag and split it open. We turned
our backs to the wind and draped it from our heads and shoulders
with our backs to the wind whenever possible. We had a line on
it with about three fathoms of slack and when we got washed
overboard we just crawled back up, pulled our sleeping bag to us,
and draped it over our shoulders once more.

We had suffered only one casualty by this time. Don and I
were washed overboard and, as he had his boots on and they
were full of water, he was having trouble getting aboard again.
I grabbed his arm and pulled. He got aboard all right but minus
one boot. He was still not too badly off as he had two pairs of
socks on, but by this time I was barefooted since the bottoms had
fallen out of my socks.

About midnight we started to see a dim flashing light that
could only be Solander Island. It appeared that we were setting
right down upon it and in a couple of hours we had drifted to
approximately three miles of it when a light northwest wind
blew up. This was discouraging indeed and we started drifting
away from the light. Just as it was starting to get daylight a light
fog and shore haze settled down and we heard the throb of
motors, then saw running lights and the dim shape of several
small trollers passed us on the way out to fish.

I dove down through the side door of the submerged pilot
house and felt around for our fog horn which is kept clipped to
the ceiling of the pilot house and managed to get out without
losing it. Don and I blew distress signals until we were blue in

the face but "no soap." After all, a hand fog horn is a puny thing when the wind is blowing and an engine is running. However, it was breezing up all the time which might blow the fog away and drive the small boats back to harbor again. About a half hour later along with the daylight it succeeded in doing just that, for we heard the boats going back in again but couldn't see them. We blew a distress signal all the time but no luck. Around nine or ten o'clock the fog lifted and an Alaska-bound four-motored bomber passed directly overhead. We waved our blanket but he was too high to see us. Not a half hour later an Alaska-bound two-motored transport passed in sight of us, but I guess he wasn't looking at the water either.

Shortly after the planes had passed over, we decided to try to rig a distress signal of some kind. We managed to twist off and break the wire rope forestays. The after stay had a rope lanyard that we cut and I managed to swim out and cut the lifts. We had already managed to get the nut off the bolt that pinned the pole to the rail. We tried every way we could to raise the pole but with nothing on the bottom to stay it to we just couldn't keep it raised.

The wind died down by noon time and we started drifting to the west again and were actually fairly comfortable with our sleeping bag wind breaker even though the sea was washing over our feet and legs. It looked as if we were going to drift right into Solander Island but just before dark we came abeam three-quarters of a mile off.

At this time we had a difficult decision to make—to let go and swim for it while we still had the westerly set helping us, or to stay with the hull and take a chance on being blown out to sea. We considered the fact that we were only about half as strong as we felt. If we could survive the pounding we were sure to take trying to make it to the island, we would only be perched on a straight up and down piece of rock with a mile more to swim to make another rocky landing and no beach. We decided to take our chances with the boat. Although we felt fairly well there was no use kidding ourselves as to our fast ebbing strength.

We started our fourth night with fair weather and a small

degree of comfort. The tide kept right on setting us to the westward and, as the land recedes to the west of Cape Cook, we were getting farther offshore all the time. We kept right on setting to the west until probably two or three o'clock in the morning when a light northwest breeze sprang up. With daylight the breeze increased and it looked as if we might be in for another nasty day.

About ten o'clock, we saw a mast round Solander Island heading more or less towards us. Needless to say we kept a close watch on her, but she seemed to be heading a little outside of us. She came close enough for us to make out that she was a cannery tender. From the time that she was within two miles of us we started to wave our blanket and Don's oilskin pants every time we would rise on the crest of a swell. It certainly was heart breaking for she passed about three-quarters of a mile outside of us. At one time we saw a man climb to the top of the pilot house. We figured he had sighted us for sure. We learned later that it was the cook, rummaging through the vegetable locker. We also learned that one of the deck hands had seen us and told the skipper that it looked like two men drifting on a log. The skipper took a look and said to forget it, as it was only a couple of black-fish playing around.

By about noon it was blowing a good NW breeze and a heavy ground swell was starting to roll. It was blowing hard enough to start us setting to the eastward and towards Solander Island again. We began to speculate as to whether we would drift between Solander Island and the mainland or swing and drift by on the outside of the Island.

We were probably four miles west of Solander when we saw another mast round the Island, and it kept bearing right for us. This was probably 1:30 P.M. on the ninth. The vessel kept bearing right down on us until we could make her out to be a schooner of some kind. She was getting closer all the time, and we kept waving our blanket every time we came on top of a swell. She was within 200 yards of us when she suddenly swung out and slowed down. She continued on until she was to windward of us and hove to. Men came pouring out of the foc'sle like ants out of a hill, ran

aft and began throwing gear out of the dory. I would venture
to say it was only ten minutes from the time they saw us until we
were aboard. She was the halibut schooner *Annie Tuck,* out of
Victoria, B. C., Joe Babcock, owner. He is an old time dory fisherman and certainly showed it in the way he gave us and the dory
a close lee.

The crew had warm, dry clothes laid out before we got below
and the cook had the coffee pot boiling. The first thing I wanted
was a cup of coffee and a smoke. The *Annie Tuck* was just out
from Victoria on a black cod trip and, as it was blowing up, she
was heading for Winter Harbor, B. C., for harbor.

I asked Joe Babcock about putting a line on the *Rebel* and
towing her in, but all she had in the way of towline was his five-
eighth-inch plow steel anchor cable. In that kind of a sea and a
heavy boat with a submerged tow, he figured he would part the
towline before he even got started; he was more than likely right.

We had our supper on the *Annie Tuck* on the way in. Needless
to say we were more thirsty than hungry. I was more worried
about the boat than myself and tried repeatedly to get through
by radio telephone to Seattle but atmospheric conditions were not
favorable that early in the evening. The storekeeper at Winter
Harbor tried to get through until after ten o'clock. He finally did
manage to get a telegram to my insurance agent and a message for
my wife. About midnight a Canadian troller laying in the harbor
managed to get through to Seattle for me and gave me a chance
to talk to the insurance agent. I had already made arrangements
for a troller with a radio phone on to tow the *Rebel* in, the boat
(the *Perry*) belonging to Vern Green.

I asked the insurance agent to call the Port Angeles Coast
Guard station and to have them send an amphibian plane to spot
the hull and to get into radio communication with us and we would
meet them off Solander Island about one o'clock, September 10th.
Sure enough, about noon the next day, while we were on our way
out, the amphibian flew overhead and started flying in ever widening circles. In about an hour he spotted the hull and radioed us the
bearing. By three o'clock we had a line on the boat and were
towing. The plane then asked if we would like to have him stand

by, but we thanked him as he had done a splendid job and could do no more.

We didn't get a line on any too quick as the afternoon breeze was springing up and a good sized swell was building up. The *Rebel* was practically submerged and the way the *Perry* was dancing around we could tow at only half speed. Even so, we parted the towline just before dark. This slowed us up for a half hour while we pulled the line in and made fast again. We arrived in Winter Harbor, B. C., about 8:00 A.M. the 11th, about 18 hours towing some 16 to 18 miles.

As the tides were rather small at the time we had some trouble getting her up on the beach far enough to dry her up, since she was drawing at least ten feet of water. It was a couple of days before we got her afloat and dry with about the whole population of Winter Harbor helping us.

I certainly have never been anywhere where I received better treatment or found a whole village more helpful. Don and I stayed there for about ten days, cleaning the boat up and getting her in shape to tow.. While there, we boarded with a very nice family.

I wish to say I don't know of a nicer fellow to be shipwrecked with than Don. Neither he nor I have suffered any permanent ill effects from our open air ride, but we did both suffer digestive disorders for a couple of weeks.

At the beginning of my story I mentioned a series of mistakes. My mistake number one was being where the tuna "aren't"; number two was "zigging" when I should have been "zagging"; in other words, being in the bunk, when I should have been on deck.

24

To Each Man His Craft

by J. T. ROWLAND

[1915]

YOU TOO, no doubt have wondered why the coasters are always waiting for a fair wind. We have all marveled at that, one time or another. Here, for example, is a fleet of a dozen sail bound east, lolling at anchor in Vineyard Haven. The weather is fine and the breeze southeast-just fresh. We come in from Wood's Hole one afternoon in our 30-foot yawl and anchor inside of them. Next morning we up-hook and away for Nantucket. The following day—or maybe the next—we come back; and the chances are that if the wind all that time has hung easterly we will find the coasters still there.

Two or three of the fleet only have left, and if our memory and powers of observation are good, we will doubtless be struck by the fact that those which have gone were the smallest and most deeply laden of the lot. The big fellows—great, high-sided three- and four-masters—are still tugging gently at mammoth hooks deep-sunk in Martha's Vineyard mud.

It seems ridiculous, somehow. Time is money to these fellows, yet here they are throwing away half their time because, forsooth, they do not find it worthwhile to try to beat to windward against a nice, fresh little zephyr which has provided our 30-footer with motive power for most of her cruise to the eastward. Surely, if we can make good our fifty or sixty miles a day to windward between dawn and sundown, these great fore'n-afters with their lofty rigs ought to find it worth their while to go to sea! Yet they don't go, and therefore most of us argue that the men who sail them are by nature a slovenly, lazy, stoop-shouldered, plodding lot.

I, personally, came to this conclusion while quite young. Still, there was always something fascinating about the coaster fleet. Their very disregard of time, and detachment from the hurry and scurry of the greedy steamers, imparted a sort of air of "hobo-esque" aristocracy. I classed them, after due reflection, not with the moving van and dray team of land commerce, but rather with the roving gypsy bands who labor only sporadically for the where-withal to meet their modest needs, and spend the major part of their lives in delightful wanderings through wooded by-ways. The old vessels, too, were such unconscious masterpieces of picturesque unkemptness. With their raking bowsprits, seamy topsides and well-patched canvas they looked, indeed, the very part and sub-stance of travel-worn voyagers from the great unknown loitering for a day, a week, a month within our harbor mouth, hence to depart unheralded and alone on their never-ending watery paths.

Compared to their mysterious spell, the charm of smug and trim little yachts or business-like, hurrying steamers was as a strain of garish ragtime breaking in upon the last quivering notes of a violinist's rhapsody. Nothing would do, I decided, but that I must in person share their lives and learn the recondite secret of their aimless voyagings. This done, I could endure, perchance, the humdrum, sordid existence of the schoolboy—feeding inwardly upon the consecrated memories of the past.

.   .   .   .

"Wall, I reckon you won't do no great sight o' harm. We're callin' in to New London for a cargo of oak knees, an' you can come along that far with us 'tanyrate. Be down to the dock here at four o'clock sharp. I cal'late to git an early start, come a fair chanct."

Thus spake the Skipper. He was a gaunt, rangey *young* man, deliberate in speech and showing unmistakable signs of acquaint-ance with the comforting weed—yet redeemed from common-

placeness by the possession of an eye as clear and piercing as an
eagle's.

Going home, I floated on air. After supper I quietly collected
the few essentials of the voyage (quite forgetful that it might
save future embarrassment to include a few shore clothes to come
home in), wrote a brief note to be left on the hall table in the
morning, and turned in. Through the night, visions of the *Genevieve,* of St. John, N. B., floated deliciously through my half-
consciousness. She was actually a foreign ship, under the British
flag; that was almost too good to believe. Also, she was a two-
topmast schooner, a true seafarer, and she boasted a high poop
deck. There was no one to tell me that this was an obsolete "bluenose" notion, that the vessel herself was about as seaworthy as a
scow and as dependent upon harbors as an open catboat, or that
her meager crew of three men and a boy consisted of three frugal,
simple, hard-working Nova Scotians—all brothers—and a ras-
cally, blasphemous Yankee mate, who had been degraded from
the deep-sea merchant marine through his inability to keep away
from the bottle. Moreover, if anyone had told me these things it
would have made no difference. It was my First Voyage!

It was not yet daylight when I was down alongside. An eerie,
brooding hush rested over the unpeopled waterfront. The tide,
already on the ebb, swirled small fragments of dirty ice along the
schooner's bulging waterline—for March was not yet gone. Of
sounds there were none save the occasional squawk of an early
rising gull and the steady chorus of muffled snores issuing with
clockwork regularity from the stuffy cabin where all hands
bunked.

It began to be quite cold. After untold ages, the family on a
gravel barge lying alongside the same dock gave evidence of
beginning the day's work. A large, frowsy woman inquired my
business with what seemed to me unnecessary asperity; but on
securing the information changed her tone, cracked a joke with
her husband and gave me a cup of steaming coffee. At least, I
suppose it was coffee; it tasted about the best of anything I had
ever drunk. Not long after that the sun arose. I began to grow

nervous. My ship was losing the better part of a fair tide. Followed a weighty discussion with the captain of the barge, as a result of which I plucked up courage to go aboard the schooner and rap loudly upon the cabin scuttle, which was almost directly above the Captain's bunk.

"Eh?—eh?—" sleepily. "Who the tarnation is that?"

"Almost eight bells, sir; you're losing a fair tide."

A long silence. Then: "Wind's fair, too, I s'pose, eh? All right, you go an' wake up the men—I'll be a-gettin' up purty soon."

The wind! What a landsman I was, never to have thought of it! There was absolutely not a breath. Again I conferred with the bargee. He tapped down his pipeful, spat reflectively over the side and studied the clear morning sky with the dignified wisdom of a savant. Maybe he was one. Finally he "figured it would come westerly when the sun got up a bit."

That was all the encouragement I needed. But as I was starting over the rail again he laid a cautioning hand on my shoulder. "You want to know where the door is when you rouse out that mate on thet-air schooner, young feller," he said. "He's a mean one, that cuss is."

Apparently complications were coming thick and fast. Somehow, though, the proximity of land lent courage. Also, I figured that a wide-awake boy was more than a match for a sleepy mate, when it came to dodging. But more important than either of these considerations was the fact that I was acting under orders from the "old man" himself. Surely that was enough. Accordingly, I made my way somewhat gingerly to the forward door of the cabin which gave access to the main deck.

Inside, the air reeked of warm humanity and stale tobacco. The boy was the first one to greet me. The day before he had been rather offish; now he hailed me as a companion in toil. Together we woke his brother, the cook; and while I was considering the most advisable method of going about the next and most hazardous part of my task the cook, in a most unexpected manner, took it off my shoulders. He was a tall, well-proportioned fellow and he had very red hair. Perhaps that had something to do with it. At any rate, he grabbed the still-sleeping mate by one hind leg and yanked him half out of his bunk.

"Rouse out, you bum," he commented sweetly. "Don't you want no breakfast?"

The boy looked at me and winked. "We'd best be gettin' out an' rustle some firewood for the cook," he said. We went.

If the fire-spitting mate attempted any comeback we did not hear it; but it was easy to see that Si (the boy) expected trouble later and it certainly did not seem likely that the mate's disposition would be improved to any noticeable degree by the manner of his awakening.

That cook was a wonder. For industry, good nature and thrift I have never seen his equal—especially for the last-named quality—either at sea or in the woods. He would be worth double pay in any lumber camp, provided the men he was feeding did not all die of hunger. However, one cannot expect three big meals a day on a lumber schooner, and a Nova Scotian at that. He had a way of making you feel just as good as if you had stowed away a rib roast: that was where his radiant good nature came in. Even the mate could not get mad at him, though he tried to at every meal.

In due course we had breakfast. It gave me a start to look at my watch and see that it was just the time that my family was having breakfast at home up on the hill—and the breeze had not come yet. So much for our early start. The regular crew were still sitting in the cabin discussing whether or not it would be worth while to work out into the harbor and anchor there to be "handier for a chanct." By nine o'clock this lying-around had become intolerable, yet the tobacco parliament was still in session aft. The bone of contention was that the skipper did not want to go to the expense of hiring a towboat and the mate said "he'd be teetolly d—d, yes teetotally, sir," if he would lend his sanction (and incidentally his muscle) to hand-warping the schooner along half a mile of docks.

I was glad to see that they evidently did not consider us two boys equal to the task. Still something had to be done. I could not stomach a whole, long, hungry day right alongside Bush's

Coal Yard with the gables of my father's house in sight up on the hill. Therefore I ventured to offer a solution in the form of the powerboat of a man I knew who would tow us out for nothing "if I asked him." I was careful not to let it appear that there would be any other consideration than my simple request: if the Skipper thought I was paying for the service it might make him feel embarrassed(!).

This worked nicely. I am not sure but that it actually saved a fight between the mate and the cook. At any rate, it got us out into the harbor, which, though tame, was a more endurable place to be hung up than at a dock. Also, it contributed indirectly to my getting some little scrap of professional standing with the mate. It came about in this way: When Fred Crocker and I ran alongside the schooner in Fred's "party launch" the mate was standing by the cathead with a coiled line in his hand all set and ready for a cast.

"Here, you!" he sung out, sending the line uncoiling through the air in my direction, "use that for a tow line, AN' PUT A BOW-LINE ON TH' END—SAVVY?"

It was what I had planned to do anyhow; so this roar did not confuse me. The summer before, while cruising, my brother had gone to some pains (and myself to some pain) to instruct me in the seamanlike art of *throwing* a bowline. It is a very nice little trick and I had learned it thoroughly—thanks to my brother's assiduity.

Now, with the flourish of the artist who is sure of his technique, I caught the end of the line, held it a moment nonchalantly while leisurely expectorating, then threw the bowline deftly, dropped the bight over the stern bitts of the launch and made a flying leap for the schooner's chain bobstay, up which I swarmed by way of the bowsprit shrouds to her "nose pole" and then into the eyes.

The mate eyed me a moment suspiciously. In flannel shirt, sweater and old pants I looked quite different, no doubt, from the young "dude" of the day before, at whom he had barely condescended to sneer.

"Ever been to sea?" he demanded.

"Yessir," I lied glibly.

"That's —— —— good; I can make you earn your salt, then. Haul in them lee fenders and look sharp, d'ye hear!"

"Very good, sir;—eh, excuse me, but which is the lee side? There is no wind yet."

The mate dropped what was in his hands and stood looking at me with chin stuck out and the most intently malevolent expression that I had ever seen on a man's face. Words seemed to fail him. When they did come his speech was so faint that I feared he must be ill—that I had literally made him sick! "A sailor," he said slowly, "a sailor generally hauls in them on the side away from the dock first. And he DON'T ASK QUESTIONS." I wasn't quite sure whether the episode of the bowline had turned out to my advantage or not.

In time we got out to the center of the harbor. Then, while the mate, aided (perhaps) by Si and me, was overhauling a few fathoms of chain cable preparatory to coming to an anchor a nice, fresh, little northeast breeze suddenly cut in from over Todd's Point.

That, to my mind, was a signal for making sail, but the Skipper only chewed on his pipe stem and said nothing. Presently the anchor was let go and much rusty chain rattled through the hawse pipe. Had I known what backbreaking labor it would mean getting that on board again I could not so blithely have seen it go. But I had won my first manoeuvre and was serenely happy.

When Fred had waved me his farewell and was chugging back shorewards the Skipper ambled slowly forward sniffing the breeze, shoulders hunched up and hands thrust deep into trouser pockets.

"Purty well ahead," he observed.

"Yes-sir"—this from the mate. "Too durn much ahead to be any use, I say! She'd just be goin' sidewise like an old crab out there in this. Wouldn't get us nowhere."

"There are plenty of harbors all the way along on both sides of the Sound," I cut in eagerly.

Both men regarded me with a sort of abstract interest which a scientist might accord to a new beetle.

"D'yew know these waters?" asked the Skipper at length.

"Yessir, I can take you in anywhere if you get out there and find she won't make her course."

The Skipper grinned in a sort of a sickly fashion and the mate swore softly but copiously.

"Reckon yew c'd do it in a snow squall?" the Skipper asked. I deemed from his tone that a reply was not expected.

In the end, the boy and I were turned to, under the mate's direction, to clean out the hold—and direct us he certainly did! That was not so bad, though, for he worked like a trooper himself. There were the usual odds and ends of junk from the last freight in her otherwise empty hold. Most of this, bits of sticks and the like, was frozen into the cemented snow and ice which had accumulated while the vessel was lying for a month or more at Bush's dock. We got after it with spades and a pick-axe (of all things to find on a ship!), heaped it into little piles and then lighted it up to deck in a bucket. By the time we got through my feet were wet and half frozen and my hands stiff and bleeding.

It did not seem quite the sort of work to put a sailor to, but I observed that Si took it all as part of the day's work, so held my peace—which was well for me! After all, there were, of course, some unpleasant features even to being a sailor, but all that would be quickly forgotten once we had gotten under way and began to list to a fresh breeze! By the time we had her cleaned out below and the decks sluiced down and otherwise made shipshape and Bristol fashion, dinner was ready—a genuine meal this time. Si and I did it ample justice, rather to the disgust of the saturnine mate, who averred that a boy was "not half a man on two men's grub." A concise statement of fact.

Gradually it grew very dark in the "house," and the next time the cook made his entrance, he was covered from head to foot with big, flocky snowflakes.

"Snowin' right smart an' breezin' some, too," he informed us.

No one seemed much surprised: the mate merely grunted,

but the captain's stock soared way above par in my admiring sight. Candidly, I was forced to admit to myself that after all he probably knew his business better than I, and I was truly thankful not to be piloting the good ship *Genevieve* up into Oyster Bay at that moment. Apparently he had smelt the snow coming.

Along towards the middle of the afternoon the wind got around into the northwest and the snow stopped with surprising abruptness, leaving a beautiful, sunny spring evening with a fair wind. Now that he had what he wanted, the Skipper was by no means slow to take advantage of it. Setting the big mainsail was a heart-breaker, and breaking out the hook another; but just as the sun sank behind the white-clad western hills we filled away and put her on a course for The Race.

That night all the stars in heaven were out. It was just comfortably cool and a gentle land breeze wafted us peacefully eastward with eased sheets and a rapping of ripples at the old schooner's bow. The little swell still coming in from the eastward lent enough motion to complete the illusion of being at sea without being uncomfortable to a very full stomach. It was wonderful: I would gladly have stayed on deck the whole night, but at eight bells the Skipper shooed me below with the injunction to get what rest I could before midnight. To tell the truth, there was a separate and distinct ache in every muscle that I had.

"Rouse out, there, matey: it's our watch," a gruff voice was saying, to the accompaniment of a vigorous shake.

I fetched up all standing in the middle of the cabin floor and caught the mess table to steady myself by, for the schooner was well listed and seemed to be traveling at a famous speed. The faint glim of a low-turned lamp revealed the mate in the act of buttoning a ragged ulster under his chin.

"It's colder than the Straits of Wan de Fusha up there," he told me, in the nearest approach to a kindly tone that I had yet heard him employ. "You want to put on all the duds you've got. We have four hours of it on end, you know."

I followed his advice, and then followed him up to the poop—being careful to ascend that sacred eminence by the lee steps. The

Skipper mumbled a course, said something about calling him if it freshened any, and ducked precipitately into his cabin.

When he was gone the mate spat contemptuously. "That is a —— of a way to start a man on his watch!" he observed, with obvious disgust. "Do you know why he didn't tell me what some of these bally lights all around us are?"

Thus directly questioned, I confessed ignorance on the point, though it *had* seemed rather peculiar considering that the mate was a stranger to the Sound.

"It's because he don't know them himself; that's the answer. There ain't no chart at all on this ——, bloody packet but a general coast sheet that shows Long Island Sound about the size of a peanut. Say, no slush now, do *you* know these lights?"

I studied them carefully and named half a dozen, beginning with the flashing white on Stratford Shoals astern and ending up with Horton's Point just visible on our starboard bow.

"That sounds all right," admitted the mate, "but how in h—— do *you* come to know so much about it; you ain't no sailor?" It dawned upon me that the mate's bluster was mostly for the gallery. Now that we two were alone he was acting quite human.

"Let me take that wheel and I'll show you if I'm a sailor," I replied tartly enough. He looked at me sharply, but stepped aside and gave me the wheel and the course, purposely throwing the vessel's head about a point off at the same time. I brought her gently back to the proper heading and had held her so for perhaps five minutes when at last the light of comprehension broke upon him.

"Oh, I savvy," he said: "you're one of these yachters. Well, that's better than nothing. Take her along, I ain't used to playing quartermaster."

This was a leading remark, and, the ice being broken, the mate loosened up and began to tell me what was nothing other than a partial biography—typical and pitiful. Only five years before he had been a strong man and a capable officer in deepwater ships. He made a voyage to the west coast of Africa in a fine brig. He went out as second mate, but on the homeward-bound passage the captain died of fever and the first mate and some of the crew were swept overboard by a boarding sea and lost, so he brought the vessel home as acting commander.

The owners, much pleased, promised him an independent command in another ship as soon as he should get his master's certificate. Then, suddenly, he took to drink. He did not tell me the reason for this, but from other remarks I strongly suspected that the loss of his wife had something to do with it. Finally, he drew a stained envelope from some inside pocket and thrust it into my hands. "Just look at that!" he said shortly. "A man ain't all bad that can have kids like that, is he? God bless them *and damn me* for ever bringing them into such a world as this ——!" And he trailed off into sacrilege the more horrible for the contrast it presented.

When I handed the photograph reverently back I noticed that the man was shivering violently from head to foot. "You're cold," I said. "Go below, man, and get warmed up. I can take her along for a while!"

"No, it ain't that," he answered in a shaken voice. Then pulling himself sharply together: "Look to them sidelights," he commanded curtly, "and see if they're burnin' bright."

Crippled, emaciated and debauched though he might be, the pride of craft was with him yet. Poor devil! So do we learn to know our fellow-man—in the still, dark watches of the night.

During the latter half of our watch the wind petered out and what little was left veered around to the northeast, so that when the Skipper came on at four in the morning we were close-hauled on the port tack and had progressed little beyond Falkner's Island.

Followed, so far as I was concerned, a few hours of deep oblivion, broken at intervals by the thrashing of booms and slatting of sails as the vessel, almost becalmed, labored in the swell of passing steamers. Then the mate woke me up. "Eight bells already?" I groaned.

"No," he growled, "Skipper's lost. Wants to see if you know where we are." It proved to be the truth. There had been a light fog for the last hour, and now with the dawn a fresh, chill

breeze from the east was driving in thicker mists from the sea
with a promise to snow behind it. Already the watch on deck
had found it necessary to clew up topsails and the schooner,
oversailed and undermanned, was tearing blindly in the direction
of the Long Island shore.

I questioned the Skipper and made out that the last light
which he had been able to see was what could be no other than
Plum Gut. It had borne broad off his starboard bow about an
hour previously and he thought that we had come at least five
miles further east since then, even allowing for the tide, which
had set in strong flood against us at the same time.

"Then New London is easy money on the other tack," I said.
"You had better go about right off before we bump Gull Island,
and stand in for the Connecticut shore."

Having asked my advice, he followed it without question, in
which I found much to admire, considering how slender a reed
it must have seemed. There was no halfway business about the
Skipper.

On the starboard tack the old schooner pointed well and
seemed to be making famous work to windward. Presently we
heard the fog whistle on the Bartlett's Reef lightship, and I told
the Skipper that we must weather that before we could swing
off for the entrance to New London harbor. It was well off our
lee bow, so the task of passing to windward of it appeared simple
enough. But a curious thing happened; we were coming up with
the lightship fast—every successive blast of its fog signal was
appreciably louder than the one before—yet its position was
fast changing from the lee bow to the weather one! To be sure,
the tide was setting strongly that way, but at our speed and the
angle at which we were headed we should at least be holding
our own over the tide.

Greatly puzzled, I glanced astern at the schooner's wake—
and saw it trailing up to windward at an angle of 45 degrees:
the old crate was making leeway like a Chinese junk! Suddenly
the lightship itself showed for a moment through the swirling
mist, a cable length dead to windward.

"Can we run inside of her?" the Skipper shouted from the wheel.

"No!" I cried. "There are reefs all around. For the love of heaven go about: we're near on top of them now!"

"No use to tack ship," he observed coolly. "She won't go to windward when she's in ballast. No freighter will—to amount to anything. She's only drawin' eight feet: you're sure we can't chance it?"

"There are no reefs showing here at low water," I ventured. "It must be half-tide now; she might go over—with luck."

The Skipper's eyes narrowed: "She's *got to*," he said quietly; "there ain't anything else."

The cook came out on deck, looked the situation over, and without an order being given, made his way quickly but without unseemly haste to the eyes. There he stood, hatless and with his apron still on, peering ahead into the driving fog, alert to give instant warning of a suspicious swirl in the water, while the old *Genevieve* with a half gale tugging at her bellying canvas tore ahead in her mad rush to shelter or destruction.

Seconds passed. Nothing untoward happened: the tension began to relax. "I reckon we fetched one of the low spots in that reef," the Skipper mused grimly.

Then, "Buoy on the weather bow!" sang out the cook. "It's a black spar."

"The eastern end of the ledges!" I yelled. "You've *got* to leave *that* to port!"

"Oh, there she is!" The Skipper ducked down for a better view. "Reckon I c'n shave *her*."

He paid the vessel off to get a good rapfull of wind; then quick as a cat, he hove her helm hard down. The schooner rounded sharply up and charged with thundering, thrashing sails straight into the wind's eye up to the buoy—then she swung off when almost on top of it into the fairway and safety!

The Skipper looked at me and grinned: "That's the only way to get one of these here vessels to go to windward," he said.

Surreptitiously—very much so in fact—I scanned a timetable about an hour later while we were peacefully lying at anchor in

New London harbor. It showed me that quite shortly a train was due to leave, going west; and further study developed the interesting fact that this train would get me home in time for dinner. That settled it!

So the cruise turned out to be regrettably short, so far as I was concerned; but at least I had learned why it is that the coasters always wait for a fair wind.

25

A Thirsty Crew

by GEOFF OWEN

[1941]

A thirsty crew's an awful thing, God wot!
The sots!
Beer pots!
The veriest curse
To sober Cap; and yet the worse
Their thirst, the more the rot
They talk when pub is not
Open to serve. Mayhap
Around the back—? God, not!
God! Wot
A place to cruise,
You inconsiderate Cap!

THE IDEA was to get *Uldra* from Scotland to Ireland during the
Easter vacation; from the Gareloch, on the Clyde, to Dublin,
on the Liffey. With two for a crew, I should have found it simple
but I found them a thirsty crew and things were not so simple.
The law of the vessel prohibiting alcohol aboard, it became imperative, for the sake of peace, to find a harbor each night. We
found the harbors but—

They remonstrated right at the start when I refused to waste
even a pint's time in that lovely inn beside the narrow mouth of
the Gareloch because there were tides to catch. They showed no

interest in my little talk about the inn as we slipped away from it. They cared not a hoot that the place had been designed by Lutyen for a daughter of Queen Victoria; that Her Majesty did not consider it stately enough and straightway built a big, square-box ugliness within a regimented park and left the thirty-six-chimneyed Lutyen beauty to become a pub.

They were sailors enough, however, to lose their sulks to join in a general praising of the brisk manner in which *Uldra* was flinging her 33-foot length down the Clyde an hour later. Gusty and strong, the wet west wind was abeam of the hills behind Dunoon and, under all plain sail, the yawl stepped out at the fastest pace I have ever pushed her. Lee deck agush, she did a nine-knot record until we halted her in the lee of Bute. We halted because we thought it wise to reef before plunging out into the rough stuff beyond. But, just as the weather topping lift was given the strain, we spied a tiny square of blue struggling out from the overcast of gray, scudding clouds. It was a feeble excuse but we made it. The staysail was sheeted home, the bow fell off and away we went—unreefed. The blue square vanished and was not replaced. The crew returned to their grumps, buttoned their oilskins up to their ears, shivered and remarked that people weren't supposed to "yacht" in Scottish waters early in April. They trusted that Lamlash, our destination on the Island of Arran would be furnished with a public house. I assured them such would be the case but I said nothing about the possible struggles that lay between us and the thirst quenchers for which they pined. Squalls off Arran are no fun, and the thought of gear giving way, forcing us to a night at sea, perhaps, was uppermost in my mind.

The squalls were bad. Really bad. And their savagery was not enhanced by the swift end of daylight. Searching for rain-hidden buoys; crashing up to and swerving agilely away from a line of surf-ridden rocks; we beat into the eye of the worst of them as we entered the harbor. The burst of wind left us as quickly as it had come; left us to flap becalmed a bare half-mile from our anchorage. And it rained as only in Scotland it can rain.

At last we anchored. Hungry though they were, the crew

would not stop to prepare a meal. They were fearful that the pubs might be closed. They were! I shall not tire you with the wearisome, one-tack talk that persisted through the slow row back; through the subsequent meal, and on into the night. Scotland, with its fool method of closing doors at 9:00 P.M., was insufferable. Enough of it! On to Ireland!

So, next morning, before the sun had risen over the distant humps of Ayre, we were heading south for the Emerald Isle of promise. A pleasant sail, close by the bird-infested peak of Ailsa Craig, on to the wide opening of Belfast Lough. Again our arrival was in darkness and we chose as an anchorage a place called Carrickfergus. The water was so shoal we were forced to anchor a long way offshore. It would be a tiresome row in our awkward collapsible dinghy—but oh! the reward at the end of it! Unhurriedly, the crew ate the evening meal, their one topic, of course, being beer and the initial excitement of it being Irish.

We rowed ashore. We *were* a long way out. It took us half an hour. The crew looked at their watches and grew worried. We landed at the wrong place, a mile out of town, and the pubs, the crew discovered, were all in town. Hurry! Hurry!

"No! Sorry! Too late!" She was a pretty colleen with the softest, singsong voice. The crew told her so. "No! Sorry!" She wore a charming dress. She surely possessed the kindliest heart. She must know, living beside the sea, the ardors of the sailor-man. She couldn't be so brutal as to—"No! Sorry! Too late!" To their everlasting indignation, the crew suffered the fizz of a raspberry soda at a roadside café!

But this was Northern Ireland; everyone knew it was almost Scotch in its mannerisms. Heigh-ho, then, for Dublin of the Free State. On the laborious row back to the ship, the crew convinced themselves that Dublin would be wonderful. Then one of them remembered the name Guiness and, with a shout of delight, the other related the story he had heard that people were shown over the brewery and, mark you, were given free tastes of the different brands of the magic stout at the end of the tour. We must start for Dublin right away. We must!

It was dead calm!

Morning brought a breeze and off we went. The day was dulled by a blanket of gray cloud. The wind went ahead. It started to rain. We lost ourselves out in the Irish Sea, thumping around in sullen, green water. We tacked and found the Skulmartin Lightvessel. Then the wind swung into the west. Despite the continued drizzle, we became gay as we considered our luck. Sheets eased, we reached southward into an interminable grayness. The rain fell harder. The crew hatched themselves in below and so regretted my parting remark about "sissies" that they refused to take an interest in the ship. Neither of them looked out when the first squall hit us.

From behind the drips off the brim of my sou'wester, I had been watching that squall. Or it might be more correct to say that I'd been eyeing a peculiar dark cloud, detached from the general murk, that had been hovering in the northwest. I'd watched its slow approach; its alteration in form from an oblong blotch to a definite arc; its change from deep gray to a fierceness of black, feather-edged with white.

It struck with a quickness that almost caught me unprepared. No warning puffs; no white lash of water; just wind and plenty of it. Instinctively, I acted on the helm and saved the jibe. Then I let the main sheet race through the blocks and away we ran before it. The smallish cloud that had predicted the advent of the squall expanded into a minatory blackness. The dark sea astern was flashing white, soon to be obliterated with the slashing hail that slanted down in a fury. The noise created by the downpour as it spattered on the sails, the deck and the windswept sea around seemed to heighten the feeling of detachment already apparent. I suppose it is the acute concentration one gives to the steering on such occasions that brings on this sense of isolation. Keyed to a tense pitch of alertness, the land, the world of things, even other ships, are lost to the mind. Your world, right then, is your ship; you and she scurrying through space together, intent on saving yourselves, oblivious to everything save the elements.

I was not thinking these thoughts at the time, although I was aware of them, aware, as I turned my head, that I *had* forgotten the outside world completely. I've had some frights here and there but the sight of the huge bow of a fast Atlantic liner not her own ship's length distance from *Uldra's* stern gave me the nastiest shock. A blackness one second, a knife-like bow ripping the water apart in two curves of white foam the next. The great cliff of steel reared up and up with alarming swiftness.

It was like one of those engulfing nightmares—paralyzing. I did nothing. Just gripped the tiller firmly and waited for the inevitable. On reflection, I realize it was the wisest course to have taken. To have jibed would have been disastrous; to have luffed would have caused a collision, for the liner swerved and crashed by on my weather side. A momentary calm, followed by a few wild minutes as the wind struck again just as *Uldra* was struggling in the mad jumble of wash, and the incident was over. At her 25-knot gait, the liner vanished quickly into the curtain of hail beyond the bow. The crew poked a nose out and wanted to know what the hell? I told them what had happened but did not enlighten them to the fact that I had, during the episode, forgotten all about them!

A series of squalls followed the first but, by the time we had arrived at the point where the land bears away to the westward, the wind had settled down to a steady, hard blow. We were some 50 miles from Dublin and, with this breeze snorting out of the northwest, those half a hundred miles would be on a reach. Running before a capful of wind is one thing, reaching can be something else. We reefed, snugging down two, and we lowered the jib. The log was put over; the ship steadied on her course and away we went. And then the clouds blew over and the sun came out. A stiff breeze, taut canvas, a stout little vessel cleaving a green, white-flecked sea at a round six knots, the Mourne Mountains rising blue ahead—what an afternoon's sail that was! Then dusk, with the mountains purple, slowly mingling into the sky. And the stars. And, right over the bow, the distant, yellow wink of the Rockabill Light. I believe the crew forgot Mr. Guinness in their enjoyment.

Only when we had slipped by the dark hump of Ireland's Eye and were heading in for Dublin Bay did talk revolve once more to the subject of thirst. The artificial harbor of Kingstown was our assigned destination but two factors made us hesitate. The wind, as we entered the wide Dublin Bay became furious; the chart of Kingstown Harbor showed innumerable unlit buoys, the kind used by steamers when turning in confined spaces. The stars had gone, the night was pitch. To have romped into that tiny harbor—complete strangers—would have been a hazardous procedure. We decided against it and, instead, beat up into the shallow water in the lee of the North Bull Sand, anchoring to await daylight. The tide was low and we lay moderately quiet. As the water rose and eventually covered the vast expanse of the sand, we bucked and rolled horribly.

A young gale had piped up by dawn and we discovered we were in for a tough time getting in our hook. The winch proved powerless and so were our united efforts. In the end, we had to resort to sailing the anchor out—a disagreeable experience both for those up forward and for poor *Uldra;* she snubbed and fretted and groaned at the sudden stresses she had to bear.

We fairly flew into the harbor. As we slammed through the popple between the stone walls of the entrance, we agreed that, uncomfortable as it had been outside, it was just as well we had not ventured in during the night. That entrance seemed narrow in the extreme and the chart had not lied regarding the unlit buoys. We let go off the yacht club. And just why we selected this spot has always mystified me. We might have known that the gale blowing would possibly shift to the northward. It did, and put us on a dead lee shore, a jolly lee shore of surf-spattered boulders less than 20 yards away!

With its change in direction, the wind decided to let us have the works. Kingstown Harbor, open to the north, became as pleasant as our anchorage in Dublin Bay. A clumsy old coastal ketch dragged her anchor to within 30 feet of our bowsprit before she stopped herself. She sat right over our anchor. We couldn't move.

Gray skies, ropes tapping, the ship jerking at her chain; wind, wind, wind. *And* a crew threatening mutiny. What a happy predicament! I enforced an anchor watch in an endeavor to arrest their incessant moans. They wanted shore leave. I refused it. The brewery must wait. The ship could not be left in this perilous position. They argued—and it was a sane enough observation—that, if we did start to drag, or the chain broke, we were too close to shore to hope to be able to claw off. But I was adamant. All through that day, that night and the following day and night, we stayed aboard, rolling and worrying. On the third afternoon, the gale began to die. Risking the harbor chop in our tiny dinghy, we rowed ashore, but not en route to Mr. Guinness. No, it was too bad but the crew's vacation was over. They went ashore to board the packet boat for England!

I know what you are going to wonder. The answer is "yes." And I found it extremely interesting and the free drinks at the end of the afternoon's entertainment simply delicious. I'll never forget that special export brand! I wrote the crew all about it.

They never acknowledged my letter.

26

A Winter Race in the '80s

by CAPT. GEORGE E. ANDREWS

[1931]

WHEN WE SPEAK of racing on the water, everyone is wont to think of trim yachts, of the races for the America's Cup, or other celebrated races. But how about a race of ships, in the winter, for honor, renown, and money? My story is of a race that was a race indeed. No weather could be considered, and no postponements. The stakes were for honor, and a great deal of workingmen's money. Long chances must be taken.

This epic race took place on the Great Lakes in the early '80s. A great iron company of Cleveland had 1500 tons of special iron ore on the dock at Escanaba, Mich. It was early December. To save great loss of time at the furnaces at lower lake ports, that cargo had to be moved to the lower lake region. Navigation was likely to close at any moment, for it was already bitterly cold in the region where the iron was stored. Shipment by rail was too expensive and all the ore had to be moved at the same time.

In this period the splendid sailing schooners of the Great Lakes were in their prime. They were beautiful ships; they were able; they could carry sail until everything was in a smother. Moreover, they were manned by excellent sailors and officers. Navigation on the Great Lakes at that time, without modern aids, was a hazardous business.

To ensure the moving of the cargo, a unique proposal was

made. Two ships were to be sent, and it was to be a race between them. If one failed, the other might carry on and beat the close of navigation. The first ship that rounded the lighthouse on the point at Escanaba and reported to the agent there would be the winner and get the load; the other would be out of luck.

Two ships accepted the battle, one the *Nellie Redington,* a beautiful three-masted fore and aft schooner of peculiar rig. She was commanded by my father, a master sailor. The other vessel was the *Thomas Quayle,* also ably commanded. My brother was first officer of the *Nellie,* and I held down the second officer's room in the cabin.

Both captains were summoned to the office of the company. There was drama in the air. We shook hands all around, as we were all well acquainted, and the manager of the company stated the conditions. Both ships were to be towed out of the Cuyahoga River at the same time. The first to report for the load and to pass the light at Escanaba was the winner. She was to get the load and the money. The freight money was $7500, and the iron had to be landed in Cleveland before the close of navigation.

I saw a sparkle in my father's eyes as the man talked. Throughout that section he was known as a very devil to carry sail—and he could carry it, for the *Nellie* was always in perfect condition. She was fast, able and superbly commanded. The other ship would be equally well commanded. Both vessels were almost alike, but somewhat differently rigged.

The *Nellie* was a three-masted topsail schooner with squaresails on the fore. She carried four headsails—jib topsail, flying jib, jib, and fore staysail. Her upper light sails were a main topmast staysail and three gaff topsails. The *Quayle* carried straight fore and aft rig, and was, in every way, a worthy competitor of the *Redington.*

"Dead heat," old-timers muttered in their whiskers, as the battle of opinions raged back and forth. Each ship had her following. The newspapers took up the battle and their columns tore back and forth in a variety of opinions—which settled nothing.

The agent at Escanaba had orders to keep the ice clear from the docks and to use ice breakers to keep it moving; under no circumstances must ice be allowed to form to any thickness at the dock; no expense was to be spared.

The two captains signed the agreement and we went back to the ship, my father making a stop at a telegraph office for a few minutes. The moment we were aboard all hands were summoned to the quarterdeck. Even the steward and the cook were there.

"Listen, boys," the captain began. "You have a real job ahead of you. All of you have heard of this race for a cargo of ore; the wages are high, but if the *Nellie Redington* shoves her nose around Escanaba Light in the lead your wages will be doubled." That meant ten dollars per day.

The men cheered lustily. There were Irishmen, Swedes and Yankees in that crew. The Old Man was known far and wide as a humane commander—but a driver in emergencies. "It won't be watch and watch this trip," he continued. "You'll be called out in all stages of weather, good and bad, to handle these big sails. In fact, we are going to sleep when we can. How about it?"

"Sing out," was the reply. "We'll stick till hell freezes over."

Next morning both ships lay at the pierhead. The wind was blowing square into the river. As the tugs moved us down the river, the captain ordered all three lower sails set and the booms bridled amidships. The advantage in this was that, laying head to wind and with plenty of time, those huge sails, with canvas as thick as shingle butts, could be sweated up like boards.

In an hour they were up and their terrific slatting sounded like thunder. The tugs puffed away and turned us loose just outside the waterworks crib. The wind was fresh from the northeast, and that was fair.

We set the three jibs on the run; and then the gaff topsails took the breeze. When the tugs let go, we were packed from boom saddles to the trucks with great, billowing canvas. The race was on.

The next morning, at Point Pelee just east of the entrance to the Detroit River, we were probably leading the *Quayle* by a mile.

At that time, sailing ships were always towed from Lake Erie to Lake Huron through the Detroit River, Lake St. Clair and the St. Clair River. Usually one tug would take three or four vessels through in one tow. When my father stopped at the telegraph office he had wired the owner of the big tug *Sweepstakes,* in Detroit, to have her meet the *Redington* inside of Point Pelee and to plan to take us through the river alone. There was nothing unfair in that; the master of the *Quayle* had the same opportunity. But what looked like a mighty good move in strategy turned out to be a failure because of treachery.

The tug came boiling out from behind the point in a smother of foam, going by us very close. As she passed she hailed us to shorten sail and announced that she would pick us up as soon as she had got the *Quayle.* As this message came down the wind, we were treated to about as thorough and fine a job of cussing as I ever heard. Did we shorten sail? We did not! The Old Man paced savagely back and forth across the quarterdeck. Shorten sail? Huh! At that very minute, the *Nellie* was doing better than 12 knots by the log. Her hatch coamings were awash and everything was in a smother—but she was stepping.

Father nodded for me to join him in his room. My brother was there, also, but we were both silent. The captain looked at his barometer. "Boys," he snorted, "we're going to have a bad blow from the south'ard; that will be fair. I'm betting it will last us through the rivers; I'm going on alone under sail." Thus did we get the edict.

We looked at him aghast. Sail through! Gosh! Well, we knew what that meant. The wind must be fair and it must hold. If it failed, we were licked.

"But, sir," I murmured, "the wind; the head current; wouldn't it be wiser to tow through with the *Quayle* and beat him sailing on another start on Lake Huron?"

"Yes, and no!" replied the captain. "I'm betting a lifelong experience against the failing of the wind. This wind will last and blow great guns for 24 hours. That's more than we need and the *Sweepstakes* can't tow fast enough to beat us. Now get out and get ready!"

That settled it. Looking through the glasses, I saw that the *Quayle* had shortened down and had a line on the tug. They kept enough sail on her to help and we went to our duties with heavy hearts; it looked as though we were beaten almost before we had started.

Always the captain glanced aloft; never were sails so tended; a pull here, a pull there, and away we bowled. Slowly but surely, the *Nellie* left the tow.

The news flew through the ship that we were going to sail through the rivers, an unheard of undertaking. Ominous shakes of the head were very plainly seen, but there could be no questioning of orders.

Away we flew. The captain called me to take the wheel so that another strong pair of arms for sail trimming would be available. I was small and light.

The long tows, the last of the season bound down, stared at us in amazement as they passed close by. All recognized the ship. Every tug roared out a salute; all knew of the race, but they had never seen a ship of our size sailing *up* the river.

It continued to blow great guns. Not a rag did we douse; everything that we could pack on her was bulging with wind, as we foamed through the narrow channels. When we came to the Port Huron rapids, the most dangerous section of the river, the Old Man still packed on the canvas. As we entered the rapids he came and stood near the wheel. He gave me a sharp look and seemed satisfied.

"Watch your step, now; don't get confused, and watch me like a hawk," he said as I spun the big wheel to the powerful current. Finally we roared into Lake Huron—and the *Quayle* not in sight. The crew gave three rousing cheers.

We had sailed out just in time, for the wind began to haul. In an hour it was nor-nor'west and had headed us. We reached over toward Georgian Bay on the starboard tack. Muttered and long-drawn-out curses emerged from the Old Man's whiskers. It looked as though we were due to lose all we had gained by our long chance through the rivers. It kept hauling and we went to the port tack and reached over toward Thunder Bay. Every soul on board our ship began to swear. The *Quayle,* on the starboard tack, crossed our bows. She was close—but she crossed. The wind had headed us and let her look up.

As she crossed, the Old Man put *Nellie* about on the heels of the *Quayle,* whose captain jumped onto the weather rail and waved his sou'wester in wild exultation.

It was now blowing harder than ever. We were carrying three lowers, upper topsail and four jibs. Long and anxiously the Old Man went the rounds of the ship on the weather side. He looked over everything carefully; the shrouds, the lanyards, the chainplates. All were as taut as a fiddle string and singing a tune. We were outfooting *Quayle,* which had hauled down her flying jib.

When night came we went about. *Quayle* promptly followed. We were now on the port tack again reaching to the westward. Slowly we continued to outfoot our rival. She did not set more canvas nor did we take any in. Then *Quayle* went back to the starboard tack, but we kept on with our port tacks boarded.

We continued on the port tack, expecting the wind to haul and free us, but it headed us. There was more cussing from the quarterdeck. *Quayle* was getting all the breaks in the wind. *Nellie* was put about. It began to snow and was growing much colder. I took a look at the amidships thermometer; it registered 29 degrees. That meant ice and trouble. Thicker and thicker it became, and *Nellie* dove like a huge porpoise into the long seas.

All night we drove her through swirling snow and cold spindrift. As we entered the Straits of Mackinac, passing Spectacle Reef, *Quayle* came bowling along from the eastward. We caught a momentary glimpse of her, and then a snow squall shut in.

To navigate the Straits of Mackinac in the night is bad enough, but to add a howling, driving snowstorm—well—

Graham Shoals, on the north side of the Straits, is exceedingly dangerous. Its approach shows no soundings, and navigating it calls for fearless and perfect judgment. The infernal wind drew to the westward and blew square down the Straits. No long leg and a short one was possible; it was just a dead beat to windward and no ship could stand very far on either tack.

Slowly we felt our way. Nothing had been seen of the *Quayle*

since the snow shut in. Without warning, Skillagalee Light flashed
out of the snow in a soft spot. In an instant the wheel was put
down. My brother got a cast of the lead; three fathoms. Gosh!
A close call! I took a look at the Old Man. His face was taut,
but, catching my eye, he grinned. We now had a landfall and it
had stopped snowing.

My father called me. "Get two hours' sleep," he said. "I'm
going through Beaver Island passage and I want you to steer
her across to Summer Island passage."

Four hours passed. Five—six—and Summer Island Light
flashed close on our starboard bow. *Then* we saw *Quayle*. She
had a great bone in her teeth, and was taking the north passage.

The Old Man called my brother and put him in the lee mizzen
chains with the lead. To leeward the heavy seas roared and
fumed over the granite rocks. The instant we entered the passage, we would have to haul up.

The mate called the soundings while the captain stood by the
wheel, and I watched him like a hawk. Five fathoms; four; four
and a half; three fathoms, and close under our lee, oh, so close,
showed the huge granite rocks. The water held at three fathoms
and then shoaled a little. The captain had heard enough; we
were nearly through. Quietly he spoke in my ear. "A half board,
Ed; touch her lightly; don't get her in irons." I eased the wheel
down and the big schooner flew up into the wind and head
reached. Gently I met her and she paid off gracefully. With a
terrific "Swish!" our stern passed the last of the huge rocks. We
were through.

Suddenly I found myself wet with perspiration. Again the
wind played havoc with us and again headed us, but it also
headed the *Quayle* this time and we went after her, splitting
tacks up little Bay DeNoque. The goal was close at hand, and
neither ship had any particular advantage. Both vessels reached
in for the light on the point around which it was necessary to
go to keep off for the ore docks. The ship that could weather
that sand point without going about was surely the winner.

My father slipped quickly to my side at the wheel. "Ed, this
race is ours," he said. "I'm going inside the light on this tack;

there's 12 feet, but it's only 50 feet wide. When they built that lighthouse they put it outside the real shoal. Don't tip our hand; squeeze her up but not too close to let the *Quayle* outfoot us. He knows he's got to go about for a short stretch and thinks that we will have to also, but we're not. You can rub the paint off her on the starboard side; nothing to leeward, though. I'm going to leave you now. We have got to carry the centerboard clear to the shoal. I am going to put two men on each crank of the winch to take up the slack of the chain so it won't jam; the bottom will shove the board up for us. Watch your step!"

All I had to do was not to tip my hand and brush that lighthouse. On we stormed. The *Quayle* went into stays when about 100 feet from the light. Before she knew it, we had lapped the light. A wild exultation stole into my heart. The lighthouse keeper was paralyzed. He waved his arms frantically, signalling us to go about—but it was too late now.

The sand boiled and spumed under our stern. I caught a glimpse of the four men at the centerboard. They were winding away like mad—and we foamed across—the victor.

The roar of our anchor had hardly died away when the *Quayle* dropped hers, and before she had stopped her sternway, her gig dropped into the water. Her captain climbed over our side and went straight to the quarterdeck with outstretched hand, a hand of congratulation. "Hank," he called to my father, "D—n your old skin, I forgot to go about in watching you shoot the chutes over there by the light!"

27

Nine Against the Sea

by CRITCHELL RIMINGTON

[1943]

THE VERY MEMORY of the first few days of December, 1942, will produce an agonized shiver on the part of any resident of the Atlantic seaboard. Simply stated, the weather was dirty. It was bitterly cold, the wind had the biting edge of a jagged glass, and all the power of a thousand furies. At sea, the gales were continuous and the skippers of inbound ships cursed mountainous seas and overcast skies. In coastal waters, conditions were worse, if anything. Those fishing boats which managed to stagger into port sat deep in the water under a heavy coating of ice; even Long Island Sound steamed like a polar sea. On shore, thermometers and oil supplies hit new lows. In a word, it was winter weather at its worst.

On her patrol to the south and east of Montauk, the *CGR 3070* was hove to. Eighteen months before, under her own name of *Zaida* and with owner George Ratsey at the wheel, she had been sailing with started sheets under a summer sky. Now she carried but a trysail, which was sail enough, even though a mizzen had been stepped in anticipation of Atlantic duty as a member of the Coast Guard's patrol working out of the Greenport, L. I., base. Designed by John Alden and built by Nevins, she was a yacht of more than local fame.

Her crew now numbered nine: Chief Boatswain's Mate Arnall, the skipper; Joseph Choate, Boatswain's Mate 1st Class; Vance

M. Smith, Boatswain's Mate 2nd Class; Toivo Koskinen, Theo-dore C. Carlson, Edward R. Jobson, James T. Watson, and Arnold Windsor, Seamen 1st Class, and Ward Weimar, Cox-swain. All were experienced in sail, particularly Curtis Arnall, who had sailed his own yacht in deep water races.

It was midmorning on December 3rd. The glass was low and dropping. The wind was Force 9, and increasing. The deck of *3070* was empty but for two men crouching in the cockpit. The others were below; the crew in the main cabin, the skipper work-ing over his charts in the chartroom aft.

Suddenly, almost as out of nowhere, a blast of hurricane force struck *3070* broadside. Down on her beam ends she went—while all of the Atlantic seemingly came aboard. In one paralyzing moment, the skipper was washed through the full length of the cabin, the pot-bellied stove burst from its moorings and crashed down on a prostrate crew member. Clothes, dishes, gear and ballast plunged about in the whirlpool which swirled through the ship. The two men on deck grabbed life lines and hung on for their lives. Buried in the sea, the trysail burst and she stood on her feet again, but the onrush of a wave later described as of tidal proportions, again sent the vessel on her side, and this time in the opposite direction.

Slowly, *3070* shook herself free and again staggered back to an even keel.

"We were in a sorry state," related Skipper Arnall. "One man had a fractured rib as a result of his being on the receiving end of the cabin stove. Three others were badly cut about the head. There was more than a foot of water above the floor boards, and the cabin was a mess. Another big sea coming aboard would have swamped us completely. Although we could find no serious damage to the hull, the decks had been swept clean. All of our ventilators were gone, as was our life raft; a spreader on the mainmast was weakened and the mizzenmast was broken above the gooseneck.

"Our first job was to take care of the injured and, although none of us will take any bows for our medical knowledge, I am happy to say that every man walked off the boat when we finally got ashore. Next in importance was the rigging, but we soon found that the weather made any major repairs out of the question. We were able to chop the rigging of the mizzen clear and cut larger ports in the bulwarks so as to more readily free any water that came aboard. At first we were puzzled as to how best to close the openings in the deck where the ventilators had been, but the answer was found in mashing tin cans to the desired size.

"The wind was NW and showed no signs of diminishing. Every man that could be spared for the job was bailing, and we were gaining on the water. We put a sea anchor over the stern but continued to make terrific headway out to sea; there was no point in putting one over the bow for she kept wanting to sail all the time. But she ran before the seas—under bare poles— in a way that was wondrous to see.

"Further examination revealed that there was salt water in the gasoline, as well as in the fresh water tanks. That spelled the end of using the engine. Our radio was all but gone. We weren't so concerned about water, as we could work into the Gulf Stream, where the incessant squalls would give us enough for drinking purposes. We checked our food supply carefully and came to the conclusion that one meal a day (which amounted to one cupful of whatever the *carte du jour* had to offer) might, with luck, see us through for a reasonable length of time.

"It was then evening. There were intermittent snow flurries, the sea was high and the wind showed no signs of abating, but *3070* was by this time seaworthy. I knew there were four things to do: give all of the crew some rest, keep the ship running before the wind, repair our tattered canvas in the morning, and then endeavor to lay a course for the Stream."

Weather reports prior to December 3rd and subsequent communications received by the Eastern Sea Frontier Command caused them to order all vessels of the Patrol in, but the full fury of the storm broke before any of them could reach port. Surface vessels of the Coast Guard were sent out to offer assistance, and after some difficulty all managed to make port but *3070*. The first message received from her was at 11:37 A.M., shortly after her knockdown, in which she stated that she was in distress between Martha's Vineyard and Nantucket Shoals. Arnall asked that a plane be sent to spot him as he was doubtful of his position and reported one man seriously injured and three other men hurt.

The Eastern Sea Frontier immediately dispatched an Army bomber and a PBY flying boat. Winds of 50 miles an hour and better made takeoff and landing hazardous. Two power lifeboats started for the *3070* but were driven back by the storm. A Coast Guard cutter also went to search. Just before dark, *3070* was located by the Navy PBY about in the position which her skipper had given. The Coast Guard cutter was notified but could not find the craft, presumably because of the thick weather and rough seas.

The morning of the 4th found the wind rising. Snow flurries continued. At noon, a British destroyer under operational orders of the Eastern Sea Frontier came upon *3070* far to the east of the position in which she had been sighted the day before, still running under bare poles. Knowing that there were injured men aboard, a transfer was considered but the seas were so high that it was not attempted, and the destroyer then took the boat in tow. It was deemed too rough to attempt to tow into the wind, so the British ship continued on her course for Halifax with the distressed craft astern.

At 9 P.M. the destroyer reported that the towline had parted, the *3070* was again lost in the dark. Their position was then about 260 miles east of Cape Cod; the destroyer turned back to seek the lost boat, but had no success.

From December 5th to December 17th all rescue efforts seemed destined to failure. The Eastern Sea Frontier had but terse reports such as these to make:

"Fourteen Canadian planes from their own bases and eleven planes of the U. S. Army Air Forces took the air in weather which made flying of great danger. They searched the area where *3070* was believed to be, and returned without result."

"Weather very bad. The area was searched by eight British planes, a Navy PBY and by Army Flying Fortresses. The British destroyer went on to Halifax. To U. S. patrol ships still hunting, a Coast Guard cutter was added."

"A Canadian plane from Halifax scanned the seas for nine and a half hours in winds from 48 to 56 miles an hour. The captain of the patrol boat notified the Commander of the Eastern Sea Frontier that there had been three shifts of wind and one of current, and he expressed doubt that *3070* could live through the heavy weather of two days previous, especially if she had been weakened while in tow."

"The probable drift of *3070* was plotted at the Eastern Sea Frontier headquarters from information on wind and sea and all were warned to keep a sharp lookout for the *3070*."

"A wireless telephone message, apparently from *3070*, was picked up. It said that the boat's condition was satisfactory and that three men were injured. An immediate request for the boat to send her position was not acknowledged. Although the District Coast Guard Officer of the First Naval District expressed doubt that the message was genuine, the station which had received it was instructed to attempt to regain contact and to instruct the skipper of the boat not to answer, but to concentrate on charging his battery until 8 :00 P.M., when all stations would be silent and listen for fifteen minutes. The stations were silent from 8 :00 to 8 :15 P.M. They heard nothing."

"The pilot of a plane reported sighting a yawl about 150 miles southeast of Nantucket. His description of the boat coincided with that of *3070*."

"As dusk closed in at 6 :00 P.M., a U. S. naval vessel came upon *3070* south and west of her last known position. They exchanged signals. The *3070* reported that she was seaworthy but in need of assistance. Rough seas made it impossible for the two craft to come close before darkness was complete. The boat's position was sent to headquarters."

"Six Navy PBY's, three Army B17's and a B25 made extensive sweeps in difficult weather. They were unsuccessful."

On board *3070* the battle had only begun. While rigging the towline from the Canadian destroyer, Koskinen went forward to rig some chafing gear. A giant sea crashed aboard, swept him overboard and then carried him back. Thereafter individual life-lines were the order of the day—and night.

The ship had been made as shipshape as conditions would permit. Watson, the seaman with the broken rib, was strapped up and lashed in his bunk where he alternated between chewing aspirin and serving as rationing director. Arnall knew that their best bet was to hit the Gulf Stream and, with the first sail to be repaired—the staysail—they started south. By the time they hit the Stream, the wind had shifted to the north, but *3070* tacked, worked her way along, fighting through one squall after another.

"It was impossible to get a decent sight," said the skipper, "but I was able to obtain a pretty good idea of our latitude. At that time the water temperature was 70°, the air about 60°. For the next day or two I did more work on 'Bowditch' than I had ever done in my life but, after getting a rough position from a passing destroyer (it was again too rough for them to give us any aid), I found that the NE set that I had figured on wasn't exactly right.

"The sea was very confused, and at times the water was seemingly coming aboard faster than we could bail. Then we got a westerly gale and lost everything we had gained. It was obvious that there was but one thing to do; to try and work south until the temperatures equalized. Ours was a long and tedious passage, but it did the trick, for in a latitude of about 33° we found S and SW winds.

"It is really amazing," he continued, "how one can improvise when one has no alternative. Having no electricity, we used the red safety lights from our life preservers to illuminate the binnacle. We made kerosene out of gasoline and motor oil. Being without cigarettes, we rolled our own (using the less vital pages of the "Bluejacket's Manual" for paper) and substituted dried tea leaves and fresh coffee for tobacco. As we had expected, the torrential downpours in the Stream solved the water problem, although we did use the precious liquid sparingly. It was essential that we keep the cabin warm and, after we ran out of coal, we had no choice but to burn locker doors and other miscellaneous wooden fittings. We hated like the devil to do it.

"There were five men available for deck work. We stood watches of one hour on and four off to keep things moving, and to insure every man getting plenty of rest. Looking back, I would say that the worst blows were at night, and it was then that the watches were increased.

"One day followed another. By the middle of December, we had just missed being rescued so many times that we put that possibility aside and were determined that we would rescue ourselves. If we had possessed a chronometer and charts, Bermuda would have been a possible objective; as it was, the Carolina coast seemed the logical alternative. Calculations showed we would have just enough food—if we were careful, and if the weather would give us any kind of a break."

The Eastern Sea Frontier's relentless search was narrowing down, and on the 17th it reported: "A B17 located *3070,* south and east of her last position. The crew of the plane saw men waving on the deck, but could not count them. The boat was under a jib only, on a course due west, about 350 miles east of Nags Head, N. C. The plane dropped supplies by parachute 150 feet ahead of her. Soon thereafter the crew was observed hoisting the mainsail and the vessel reversed course for five minutes. The plane's crew believed that the supplies were picked up for the mainsail was lowered and *3070* returned to her course. All ships in the vicinity were warned to be on the alert and a destroyer took up the search."

For the next five days, planes, blimps and surface vessels searched fruitlessly. But, on December 23rd, came a flash which read: "Shortly after midnight, in thick weather, a Coast Guard cutter found *3070* about 25 miles off Ocracoke Inlet, N. C. The crew appeared to be all right, but indicated that they needed water and food. Contact between the vessels was lost in a rain squall. Blimps, planes and other surface craft were dispatched. At 2:45 P.M., a blimp sighted the boat and notified the other searching craft. There were six men on deck gesturing wildly for food. The blimp dropped an emergency kit and an individual ration kit. The men aboard picked up the emergency kit and were seen to dig into it. The blimp hung above the boat until surface craft arrived, took off the crew, put other men aboard, and took *3070* in tow."

Arnall's account of achieving their long-sought landfall and their subsequent rescue is modest. "On the afternoon of the 22nd, I told the men to get their life jackets together as I hoped to sight land within the next six to eight hours. The life jackets would be necessary in the event we did a 'dead pan' landing. At 10:00 P.M., we came upon a flashing buoy—the first thing associated with land that we had seen since we passed Montauk on November 27th. I planned to lay off it until morning but, shortly thereafter, a patrol boat came by and said they would pick us up in the morning. We were given instructions to keep to the south of the buoy, but the combination of wind and tide set us upon it, and as a result we were forced to make sail once more. The visibility was poor and the cutter lost us. But they had reported us and we were picked up early the next morning.

"When we hit the buoy, my guess was that we were near Cape Lookout; actually, we were between that and Cape Hatteras. I'm afraid it was hardly a landfall that would win an ocean race, but in view of the circumstances, it wasn't quite as bad as it might have been."

28

Goodbye Pacific, Hello Maine

by IRVING JOHNSON

[1945]

HOW WOULD YOU SPEND a 30-day leave after four years with the Navy in the Pacific? You'd go sailing along the Maine coast if, like me, you wanted to get acquainted with your family quickly and they were tired of staying ashore. My family consists of Robert, six, Arthur, nine, and my wife, Exy, all of whom are used to life in a schooner. The two boys had spent no more than the first six weeks of their lives on land until war forced them ashore. Exy and I had sailed the *Yankee* three times around the world.

Part of my leave was already used up crossing the country and stopping just long enough in the mountains to get mixed up in some real snow. Now to find a nice little cruising boat which the boys could help sail. Wouldn't that 36-foot, marconi-rigged, Casey ketch which my brother and I used to own about 18 years ago be just the boat for us? She had a double cabin forward for the boys, main cabin amidships and galley and toilet aft. And, best of all, *Bonito* was already in Maine waters where we could start real cruising right away.

Her present owner informed us that she was not yet in commission, and that her sails had burned last winter but new ones were being made. However, if I wanted to push things along I could get her ready in time and ought to be rewarded with a sail after four years at sea. John Robinson was able to hurry the sails and we shoved off for Maine with loaded sea bags and high hopes.

We arrived in West Southport, near Boothbay Harbor, to find only the cover off and the starting battery aboard, but *Bonito* looked good to us, anyway, lying at her winter mooring in beautiful little Hendricks Harbor. We stayed ashore that night and started cleaning her up in earnest the following morning. While a couple of local men tied her up at a little fishing dock and cleaned the bottom at low tide, my wife scrubbed her inside from stem to stern. I explained that this would give her a chance to learn the whereabouts of everything and plan the stowage of our gear. I got after the various hull openings, which had been closed for the winter. It was a good chance to make sure all were clear of barnacles and grass. On deck there were the manila parts of halyards and backstays to renew, booms to come aboard and sheets to reeve off. I always find cruising more fun after fitting out a boat, anyway. Meanwhile, the boys scoured the mud flats at low tide, finding exciting things like starfish, clams and old paint pots.

That night we ate dinner aboard, cooking on the smallest size No. 1 Shipmate. It is a fine stove for the Maine coast and, with good kindling wood, is no trouble to light and gets hot quickly. Exy was delighted with the position of the galley, aft near the companionway rather than shut away forward where she wouldn't know what was going on and where ventilation is apt to be inadequate.

The following day we started to bend sail with hopes of getting under way. First, the combination lazyjacks and lifts were rigged, then the new mizzen. The mizzen set well; next came the mainsail. Bending sail went along fine until the last few feet were taken up on the halyard. The after end of the main boom barely cleared the deck! Somebody had slipped badly on the measurements. Here we were with a brand new mainsail whose leech was 28 inches too long. I had brought my palm and needle and a few other tools for minor repairs, but was out of practice and not anxious to shorten the entire foot of a mainsail. Finally, a fellow named Luke in East Boothbay, who had a sailmaker's sewing machine and a loft, was persuaded to tackle the job. The jib was too long also but, with the tack secured to the bowsprit, it would set well enough loose-footed, so I decided to use it that way.

Lots of things about *Bonito* took me back 17 years to summers of Maine cruising with my brother, when we would take turns piloting and handling sail, both of us learning the Maine coast and trying to identify every yacht in sight. I wondered what *Bonito* thought of my coming back after all these years, with a wife and two boys and a few gray hairs. There had been a couple of hundred thousand miles of sailing and four years of war since I had been aboard. Some things about her hadn't changed. She had obviously been used mostly for day sailing out of Boothbay, as we found the charts were those my brother and I had bought in 1926. This didn't worry me much as I figured I knew the coast quite well and only a few buoys would be changed. That proved to be the case until we got a fog one day. "Knowing the coast" in no way replaces up-to-date charts.

The topsides paint and varnish were in good condition and we decided not to touch them now, so that we might get in some sailing while my leave lasted. There would be ample time for painting and varnishing after the cruise. She must have had a good winter cover on her to keep the bright work looking so well. Down below, after my wife's washing, she was clean and bright.

Much as we liked Hendricks Harbor, there seemed to be no reason for waiting there for the mainsail. Roscoe Rand had told me some about the harbor's busier days and shown me pictures of his father's husky, broad beamed, wide-sterned cargo and fishing schooner which had been built close by. Hendricks Harbor was her home port along with 40 other schooners. It was hard to imagine 40 schooners loading and unloading, coming in and getting under way in that tiny, quiet little harbor. You would suppose it had always been just a little cove for a few small sloops, an assortment of skiffs, some lobstermen's boats and maybe one *big* yacht, like the 36-foot *Bonito,* at a mooring. But Roscoe pointed out, at low water, the remains of several stone piers which used to border the harbor. Once you got a big schooner in that narrow, crooked entrance with two spindles and a buoy all within 100 feet, you would have perfect protection. At low water, there seems to be only a trickle of water at the entrance. The schooners liked to winter here and were never bothered by ice. The Rand family still owns most of the east side of the harbor which used to be covered with racks of drying fish. Today there is a nice little Southport Yacht Club building and a convenient float at the northeast end.

The following morning we came in alongside the little float at high water, took on water, ice, gas and oil. Then, under power, *Bonito* slid through the narrow entrance, north about Southport Island and down through the drawbridge which connects the island with Boothbay. It was a really beautiful Maine day with a little snap in the air which was exactly what we had come to Maine for. The pine trees and rocks on little islands and coves stood out with the clearness and beauty I had often remembered in the Pacific while looking at the languid palms and coral.

We set jib and jigger, shut off the motor, relaxed and enjoyed the lovely cruising feeling when everything is going just right. Four years away from this sort of thing made us appreciate it even more. We tried to point out the charms of the Maine coast to Robert and Arthur who, of course, couldn't quite comprehend what we were so excited about.

We eased out of the harbor close hauled, sailing nicely past Squirrel Island, and then headed southeast for Ram Island Light. As we came closer, with our bowsprit still pointed straight for the rocks, the boys became excited over our prospects of going aground. Suddenly, to their surprise, a narrow, deep water channel showed up between the lightkeeper's house and Fisherman Island. We swung sharply to port and glided through between the rocks, missing the lobster pot buoys by inches on either side. It is so much more fun than cruising through the half-mile-wide passage one normally would take.

What a change this was from a month ago! My crew had shrunk from 275 to 3; the *Sumner's* 350 feet to *Bonito's* 36. Calluses were now growing on my hands, where they belonged, instead of on my backside. Operation orders, communications, signals didn't exist here, just the boat and the breeze. I looked at the chart again to find the next narrow place with deep enough water. It's Little River, so we made for it. Sailing into such a narrow place with many rocks, reefs, lobster pots and an occasional boat for obstacles is exciting and good sport. It is really beautiful 'way inside and a number of lobstermen have their homes in there, close by their little docks and moored boats. Beating out against the wind dead ahead is out of the question so we powered a short distance till there was room to sail, and squared away up the Damariscotta River.

The wind by now had come up fairly strong and the tide was flooding, so we jibed along up the river making good time. My wife disappeared below to putter around the stove, and in a surprisingly short time she had a lovely chocolate cake cooling on the cabin floor. We were all cautioned about its location, but she claimed that was the safest place for it and shortly nearly stepped on it herself. She had scoured Boothbay to get someone to make a suitable cake for me as this was my birthday, the 4th of July. In desperation, just before leaving, she told her sad story to the proprietor of a bookshop and was allowed to copy a chocolate cake recipe out of one of the cook books. Here was the handsome result, baked in a basin which would just fit in the tiny Shipmate oven.

Several times Exy was called to the hatch by the boys who wanted mother to see some pretty little cove or some bare granite rocks close by. Another time it would be a perfect boy's island that tickled their imagination. They were beginning to catch on to Maine. Such a wonderful day with everything going beautifully and a strong fair current, we jibed our way clean up to Damariscotta.

Not wanting to get sucked through the bridge by the strong current, the boys and I went forward to rig the heavy anchor. The large anchor warp was down below and 'way forward but small boys are just made for crawling into holes like that and pushing the end up through the deck. Then they stood by halyard and downhaul and let go smartly when ordered. Exy, at the tiller, rounded her up. With plenty of scope, she held nicely with the water racing by.

"Father, can we go out in the dinghy?" The boys immediately wanted to row somewhere every time we dropped anchor, but they must help me furl sail and wait a little while till the current eased off as I was sure they would get sucked upstream under the bridge. A little later, they cast off with Arthur rowing hard across the current to explore a large cove on the west bank. I have often wondered how many miles Arthur rowed during the cruise, also how many times the younger Robert, sitting in the stern, advised him how he should do it and where he should go. Sometimes Arthur would report "trouble with Robert" or announce that he would never take him again but his memory proved rather short in this respect. They were at just the age when handling a dinghy on your own is paradise. You get away from grown ups and she's all yours.

They seldom came back empty-handed. Their collections included fish, shells of all sorts, queerly shaped sticks and stones, various feathers, but the biggest prize was a large dead sea gull which was brought dripping down into the cabin to show their mother. Arthur's rowing improved each day. They learned where to put weight in a boat, how to handle the painter, and Robert became quite proud of his ability at making fast with the right kind of final half hitch around a cleat. They also learned how a skipper hates to have a dinghy bang into the side of the ship.

In the morning, we all went ashore at the old steamer pier to explore the picturesque town which had prospered in the days of sailing ships. About midmorning, the tide started to ebb so we headed downstream, being especially careful to stay in the channel as it is no fun going aground on a falling tide such as the Maine coast has. However, there were several little islands with deep water behind them which looked much more interesting than the wider parts of the river. About lunch time we picked out Seal Cove and approached dead slow when it seemed as if our mast would surely touch the power wires which cross

overhead about halfway in—we cleared by four or five feet. We
anchored, and the boys immediately started rowing. They picked
out a tiny island to have lunch on, where we picnicked at the
edge of the pines and watched the tide go down.

Planning to pick up our mainsail the following morning in
East Boothbay, we started out of the harbor at slow speed under
power, staying carefully in the middle of the cove entrance where
the chart showed 21 feet of water. The low tide had uncovered
many rocks, and Robert declared: "This is dangerous, Father.
We might bump on a rock."

I assured him I had been at it quite awhile and expected to get
through a place like this with care and the large scale chart on
my knee. About 30 seconds later, there was a bump and the bow
slid a foot and a half out of water.

"See, didn't I tell you?" Robert yelled. "I told you it was
dangerous, Father."

The engine was shut off and I checked the chart with special
interest, as my work for three years in the Pacific had been
hydrographic survey for the Navy. A few soundings were taken
and, of course, some pictures of *Bonito* with her bow in the air.
I definitely try to avoid running aground but it must be expected
sometimes or you are missing a lot of fun cruising in confined
waters. In an hour, we floated clear of the uncharted rock—mind
you, I've been on charted ones, too—and went on our way. Two
things to keep in mind in tight spots and strange waters, are:
do most of your fooling around on a rising tide and take it
slow. In Maine, it is a good thing to watch for kelp on rocks or
for lobster pots, which are often placed near them, but neither
can be depended upon. If I hadn't been assuring Robert that I
was such a good navigator and paying such close attention to the
chart, I might have noticed kelp around the four-foot shoal we
bumped on.

The mainsail was not ready but East Boothbay is an easy
place to spend an extra day. The boys investigated the shipyards
and docks, poking around boats and gear. But when they discovered the old tide mill, last of its kind in the United States, I
knew where they would be found if we ever lost them. It was

being dismantled and the sport of scrambling around among the rotting timbers and rusting shafts over a roaring sluiceway was too much for any boy to resist.

Early next morning, with the mainsail aboard but not bent, we powered across the Damariscotta River to go through the South Bristol Gut at high water. The chart shows two feet of water but with a good tide there is plenty to spare. Arthur woke up the town blowing for the bridge keeper to open the draw. Finally the keeper woke up, too, and let us through the tiny opening as a brilliant Maine day was beginning. Just beyond the bridge we rounded up alongside a moored schooner to have breakfast and bend the mainsail. This time it made a nice fit so we slid out the narrow winding passage south of Davis Island and headed for the open sea off Pemaquid. In contrast to my recent Navy experience, we didn't have orders to go to any particular place. We would just sail in an easterly direction and let the wind settle the rest of it.

Two wide-awake boys in a 36-foot ketch have got to have something to do during an all-day open water passage. All the halyards had been coiled down and Arthur had whipped every rope end with needle and sail twine. I started to show them some knots and the boys solved the rest. They got the idea of tying each other up and seeing how long it took to get free. Then Exy and I each had to tie them up. Some of the complicated entanglements took a struggling boy a half hour to get loose and they had good fun at it.

The boys would steer for short periods, but this steady going on a straight course was not exciting enough to keep them interested long. We called Arthur the mate and Robert the engineer, and in reply to the most persistent questioning maintained that neither position was superior to the other. Arthur learned to get the anchor ready, set the jib, handle lines and help furl sail. Robert felt very responsible about the motor and never shifted the wrong way. He turned out to be a better helmsman than his older brother and would really concentrate on good steering. Arthur would get too many ideas of his own unless things were exciting.

With the nice southerly breeze we made good time and slipped into the little cove on Matinicus Island before supper. Arthur promptly made friends among the fishermen while the rest of us went for a walk across the island. Seeing chickens at one farm, we stopped to ask for eggs. Mrs. Young, Aunt Marion to everybody on the island, recognized us immediately as part of the *Yankee*. She wouldn't take a cent for the eggs and was soon telling us stories of the island. There are as many Youngs on Matinicus as on Pitcairn Island, and in many ways the resemblance goes farther than that.

Back toward the harbor a Mr. Young insisted on giving us a huge lobster. Realizing we didn't have a pot big enough for it, he had his wife boil it. By the time we rounded up Arthur to go back aboard, one of the fishermen had given him a whole mess of fish, nicely cleaned and filleted. Matinicus had given us a real welcome after four years away.

We were ready for some excitement the next day as we sailed toward Vinalhaven Island. Skirting the west side through a mass of islands, we approached a place called "The Basin" near Leadbetter Narrows. I remembered the fun to be had here 17 years ago and wanted to show it to the boys. The sea rushes in the narrow entrance at high tide and roars out forming excellent rapids at low tide. We used to carry the dinghy in to the Basin and have a wild ride out. This time as we sailed in near the racing water we heard a woman's voice crying for help and soon came upon a girl in a tiny dinghy without oars. As she was trying to row across the rapids they had been jerked from her hands. We passed her a spare pair we had aboard and eventually found her oars some distance away. The boys were impressed at what can go wrong in a dinghy.

A hundreds yards south of the rapids is a quiet, lovely little cove. We anchored *Bonito* there and rowed around the point to the rapids. After landing on the rocks at the right I found that I could carry the dinghy on my back, so, looking like a strange sort of turtle, according to Exy, I got it over the rocks to the higher, quiet water inside the Basin. One look down the chute of roaring water made the dinghy seem pretty small and the water was just as wild as I had remembered. We put a life preserver on Arthur and he and I started through. Bouncing and swirling through waves and eddies made us whoop with excitement. It was more fun than ever with a small boy along. Then the boat was turtled over the rocks again so that Exy and Robert could have a turn. Robert gasped for breath as some of the cold water of the bow wave dashed over him but he wanted to do it again.

Under way again, we set our course for North Haven through Fox Island Thoroughfare. As big black rain clouds approached, the wind dropped flat. We had the engine going and the main and mizzen furled when down came a squall that we heard about all up and down the coast for the rest of our cruise. Dinghies were blown off docks and considerable damage done. Alongside of us a smart little cutter named *Survivor* had her jib blown clean out. As our jib was brand new, it seemed as though it might yank the forestay out at each jibe. My wife was below holding two boiling pots on the stove while *Bonito* careened through the Thoroughfare almost to the anchorage.

Then it blew harder and the jib thrashed like mad. I hated to send Arthur forward to let go the jib halyard in that wild wind and rain, but he was the only one there and he is an expert at holding on. I was mighty proud of him as he doused that jib and then tried to capture the sail lashing about the deck. He soon realized that was no job for him, so forced his way aft almost on hands and knees. Dousing sail had taken some speed off her, so I thought Arthur could steer. He braced himself in the cockpit while I watched a minute to see if he was going to be able to handle it.

Then I beat it forward to throw a line around the jib and get the big anchor ready before we were 'way past the anchorage. I had told Robert to stay down in the cockpit and not move, for it seemed as though his 50 pounds might go flying through the air. But now he came scrambling forward through the rain and spray, eyes as big as saucers. "The mizzen boom crotch is going, Father," he yelled above the wind. His mother had seen it start to go from her battle station at the stove with two boiling pots, and had sent him forward with the message. You could see he felt it was a life and death matter. I grabbed his coat and bundled him into the cockpit again and got the boom crotch just in time. We were already past the normal anchorage, but rounded up in a good spot and let go the big hook. The boys proved they had what it takes in a squall. I like to think that some of their early training in *Yankee* was showing up.

Ten minutes after anchoring, the sky cleared and the sun came out. The Maine day was sparkling now and looked innocent of all evil.

In the morning a nice southerly eased us along through the Thoroughfare, eastward bound. We crossed over to Deer Island and sailed through its Thoroughfare till near the eastern end where the wind backed towards southeast, which decided us to head up Blue Hill Bay. The wind seemed to suggest Seal Cove on Mount Desert Island. Knowing that Roger Griswold used to have a summer place here, I was not surprised when a big, burly figure appeared on the shore and hollered "Hello." Roger was just back from the wars in Europe and starting to get his wonderful old barn in shape to live in again. That night our talk went round and round from his old schooner, the *Lloyd W. Berry,* to the last war, this war, and the *Yankee.*

The next morning the fog came down thick and we were glad of our coal fire in the Shipmate. The only place we had been able to get briquets was in Boothbay and they are ideal for a fairly short quick fire, but you can't beat coal to keep things dry and cheery on the foggy cold days. The boys rustled up some good kindling wood on shore. I was determined to get everything possible out of my leave, so we set out northward along the coast of Mount Desert with visibility of about 100 feet. With care this would keep a small craft off the rocks along this part of the coast, so it was sort of fun for a change. It was time to be thinking about getting back to the westward. Orders were to report in Boston, "Headquarters, First Naval District," on July 14th. But we couldn't do much about that today, and the question now was: Could a Maine fog be called an act of God and extend a leave?

In mid-morning we felt our way into Sawyer Cove. When

someone appeared near one of the cottages there I yelled to ask if he knew where Sam Morison lived. "This is he," came the answer; "Who's calling?" I yelled back, "Johnson from Iwo Jima" as that was where I had last seen him just six weeks before. Commander Morison was writing the history of the Navy in World War II. He had a yeoman with him and was working on some of the material under ideal conditions. We enjoyed the ideal conditions too—an open fire and the good company of the Morison family.

Shortly after noon the visibility increased to half a mile so we headed across Blue Hill Bay, hoping for still more clearing. A large air bubble in the flat top compass made it jump around as much as four points whenever the going got a bit rough. Soon the carburetor clogged up from sediment sloshing around in the gas tank. It is hard enough to keep some track of your position with a poor compass when going under power, but it is twice as bad when beating to windward. While I was below trying to get the carburetor off, the fog shut down again and it was mostly by guess and by God that we found the spar buoy we were looking for and still more surprising that we kept finding them that day. Each time, just as we'd begin to wonder if we'd missed the buoy entirely, it would slip dimly into view. The wind must have stayed pretty true, as we had to steer more by it than by the compass.

When getting ready to sail I had forgotten to look for a sounding lead. Now I began to want some soundings to check our position, and no Navy fathometer was clicking for me. There wasn't any lead either, so a couple of old turnbuckles wired together had to serve. I could quickly measure off the depth by hauling in a fathom at a time with my arms stretched out. The soundings and lobster pots helped guide us from one buoy to the next.

Presently the breeze freshened, making a nasty chop against the ebb tide. Rain also came in with a very thick fog, so we scudded for the lee of a little island and anchored long enough to dry out over the coal stove and have a good cup of hot cocoa. When we got under way again it was nearly low tide, which made

the water smoother and was a better time to be fooling around
when there is any chance of going aground. We were trying for
the eastern end of Eggemoggin Reach and finally found our way
through the tiny passage between Harbor Island and the mainland. It was clearer in back of the islands and we could easily
make out the big fish weirs sticking way out of water at low tide.
We sailed between them and up the Reach a couple of miles to
an anchorage back of Little Babson Island, where the Guilds
welcomed us ashore at their island paradise. We all had baths
and enjoyed the place immensely. It is just about what one would
order if he were to pick out the ideal private Maine coast island.

In the morning we started up Eggemoggin Reach, but about
halfway a strong, clear northwesterly wind said *no* with a puff
that slid a new coil of manila and a fender over the side. That
coil of manila was as good as gold, so we quickly doused mainsail, jibed her over, and headed back. With Exy steering and the
boys as lookouts we succeeded in picking up both the coil of rope
and the fender in one run. It was really fresh by this time. Exy
says the only good thing about beating to windward in a chop
is that it feels so good when you stop. We weren't going to get
much nearer First Naval District Headquarters that day, but
neither the *Bonito* nor her crew wanted to drive up Eggemoggin
Reach in that blow.

Heading down the east side of Deer Isle, we came to the
Thoroughfare and started to beat through it. It was smooth
here and quite different from the lashed up surface of the
Reach. A big ketch was coming the other way with everything
set, loving the fair wind. Anchoring for the night in Stonehaven
seemed like a bit of old times. Our little ketch was right in the
middle of four old-time schooners, part of Captain Swift's fleet
of nine schooners now sailing paying guests out of Camden.

One of the best parts of the whole cruise was taking the boys
aboard these schooners, one after another. There was enough
memory of the *Yankee* still with them to make the deck of a big
schooner feel just right and faintly familiar. Yarns were swapped
about the day's fresh breeze. Arthur and Robert were so enthusiastic about pumping bilges, thereby saving the crew considerable

labor, that they got all four of us invited to have supper aboard. At other schooners the boys were given nickels, candy, and fruit. With the influx of four schooner loads of vacationists, the town put on a rip roaring dance. Apparently a large part of the population showed up to see the fun, and the mixture of old and new dances and people was fascinating.

About five-thirty the next morning the *Bonito* was under way in a flat calm, heading westward through Deer Island Thoroughfare. This was the day the Navy ordered. We had breakfast in North Haven where we picked up a few provisions and some more gas. Heading for Two Bush Channel across lower Penobscot Bay with the motor grinding out the miles was the dullest part of our cruise. It seemed as though nothing could happen and we were all a bit sleepy. Suddenly we struck something that felt just like going aground again. Arthur shut off the motor in a second, as I had told him to do when we ran aground in the Damariscotta. Robert asked, "Father, was that another rock we hit?" I was wondering what it was myself when a 40-foot log slowly came to the surface astern of us. It floated just awash and we had ridden right over it.

A few miles more and the carburetor clogged again, but before I could get it off a breeze sprang up and we thankfully set sail. Along with the breeze came a big double-ended racing cutter with her parachute set and drawing. We headed for the spindle on Old Man Ledge and for the first time in my life went by this particular spot at low tide when Old Woman Shoal can be seen. Coming past Shark Island the boys wondered where the shark was, but just then a whale spouted close by and they didn't wait for an answer. They wanted to run over and bump him. We rounded Pemaquid Point, and it came time to pick an anchorage for the night. There seemed to be a little cove just north of the Thread of Life between Hay Island and Christmas Cove. Sailing for the tiny anchorage under jib and jigger, we barely missed the one-foot spot in the center of the entrance and rounded up between the lobster pots where there was just room for us.

In the morning it was blowing real fresh from the south-southwest, so everything was lashed down and prepared for a

thrash to windward. Under full sail we tacked toward Pemaquid, luffing her a little over the steep seas, keeping the rail just
out of water. This kind of sailing is where a tiller comes in handy.
A boat of this size or smaller can often be worked over rough,
snarling seas with hardly a bit of spray coming aboard—not
quite the fastest way, but a pleasant one. Passing to leeward of
Damariscove Island, we could lay the course for the bell off
the Cuckolds and that is where it really got rough. By this time
full sail was actually too much for her, but it wouldn't be long
before we could start sheets, so we hung on, the boys keeping an
eye on the lee rail to see how far under it went as the bigger
seas swept by.

She really scooted, however, when we started sheets for the
home stretch up the Sheepscot River. The wind sure put a roaring climax on our cruise. We had to go into tiny Hendricks
Harbor, so doused main and approached the entrance under jib
and jigger. The motor refused to go, so Exy wiggled her in
around beacons, buoys, and rocks. Such a crowded place is not
ideal for shooting moorings under sail. Obviously we would
get but one chance. Besides, a lot of critical fishermen were looking on and my mind went back to the days when the harbor was
home port to 40 schooners. Exy rounded her up smartly and I
was thankful when we made it. As one of the fishermen rowed
by later he paused a moment to say, "Didn't think you'd make it.
Guess somebody aboard there must know how to sail."

Sails were harbor furled and the covers put on. Then the
inevitable, "Father, can we go out in the dinghy?" It was most
time for supper, but they might as well have their last chance.
When I went on deck to call them, I was horrified to see them in
the harbor entrance riding the breakers over a snarling reef. I
yelled at the top of my lungs, but they couldn't hear me because
of the breaking surf and their own laughter. Time and again they
were thrown straight over the rocks.

I was about to swim to a dory close by to go after them when a
fisherman who was closer relayed my call and got them to come
back. The fisherman turned to me to exclaim, "Damnedest thing
I ever seen. Breakers throw them right up in the air." Back

aboard, bubbling over with excitement, the boys wanted a quick supper in order to head back for more. After they had cooled down a bit, I carefully explained the difference between that kind of breaker and those in the rapids from the emptying Basin at Vinalhaven. Exy hopes they got the point. She says she wonders where they get such ideas.

29

On the Starboard Tack to Bermuda

by HERBERT L. STONE

[1932]

THE STORY of this year's Bermuda Race has many sides. First, there was the record-breaking drive of three days in a hard sou'-wester and heavy seas, with all hands carrying on without a let-up to smash their way to St. David's Head in faster time than it had ever been done before in a Bermuda Race. Then there was the unfortunate burning of one of the entries, the schooner *Adriana,* and the gallant rescue of all but one of her crew by the British cutter *Jolie Brise,* which Bobby Somerset, commodore of the Royal Ocean Racing Club, had sailed across for the race. Finally, there was the long anxious wait for the stragglers that found the going too heavy, or suffered minor casualties that delayed them long after the leaders had finished and brought them in with weary crews.

It was a hard race, chiefly because it was a fast race. Not that there was much to do in the way of sail handling. The boats, at least the leaders, sailed on one tack from Montauk all the way to St. David's Head. But to drive any little boat 625 sea miles in three days, with wind and sea forward of the beam, means wet work and slamming through heavy seas at an average of nearly 8¾ knots for the entire distance. After the first two hours the speed of the leading yachts did not once fall below eight knots. Often it was over nine. Only those who have sailed ocean races realize how wet a little ship can get when driven at this speed into a rough sea. Decks were washed constantly, cockpits were filled frequently, while getting about on deck was always precarious. Skylights were battened down and the air below was foul, while many stomachs labored no less than the boats. Sights for navigation were difficult until the last day, and cooking on most of the racers was a lost art, or of a very sketchy character. In other words, it was a race one was glad to have sailed in, but gladder still to finish.

Highland Light set a pace that will hardly be beaten by a boat of this size in this race. She sailed so fast that she arrived at the finish before the tug had established the line. The race committee had hardly camped out at St. David's Lighthouse, expecting at least a 24-hour wait for the first boat, before the tall, slim sails of the Boston cutter lifted off Northeast Breaker. She beat up the last six miles to the finish like a cup racer off Newport, going like a train of cars, with everything set that would draw. Just under nine knots she had made from start to finish. The nearest approach to this mark was in the race of 1909 when the schooner *Amorita* covered the course from Sandy Hook to St. David's in 78 hours 19 minutes and 15 seconds. Though the latter course is 45 miles longer than the one from Montauk, *Amorita* was a much larger yacht, 100 feet in length, and her average speed only 8½ knots against 8¾ for the much smaller *Highland Light*.

Twenty-seven yachts started in the race, an exceptionally creditable showing for a year when economic conditions are as stringent as in this. Fourteen of these were in the larger Class A, and 12 in Class B. A last minute entry was the schooner *Adriana*. As she was too large to fit in any of the regular classes, she was allowed to start in a special class, racing against the best corrected time of the fleet.

The caliber of the fleet was exceedingly high, and interest was heightened by the entry of two British yachts from the Royal Ocean Racing Club, "Bobby" Somerset's *Jolie Brise,* which raced here in 1926 when she was owned by E. G. Martin, and the *Lexia,* a new boat last year, owned by Major T. P. Rose-Richards, and a contestant in the last Fastnet Race. Both had crossed the Atlantic by way of the West Indies to take part in the Bermuda Race. Then there were two Bermuda boats at the starting line, our old friend the *Dainty*, with a new jib-headed ketch rig and sailed by Alfred Darrell, and the ketch *Zena* sailed by Wilfred Darrell. In the fleet, also, were six new yachts, sailing their first race and of which very little was known as to their speed capabilities. These were the schooner *Barlovento*, owned by P. S. duPont 3rd; the schooner *Brilliant*, Walter Barnum, owner; and the *Mandoo*, built for D. S. Berger, all in Class A. In the smaller class the newcomers were the schooner *Sonny*, Albert D. Phelps, owner: the yawl *Ayesha*, built for John R. Hogan; and the new Wells cutter, *Cyclone*, just down from Nova Scotia, where she was built.

All in all, it was a brave fleet that shoved off that gray afternoon from Montauk Point, where the starting line had been moved from off New London, shortening the course by some 20 miles. The change did not provoke much enthusiasm, for it meant getting underway in the early forenoon and, as the wind was fair, a wait of several hours off the Long Island headland for the starting gun at 3:10 P.M., with all hands impatient to be on their way.

The fresh westerly breeze of the forenoon had backed to sou'west by west as starting time approached and the sky clouded over with a hard, leaden aspect to windward, giving a hint of the rain and wind to follow.

By starting time the wind had eased off a bit, but the direction was fair so that the fleet could lay the course, SE by S, with started sheets. Frank Paine had *Highland Light* on the line at the gun and he, along with *Grenadier* and *Barlovento*, probably got what honors there were at the start. The adverse tide played hob with the starting plans of many of the other skippers. But the start does not mean much in a race of this length. George Roosevelt's *Mistress* got away late, but with everything drawing hard, she started to overhaul the boats ahead of her in short order, gradually working up with the leaders. *Jolie Brise* got away with the leaders, breaking out a big, tanned jib topsail that pulled her along in good style. *Lexia* had the wrong combination of head sails and dropped back until a big genoa jib was substituted for the three first used, when she began to move properly.

Five minutes after the large class was away, Class B started. *Dorade,* last year's Transatlantic and Fastnet Race winner, stepped out in the lead, followed by Philip LeBoutillier's *Viking,* and Jay Wells' new *Cyclone.* These three soon caught and passed the laggards of Class A. By nightfall, the fleet was strung out with *Highland Light* leading, closely pressed by *Barlovento, Grenadier, Teragram, Brilliant* and *Malabar X.* At this time the wind was moderate and the sea fairly smooth.

With the coming of darkness, the wind began to harden, with now and then a spatter of rain. Some time before midnight a hard squall swept the fleet, bringing light sails down on deck in a hurry. On some boats mainsails were lowered, only to be set again when the heft of the squall had passed, leaving the wind more to the westward. From this point on the boats really began to step out, reeling off the knots with the regularity of a steamer. Gradually the wind backed to sou'west and hardened, while the sea began to make up rapidly. It was blowing, perhaps, 20 miles an hour, and up to 25 or 30 in the puffs, but on the whole it was remarkably steady, except for occasional squalls. It was too much, with the wind forward of the beam, for light sails, and the fleet had all it could stagger under with lowers, while mainsails were reefed or foresails stowed on some of the boats. The smaller craft, of course, suffered more in this respect than the larger ones, although all had more breeze at times than they wanted.

It was about three o'clock on the morning of the first night out that *Adriana* burned. A tile heating stove in the cabin became overheated and set fire to a locker containing oilskins and hemp rigging. When discovered, it burst out fiercely, and when extinguishers failed to make any impression on it, the cabin was shut tight and distress flares were burned. The watch on *Jolie Brise,* some three miles ahead, saw a rocket (a Very pistol was used, I think) and Bobby Somerset immediately turned back to give aid, burning flares to show that the distress signals had been seen. On reaching the burning yacht, Somerset decided to go alongside and take off the crew, as to launch a boat would have been too slow and dangerous an undertaking. With rare seamanship, *Jolie Brise* was ranged alongside the *Adriana* to leeward, and as the two vessels came together with the heave of the sea, those on the now-blazing yacht jumped to the British boat, being helped aboard by the latter's crew. *Jolie Brise* was forereaching at about four knots as she went by.

Clarence Kozlay, at the wheel of *Adriana,* keeping her under control until his ten shipmates were rescued, delayed too long. When he jumped it was too late and he fell into the water between the two vessels. In the darkness he was swept away and drowned, the first fatality in these races since they were inaugurated.

Jolie Brise had her rail and stanchions smashed when the yachts came together. After cruising about for several hours in a vain attempt to find Kozlay, she bore off and started back to Montauk, where the ten rescued men were landed early Monday morning. Somerset, of course, abandoned the race and went to Bristol, R. I., for repairs to his damaged ship. It was a gallant piece of work, executed with rare skill and courage.

It blew hard the second day out. Noon positions showed that the leaders had done from 175 to 180 miles in the 21 hours since the start. Thereafter the pace was to be even faster. The Gulf Stream brought its usual confused sea, but the squalls, except in rare instances, carried nothing vicious, though some of the boats shortened down for a few of them. By noon the second day, runs of from 212 to 222 nautical miles for the 24 hours were hung up by the larger yachts, the latter figure being turned in by the *Brilliant.* It was wonderful going, but wet and uncomfortable, particularly below. There was not much to do on deck but sit and steer as the boats drove to the southeast, with now and then a pull on the sheets as the wind backed a bit more. The third day brought hardly any slackening of the pace, and many runs of over 200 miles were recorded. While the wind eased off a trifle, the sea was smoother and steering was easier.

At this time *Highland Light* was some 25 miles ahead of the

fleet, with Bermuda almost within sight at noon. She tore down
on the Northeast Breaker buoy, marking the corner of the outlying reef, and hardened her sheets for the beat up to the finish.
She crossed the line at 3:34:43 P.M. (Bermuda time), less than
three days after the start. *Mistress,* well sailed all the way, was
her closest competitor. She shaved the buoys around the reef to
finish at 7:20:51 P.M. In sight, behind her, came *Barlovento*
and *Malabar X,* followed by *Teragram* and *Brilliant,* with
Grenadier and *Water Gipsy* treading on the latter's heels. It
was a stirring finish with only one hour and ten minutes separating these six schooners. Three hours later *Lexia* finished, in a
softening wind, and about 1:30 A.M., the little *Dorade,* first in her
class by a margin of ten hours. She had, as always, sailed a fine
race.

Malabar X, sailed by her former owner, John Alden, passed
Barlovento on the short beat up from Kitchen Shoals buoy,
getting the gun 5 minutes and 22 seconds before the duPont
schooner. So far, she had saved her time on all those ahead of
her. But there were others with larger handicaps still out. Would
they beat her time? Neither *Teragram* nor *Brilliant* did it, but
Grenadier was in sight, and dangerous. It was dark when
the last named crossed the line, shortly before nine o'clock, with
over an hour's allowance on *Malabar.* It was going to be close—
a matter of minutes only—perhaps of seconds. With no communication with the shore, the crews of neither boat knew which
had won, or if perhaps some other smaller yacht would slip in
during the night to save her time. It was only when they dropped
anchor in Hamilton Harbor the next morning that the actual
standing was known. *Malabar X* had saved her time, but only
by 3 minutes and 17 seconds on *Grenadier.* It was one of the
closest finishes in the long record of Bermuda races. *Water Gipsy,*
hard driven all the way, took third place on corrected time and
Teragram was fourth. *Highland Light,* in spite of her record-
breaking run of 71 hr., 35 min., 43 sec., had to be content with
fifth place on corrected time.

In Class B, the little *Twilight,* with an allowance of 17 hours
33 minutes, figured winner of second place, with the new yawl

Ayesha third and the *Viking* fourth. So close were the boats in this class that only five minutes separated third and fifth place in the final standing. It was a great race—perhaps the fastest that will ever be sailed for years to come. (Ed. note—record unbeaten through 1951.)

Of the unfortunate tragedy, with the loss of a well-known and much-liked yachtsman, most of the crews knew nothing until they finished, except those on *Mandoo* and *Sonny,* both of which stood by the burning yacht when they sighted her, after the crew had been taken off by *Jolie Brise.* But with the universal regret at the occurrence went admiration and praise for Somerset and his crew, who, by their prompt and efficient action, upheld the best traditions of the sea.

In view of the many conflicting reports regarding the adventures of the *Curlew,* the following explanation, given by the yawl's navigator and approved by her crew, is published as an authorized account of the facts—an account which her crew feel they owe to yachtsmen and to the government authorities for the concern and inconvenience inadvertently caused by them, and in an effort to clear up the unpleasant publicity which followed.

The crew of the *Curlew* entered the race admittedly green to ocean racing, but they had experienced three years of coastwise cruising in their boat and had full confidence in her, as well as a realization of the rigors of ocean racing, for which the boat was adequately equipped. Rumors of *Curlew's* unfitness for the race reached the committee before the start of the race, and the committee's inspection was, therefore, doubly rigid. The boat was declared sound and properly equipped. That this inspection was not faulty was borne out by the fact that the boat withstood two weeks of hard weather without leaking, and her crew returned in good health, with ample food and water remaining. During the two weeks' interval, her experience might have been that of any boat of 46 feet overall length under the prevailing conditions.

For the first three days *Curlew* did well, reaching a latitude of 100 miles north of Bermuda, but being driven to leeward and to the eastward by the fresh head wind and steep seas. All on board lent willing hands to reduce canvas in the squalls and the boat behaved well. On the fourth day, those who were in or near Bermuda will recall, it blew very hard from the southwest. *Curlew's* crew estimated the velocity at 40 m.p.h. In these conditions, under reduced canvas, *Curlew* was driven farther to the eastward, as it was anticipated would be the lot of the smaller boats by those who had already reached Bermuda. Added to these circumstances was the eastward set of the currents around Bermuda, which navigators making landfalls on the third day estimated to be between one and two knots. The net result of adverse wind and current brought *Curlew,* at the end of the fourth day, to the latitude of Bermuda, but 100 miles to the eastward.

Under reduced canvas, *Curlew* could not hope to beat against the strong southwesterly, high seas, and adverse current; so they tacked north and south, awaiting a shift of wind, meanwhile being carried to leeward about one mile per hour. For three days there was no let-up in the wind, and *Curlew,* being carried to leeward about 30 miles per day, reached a position 200 miles east of Bermuda. Overdue, and with only one week of their vacation remaining, the crew decided to ease sheets and sail for the steamer lanes and home. At the end of the eighth day *Curlew* turned in a good run of 160 miles, and then the wind dropped. Had they waited one more day they would have made Bermuda about the same time that *Spanish Rose* came in.

The calm was followed by some nasty weather over the Fourth of July weekend which made it impossible for them to get to the westward, but allowed them to make northing toward the Atlantic steamer lanes where they hoped to be reported.

On the twelfth day out, they reached the steamer lane and sighted four tramp steamers in the distance. Flags were hoisted but were not distinguished. Distress signals were considered, but not being in distress and not wishing to create a needless sensation, they were not used. On the thirteenth day, a landfall was made on Davis South Shoal Buoy, south of Nantucket, and a course was laid for Newport. It was then that the Coast Guard sighted *Curlew* and hove alongside, advising that a search was being made for her and found that she needed no assistance.

BERMUDA RACE. STARTING FROM MONTAUK POINT, JUNE 25, 1932

Class A

Yacht and Owner	Elapsed Time	Corrected Time
Malabar X, R. I. Gale, John G. Alden	75:42:29	69:48:48
Grenadier, H. A. and S. Morss	76:47:28	69:52:04
Water Gipsy, William McMillan	76:57:52	70:57:04
Teragram, George W. Mixter	76:13:24	71:33:24
Highland Light, F. C. Paine	71:35:43	71:35:43
Brilliant, Walter Barnum	76:42:07	71:37:21
Mistress, G. E. Roosevelt	75:10:51	72:10:24
Barlovento, P. S. duPont, 3rd	75:47:51	72:15:18
Lexia, Major T. P. Rose-Richards	80:08:26	76:14:48
Vamare, Vadim Makaroff	89:28:11	77:31:15
Discovery, J. H. Nichols	98:37:46	91:43:00
Mandoo, D. S. Berger	97:10:58	92:13:22
Sea Witch, E. S. Parsons	123:35:15	116:04:39
Jolie Brise, Robert Somerset	Withdrew	

BERMUDA RACE. STARTING FROM MONTAUK POINT, JUNE 25, 1932

Class B

Yacht and Owner	Elapsed Time	Corrected Time
Dorade, R. Stephens, Jr.	81:33:33	72:11:10
Twilight, Edw. S. Bradford, Jr.	98:09:55	80:36:10
Ayesha, John R. Hogan	97:56:33	82:10:46
Sonny, Albert D. Phelps	95:08:40	82:11:55
Viking, P. LeBoutillier	91:24:26	82:15:52
Malabar V, Herbert Parsons	94:53:17	82:56:21
Duckling, Chas. H. Atwater	119:00:08	99:12:47
Zena, C. H. Masters	127:35:15	105:22:14
Amberjack II, Paul D. Rust, Jr.	Withdrew	
Cyclone, F. Jay Wells	Withdrew	
Dainty, Alfred A. Darrell	Withdrew	
Curlew, David Rosenstein	Withdrew	

30

Sun, Keys, and Tropic Seas

by SHELDON VAN AUKEN

[1949]

THIS STORY is not of hazardous adventure but of pleasant sailing, of beachcombing and exploring among the islands south of the tip of Florida. Also, it is the story of sailing on a shoestring; the cruise that anyone with a boat and vacation can make.

There are no anchoring fees in the lee of an island. In seven weeks, the one-cylinder Palmer auxiliary burned just short of seven gallons of fuel. The few needed repairs were contrived aboard. Food costs were, if anything, less than on land, owing to the mackerel, grouper and, especially, crawfish which came out of the sea into the galley. The entire expenses of the cruise, therefore, came to under $50; the gasoline, half a dozen charts, two giant straw hats and a bottle of sun oil, five gallons of alcohol for the stove, two or three spoons and handlines—I can't think of anything else.

The vessel which was our home for seven weeks was a stoutly built, gaff-rigged sloop, 18 feet l.w.l. (and on deck), 7 feet beam, and 3 feet draft. Below was a surprisingly roomy cabin with two seven-foot bunks, sitting headroom, one-burner stove with its invaluable pressure cooker, book-shelf, head, and chart table. However, the stout little *Gull* was not the perfect craft for the Keys. Even three feet of keel can be too much in these waters; a centerboard is preferable. Her short gaff rig was perfect for the open sea; a marconi rig with more area would have been better for

Keys sailing. A few more feet of length would have provided more stowage space and room for a good-sized icebox. Nevertheless, *Gull* was a fine little ship, and her sturdiness and stiffness were often reassuring.

At the moment our story begins, *Gull,* under all two of her sails and clipping off about one knot, was proceeding southwards through lower Biscayne Bay. I drooped languidly over the tiller; my wife and co-skipper, Dave, lay prone up forward, staring over the side into the cool, translucent world below. In the center of a cloudless sky burned a fierce sun. Astern, Miami was being swallowed in shimmering haze. Somewhere ahead lay Feather-bed Bank and the beginnings of the Keys.

Helped by the engine when the wind dropped completely, we sailed on all the hot afternoon; through the short well-marked channel of Featherbed Bank, across Card Sound and Barnes Sound, following, generally, the Intra-coastal Waterway. In the lower part of Barnes Sound we turned off toward the Key Largo shore in which is a perfect little cove with a depth of four to five feet and a grassy bottom. On an earlier voyage, we had discovered this anchorage and named it on our charts "Five Pelican Cove." This afternoon only two pelicans watched us drop the hook, but everything else was just the same; the desolate beauty of the encircling shore, the stillness, our pleasure at being just where we were.

We had heard of the Keys mosquitoes and, after we had lightly but only temporarily spliced the main brace, following a swim overside, we draped a large mosquito bar over the boom to cover cockpit and hatch. In the cool of the evening we settled down to salad, coffee, and a cheddar cheese, with splendid red sunset and one lone frigate bird hovering like a sentinel. Suddenly, a drone filled the air; the mosquitoes had arrived. They penetrated the cockpit defenses in seconds. We jumped below, slamming the screens and thanking the gods that we had screens to slam. All through the night, across the still reaches of moonlit water, the air was filled with the muted tenor frenzy of billions of bugs—the Mosquito Madrigal.

Early next morning, before the last of them were gone, we

decided to leave our too-sheltered cove. With a few random sprays of DDT through the hatch, we popped up on deck, made sail, and slid out into the bright water of Barnes Sound. *Gull* sailed herself in this gentle to moderate breeze, and we let her pick her own course while we breakfasted and swabbed down the decks. *Gull* had sailed steadily north for about an hour when we decided aloud that one of us should bring her about. Just at that moment she came up gently and fell off on the other tack, which she held for another hour. We resumed our southward journey through Jewfish Creek, with its courteous bridge tender, across Blackwater Sound, Tarpon Basin, and Buttonwood Sound, following the clearly marked Waterway, and anchored in the lower part of Buttonwood in the lee of tiny Pelican Key. After dinner and a windy-looking pale gold sunset, we sat topside in the brilliant moonlight, listening to the moan aloft of the rising wind. There were no mosquitoes out this night. By morning the breeze had moderated and we got underway early to make Tavernier before the breeze freshened. A moderate to fresh northerly in the early morning meant fresh to strong by early afternoon.

Gull fell away from Pelican Key on the port tack and, circling wide to avoid the bar which stretches to the north, was soon traversing the short dredged channel of Baker's Cut into Florida Bay—a shallow, island-dotted part of the Gulf of Mexico. With a fair breeze and following sea, *Gull* charged down toward Pigeon Key, and the double-ended dinghy astern charged down on *Gull*. The seas were so large and the disturbed water so milky that it seemed inadvisable to take the short cut into Tavernier, which would entail threading the sandbars between Pigeon Key and Key Largo. We held to the marked channel until we had rounded the Pigeon, when we set a course for Hammer Point and the entrance to Tavernier's Community Harbor.

For yachts entering Tavernier for the first time, a clear, quiet forenoon, when sandbars can be seen, is best. A bar stretches east and west across the opening of the cove; approximately in the middle lies a dot of mangrove brush perhaps five feet across. It is necessary to locate this keylet and the southernmost of two prominent fish houses (with piers). The right tangent of the keylet must be lined up with the fish house. Sail on that line, passing the brush port-side-to, within a few feet, and hold the course until the shallows on either side are passed. Inside are four feet of water and grassy bottom.

We rounded up to anchor near a trim sloop with the name *Beachcomber* on her stern. Her owner came sculling fast from shore. Pipe all hands; break out the rum! He came aboard like a boy, despite his 60-odd years, and it is difficult to say who was the more joyful in this reunion—brown old Cap who had taught us practically all we knew of sailing, or the crew of *Gull*. In a matter of moments, we had the charts spread in the cockpit and were planning voyages on to the south where Dave and I had never cruised.

Since *Beachcomber* and *Gull* were to cruise in company for the next several weeks, it may be interesting to analyze briefly the basis for the unqualified success of the cruise. It must have been pleasant for Cap to have the companionship of enthusiastic amateurs. We were companions, respectful audience, and pupils. Cap had followed the sea all his life. He had first come down to these keys in a sailing canoe, without even a chart. We appreciated in Cap not only his sea lore but his deep, simple philosophy of nature and man.

Cap filled his 200-lb. icebox, and we stocked up on groceries. I found some scrap iron for extra ballast in *Gull's* forepeak. Dave and I struggled the length of the pier with armloads of groceries, piling them atop a heap of the 60 pounds of scrap, a five-gallon drum of gasoline, and six one-gallon water jugs. A powerful young fisherman, surveying the pile and the dainty 10-foot dinghy that was to carry it back to *Gull*, observed scornfully, "That's a hell of a dinghy!"

"It's a good dinghy," I replied.

"Good for what?"

"Well, for riding a surf."

"But it won't carry nothin'; you'll have to make two trips."

Knowing the buoyancy of the little round-bottomed double-ender, I said nothing and began to load. In the ends went jugs.

Amidships went, first, the gas and then, carefully, the scrap. Dave got aboard with the groceries; I followed. The fisherman looked on, astonished, "Gee, it sure holds a lot, don't it?" "It do," I said.

Later the fisherman expressed his highest praise in the genial threat to steal it if he had a chance.

Next morning the breeze was a fresh easterly, and *Beachcomber* sailed out the channel followed by *Gull*. We cruised south in leisurely stages, following the Waterway through the dredged cuts, otherwise wandering where we pleased with a glance at the chart and considerably more than a glance at the color of the water. One cannot depend entirely upon the charts for, with every hurricane, the sandbars shift. As long as the sun is bright and water clear, sandbars stand out with beautiful clarity. Occasionally we misjudged and felt the nudge of the bottom. We saw many yachts proceeding toward Key West, never varying from the red line of the Intracoastal Waterway charts, and we wondered if they did not regret not seeing the Keys more intimately.

The first night out of Tavernier we anchored in the lee of Lignumvitae Key, higher than most, and one of the most beautiful. Aside from the long, narrow keys that stretch, one after another, between the Atlantic and the Gulf down to Key West, there are two groups of Florida Keys. The northern group may be said to end at Lignumvitae or at Bowlegs Cut just beyond. About 35 miles to the southwest begin the Big Pine Keys, which continue on to Key West. Between the two groups are a few small keys, spaced just right for easy runs. From Bowlegs, after some complicated weaving in and out among the sandbars, we anchored close in to the northeast side of Channel Key. As always, the two boats were alongside, both swinging to *Beachcomber's* big anchor.

Here occurred my most harrowing experience of the cruise. We were all bathing in the warm shallows off a little beach, and I decided to spear one of the wily mangrove snappers which lurked among the mangrove roots along the shore. Only I was going to try a new method, all others having failed: I would swim with a breathing-tube mask over my face and a light spear or grain in my hand, ready to thrust it among the fish as I floated over them. This I did, darting futile thrusts among the contemptuous fish. Then, glancing up from the bottom, I found I was about to collide with a peacefully drifting ray, about three feet in diameter and about ten inches away. He and I looked one another steadily in the eye, at least one of us attempting unobtrusively to swim backwards. There was a long moment; and then we turned simultaneously and proceeded on opposite courses.

These stingrays never seem desirous of attacking, and a slap of the water will send one rushing away, but do not slap the water if you are within reach of the long, vicious tail which lashes out like a whip. When the sun is hot on the water, they will float awhile and then spring into the air to smack the water with a crack like a three-inch gun. The biggest we saw measured five and six feet from wing to wing. Big sharks do not enter the shallower parts of the Keys area, nor do the huge barracuda which may be encountered around the reefs in the Atlantic, though small barracuda (up to three or four feet) and little sand sharks are common. The one really deadly creature likely to be met in the shallows is the moray eel—especially in the vicinity of rocky ledges. Happily we never saw one. We were told, however, that if a moray got on our fishing line, we should immediately cut the line adrift; and, if we met one while we were in the water, we should expect him to attack. For this reason, when we waded in the shallows for crawfish or shells, we trailed the dinghies after us. We also wore sneakers as a protection against sharp coral and spiny sea urchins.

Next morning, after a cool dawn swim and a breakfast of crawfish and eggs, the Admiral directed us to lead the way through the sandbars to the south. We endeavored to interpret every slight shading of the color of the water, every little ripple where the tide flowed over a bank, and we emerged successfully on the other side. The two boats then sailed side by side, *Gull's* boom so close to Cap that he could reach up and pat it. The tall marconi main of *Beachcomber* had a reef to keep her from running away from us. Thus, for tranquil hour after hour, we sailed on, sometimes talking between the boats, sometimes with no sound but the cool rippling at the bows. At noon we dropped sail, Cap tossed a line, and we drifted together while we ate cheese sandwiches and drank a cold beer from *Beachcomber's* cavernous icebox. Then we sailed on, across Grassy Key Bank, past Burnt Point, until we reached Bamboo Key off the larger Fat Deer Key.

This key was the first one we explored thoroughly. Most of the Florida Keys are but a few feet above sea level, and from a little distance appear to be groups of trees growing out of the water. But, as one approaches, they are seen to be dense jungles of mangroves and other trees. Pushing the dinghies under low-hanging mangrove branches into a little cove, we found a minute beach and made our way inland. The jungle suddenly gave way to a broad, grassy plain at the center, full of bright, blooming shrubs and dotted with orange flowers, beautiful in its utterly secluded peace. The only sounds were the high, clear whistles of red-winged blackbirds and the occasional rush of wings of the blue herons which nested in the mangroves. On the windward side of the key we found a break in the encircling mangroves and a stretch of windy beach. We found a magnificent red pen shell for Dave's collection, as well as lesser shells and other flotsam left through the years.

In the evening we followed our customary routine: dinner in the cockpit just before sunset; then, with the arrival of the mosquitoes, down to *Beachcomber's* roomy cabin for an hour of boat talk or reading old *Yachtings,* and so to bed.

The fish had a hammer in his starboard fin and he again smote the *Gull* just below the waterline. I turned uneasily in my sleep, aware of resentment against this persistent fish. Suddenly I was wide awake; that hammering was the dinghy alongside. As I swarmed topside, my only thought was that we were adrift. But there, in the light of a large and misty moon, was the key just where it should be. What, then . . . ?

"Good sailor," said Cap from the bow of *Beachcomber,* "I was wondering if you were going to wake up. You're sitting in the mud!" Cap, of course, awoke the moment *Gull's* keel had touched. He had gone out in his dinghy to get the anchor, and was now preparing to pole us to a deeper spot. He was pleased that I had awakened and had me hoist *Gull's* jib—at which Dave shot out on deck. We pushed hard with our poles; the jib pulled; we moved. In a few moments we were re-anchored in the hole Cap had found. A fresh easterly breeze had blown the water out, reducing a one-inch margin of safety to one inch too little.

From Bamboo Key we cruised down to the little village of Marathon on Vaca Key, sailing in for ice and groceries and then continuing on for the long jump to East Bahia Honda Key. Here there is a long break in the sheltering keys, and strong tidal currents sweep in from the Atlantic and out again. The moderate easterly breeze blew steadily and our course was a little north of west. For the only time in the whole cruise land disappeared, but in an hour or so, out of the sea ahead, there rose and seemed to float in air the treetops that marked East Bahia Honda. We were no longer even approximately cruising the Intracoastal Waterway, which follows Big Spanish Channel out into the Gulf and then in to Key West. We decided to wander about among this maze of southern Keys, trusting to find some sort of hole in which to anchor at low tide, and to attempt to reach Key West this way in spite of *Gull's* keel.

Early next morning, we got underway with a fair breeze and, pausing now and then to explore the beaches or shallows of some interesting key, made our way across Big Spanish Channel. As the sun climbed higher the breeze freshened and dark squalls built up around us. We kept a wary eye on these and observed without pleasure that one of them was aiming for *Gull*. Cap had told us that when we saw a squall with dark fingers, and when those fingers were working, it was time to get the canvas off. So now we divided our attention between the squall and *Beachcomber*. Had she been out of sight, we would have anchored. But we held on, ready to let the sheets fly in a moment. "No," I said again, "the fingers don't seem to be working. Or are they? You stand by the peak halyard ready to drop the peak the minute I give the word."

At that moment the breeze was suddenly gone. There was

not a breath. We heard a low roaring sound, growing in volume. "Drop that peak!" I said sharply, and what seemed like
a hurricane was upon us. The wind was terrific; rain slashed at
us in horizontal lines. The peak was dropped and I eased the
sheets; the flapping of the canvas was a pistol-shot obligato to
the overwhelming roar of wind and driving rain. We could not
see a hundred yards in any direction; the waves were whipped to
white froth.

And then suddenly the squall was gone. We were astonished
to find that, although one side of us was soaked, the lee side of
our clothes was quite dry. We also discovered that, on the handline customarily out stern, we were dragging a two-foot grouper.
The breeze was steady but uncomfortably strong, and we were
glad to see Cap's anchor go down in the lee of Porpoise Key. We
were in for a blow, and for four days we were unable to leave
this shelter.

Wind-bound though we were, we were not bored. We read
and napped and effected minor repairs. Porpoises—a bull and
two cows—leaped and frolicked about Porpoise Key. Exploring
in the dinghies, we found on the south side of the key a narrow
channel, nowhere less than four feet deep, leading into the mangrove. In this creek, if need be, we could ride out anything short
of a hurricane.

Eventually the wind moderated and we sailed northwest along
the coast of Big Pine Key. Not far from Porpoise begins the
Little Spanish Channel, known to us as the "Picket Fence"
owing to the incredible number of fingerboards which mark its
devious twistings. On the chart the little triangles overlap, so
close are they, and in an air line distance of less than 25 nautical
miles the red and black fingerboards go up to Nos. 98 and 85,
respectively. And along the Picket Fence we sailed. I think no
boat with more than three feet draft could successfully cruise
the Little Spanish Channel and even three feet is rather too
much. We were forced to hunt a hole and anchor when the tide
was out. Sailing only near the flood, there were several places
we just scraped across by getting most of the weight up forward.

In the lee of a tiny nameless key, located just about in the center of a triangle formed by Big Torch, Raccoon, and Knock-emdown Keys, we anchored for the night. Around us were count-less Keys: Content, Tarpon Belly, Toptree Hammock, Little Crane, Cudjoe, and Happy Jack—to mention a few just for the pleasure of writing their colorful names.

Most of the time a fresh breeze helped us, in spite of our twistings. By 1100 we had traversed the worst and shallowest section of the whole channel, the Inner Narrows between Snipe and Saddlebunch Keys, where our keel stirred the mud from beginning to end. I suspect we made it only because the breeze kept us heeled over and because I kept my weight well forward: it was that close. Then the water deepened and our mud trail disappeared. And when, at noon, we anchored in three feet one inch of water (and 10 feet of mud), we could see Key West less than five miles away. Since the breeze was again freshening un-comfortably, we decided to stay where we were until morning. We calculated that of the 17 days since Miami, the breeze had been fresh or better for 14.

Next morning we sailed in—with a fresh breeze. Key West Bight, in the northwest corner of the island, is the easiest harbor to enter and is close to such facilities as ice houses and grocery stores. We were allowed to tie up to the pier for the several days of our stay without charge, and everything we needed was within walking distance. Dave and I found the city more charm-ing than we had any right to expect, a lovely, faded relic of the past, blended of the Old South and proud Spain. We wandered streets made colorful by flowering trees and the old, balconied houses. We dined on turtle and conch steaks and then, footsore from unaccustomed walking, limped through dark, windy, fra-grant streets back to the harbor.

The tourists who rush down the overseas highway from Miami often find little to amuse them in a cursory glance around the old city, and usually are back in their expensive hotels before nightfall, having seen Key West and the Keys. But we lingered, delighted with the time-mellowed charm of the town, so pleas-antly different from anything else in south Florida.

At length, we stood out of the Bight into a fresh head wind, and sailed back the way we had come, through the Narrows, to an anchorage in the lee of a nameless key just east of Johnston and south of Sawyer Key. With appropriate ceremonies—the passing of the rum—we named it "Cap Key," as who has a better right to a key named for him than Cap'n Frank Watson, who has wandered these waters for years. Two large, furry coons sat curiously on shore and witnessed the proceedings.

From Cap Key we sailed out the Johnston Key Channel into the Gulf of Mexico, then northeastward to what was perhaps the most interesting of all the Keys to us: Sawyer Key. It is distinguished by a broad, sandy beach, and is unusual also in being rather like an atoll—really a circle of keys and keylets with a lagoon in the center. On the beach we found many shells for the collection, and in the clear shallows we found crawfish. When the beachcombing and dinner-hunting were finished, Dave and I rowed through a pass into the deep, still lagoon. As always among these keys, we were awed by the untouched wildness of the scene: a great white heron flying low over the water, the broad back of a turtle, the shadowy grace of sharks beneath the surface, the dense jungle on shore, and the profound stillness. We spoke in whispers, the boat moved with scarcely a ripple, and the only break in that sun-drenched silence was the strange lost cry of some bird.

The cruise was not yet half over; nearly another month was to elapse before *Gull* proceeded up the Miami River to her home slip. In the month *Gull* and *Beachcomber* sailed leisurely about through the Keys, working gradually north and east. We did the same old things—we fished and prowled the shallows, we wandered along the beaches, we read and talked. Of course, there were variations. Every key, each stretch of bottom, was unknown territory and full of potential wonder. The quest for shells continued with exciting finds, and a subsidiary collection of tropical feathers was begun—but only feathers that were found on the beach or in the water.

This second period saw the belated arrival of summer weather. It was marked by a cessation of the eternally fresh breeze and the frequent northerlies, and a substitution of hot forenoon calms and sudden squalls. With the change arrived a new pest, the horsefly or deerfly, which, in spite of his bulk, lands like a feather and takes his vicious bite. In spite of flies and calms, wicked squalls and occasional ominous-looking waterspouts, this was the weather Cap loved. We learned from him the charm of ghosting through scarcely rippled water. The boats barely moved, much of the time the tillers were tied or simply abandoned, and we watched the bottom. I suppose it is the nearest thing to the flying we dreamed of as children, easing along soundlessly, the bottom a fathom or two from our eyes and the water as clear as air. Once or twice *Gull* and *Beachcomber* became a ketch. Still lashed together, *Gull* on *Beachcomber's* quarter, we set all sails and weighed anchor. There was much amusement among the crew at this combination. The ketch, *Beachgull* we called her, sailed or drifted for miles along our way. But it was companionable, we had always the shade of one of the sails . . . and then, we weren't going anywhere anyhow. The *Beachgull* was a pretty good vessel for summer in the Keys, especially since there was only one icebox.

To us, the joy of the voyage lay in the easy companionship, in the wild beauty that stretched around us, and in the cessation of that hurry and strain which is part of civilization. There is a peace and a deep contentment in this sort of idling close to nature. It seems to me that such peace could not be found along a highway, nor in a 20-knot cruiser. But, however one may feel about the choice of a vessel, as long as she does not draw too much water she can wander the Keys—and, if she leaves the "red line," she will not travel far at 20 knots.

Ahead of *Gull* lay as yet "undiscovered" keys and then the voyage back to civilization through the last storm in Biscayne Bay. But let me leave *Gull* and her crew in the Keys. The little sloop is easing across from one key to another. The crew, in an absolute minimum of clothing and as brown as Tahitians, is unaware of any news later than two weeks ago but very much aware of the wind and the water, of the bottom gliding not far below the keel. The anchor goes down in the lee of a key. The crew swims overside and emerges to prepare a freshly caught grouper for the frying pan. The sun drops lower; dinner is spread in the cockpit. A little talk topside and then, with the drone of the first mosquito, the crew secures. Not long afterward the cabin lamp goes out, and then there is no light anywhere but the slow, bright stars above and in the water.

31

Bermuda Passage

by ALEX W. MOFFAT

[1936]

THE SKIPPER LEANED OUT the pilothouse window peering into the blizzard, his cap and eyebrows white with snow. The pitching was easier as we came under the lee of the beach, with less spray to add to the coating of ice forward.

"Stop her."

The engineroom telegraphs jangled, followed by silence except for the seas hissing along the side, a cotton wool silence muffling sound and sight alike in swirling snowflakes. I held the course while *143* lost headway, listening. A faint, brief sound, a mere punctuation in the silence, came from somewhere up wind; men on deck pointed. Again it sounded.

"Slow ahead, port and starboard. Steady as you go." She gathered steerageway and forged on into the smother, until with appalling suddenness, the end of a breakwater loomed on our starboard bow, bringing a startled yell from the crew. It was a perfect landfall for the new Skipper. Of the whole crew, he and I were the only two who knew that the change of course after we passed Race Rock had been for the Harbor of Refuge at Point Jude. All hands had expected Bermuda to be the first landfall.

Delayed by a broken steering gear, we had departed six hours after the rest of our detachment, under orders to overtake them at sea. I admired the Skipper's decision to put in for temporary shelter instead of proceeding to sea with an unorganized ship and a seasick crew, most of whom were from west of the Mississippi and this their first introduction to salt water.

Slowly we slid through floe ice toward the sound of an auxiliary engine exhaust up ahead which sounded suspiciously like that of a subchaser. Then we were among our own detachment, whose C.O. had had the same idea as our Skipper, who smiled grimly as he gave the order to anchor.

For two weeks past the State Pier at New London, fitting-out base for the chasers scheduled for foreign service, had buzzed with rumors. Of the 70 110-footers gripped in the ice alongside the pier, 12 were being made "in all respects ready for sea." Officers came and went, truckloads of stores were dumped on the stringpiece, lists of all kinds were checked and rechecked, inspections, from medical to engineering, filled every hour of the day. As quartermaster of *143,* one of the glamorous twelve, I had little to do but stand by to handle stores aboard, and to try to keep warm practicing semaphore by which the rumors were circulated. Some said we were bound for the Mediterranean, others said for France, still others that we were to sail the very next day for a secret destination under sealed orders.

Most of our boys on *143* were a draft from the Great Lakes Naval Training Station, an alphabetical draft whose qualification for the service appeared to be that their names began with "H"; a fine, husky lot, anxious to make good but bewildered by the confusion and absence of authority. For two weeks we had been without a Skipper. The second in command spent his time ashore when not attending the officers' training course, of no help to the petty officers who were doing their best against odds to get the ship ready. The gunner's mate, an amateur woodsman, was trying to teach the rudiments of cooking to the poor devil who had been assigned as ship's cook. My own claim to seafaring experience was limited to the ownership of a small sloop in Long Island Sound, but of Navy procedure I knew as little as the rest of the crew.

This, then, was the situation on a morning of snow and gale with the mercury at 8° below zero when a strange officer crossed

the boats which lay between us and the pier to come aboard.
I took his salute at the rail, certain from his appraising scrutiny
that this, at last, was our new Skipper. He was tall, lean and
brisk, with a quiet voice.

When he found that the executive officer was ashore he
ordered me to muster the crew. It was five minutes before the
last man had taken his place in line along the rail, some surly,
some hopeful, but all looking sloppy and uncared for. I suddenly
saw my shipmates through the officer's speculative eye as he
looked them over. Then, instead of giving the order himself he
called out the machinist's mate, the only chief petty officer in the
crew.

"Call the crew to attention, please, and report to me."

Jack called, "Attention!" Some of the boys straightened up,
others went on talking. At last Jack reported, apologetically,
"The crew is at attention, sir."

The officer produced a paper from which he read the orders
making him our commanding officer, then said, "At ease, men."
For a full minute he looked at us before he spoke again.

"We sail for European waters early tomorrow morning with
the first detachment of subchasers to serve in the war zone. I
shall do my best to make this a happy ship, which means a well
disciplined ship. You can make it so. Play square with me and
I shall play square with you." He paused and then smiled a
warm, personal smile which removed many uncertainties about
the future.

"Dismiss."

The petty officers were summoned to the cabin. Within an
hour order began to come out of chaos.

That night at Point Jude was bitter cold, for although the
wind dropped so did the temperature, to 10° below zero. Hot
food helped to restore morale which had already improved
with growing confidence in the new Skipper. By midnight station
bills had been posted, watches organized and routine duties
assigned. When I came on deck for the morning watch, the stars
were out and the decks cleared of snow, even at that hour of
lowest vitality auguring a better day.

From the division commander a flag hoist ordered us to weigh anchor at 8 :oo a.m., augmented by a semaphore message that we were to meet, off Newport, two seagoing tugs which were to escort us to Bermuda. Fortified by a hot breakfast and a day calm and crystal clear, we shoved through the ice to open water, presently to be joined by the comforting presence of our two tugs and a third flying the French flag, which had elected to join the convoy.

The Skipper examined the tug *Mariner* with particular interest.

"If that isn't the old *Knickerbocker* under a new name, I'm a Dutchman," he said, putting down the glasses. "New paint and new nameboards, but still the same old crate, wished off by the Navy on the Army Transport Service."

"What about her, sir?"

"One night in Smithtown Bay, tending target rafts in a northwester, she opened up and started to sink. My S.P. boat was anchored near enough to hear "S O S" signals on her whistle, so we came along and escorted her into Port Jeff where she was beached. The next day I helped her engineer officer caulk a seam in her bilge with a whole pair of dungarees. The Navy condemned her. How she happens to be under the A.T.S. flag now I don't know, but paint and putty has sold many a wreck. You and I, we're lucky to be aboard *143.*"

The other tug was named *Cherokee*. Little did we know that when we lost sight of her at dark that night neither we nor anyone else was ever to lay eyes on her or her crew again. All day the barometer rose; and a long swell came out of the northeast under a sapphire sky. At noon the Skipper took an observation and found that his executive officer had never learned to navigate.

"Get the positions of the other vessels when they report," he told the radio operator. When the positions were handed to him he was still at work over his figures. I noticed that the latitude and longitude he gave Sparks to send as our position was not taken from his own figures but was a slightly modified average of the other positions reported. So far as the rest of the crew was concerned he was an ace navigator but I wondered at the time what might happen to us if we separated from the convoy or our radio became disabled. He spent the rest of the watch studying Henderson's textbook on navigation.

The crew began to function in spite of seasickness and the ship was cleaner than she had ever been. When darkness came we felt as though we had been to sea all our lives, the sense of adventure strong in us, a small, isolated world in an immensity of heaving ocean among the scattered lights of the fleet.

At midnight the glass began to fall and at dawn it was obvious that we were in for a northeast gale; the swell was heavier; there was weight in the wind and low flying scud overhead. The eastern horizon, banked with dark clouds above a low lying streak of red, indicated a sunrise stillborn. Of our fleet there were in sight only four chasers and the tug *Mariner* on which we kept station at eight knots, rolling heavily in a quartering sea.

The day dragged its weary succession of watches, the glass still falling and the wind beginning to sing in the rigging as seas crested with whitecaps slapped occasional spray across the deck. Water warmer than the air as we approached the Gulf Stream gave welcome relief from the cold. For the first time I sweated at the wheel, thanking God that I was immune to seasickness. Even the Skipper had taken time from his navigational studies to go to the rail. Sparks picked up a message from the *Cherokee* reporting engine trouble, her position about 50 miles astern of our noon dead reckoning. No observations were possible.

At dark the *Mariner* flashed us a signal to reduce speed for the night which, for a while, made steering easier. All hands were on deck by choice. The Skipper had every man in his lifebelt and the sick ones secured by heaving lines. He himself had a long line tied under his arms, the other end fast to the signal mast. He was everywhere, covering hatches, plugging ventilators, securing deck gear, removing weather cloths, doing the work of three and pausing only to be sick.

The night was endless and steering increasingly difficult as the seas grew steeper and higher. With the boatswain's mate, I took 15-minute tricks, trying to keep the ship from broaching to, occasionally relieved by the Skipper who wanted to find out how she handled. From time to time a crash told of more damage on deck from solid water coming aboard. Once when the Skipper came in to ask for reports Sparks told him the *Cherokee* had sent an "S O S" signal that she was sinking and could not keep afloat till daylight. Our engineroom reported that we were taking more water than the pumps could handle.

The Skipper yelled back down the tube, "All the ventilators are gone but we have the holes plugged now. Rig up a strainer if you can't keep ahead of the water and put it on the circulating pump inlet. Don't forget to shut the seacock before you pull off the hose. That ought to give you enough capacity."

It was nearly dawn before the electric lights were short circuited but, thanks to low tension magneto ignition, the midship motor still continued to turn. The Skipper put his mouth to my ear. "Fetch her up the next time she broaches. Time we hove her to."

For a space she lay almost on her beam ends in the trough of the sea, then staggered up out of it, taking a cuff on the side of the pilothouse, as the next sea surged under her, which showered us with broken glass from the windows. For the first time we felt the full force of the gale which sang a new, wilder note to the creaking of the hull beneath us. Water six inches deep washed over the pilothouse floor.

"Hold her that way if you can. Take them diagonally."

She was easier to steer. Although each sea slammed the bow off a couple of points she rallied and climbed sluggishly up the face of the next one.

Dawn revealed a frightening seascape like nothing I had ever seen—racing seas, backs streaked with foam, and rearing crests which folded like breakers on a shoal. From time to time a crest would be plucked off by a fiercer squall to be transplanted bodily to the back of the next sea to leeward. In the limited visibility only the *Mariner* was in sight, hove to on our starboard beam a half mile away. She was down by the head, taking terrific punishment, the radio shack on the boat deck crumpled like an old cardboard box, her life boat gone and the funnel swaying crazily. No sign of life appeared on deck.

Our condition was not so bad. The crew were all accounted for on deck except the second officer, still in his bunk in a coma from seasickness. A manhole cover aft had carried away and the lazarette was awash to the deck, which helped to keep the propellers buried, though all food stores but the canned stuffs were ruined. Decks were swept clean of ventilators except for the two above the pilothouse, packed with signal flags. The wherry was still in its chocks, split from end to end. The shattered hatch of the radio room, which had received enough salt water to put both the spark set and the radio telephone out of commission, was partly protected by a collision mat over the forward end of the deckhouse. The aerials had flogged themselves into a braid streaming out to leeward from the masthead.

The Skipper finished his inspection. "All stripped for action. Bring on your submarines!" He slapped me on the back. "How's your courage, Chad? Want to lend a hand with the sea anchor?"

We might just as well have set out a rubber boot for all the good it did us. She was too high forward and too low aft to lie head to it; the drogue would not hold her head up at all. When we tried to see how she would handle stern to the sea we were dangerously swept even before we got the drogue out. After two hours of weary work we abandoned the effort, and the drogue, to return to our former angle. We were nearer the tug, which had now lost her funnel and was awash forward, each plunge showing her propeller still turning slowly. Some of the crew were clinging to the bitts on the stern, waiting. Obviously she could not live much longer and I wondered what our Skipper proposed to do.

A man on the bridge shouted, "Look at the yacht!"

Where she came from nobody noticed, but suddenly there she was, a big, single-funneled steel steam yacht painted Navy gray, abeam of the tug three seas to leeward, rolling her bulwarks under. The Skipper grabbed the glasses. *"Wadena,"* he said, "Must have answered an "S O S" after our radio quit. A sheer miracle they found her. Watch this."

From our wild little platform we watched an unsung rescue at sea, a piece of seamanship superb in planning and execution which went off as though rehearsed.

A ring buoy carrying a light line, put over the *weather* side of the yacht, went to windward as if driven by power.

The Skipper said, "That will give you an idea how much leeway the ships are making. The buoy stays still while the sea carries the two vessels down wind, the yacht away from it and the tug down on it. Look, they are picking up the line the first try!"

The men on the stern of the tug hauled aboard a block in the bight of a heavier line. When this was made fast a life raft on a painter was sent across. Three trips it made, each trip dragging back men who were scooped in over the rail of the *Wadena*. On the last trip, had we known it, was the able officer who subsequently replaced our executive. Within ten minutes the *Mariner* wearily lay down. Four seas passed over her. Then she was no more. The whole episode was unreal.

"Get our position before the yacht leaves," the Skipper shouted to me. I grabbed the semaphore flags, but could get no reply. Flying "Proceed" from her signal yard—the *Wadena* disappeared as suddenly as she had arrived.

The Skipper looked white and drawn, "O.K., Chad. We'll make it anyhow," he said.

With darkness approaching, the wind increased in velocity. Wild squalls screamed out of the murk which flung the little ship quivering broadside against the seas, half burying her under the press of wind and water. The crew, except for the helmsmen and the engineers, were lashed along the lee side of the house, most of them in a torpor of misery, drenched, weary, too seasick to feel hunger or thirst, too numbed to know fear. So appalling was the desolation, the force of wind and sea, the helplessness of our position, that darkness was a mercy. Loneliness gave place to the conviction that no structure built of wood could survive the wrenching onslaught of the great, invisible seas which assailed us out of blackness, lifting, battering, dropping us in an endless succession of dizzying falls, blinded and choked but hanging on.

Without lights except for the occasional gleam of a flashlight, it was impossible to check our condition. The ship was lower by the stern and making water fast. With the utmost difficulty, the hand pump on the deckhouse was kept in motion. Steering was no longer possible. With hard left rudder the average position was beam to the sea, the course SE.

The midship engine continued to run. One at a time six indomitable engineers were lowered on a line down the black pit of the engineroom hatch opened for an instant between seas, each in turn to stand with a hand on the air valve for as long as he could breathe in the emulsion of sea water, cylinder oil and battery acid thrown by the open cranks of the engine. All night long, kicking the engine over by compressed air to help the failing ignition, on the job for one minute, up for air for five minutes, vomiting, soaked with oil and burned with acid, for hours without end repeating the same routine, somehow they kept *143* going.

Perhaps the sea was no worse that next dawn, but it looked more terrifying because we were exhausted. Only the barometer gave promise of improved conditions, up three-tenths since nightfall. All hands had been without food or water for 40 hours and it was beginning to show in bloodshot, sunken eyes. With the Skipper, I crawled aft to the lazarette. He tended the line while I lowered myself in search of canned food under water turned opaque by flour gone adrift. After three tries I decided that the canned goods were under bags of coffee and sugar which I could not move. Until we could clear the compartment there was no food to be had. When the Skipper hauled me up my foot was stuck in a nest of buckets which proved a valuable find. Between seas we opened the galley hatch, but the water was up to the top of the stove. Two men were put to work bailing with buckets while a third opened and closed the hatch. After a trick at the hand pump I went back to the pilothouse. The glass showed signs of a further rise.

From the edge of visibility a great sea marched toward us,

towering above the intervening seas, a mountain of water lifting its ridge to the low flying scud above. We slid sluggishly down in the trough before it, cut off from the wind as it reared above us. It is all over now, I thought; she'll never come out of it. A lip of water rolled us toward the face of a cliff of water just as the crest broke and roared down over us. In the instant before the pilothouse filled with solid, swirling water I was aware of a cracking impact on the roof and a rending of woodwork which was lost in the roar of the descending avalanche. Holding my breath, I clung wildly to the wheel and felt my legs twisting as they were dragged out the lee window. Whether *143* was on her beam ends or bottom up I could not tell. Then, miraculously, I got a lungful of air and realized that the door had burst, freeing the pilothouse, and that we were afloat. On my feet again, my head bumped the overhead. The whole structure was crushed down and to starboard, flapping with the motion of the ship. The wheel was jammed by the bending of the vertical steering shaft, but by some magic the engine was still running.

Thoroughly frightened, I crawled out on the bridge where the Skipper had been. He was nowhere to be seen and I felt a sudden, cold dismay. The crew, wild-eyed, were picking themselves out of the scuppers, so far as I could see all accounted for. The Skipper's line led overboard, taut. Just then he came to the surface and as *143* forged ahead was dragged by his lifeline against the rail aft. As the ship rolled back he was over it and on his feet again, coming hand over hand to the bridge, unhurt.

The first job was to get under steering control. Continuously washed by seas, we managed to rig the six-foot iron tiller to the rudder head and set up the bolt. Next, some makeshift tackles were secured to the quarter bitts and two men lashed to the rail on each side to handle these improvised tiller lines. Then, with great difficulty, the steel steering cable which held the rudder rigid to the jammed gear was cut with a hacksaw. All measure of time was lost in fatigue and weakness. When the job was at last finished some of the weight had gone out of the wind and the seas had lengthened.

Hour after hour, pumping and bailing, the level of water went down. The Skipper encouraged the men, setting the pace and spelling the exhausted boys at the hand pump. The wind went down with the sun. At last we reached the canned goods.

Out of the Gulf Stream we found longer seas and clearing skies. The wind, moderating, hauled through south to west and died at sunset. Before dark the quarters were clear of water and a fire was going in the cookstove. For the first time, we could peel off wet clothes in balmy air, grateful to the skin. Our battered pilothouse was lashed in place but the bent steering shaft could not be straightened, so we steered by tiller and conned the ship from the bridge, indicating with a semaphore flag to the men aft which way to put the helm to keep an approximate compass course. Water, food and rest put the crew in buoyant reaction of spirits, even the worst of the seasick cases rallying to join in the conversations about shore leave in Bermuda. Not a vessel showed on the wide horizon and nobody spoke of the other chasers, whose possible fate was uppermost in everyone's mind.

The Skipper was absorbed in working a dead reckoning position. His afternoon fix, he confided to me, put us in Lake George, New York. He estimated that in spite of the easterly set of the Stream we had been carried 120 miles west of the base course. He was worried and so was I.

At sunrise the next morning all the wet gear was brought on deck to dry in the brilliant warmth of a summer sun as we monotonously dragged our wake across the immensity of a calm, empty sea. Ship's routine was fully restored. The Skipper worked morning, noon and afternoon sights and obtained a line of position which he said was much too close to where we ought to be for him to have confidence in it. To the rest of the crew, all was as it should be.

The Chief brought the gasoline report up to the bridge late that afternoon. "When do you plan to make Bermuda, Sir?" he asked. "We have only eight hours left in the tanks."

The Skipper looked at his watch as though we were running on a railroad schedule.

"Within an hour we should pick up Gibb's Hill Light," he answered gravely and called up to the man in the crow's nest. "Keep up a sharp lookout for a flashing white light."

Dusk fell rapidly on a stately sunset. Thirty minutes later a long drawn hail from aloft brought a cheer from the crew, "Gibb's Hill Light one point on the starboard bow!" I was the only one watching the Skipper's face. It was the only time I ever saw his emotion caught unawares. It would be hard to say whether astonishment or relief or gratitude predominated.

At last we raised St. David's Head, bathed in moonlight, and closed with some lights on a group of small vessels drifting a few miles offshore. They proved to be our French tug with three chasers in tow. The rest of the night we lay waiting for a pilot, silent and motionless on an ocean as tranquil as the gentle breeze which wafted to us the exciting odors of land.

The beauty of Bermuda in the light of dawn was surcease from cold, from fear, from struggle with the relentless sea. From that time, born of dangers shared and overcome in a common cause, there grew that indefinable spirit called morale that comes to good ships' companies. Compounded of pride without conceit and confidence without cocksureness, *143* had found herself. Of the whole detachment only two chasers had reached Bermuda under their own power; one of them had to be *143*. Of course she would, she was a good ship, with the best Skipper in the fleet.

Coming alongside the stone quay of His Majesty's Dockyard under the curious eyes of the British, the Skipper laid *143* neatly near the upper corner of the dock and rang for reverse. The engine coughed and died. A yell came up the voice tube that could be heard ashore, "No more gas, tanks dry!" With awful deliberation we rammed the dock.

The British sailors looking on were probably amazed to see an officer and an enlisted man shaking hands on the bridge of their vessel.

32

The Longest Way Home

by WILLIAM H. TAYLOR

[1941]

EVERY TIME, on a cruise, I hear somebody (myself, for instance) beefing because the ice is running low, or the engine's acting up, or the wind's from the wrong quarter, I know the complainer is getting old. If he'd just think back to some of the discomforts he put up with, some of the boats and equipment he was delighted with and some of the misadventures he survived in his early cruising days (unless he was unlucky enough to be born with a silver yacht in his mouth), and the fun he had in spite of it all, he'd feel better.

I have in mind, specifically, a cruise made about 1921. It wasn't a spectacular voyage. In fact, its sole claim to fame is that it was probably the longest cruise, in point of time, ever made from Boston to New Bedford *via* the Cape Cod Canal. Let others write lyrically about reeling off 200 sea miles a day. I give you a different sort of cruise; a cruise that, covering less than 80 miles as the navigator's fancy flies, took 11 days—or two months, depending on how you look at it.

It all happened because, as a youngster in the sophomore stages of both a college and a nautical education, I was bitten by the then-epidemic Maine sloop bug. So, thanks to indulgent parents, one fall day I found myself the owner of one, stored for the winter in an East Boston boatyard. She wasn't exactly a Friendship, which was what I'd had in mind, but she was reputed to

have been built by "one o' the Morse boys" nine years previous
as an improvement on the old clipper-bowed Friendship model.
The "improvement" part is debatable but she was a good little
boat for what she was.

She was 28 feet on deck, beamy and pot-bellied as a depot
stove, with a really handsome bow of the then modern fisherman
type and a stern that cocked up out of the water like a duck's
tail. In fact, I think her designer, if any, had a duck in mind, a
chunky, tough, seagoing little duck. She could ride out anything,
if you had sea room to leeward. Sound and tight, she was, though
planked with the widest planks I have ever seen twisted around
the rather sudden curves of such a fat little boat. Gaff-headed,
of course, with a rig of fisherman simplicity and a sail plan that
might have balanced if the bowsprit had been ten feet longer.

The former owner, a little old Down East lighthouse keeper
named Day, had been frank, though perhaps a trifle prejudiced.
She steered a mite hard, he said, and showed me a goodly length
of iron pipe to be slipped over the end of the tiller for extra lev-
erage when you needed it, which was always. He admitted her
sails were "kind o' tender," which was no exaggeration.

The engine, he said, wanted a mite of overhauling but it'd run
if you knew how. It was a two-cylinder, two-cycle, ten horse
make-and-break Mianus, coupled direct to a huge three-bladed
wheel. Day pointed out a spare igniter which he said would come
in handy, and he was right. The procedure was to clean and
adjust both igniters before you started and overhaul the third
as you went along. By the time the spare was ready, one of the
others would go dead and, by the time you'd replaced and fixed
that, it was time to put it back in place of one of the others. *Ad
infinitum.* You got used to it.

Her cockpit was small; her cabin, by my standards then, more
than adequate, having two big bunks with spring cushions (the
springs stabbed you in odd places but you got used to that, too) ;
a rusty coal stove complete with built-in backdraft; an enamelled
bucket by way of plumbing, and—well, that's about all except
for a small locker or two. The good sloop *WaWa* (Hiawatha

for goose, I believe) was no luxury liner, but we weren't paying luxury prices.

She was laid up in a little back-crick yard on the marshes between East Boston and Winthrop that was run by a beefy, red-faced old pirate, name of Benner. He's probably dead now. If he is, I know where he's gone. If not, I'll be glad to direct him. But that fall day he sounded most accommodating. Just a cheap outside paint job, and rig her? Sure. Have the engine gone over? Sure, he had a fine mechanic did such jobs for him; cheap, too. Wanted her in April? Kind of early, but, sure, he'd have her ready. Whole job wouldn't run over $40, way he figured it.

We mistook him for an honest man and went back to college, happy. We'd stop in Boston on our way home for April vacation and sail her home—an easy two-day cruise—"we" being Gardner Akin, who was my roommate, and myself. Both of us had owned boats and cruised up and down the coast every summer for years and were quite a handy pair of nineteen-year-olders in a boat.

Came April, and one fine spring morning we rolled up to the yard in a taxi loaded with boots, oilskins, heavy clothes, canned beans and a few other stark necessities. The idea was to get her home and then fit her up with new sails and whatever else she needed.

We looked at the creek, but no *WaWa*. We looked in the yard and there she was, just where we'd left her. Her engine had been overhauled, her mast varnished and her deck painted (badly)— which we hadn't ordered. Nothing else had been done. Friend Benner mumbled something about "Spell o' bad weather. Too damn early to put a boat over anyhow. Better leave her till later." Then he retired to aid some cronies in their project of spitting tobacco juice at a hot stove in his office.

Disappointed but determined, we turned to, and in two days of blistering hard work we painted and rigged her, all set to go. We interviewed Benner again.

"The bill's $80," he said.

I protested that he had agreed to $40, and that, besides, Gardner and I had done most of the work.

"There's yer boat, young feller," he growled. "Right up there on the railway, and there, by God, she stays till I get my money."

And there, by God, she did stay until he got his money, which involved telephoned explanations and a money order from home, and another day lost. Eventually, she got afloat, and very handsome she looked. But the engine wouldn't start.

No matter, said dear old Benner. He'd get the feller that overhauled it to come down next day and start it and pilot us out of the crick, which was crooked and shoal and unmarked and no stranger could possibly navigate it. Only cost us another five dollar bill. And so it was decided. Easter vacations don't last forever. Two friends, Al Bowers and Mouse Jackson, from M.I.T., were going along with us for the trip and, with a full crew, we'd drive her right through.

The mechanic—he looked like a younger edition of Benner—showed up a few hours behind schedule, finally managed to curse and beat the engine into activity, and disappeared again, saying the tide was too low to get out of the creek now and he'd be back when it flooded. It was past high water when he showed up again (fools we were not to have gone without him!) and getting dusk. He had a friend with him, also what was left of a gallon tin of what they called "Egyptian wine," the local variety of block-and-fall. With great assurance he started the motor, took the helm, and put us hard and fast on a mud flat a hundred yards downstream, on a falling tide.

Two or three hours later, the can of Egyptian wine being dry and the mud flat reasonably so, they left us, squishing knee deep in soft muck. I forgot to mention that I'd had to pay the five dollars in advance. (If anybody wants to sell the Brooklyn Bridge, see Taylor.)

Taking thought to the ways of college deans with students who overstay their vacations, also to the hazards of rotten sails and dubious engines, we knew we were licked. Around daylight, *WaWa* floated and we made sail (the engine wouldn't start) and went back to the dock. Just below the boatyard, a tiny creek made down through the marsh. Into this, on the top of the tide, we warped the sloop and moored her solidly in all directions. As the tide went out, her keel settled in the mud and the steep banks of the creek just nicely cradled her bilges. She couldn't have been more comfortable in a feather bed, and there we left her. Benner said he'd keep an eye on her and wouldn't charge us nothin', which he didn't, because we carefully ducked him when we came back for her in June.

So, up to this point, this tale of woe has been just a preamble to the eleven-day cruise I started to write about. It was a useful part of the educational processes youngsters who have led sheltered lives have to go through when they get out into the world and meet strange people—people like old Benner and his mechanic-pilot, whom may the Devil prod incessantly with red hot pokers.

By June, Gardner and I had forgotten the worst features of the April fiasco. Of course, we knew the boat wasn't really equipped to go anywhere. Her sails were rotten and of gear she had rather less than enough to scrape by on: an uncertain box compass, a few rusty tools, a frying pan and coffee pot and such odds and ends as had sufficed the undemanding Captain Day. We'd attend to such details when we got home. Meanwhile, it was just an easy two-day trip (they *never* learn), the weather ought to be good by now, and we'd yet to see the sailboat we couldn't take anywhere within reason. Se we grubbed up (bread, butter, eggs, canned beans and hash), filled the water jug and, at high tide, kedged *WaWa* out of her mud berth.

Wanting no more truck with pilots, we started at dead low water in the morning, chugged down the middle of the narrow channel between the bare mud flats, and cleared the mouth of the creek before the motor, which had been doing badly, stopped altogether. We made sail but what little air there was was dead ahead and we drifted around most of the afternoon, making little progress either toward home or in our efforts to start the motor, which was so stiff we could hardly move the flywheel.

Late in the afternoon we put our helm up and drifted into the Winthrop Yacht Club anchorage, no nearer home than when we started but at least two miles as the crow flies from the Benner boatyard, for which we thanked God. A sympathetic club steward found us a mechanic who agreed to come down in the morning and wrestle with the Mianus. The trouble, he found, was that our Egyptian friend had set all the bearings up too tight, put in oversize piston rings, and left the shaft out of line. After uncoupling the shaft, he finally got her started and then let her run idle, practically wide open, for an hour or so. This treatment limbered her up so we never had any more trouble starting her—only in keeping her going. So, along in midafternoon, we pulled out of Winthrop.

It was a dull, dead, gray afternoon, stark calm, as we chugged intermittently into Nantasket Roads. "Intermittently" because the engine had now developed a habit of blowing out the head gasket of the forward cylinder. Fortunately, one of Captain Day's legacies (he must have had the same trouble) had been a big roll of soft asbestos gasket material. I don't remember how many head gaskets we cut out that afternoon nor how many times we removed and bolted down the head, but invariably, sometimes after just a few revolutions and sometimes after five or ten minutes, she started squirting water into the forward cylinder again. In Nantasket Roads, we used the last of the gasket stuff—and it blew out again.

At dusk, a little air ruffled in out of the northeast and we wanted to put the rags to her and take advantage of the fair slant for the Canal. The trouble was that "rags" was too painfully accurate a description of our sails, and what weather sense we had told us that light breeze might turn into something nasty. The prospect of being caught on a lee shore in a no'theaster, with the sails blown off and the motor dead, seemed uninviting; reluctantly we anchored in the lee of Nantasket, warmed up a can of beans in the frying pan and rolled into our bunks. With two days' hard work behind us, we were still in Boston Harbor and less than six miles nearer home than when we started.

As it turned out the light no'theaster held all night and would have fanned us well down toward the Canal by morning, if we'd risked it.

We sailed soon after sun-up, and the last of the breeze left us abeam of Boston Light. In desperation, I lifted the cylinder head again, wadded up a crumb of wet asbestos, tamped it down in the blown-out spot and bolted the head down hard. This scientific repair lasted all season, and it was fully half an hour before the motor stopped again.

It was a plugged feed line this time. We could get the thing to run for a minute or two at a time and, with this and occasional catspaws of air, we worked her into Cohasset, where another mechanic took the line and carburetor apart and, for the time being, opened them up to traffic. We were under way once more late in the afternoon but the weather looked owly again and by now we'd lost faith in everything, so we holed up for the night in Scituate, the motor having stopped only once—igniter trouble —en route. It was our best day so far, with a dozen miles made good.

It was breezing on fast out of the southeast next morning when we motored down Scituate Harbor, turning in a reef just to play safe. It was half tied down when we swung around the jetty and plunged into a heavy sea and, of course, the engine stopped dead again. It was a grand scramble then, with the sea breaking high over the jagged rocks a few yards under our lee, to get sail drawing and fill away, but somehow we made it and she clawed off just when it seemed as though the next sea would surely land her on top of the jetty.

For the next few hours we really had a grand sail, sloshing along into a rising wind and sea under reefed mainsail and jib— a long port tack down the beach and a short offshore hitch to keep sea room. We were well soaked through but enjoying every bit of it and making hard-earned progress toward home when, off High Pine Ledge, the foot of the jib split clear across. Then it was out on the bowsprit, and a merry job, mostly under water, of stowing the jib. Without it, however, she just lay to comfortably under the reefed mainsail, so I had to swarm out again and hoist a few feet of the head of the sail to keep her bow off. We wallowed and thrashed another two slow miles to windward, until we could ease sheets and drive her in past the Gurnet with a smashing breeze over the quarter.

Just inside Goose Point, the Plymouth Harbor channel runs to the east of south, narrow between mudbanks that dry at low water, and we were short-tacking laboriously up this slough when the Boston-Plymouth excursion steamer took a notion to start home. She was using most of the channel. We couldn't hold a luff long enough for her to pass, and there was no room for us to tack either side of her. It looked like the mud for poor old *WaWa* once more, but Gardner dove into the cabin and gave the flywheel a spin. Astoundingly, our little cast iron joker started with a roar. I put her into the wind and we skinned through between the mudflat and the steamer's guard rail. The motor died again just as we cleared her stern. We filled away and, a few minutes later, laid her neatly alongside the town pier and doused our watersoaked canvas.

In four days of hard, uphill work we'd made less than 40 miles. Our hands were blistered raw, we were wet and sore and weary, and we were dirty. We'd started with one cake of soap and a towel but *WaWa's* water supply wasn't adequate for much washing even if we hadn't been too tired to care. Salt and dirt and engine grease and smoke were ground into our hands and arms and faces and hair. We were nearly out of grub and, having started with little cash and contributed to the support of two machine shops en route, we were broke.

It was at this point that we met Old Man Haire, and if ever a man restored two youngsters' flagging faith in humanity it was Old Man Haire. Old Man Haire ran a restaurant opposite the dock and he was sitting alone behind his counter, a huge, stooped, bony frame of a man with a round black skullcap on his old bald head, when Gardner and I, having snugged everything down and rigged makeshift fenders against the barnacled piling, went looking for something to eat. We hadn't the price of a meal between us, and didn't look as though we ever had had or would have. I don't know why he didn't chase us out when we came dripping into the restaurant, dirty, soaked, weary and disgusted, lugging a couple of gallon jugs which, if refilled, would constitute the *WaWa's* total water supply. Maybe we looked honest under the dirt, or maybe the old boy had been in such scrapes himself half-a-hundred years earlier.

We told him who we were, and how and why, and he took us right under his wing. He showed us soap and hot water and towels, and staked us to a phone call home to New Bedford and to two colossal meals of steak'n'taters'n'onions'n'everything, than which no meal ever tasted better. He even loaned us money to buy supplies with. He was quite a man. If I ever get to Heaven, I expect to find him dishing up short orders and seafood specials over a cloud counter somewhere.

Life seemed a good deal less desperate by the time we got back to the boat late in the afternoon, though by then it was blowing a real old-fashioned southeast gale, with sheets of rain. It wasn't a bit better next morning but we were in a fairly snug berth. Also, we had company. Two ancient fishermen in a decrepit "sloop boat," the *Beulah Maude,* were tied up next to us. They were gill-netting, chugging out evenings, when the weather looked good, to make a night set in Cape Cod Bay and pick up fish enough to keep them in grub, gas and tobacco. But only when the weather looked good.

"The old gal's a mite weak in the stummick," the skipper explained resignedly. "We have to pump too durned much when it gits rugged." Currently, they were, like ourselves, pretty much out of everything and with no prospects until the weather cleared, which we agreed wouldn't be for another day or two at least. We made a congenially dismal quartet.

I was reasonably contented. I had all summer. It had to clear some time and the remaining 40 miles couldn't be much worse than those we'd already lived through. But Gardner, the able shipmate who had cheerfully stuck with me through all this, was booked to sail for Europe in a few days and, when the third day found our southeaster unabated, his family drove over to bring him home. It was going to be lonesome without him. Besides, I needed a new crew and some money; thoughts of home and Mother and a hot bath overcame my "stick to the ship" principles. We doubled up *WaWa's* dock lines and fenders, asked

Beulah Maude's boy friends to keep an eye on her and I rode home, too.

Next day, Father drove me back, with a new crew, John Allen, who, like myself, didn't have to be anywhere special until the fall. Also, we brought Bill LaCasse, a first class marine engine man. Bill shucked off his coat and ripped out the gas tank, the piping and most of the detachable parts of the Mianus. When he got through and put everything back together again, he said: "Now she'll run," and went home.

And run she did. She actually went almost half a day without stopping and all the rest of the way home the only thing that bothered her was her igniteritis which, as I've said, was a chronic ailment that even old man Mianus himself couldn't cure for keeps.

Meanwhile, we had to lay over another day in Plymouth, because the gale had been followed by a burgoo fog that obscured even the mud flats across the channel. (And when you can't see mud flats in Plymouth at low water, it's *really* thick.) It was still thick next morning (the ninth since we'd left East Boston) but it looked brighter overhead and we started. Sure enough, the fog burned off and we had a nice motor boat ride down to the Canal in a flat calm.

About two-thirds of the way through the Canal, when we were beginning to think that maybe the jinx had left us, the motor died and there was nothing for it but to anchor and hope no big steamers came through. What did come was the Canal patrol boat, her crew annoyed with us for being anchored in the middle of their ditch. I don't know what they thought we should have done.

"We got orders to get you out of here," the skipper said. With some 200 horsepower working on the far end of that towline, the poor little *WaWa* sat up on her duck-tail stern, her bowsprit pointing skyward, and, though she groaned and complained about it, she traveled as she never had before. Her progress was accompanied by a loud gurgling sound we couldn't explain until we discovered a geyser spouting under her after deck and running down into the bilge. *WaWa* had a square, open-topped rudder port and, skating along on her tail like that, it made an elegant waterspout.

When the Canal launch dropped us off Monument Beach, there was a nice little sou'west breeze, so we made sail and worked her into Onset where, late that afternoon, we got a garage job done on the igniters that lasted for several hours running. Next morning we found the usual fresh Buzzards Bay sou'wester kicking the shallow upper end of the bay into a straight-up-and-down chop. We tucked a reef in the mainsail and drove her into it, under sail and power, with the spray flying masthead high, until our decayed mainsail let go at the leach and started to rip in along the reef points. We got it off and headed her straight for home under power alone. If you've ever tried to plug a short, fat boat square to windward in one of those upper Buzzards Bay chops, you'll readily understand that, while we were piling up mileage vertically, we made practically no progress horizontally. After a while, we gave it up and swung off for Marion where we laid the sail out to dry in the afternoon sun.

Neither of us was any great shakes as a sailmaker and the canvas was so far gone that every needle-prick started a new tear but we got it basted up after a fashion. Fortunately, the next day the air was light.

The eleventh and last day of *WaWa's* Odyssey we covered the last few miles. We motored most of the way and repaired igniters three or four times but a little breeze sprang up eventually and we did manage to make the last couple of miles to our mooring at Salters Point under sail.

I wouldn't want the reader to get the idea that this perilous voyage soured us either on the boat or on cruising in general. We cruised in her for the next two seasons—in fact, until the pinch of having to earn my own living made itself felt. A little fixing up below and above decks made a comfortable small cruiser of her. She'd take what came in the way of weather and, with a new suit of sails, she was a satisfactory though by no means a brilliant sailer. The engine never was worth a damn. When the igniters weren't giving trouble, it was because something else had busted so we couldn't run it at all—except for the last trip we made in her. Coming home from Nomansland after a late fall codfishing trip, for no reason at all, she ran all the way to New Bedford without a skip. That winter I sold her.

33

A Line Squall Off Cape Hatteras

by A. C. STRONG

[1934]

Temptress, returning from a winter's cruise, anchored off old Fort Marion, St. Augustine. We were in from the Little Bahama Bank, British West Indies, and we hoisted the yellow flag. It was practically an entrance in distress, for we had eaten ourselves out of house and home during the last weeks in the islands.

No one paid any attention to the quarantine flag. There was enough gin and vermouth left for cocktails, however, authentic Dutch gin and Italian vermouth, and it was cocktail time. Thus fortified, the skipper rowed ashore.

There was a flurry in the Custom House, and notable goings on in a grocery store. Fresh tomatoes and asparagus, new potatoes, baker's bread and fresh meat came aboard along with the Custom Officer and the *pro-tem* Port Doctor. The doctor brought a stethoscope, tongue depressors, and a thermometer in a black bag full of pills; and if Bert, Bob, Don and the skipper had not looked so offensively robust and tanned, he would have used them all. Obtaining pratique at St. Augustine was a novelty for all concerned.

Next day, Bob and Bert steered a Ford towards Chicago, while Don and I explored the old town and sat on deck in the pleasant spring weather. We were waiting for a new shipmate from North Carolina. Sonny joined in a few days, and we waited again, with an ear to the radio, for the wind to haul easterly.

We sailed for Charleston at daybreak on May 5th. This was Sonny's first trip to sea and St. Augustine Inlet is a proper preface to the sea. It is not much better marked than when Ponce de Leon sailed in (he must have been a navigator). The shrimp fleet, going out, all passed us, and we followed until they lost us near the lighthouse. The devious way out had two rusty red, third-class nuns, where the channel rounds a spit. There were breakers on either hand, and tide rips and confused currents made smacks behave like corks. Smacks and yachts. Then, after passing the lighthouse and the land and having lost the fleet, we discovered the black can buoy. It was craftily hidden in the curve of ground swells, two miles to seaward, and beyond it was the sea buoy rolling in the ocean. We crossed the bar.

A delightful three days' sail followed, out of sight of land. The sea was smooth. Gentle to moderate easterly and southeasterly breezes kept the balloon staysail pulling like a team of horses. And there were calms and the need of a gasoline breeze. On the third day, Charleston's lighthouse appeared ahead, and Charleston's afternoon southwester shoved us briskly up the ship channel.

All the romance a town possesses is presented to the sea. Auto tourists entering Charleston, or any other town, discover it to be surrounded by frightful suburban rubbish, gasoline pumps, and hot dog stands. Not so the mariner. Charleston's waterfront is like an old print or a painting by Van der Velde. Stately white mansions on Bay Front lead to the Battery, where, under ancient trees, a few old cannon justify the name. The Custom House is a classical model for all custom houses, the Carolina Yacht Club looks exactly like a yacht club and, beyond the shore line of docks and old warehouses, the lovely spires of St. Michael's and St. Philip's rise above the town. A bark and several brigantines are needed in the foreground but there were yachts, a famous English cutter, a sloop, two schooners, a yawl, and the ketch *Temptress* to point the view.

It is easy to linger in Charleston, especially in the spring. A very pleasant week passed, and the wind hauled around again southeasterly. "He who drinks Goose Creek water for two weeks never leaves Charleston." We filled the water tanks again and sailed in time.

On May 15th we took our departure from Charleston sea buoy for Frying Pan Lightship. Friends in the schooner *Sea Horse* had sailed three days before. I had a hunch that we would beat them to Hampton Roads. Late that afternoon the *Hector* buoy came abeam. It is a convenient wreck about 50 miles from Charleston, on the course around Cape Fear. It gives an irrefutable answer to the skipper's guess on leeway, on time signals and on the patent log.

May 16th, at sea. A broadcast receiver is useful for coastwise cruising. The range at sea is remarkable. Sopranos and crooners are next-door neighbors (damn them!), but there is useful information to be had. At noon I received time and weather not only from Jacksonville, but from Miami as well. They agreed on both: "Hatteras to Florida Straits, Moderate S. Fair weather." There was a high along the Carolina coast. Our glass had been rising ever since leaving Charleston.

"Well," I said, "let's sail around Hatteras."

The ship's company was delighted. Don is a salty youth, and Sonny had taken to the sea. I suspected that glass, but here was our chance to beat the *Sea Horse.* Noon sight, Lat. 33° 25' N.

The Frying Pan soon appeared ahead, a chunky lightship tailing to the Gulf Stream. We steered for it ENE to give it a wireless on change of destination. The southeasterly breeze was light and the lightship appeared on the starboard bow. The course was changed a point to windward, and presently she was on the starboard bow again. During a three-hour hare and tortoise race with the Stream, we changed our course from ENE to SSE and, close hauled to the little breeze, finally slid across her stern, going sidewise like a hay stack. We blew a conch shell. The crew of the lightship popped on deck. They goggled over the stern at our crab-like maneuver. Could we send a message ashore? We could.

"I'll send over a small boat," said the captain of the Frying Pan. We doused the balloon staysail and came about. The lightship receded southerly, as two sailors pulled over in a yellow dory.

"Say, buddy," I said, "how fast does the Gulf Stream flow hereabouts?"

"This here Gulf Stream," said buddy, scratching a chest like an astrakhan muff, "flows four knots." Thus proving again that natives are nearly always wrong about local phenomena. Our anchored mariners took the message and a bundle of newspapers and magazines. They gave us a typed slip: "Hatteras to Florida Straits, mod. S. Fair weather." That made the day unanimous.

As we jibed over and headed for Cape Lookout Lightship, the dory gained the Frying Pan. Against four knots? Well, hardly. The lightship receded, and the southeast breeze freshened a trifle that night. Fair wind and fair tide.

May 17th, at sea. The log reads: "A high dawn. Wind? Chinese lantern sunrise." For an instant a collar at the sun's lower limb stuck to the horizon. An hour later a steamer suddenly appeared over the bow. She loomed vertical and grotesque, with great stacks and masts. High visibility and refraction. Easterly blow coming? The breeze hauled to south as predicted. It was very light.

At 9:30 A.M. Cape Lookout Lightship was abeam and nearly hull down. We had averaged only 4.2 knots since leaving the Frying Pan. The sails slatted. Took the main and jib off. The light air filled the balloon staysail. The mizzen made pretenses. Logged 2.5 knots. There was gasoline only for emergencies. The noon weather report read: "Southerly winds, shifting to moderate NE; overcast." I didn't like the "shifting," or the "NE," either, and the weather man's idea of moderate often turns out to be fresh. But I'd rather be at sea than run back to Beaufort and attempt that entrance in a blow. We held our course. The light air failed, and we ran the little motor all afternoon. I wanted to get around Cape Hatteras before the weather changed.

Sunset with mares' tails. There were angry clouds that night. A fine breeze came in from the SW. We saw lots of traffic rounding Hatteras, and the ballooner hid the lee sidelight.

Took the ballooner off, furled the team of horses and we slowed down perceptibly.

May 18th. Off Hatteras. 12:35 A.M. Diamond Shoal Lightship and Hatteras Light in line. Hatteras on the horizon. Many steamers. 7:00 A.M. Red and angry sunrise. Bar. 30.20, steady. We held a northeasterly course. Just as well to get offshore when the radio and sky agreed. 8:00 A.M. Morning sights put us seven miles east of our D.R. position. Gulf Stream or bum observations? But I'm always gratified when sights taken from a bobbing cork may be charted on the adjacent ocean.

I was thinking pleasant morning thoughts while at the wheel, digesting a notable breakfast of coffee, grits, bacon and eggs. Just then I looked ahead. Digestion ceased. Far ahead on the northern horizon, and extending as far as I could see on either hand, was a low roll of white clouds. There was a high haze above it.

"Line squall coming! Stow that ballooner! Get the fore staysail on her . . . Slickers . . . and secure a few frying pans in that galley!"

The Pilot Chart of the North Atlantic Ocean, November, 1929, has an article on the back entitled "Line Squall." Ample time to read it before the squall hits.

"The characteristic long cloud roll may extend in an advancing line for 1000 miles. . . . In many line squalls this rolling cloud is obscured by larger cloud masses, and it is often not clearly seen. . . . The violent rolling motion peculiar to clouds in a line squall is limited to the first 2000 to 6000 feet, while above it the intense vertical currents of thunder storms may reach 20,000 feet or more. A most amazing state of turbulence is often revealed by the motion of cloud fragments, just after the passage of a line squall. . . . Some or all of the following characteristics are observed, although all of them seldom occur in the same line squall.

"Sudden change of wind direction; heavy rain (or hail or snow); thunder and lightning; rapid fall of temperature; rapid rise of relative humidity; very rapid rise of barometric pressure.

"These phenomena result from the advance of air masses of

recent polar origin, along a 'polar front,' like the advance of a battle front; and an area covered by warm air of recent tropical, or sub-tropical origin is overcome. . . . The speed of advance is usually 25 to 35 m.p.h., but in some cases up to 60 m.p.h. or more. . . . The barometer rises rapidly when the line squall passes overhead, and the wind suddenly changes its direction clockwise (in the northern hemisphere) from 90° to 180°. . . . The chief characteristic is a rapid fall of temperature, 20° or more in a few minutes."

We had ample time to snug her down. A picture was taken of the advancing squall, and of the skipper prepared for the worst. The sea was smooth, the southwesterly breeze still held, and the line squall approached from the north. Just before it hit us, we saw two steamers in a haze, far off the port bow. They were heading southerly under the advancing front. Smoke from their stacks rushed in a horizontal plane ahead of them. Scudding before the squall, the steamers looked windy and indistinct.

Then the rolling cloud line passed over *Temptress*. She crossed beneath a covered way, which extended from the east to the west, a covered way with a turbulent roof. And then the wind suddenly shifted from SW, Force 2, to NE, Force 4. At once it was cold and the barometer rose .06 inches.

I kept her on the port tack as the wind hauled. We sailed east, close hauled and very fast. The wind gradually increased. We tacked and tied two reefs in the mainsail before the sea made up.

A course full and by (NbyW) paralleled the beach and left nothing for leeway. I have no illusions about the weatherly qualities of the *Temptress* (or of any other small yacht) in a really bad sea. The sea made up and I started the motor. We beat to windward the rest of that day on the starboard tack. The wind increased, possibly to Force 6, but I have never seen shorter or steeper seas with so little wind. They were portentous seas, and they came in series. *Temptress* would rise to the first two, then the third would stop her dead, and she would fall off to leeward. She is a dry boat, but that day she lost all the varnish on her booby hatch, not to mention the bowsprit, and torrents of water rushed aft. *Temptress* had not been sailed hard all winter, and the tropics had dried her topsides. We pumped her every hour that day, and we always wondered if the pump would suck.

The seas became worse, and I didn't dare to drive her. The motor was kept idling, and we sailed her very scant of wind, looking for the beach to leeward. Steamers passed to leeward; so far, so good. A freighter came up astern, under slow bell. It was heavy going for her, too, and we kept her in sight for hours until she melted in the haze two points to windward. If we could only do as well.

Noon weather report, Norfolk, "Fresh NE and E," which was no news. We prayed for the wind to haul easterly, but it stayed in the NE and blew some more. Cloudy all day.

The line squall hit at 10:00 A.M. and we raised the beach about one o'clock that afternoon. I said it was a steamer, but it wasn't a steamer, it was a large building on the beach. At two we raised Bodie Light in the NW. The Platt Shoals in this vicinity have six to eight fathoms over them. And now the seas became really bad. If the motor failed, I might have clawed offshore on the port tack, but I do not know. A motor is a life saver in any small yacht.

We were close to the beach near Nag's Head at five. I could see the breakers. We tacked and stood offshore for an hour. The seas seemed worse on the port tack. We came about and tried it again, but we were too close to the beach. At dusk the white dunes of Nag's Head glowed in the failing light. They were dead ahead. Tacked and put to sea for three hours. My watch below, and I could sleep with the open ocean ahead. We were clear of all shoals. Bodie Light bore SW½W at 10:30 P.M. We tried the starboard tack again. The seas were not quite so bad, though they were steep enough, and we should raise Currituck Light before we went ashore.

May 19th. On a lee shore. I slept the rest of my watch below, and Don raised Currituck Lighthouse at 2:30 A.M. It was abeam by four, and then the wind hauled a point. We could sail north.

False Cape whistler was abeam at 7:15 next morning and we

began looking for the land. Found it at eight o'clock and it was not a pleasant sight. The seas had let down a trifle, or we had become accustomed to them, and the little motor chugged sedately until it coughed a few times, about ten o'clock—and died. The gasoline tanks were empty.

By that time Virginia Beach was abeam and Cape Henry Lighthouse appeared dimly over the port bow. The breeze was no fresher, so we shook out the reefs in the mainsail, and windjammed up the coast, N½W with started sheets. Good old crock!

At noon Cape Henry was brought abeam, and we sailed into the bay in a nasty tide rip but, oh, my fellow yachtsmen, with eased sheets. With a fresh breeze it is an afternoon's sail into Hampton Roads.

Temptress lay at anchor in Hampton Creek by five—three and a half days out of Charleston. We had beaten the *Sea Horse* and *Old Ocean* as well.

34

A Mutiny in the South Atlantic

by HERBERT L. STONE

[1915]

In this day of steam, submarine cables and wireless, bringing into closer touch all the ports of the civilized world, mutiny on the high seas is virtually a thing of the past. There are still, of course, isolated cases of crews refusing duty, of an occasional murder of an officer or a seaman, and of a vessel having to return to port on account of insubordination, but these are cases where there is no organized attempt to get control of the ship and that entail no great loss of life. If the port of missing ships could give up its story, it might be found that mutiny was responsible for the posting as "missing" of some ships in recent years; but stress of weather, overloading and improper stowage of cargo, or fire, are the more probable causes of their disappearances.

We forget quickly, however, and probably no one outside of those intimately connected with the tragedy recall a mutiny that for its fiendishness and bloodshed was the equal of any that history can produce. Yet it happened not so many years ago, and the captain of the ship and a number of those aboard of her on that memorable voyage are still alive.

It was in the latter part of January, 1886, that a news dispatch from the island of St. Helena in the South Atlantic reported the landing on the island of a ship's boat containing 17 persons, five of whom were badly wounded, survivors of the American ship *Frank N. Thayer*, which had been lost some 700 miles to the south'ard in a mutiny in which seven of her men had been killed. Here is the full story of the tragedy as it was told me by the captain himself some months afterwards.

The *Frank N. Thayer* was a fine three-skysail-yard American ship sailing "deepwater" out of New York and Boston under command of Capt. Robt. J. Clarke. She had discharged a cargo in the Far East and loaded hemp at Manila for New York. She carried a crew of 22 men all told—16 forecastle hands, a carpenter, two mates, cook, steward and the captain. Besides these Captain Clarke had with him his wife and seven-year-old daughter.

Anchor was weighed at Manila on November 1 with everyone in high spirits at being homeward bound once more, and it was a cheerful gang that manned the capstan bars to heave short that morning. The forecastle hands were mostly Scandinavians or "Dutchmen," as all North Germans are called in American vessels, but among them were two Malay Indians, shipped at Manila to take the places of two deserters. It was a common practice in deep water vessels to ship Malays for the homeward passage from the Far East, and they usually made excellent sailors. The two on the *Thayer* were swarthy, silent little devils, fair sailors though taciturn, and for the first two months required no more of the mates' attention than any of the rest of the crew.

A few days out from Manila one of the Malays came aft and in a broken Spanish *patois* complained of being sick. After looking the man over Captain Clarke gave him a dose of salts from the medicine chest. This he refused to take, and, to prevent any shirking of duty, he was given a cut over the shoulder with the end of a clewline coiled on the pin rail. Thus admonished, he swallowed the dose and went forward sullenly.

Nothing was thought of the incident, and the *Thayer* bowled down the China Sea before a favoring monsoon, had a fair passage across the blue Indian Ocean, round Good Hope, and into the South Atlantic, where her nose was pointed northward. New Year's day found the ship some 800 miles south of St. Helena with yards trimmed to the fair South East Trades.

There had been no more than the usual friction of a deep
water voyage between the mates and the men forward, but on
the evening of January 2, as the watch going below tried the
pumps at eight o'clock, as is the custom on wooden vessels, the
mate had occasion to speak sharply to one of the Malays. He
answered back and the mate struck him, but the watch turned in
and the incident was apparently forgotten.

It was a glorious night, the ship bowling along under royals
and skysails in the strong Trades, the sky studded with stars
and overhead the constellation of the Southern Cross. Captain
Clarke remained on deck until late, smoking and enjoying the
evening. It was after ten o'clock when he went below, leaving
the deck to the second mate, and turned in with no more thought
of trouble than he had of piling up on Diamond Shoals before
morning. Subconsciously he heard the watch changed at midnight, and turning over dropped off to sleep again. How long he
slept he does not remember, but he was awakened suddenly by
hearing a voice call, "Cap'n Clarke, Cap'n Clarke!"

He sprang up, thinking the mate wanted him for a squall, or
something, and without waiting to dress, started up the after
companion steps, just outside of the door of his room, his eyes
heavy with sleep. As he reached the top step a figure sprang
on him from behind the companion door and he received a blow
on the head from a sheath knife that laid his face open from
forehead to chin. Staggered for a moment, the captain blindly
grappled with his assailant, and began a struggle on the steps
for the possession of the knife. Down the steps they fought, the
captain dragging his assailant after him till he could reach the
firmer footing of the cabin floor. As they reached the bottom
step, however, Captain Clarke slipped in the blood from his
wound that was already blinding him, and his adversary, wrenching himself free, plunged his knife deep into the captain's left
side and abdomen and jumped back up the stairs to deck, leaving
Captain Clarke for dead. As he jerked himself free the captain
recognized in his assailant one of the Malay Indians.

The captain was a powerful man of great vitality, and though
badly wounded he staggered to his room in the dark and got out

his revolver, merely telling his wife that he had been hurt, returning to the passageway containing the companion steps. As he had received no help from the man at the wheel—the only man at hand—and getting no response to his call to the mate, he supposed that the former was also concerned in the attempt on his life and called out to him to shut the companion doors.

"I can't, sir," answered the man.

"Why not?" asked the captain.

"Because there's some one there by it," was the reply.

Captain Clarke then backed into the cabin and shut and locked the door between it and the passageway from which the companion steps led. Then he staggered through the forward cabin to shut the door leading from there to the pilothouse and poop deck. As he came back he stumbled heavily in the dark over some one on the floor of the vestibule, and calling to his wife for a light it was seen that it was the body of his second mate, W. Davis, lying dead on the floor outside of his room. Getting no response to his call for the mate strengthened Captain Clarke in his opinion that his entire crew was in mutiny and that his first mate was dead also, as he would have made some effort to aid him were he alive. Making his way back into the after cabin, Captain Clarke heard some one at the passageway door which he had first locked.

"Who's there, and what do you want?" he asked.

A man answered: "Hide me, Captain; hide me!"

Thinking it was one of the mutineers, Captain Clarke pushed back the sliding panel in the door and saw one of the sailors, Hendricsen by name. Covering the man with his revolver, he asked what he wanted. The man only replied as before, asking to be hidden. Though the sailor was apparently laboring under fright the captain, in his state of uncertainty as to the extent of the uprising, was afraid to trust him with no more explanation and fastened the panel after ordering the man to go away. A bathroom opened off this passageway, and this the sailor entered, locking himself in.

By this time the captain was very weak from loss of blood, both wounds being very painful and the lower lobe of one lung protruding from the wound in his side. He sank down on the transom in the after cabin while his wife attempted to staunch the flow of blood and bind his wounds, the captain as she did so attempting to cover the door and skylight with his revolver. As his wounds were being treated the little party in the cabin could hear some one going around on deck closing the wooden shutters of the cabin windows and fastening the doors on the outside. Facing the balance of the night locked in, shut off from any outside help and in the belief that the whole crew was in mutiny was not a cheerful prospect. The Chinese steward, Ah Sam, was the only man besides the mates and the captain's family who berthed aft, and he was called, but at the first sight of the blood-stained cabin he had run to his room and locked himself in. It was only by threats of shooting that he was finally induced to come out and assist Mrs. Clarke in dressing her husband's wounds. He was absolutely useless for defense. In this state they waited for daylight.

While all this had been going on below the mutineers had been equally busy on deck. This is what had happened:

When the watch had been changed at midnight the second mate had not gone below at once, but with the mate sat on the booby hatch on the poop deck talking over the work laid out for the next day. The wheel had been relieved and there was absolutely no sign of danger when the two Malays, on their bare feet, skulked aft in the shadow of the rail, climbed the poop ladder, and crawled up behind the mates, falling upon them with their sheath knives and stabbing both several times in the back. The second mate had only life enough to stagger to his cabin without a cry, where he fell dead at the door of his room. The first mate, wounded to the death, made his way forward to get help from the men, and fell through the foc's'le door, where before dying he told the sailors that the two Indians had stabbed him. Seeing the mates stabbed, the man at the wheel called out for Captain Clarke. At his cry the captain had come on deck, but, as one of the Malays had been lurking close to the wheel waiting for the captain, the sailor did not dare utter a warning or tell the captain the true state of affairs, while the other men of the watch, seeing the commotion, had followed the mate into the foc's'le.

Realizing that they had only the Indians to deal with, six of the sailors of the mate's watch made a half-hearted sortie armed with capstan bars, but the Malays jumped upon them with knives from the corner of the forward house and stabbed four of them, the other two running aft; one, Hendricsen, into the after companionway, where he asked the captain to hide him, the other jumping into the main rigging and running aloft, unseen by the Indians. The wounded men made their way back into the foc's'le, where they locked the door from the inside.

The foc's'le was divided into halves by a solid bulkhead, so that the starboard watch had no communication with the port watch, and the Malays had taken the precaution to lock the door of the starboard foc's'le on the outside before the watch was alarmed. Then they locked and barricaded the door of the other foc's'le on what remained of that watch, all four of whom were wounded.

The Malays had now complete possession of the forward part of the ship and went aft again. Finding that they could not get the man in the bathroom, they stabbed the man at the wheel, who offered absolutely no resistance, and from the bathroom window Hendricsen saw them throw his body overboard. Then they went forward, opened the door into the carpenter's room in the after end of the forward house and killed him, and then the lookout on the foc's'le head. The Chinese cook in the galley was now the only one not accounted for, and they locked him in from the outside and by threats forced him to cook for them during the time they had charge of the ship. The cook said later that he tried to poison them by putting sulphur from matches in their coffee, but that it had no effect on them.

This was the true state of affairs when morning dawned on January 3, though Captain Clarke only had cognizance of what had actually transpired before his eyes. The captain lay between life and death, propped up on a cabin transom with a revolver in his hand, and, as no concerted move was made on the cabin during the hours of darkness, he surmised that the Malays were the only ones in the mutiny. When daylight came he fired a few shots through the skylight to show those forward that he was alive, in the hopes that some help might come from them, but the men who were left were craven. While eight of the watch which had been below were still uninjured, they made no concerted movement during the next two days to break out and aid the after-guard, though they knew that the captain, or at least his wife and child, were still living.

All that day the Malays had charge of the ship, which lay with sails aback in the light South East Trades, and prowled around the quarterdeck peering cautiously in at the skylights to get some token that the captain was dead, and all the while the captain sat propped up on the cabin transom suffering intensely, but the flow of blood stopped by the use of absorbent cotton. He got the steward to call to the sailor in the bathroom to know if he was of the mutineers, but for some reason could get no answer. Late that afternoon the captain saw through the skylight the sailor hiding aloft. He was discovered at about the same time by one of the Malays, who started aloft after him with his knife fastened on the end of a bar. The sailor kept him off, however, with a block on the end of a lanyard. The captain then made up his mind that he only had the two Malays to deal with.

Another night of suspense followed, but in the morning the fresh water in the cabin became exhausted. As there was an extra cask in the bathroom the captain, though very feeble, staggered to the door, revolver in hand, and called to Hendricsen to unlock it. Covered by the pistol, he opened it, and then told what he should have told the first night, of everything that had taken place on deck, of the wounded men forward and of the death of the two mates. With Hendricsen in the cabin something more could be done. Directed by the captain, he stood upon the cabin table until he could see out of the skylight, and with a rifle from the captain's room kept up a fire upon the Indians whenever they appeared. They had, however, built a barricade across the roof of the cabin, just forward of the skylight, made out of a door on edge, some planks, and the mattress and pillows from the murdered carpenter's room, and with their knives lashed to the end of rods ten feet long they prowled around the ship looking for other victims.

With the rifle Hendricsen finally dislodged them from their barricade, and they sought refuge in the alleyway between the cabin house and the rail. Then, firing at random through the wall of the cabin house and through the shuttered windows, where they figured the Indians were standing, they finally succeeded in wounding one of them. With a wild yell, he ran forward. The men fastened in the forecastle saw him shove a plank overboard and then jump after it himself. He was seen no more.

Captain Clarke now had a hole cut in the after companionway doors with an axe and made Hendricsen go through with the gun after the other Malay, while at the same time the man aloft started down the rigging. Realizing that the game was up, the remaining Indian ran forward and disappeared round the end of the forward house, no one at the time knowing what had become of him. It took but a minute to liberate the men forward, four of whom were wounded and eight well.

Captain Clarke was gotten on deck, and with the ship in charge once more the foreyards were swung, her head paid off, the yards squared and the ship was put on her course. Including the Indians, seven men had been killed, four sailors and the captain badly wounded. It was still a question whether the captain would live, and the well men were badly demoralized. They had not been in charge long when smoke was seen coming from one of the hatches, and it was known then that the Malay had disappeared down the forward hatch and set fire to the ship. The captain prevailed upon Hendricsen and another sailor to lead the crew into the 'tween decks to dislodge him, but the Malay hid behind a bale of hemp and held them off with his knife until the smoke got so thick that they had to retreat.

Rigging the deck pump, they fought the fire with a will, but there were only eight well men left besides the Chinamen and they could not drown it out. Just before the fire got out of their control the Chinese steward claims that he saw the remaining

Malay climb out through the forward hatch and with a wild yell jump overboard, where the sharks undoubtedly got him.

All that afternoon and night they fought the fire, but by eleven o'clock the flames had eaten through the deck and they saw that it was all up with the ship. They loaded two of the boats with a scanty supply of provisions and 200 gallons of water and started to put them overboard with tackles rigged from the fore and main yards. The smaller boat swamped in the launching and the entire crew of 17, including five wounded men and the women, got into the larger one. This was about midnight. They hung around the ship until ten o'clock Tuesday morning, January 5, hoping against hope for rescue, but when the ship had burned to the water's edge they headed for the island of St. Helena, a mere speck in the South Atlantic 700 miles to the northward, in a deeply laden boat 27 feet long, with the only navigator a wounded man who might die from exposure at any minute. With oars for a mast and blankets rigged for a sail they made fair time before the favoring South East Trades. They sighted the island at 3 P.M. January 10, and landed at Jamestown at 3 A.M. of the 11th, having been in the small boat over six days. The wounded men went to the hospital, where all eventually recovered and Captain Clarke, after some months, came home with his wife by steamer via London.

35

Faatoai to Papeete—Personally Conducted

by PAUL J. HAAREN

[1925]

HERE'S THE TALE of a winter cruise you won't find listed in any of your guide books—the twice-weekly cruise of the good schooner *Faarora* from Papeete to Faatoai.

The fare is seven francs, the distance about 20 miles. The skipper a native from the island of Rapa; the engineer a half-cast Tahitian; the deckhand, God knows what; the cargo, the same. The passengers . . . but here, wait a moment! Let's get organized.

No need to tell you Papeete is in Tahiti. Faatoai is a South Sea village that straggles along beyond Oponohu Bay for a hundred yards on either side of the road that skirts the edge of the island of Moorea, the sister isle of Tahiti, 14 miles away. Faatoai was the summer capital in the days of King Pomare. No doubt swift and mighty double war canoes cut the waters separating the summer and winter residences in the old and glorious days. But now, in these days of rapid and luxurious communication, the only way to get to Faatoai from Papeete or from Papeete to Faatoai is by a stubby little 40-foot schooner. Thereby hangs my tale.

I am already in Faatoai. No matter how I got there. Now I fain would go back to Papeete to watch the monthly steamer from San Francisco dock, to collect my mail at the post office. Then, with several boon companions who will be in town for the same reason, I am to make several social calls that will end eventually in our achieving a most beautiful state of intoxication. But I must not get ahead of my story. I am still in Faatoai.

It is six o'clock, an unearthly hour to my city-bred manner of thinking. But to the natives of the village, who have been up and stirring since daylight, it is quite late. Llew and I gobble our melon and dunk our chunks of Chinese bread into huge bowls of coffee. That constitutes the rite known as "café" even down here, ten thousand or so miles from France. Then away to the wharf and the *Faarora*.

The *Faarora* sails at seven, so we have a good half hour to spare. The rickety wharf is swaying under the weight of several score natives. Some are voyaging to Papeete. Others are there merely out of curiosity. But all stand about or sit on the boxes that strew the wharf, and gossip. We add our weight to the wharf just long enough to traverse its length. We hop aboard the schooner, pick out good vantage points (the necessity for which you will soon understand) and await the arrival of Fowler.

Seven o'clock . . . then seven thirty. But no Fowler. Llew makes a remark in native to the Rapa skipper. The skipper replies—and a guffaw of laughter goes up from the crowd. It must have been a wise crack. Fowler must have had a bad night. A light was seen burning in his house way down the road until a late hour the previous evening. But *aita pea-pea*—no difference, he'll show up soon.

A character—Fowler. English; not so old, forty at the most. During the war an R.A.F. officer; skipper of a blimp patrolling the English Channel. Now he's owner of a chubby little schooner in the South Seas, is a trader of sorts, has ideas of his own, lives as he likes and more power to him.

The wharf is only three feet wide but Fowler rides his sea-going bike right down to the very edge of it. A native grabs it and swings it aboard. His raincoat follows, then his tin box of money and accounts. It has funny cork bobbers all around it to float it in case the boat goes on the reef. No use losing ship, tin box, money, accounts and everything. Fowler flirts his floppy

panama hat that looks like nothing at all and hops aboard. A
greeting for us. A nod to the skipper.

"Cheerio, Fowler—let's push off." . . . And we do.

First stop, by rights, is Maharipa. But the Chinks who live
down at the foot of Cook's Bay sent word last night they had
some cargo for Papeete. So out to sea through the pass at
Oponohu and in again at the very next one, into Cook's Bay.
There are sheer cliffs on either side of the bay that seem fairly
studded with caves. Llew's father has some great tales to tell
about these caves. They are the burial caves of the old people.
They are full of little stone *tii*. In them repose the bones of
mighty chiefs with their weapons of war, canoes and, some even
say, treasures of pearls.

The schooner noses as far as possible into the shallow water
at the foot of the bay. Then over the side with the small boat.
Pini, the deckhand, gets ample help from the small boys who
have managed, as usual, to stow away at Faatoai. Three times
the boat comes back laden almost to sinking with matting-covered
paddies of rice. On the fourth trip, back comes the boat one-
half filled with rice paddies, the other half with three Chinese
who, at every lurch of the boat under the oar strokes of Pini,
glance apprehensively over the side down through the water,
which is so clear they seem suspended in space. The last of the
rice paddies is flung into the hold, the hatch-covers stamped
down and the boat hoisted back on deck.

The Chinese had seemed to vanish as soon as the small boat
touched the side of the schooner. They had scrambled aboard
and tumbled down into the cabin, where they would stay nested
together like a knot of worms until the schooner put the pitching
channel behind her and was floating serenely on the calm water
inside the reef at Papeete.

Up anchor . . . and on to Maharipa. We should go out
through the reef and in again at the next pass, but Maharipa is
only around the bend of the bay and Fowler decides he will save
gasoline and time by taking a chance through the shallow water
of the lagoon.

We go at quarter-speed. Pini, the deckhand, sits astride the bowsprit and waves his arms to port or starboard to guide the skipper in avoiding huge hummocks of yellow mushroom coral. Fowler, in the bow, runs from side to side. Pini's eyesight might be all right but Fowler doesn't credit him with too great a sense of responsibility. Suddenly Pini hollers. I think we are surely headed for something terrible, but that is only Pini's way of telling the skipper we are in deep water. Although the engineer's head is stuck up through the hatch of the motor room and the skipper and the engineer have been conversing unconcernedly the while, the skipper now yanks the fishline that is attached to the bell in the engine room. Yank . . . Down goes the engineer's bushy head. Chug-a-chug, chug-a-chug, goes the heavy-duty gas engine. We gather speed.

Yank . . . The clutch goes into reverse. The water astern churns yellow. Pini flings the bowline wharfwards—anywhere. It lands among the crowd on the wharf. Someone grabs it and twists it around the end of a coconut tree spile that also acts as a mooring bollard.

Yank, yank . . . The engine dies down. We're in port.

Maharipa is the stamping grounds of one Mike Foley. Mike isn't Irish. Where he got the name—search me, for Mike is the Jewish King of Moorea. A newspaper man with a nose for nonsense had visited these parts some few years ago, taken a picture of Mike with his native woman, and written a story about King Mike and his mythical South Sea Kingdom that appeared in the Sunday magazine section of a well-known string of newspapers. Poor Mike! The news leaked out to Tahiti. Copies of the sheet followed. Mike was ragged every time he set his nose in Papeete. But Mike should worry. He had a native woman who owned a nice little strip of coconut land. The trees were producing nicely. Mike was shipping a couple of sacks of copra every schooner trip, together with an odd pig or so, and the rumors had it that Mike had cleared quite a neat little plot of land which was already set out in flourishing vanilla vines. All hail Mike, King of Moorea.

Mike was there, in all his bespectacled glory. We held long and earnest discourse with Mike on the current price of copra, the state of the weather and the advantages, both mental and moral, of an occasional trip to Papeete for a bang-up bust. Friend wife, as we shall designate Mike's woman, meanwhile hung in the offing. Something was amiss. Mike at last gave her his attention. Mike's offspring, a coppery imp of about five who had been left in charge of the Mike family's horse, was inadequate to the job, it seems. Even now the horse was dragging said offspring indiscriminately about under the coconut trees, said offspring's point of contact with said ground being said offspring's belly. Mike turned his attention to the horse and offspring, while we turned ours to the schooner.

Fowler, it seems, was having the devil's own time. Freight was running heavier than usual. What to do with the damn stuff? The hold was full of copra from Faatoai and paddy rice from Cook's Bay. And here were more copra, more pigs, more chickens and endless bunches of bananas, fei and what not. The cargo was disposed of in the only way it could be. . . . It was piled about the forward deck, amidships between cabin and stanchions, and far back even into the clear space of the afterdeck ordinarily reserved for passengers. Now, all the passengers were standing around on the wharf. But wait until the schooner pushed off again and the scramble for places began.

Fowler gave the skipper the word. The skipper gave the engineer the word. The motor chugged over. Pini must have got word from somebody or else he just acted on his own initiative. Anyway, he cast loose, and the passengers, including ourselves, made a wild dash and clambered across the widening space between wharf and schooner as best they could.

The passengers were mostly natives. Single male natives, single female natives, and whole families of natives—about 20 in all. In addition, there were the Chinks nested together down in the cabin. One more had joined them at Maharipa and had already entwined his frame amongst the bags and bundles that constituted the baggage of the passengers. The baggage of those who had come aboard at Maharipa was simply thrown in through the hatch to mingle with the other baggage and the Chinese as it would. How the Chinks could breathe in that hole is beyond me.

To the stifling heat was added the fumes of the gas engine which, mingled with the already foul air, made what was bound to happen doubly certain. But the Chinks have their own philosophy about such things. Might as well get sick down there as any place else. They'd be free of the terrifying sight of the leaping sea.

One of the new passengers was a Russian. How he had landed in Tahiti no one knows. He had come to Moorea from Tahiti with an old-time sour-dough from Alaska. They got hold of a small bit of land apiece. There they lived side by side, each in his own little shelter of thatched coconut leaves, each clearing his own bit of land and each raising his own patch of vegetables and living as best he could. They were model neighbors until the memorable day when they had a falling out, three years ago. Since then each continued to live in his own shelter, to raise his own vegetables and to live as best he could. But as an added feature to their otherwise colorless lives, each never lost an opportunity to vilify the other with the most horrible oaths imaginable across the high fence they had jointly built to shut out the sight of the other. All this to the speechless and unbounded amazement of the neighboring natives, who were utterly at a loss to account for such strange behavior.

The Russian had a nasty tongue, with a jeer or a snarl for everything. He spit down into the cabin onto the Chinese. He pushed an unresisting native out of a cozy nook he fancied for himself. But when he began poking his head down inside the engine compartment, Fowler had gone up and whispered something in the Russian's ear. Whatever it was Fowler said, its effect was immediate. The Russian sat quietly in his place until he found fresh diversion in the shape of Old Man Squeegee at Vaieri, the next port of call.

It was much the same as Maharipa—the wharf a little more rickety, less people standing about, perhaps, but this was offset by the appearance of Old Man Squeegee. That's what Fowler said he was called. He came meandering down the shaky wharf in a preoccupied sort of way. A big, floppy native straw hat was on his head, which, we saw when he removed the hat to mop it

with a turkey red bandanna as big as a table cloth, was as bald
as a billiard ball. The legs of a pair of dirty yellow drill trousers
were stuffed into heavy mush-boots that laced to his knees. The
top of the trousers were anchored to his middle by a three-inch,
harness-leather belt fastened with a brass buckle that shone like
the sun and must have weighed five pounds. He had no shirt on
and his old hide hung from his frame in huge loose folds like that
of a rhinoceros.

Squeegee hailed from Los Angeles. He had shown up in
Papeete, by means of a third-cabin passage, with only the clothes
he stood in, a blanket and two plugs of chewing tobacco. He
swapped the blanket for a pipe and the straw hat and elected
himself a member of the beachcombing fraternity that hangs
around the waterfront in Papeete. From beachcomber to plantation owner is quite a leap, but Squeegee did it. Here's the story
as Fowler told it to me.

In some way Squeegee managed to get chummy with an old
and odd Frenchman who owned a nice little coconut grove on
Moorea. Then he went over to Moorea to live with the Frenchman. Now it seems that the Frenchman, years ago, had brought
a woman from Papeete to Moorea to act as his housekeeper. She
got no pay, but the Frenchman, to show his appreciation, had
willed her his property against the time when he should die; all
of which, in Tahitian usage, is fair enough.

But somehow or another, soon after Squeegee had gone to
live with him, the Frenchman took sick and had to be taken to
the Government hospital in Papeete. Here, while he lay at
death's door, he was nursed and waited on hand and foot, by old
Squeegee. But the Frenchman, for all Squeegee's attention, died,
and then the dirt came out. It seems while he was lying in the
hospital the Frenchman had found it pleasing and expedient to
alter his will. And when the native woman objected to Squeegee
returning to Moorea and setting himself up permanently in the
place where she had lived for years and which she believed was
now hers, she was astounded when Squeegee told her to act nice
or get t'hell out. The plantation was Squeegee's. Squeegee had

the will to prove it. And here, before us, stood Old Man Squeegee in the flesh.

The natives evidently would have nothing to do with him.
He spoke a few words to Fowler, who acted as if he hadn't heard.
Squeegee saw us and sidled over to have converse. But Llew and
I were suddenly very interested in nothing at all. Then he spied
the Russian. And this was just what the Russian had been waiting
and hoping for.

"H'lo, there—Roosian. Hev ye seen my new place?"

"Your new what?"

"My new place—my plantation."

"Oh, that's what it is—a plantation."

"Sure it is. Why don't ye come over an' call on me some
time. I'll crack out a bottle."

"Oh, you will, will you? . . . And how do I know you won't
fix the bottle for me like you did for the Frenchman."

"Fer the Frenchman! . . . What do you mean?"

"I mean you're an old ——, you blankety blank blank."

"Why you blank blanked Bolshevik," raved Old Man Squeegee. "They ought to send you back to Roosia with the rest of the
blank blanked Bolsheviks."

"And you, you old blank blank," chorused the Russian. "They
ought to ship you back to the States, where they are looking for
you, you blank blank jailbreaker . . ." etc.

As the *Faarora* pushed off, Old Man Squeegee stood on the
edge of the wharf shrieking maledictions at the Russian and
shaking his skinny fist in the air with such vigor that the folds
of loose skin across his belly twitched and quivered like a slack
sail in a gust of wind. The Russian stood on the taffrail howling
back at him until a kick in the pants from Fowler silenced him
and he took his seat with a leer of fiendish delight at having successfully baited someone.

There was one more stop . . . Afareaitu. A big load of firewood, done up in small bundles, was sitting on the wharf waiting
for us. But Fowler absolutely refused to take it. It would have
to wait till next week. The only reason we put in at Afareaitu at
all was because that village was the residence of the *gendarme*

for Moorea. Fowler had some business with him and disappeared up the wharf toward his house.

Thereupon a slapstick comedy was enacted for us at the landing. The Chinaman who owned the wood would not take no for
an answer. When Fowler disappeared he and his Chink hench-
men began loading the wood onto the schooner as fast as they
could. There wasn't a clear space on the ship, but this didn't
bother the Chinamen. They piled their bundles of wood on
top of bunches of bananas, fei, taro and other perishable stuff
regardless of the damage done. And as fast as they piled it on
board the Rapa skipper, the Tahitian engineer, Pini and several
other big buck natives, who jumped to for the fun of the game,
hove it back on the wharf.

It rained wood. The bundles flew around like cannon balls.
The bark fastenings came undone. The loose sticks bounced all
over the wharf. This gave the crew an idea. Instead of heaving
the bundles back onto the wharf they hove them back *at* the
wharf. And more often than not the bundles missed the wharf
and landed plunk in the water to bob around exasperatingly just
beyond the reach of the Chinamen.

In the midst of the melee Fowler and the *gendarme* came
running down toward the beach. The skipper told Fowler what
had happened. Fowler told the *gendarme*. The *gendarme* turned
on the Chinks who were pulling his coat tail and jabbering like a
mob of monkeys. He shut them up in short order, administering
a judicious kick here and there amongst them. He knew his
business, that *gendarme*.

We cast off and headed for the pass in the reef. As we made
the open sea I could still see the Chinks fishing from the wharf
with long poles for their bobbing bundles of wood.

And now for a straight run of 14 miles across the open sea to
Papeete. The current was setting one way, a stiff wind another.
A nasty chop wrinkled the sides of the big swells that came
whooping at us. The little schooner bounced around. Occasionally
a big sea would catch her broadside and swash over the side. The
bananas, fei, taro and everything else on deck were soaked. The
pigs, their feet tied together, were lashed to the deck up in the

bow to prevent their washing overboard. Scores of bananas tore
loose from their bunches and bounced around the deck. The
natives snatched them up and ate them. The gasoline fumes
from the engine seemed to hang over the ship in a pall. Some of
the native women began to get sick, and the children who weren't
sick whimpered with fright.

Llew beckoned me over to where he was looking down into
the cabin. Together we peered in. There were the four Chinese,
their faces pales as corpses', all snarled together perfectly motionless. They looked like so many dead men, but they weren't
dead—far from it. Every now and then one would twitch and
squirm convulsively as he proceeded to give a demonstration of
the fact that he was very, very seasick. Evidently they didn't
care where they got sick, when they got sick, or who knew they
were sick. I thrust my head over the side to windward and gulped
for air.

And all through it, Pini the deckhand slept. He had found a
comfortable roosting place and had proceeded to curl up. No
more work till Papeete. The engineer was down in his cubbyhole
nonchalantly oiling his engine, utterly unconscious of the fumes.
The skipper from Rapa was perched easily on the wheel box
blithely spinning the wheel from side to side to meet the onrush-
ing combers—with his bare feet.

Rapa is an island famed in the South Seas for its good coffee
and excellent sailors. They tell me it is a bleak place and that
during the war, when it was cut off from the rest of the islands,
its inhabitants ran entirely out of clothes and almost starved
to death. There are few women there. The boys, therefore,
either move to other islands more profuse in women or ship on
board some sailing ship as seamen. As sailors they are utterly
fearless and tireless, and captains are keen to ship them.

This particular Rapa man had been on board a British ship.
He could speak a little English—a fact in which he took almost
as much pride as he did in the huge British coat-of-arms tattooed
on his chest in red and blue ink. On one forearm was the British
ensign, on the other the British Jack. He invariably steered with
his bare feet, the while sitting on the gearbox and puffing away

ON & OFF SOUNDINGS

EDITED BY
WILLIAM H. TAYLOR

INTRODUCTION BY
HERBERT L. STONE

A new selection of wonderful stories from the files of YACHTING magazine. "Bill" Taylor has chosen a well balanced group of fascinating tales of sailing on and off soundings which provides just the kind of reading that sailors love. A companion book to JUST CRUISING.

at a vile native tobacco cigarette. Fowler said at first it nearly gave him heart failure to see him steering this way, even when negotiating the most difficult pass in a reef. But he never seemed at a loss, never scraped the bottom, and unless something unforeseen happened would never pile the ship up. There had been many a tight squeak, as for instance the time when the motor failed just as they were coming through the reef. The schooner was drifting back fast in a nasty sea, but the skipper got sail up and slanted out along the reef, just grazing it, the combers breaking on the reef right under the rail.

Another time he had lost his rudder and was going onto the reef with a whole boatload of native women and kids. Luckily the sea was fairly smooth, but the big swells threatened to lift the boat up and drop her on the jagged coral any moment. The skipper broke out the long sweeps and, pressing the native men passengers into service, not only held the ship off but worked her slowly along the reef until he reached the pass and allowed himself to be washed through into the lagoon.

But here we are going through the pass at Papeete. The little *Faarora* kicked up her heels at the sea for the last time and glided into the smooth lagoon. The engineer tooted deafeningly on a whistle large enough for an ocean liner. The passengers began to sit up and take notice. The pigs stopped squealing. The chickens shook themselves to dry their feathers. A Chinaman, astonishingly soon, thrust his head up through the cabin hatch. A screech of derision met him and the bucks showered him with bananas. He ducked back with a sickly grin.

Yank—on the fishline. The motor slowed down. We slid alongside the stone embankment.

Yank—on the fishline again. The motor reversed. A line shot out from the bow. Pini was up and at 'em again. He hollered at a little brown imp on shore. The imp slipped the noose over the iron cannon embedded, muzzle upward, in the earth.

Yank; yank . . . the motor gave a last chuggety-chug. A long plank about six inches wide was laid from shore to ship. There were 20 feet of harbor water between us and the shore, and this was the only fresh suit of whites we had with us. But we teetered along, bag on one hand, catching the air with the other. Fowler met us at the shore end. The pay-as-you-enter way of doing things hasn't reached Tahiti as yet. We forked out a dirty five-franc note and two dirtier one-franc notes, gladly. Little enough for a 20-mile personally conducted cruise. The trip took some seven hours to accomplish—a little less than three miles an hour. But it was worth it. Look at the fun you had! And anyway, you can't expect too much for seven francs.

PART II

PART II

36

Singlehanded Ocean Cruising

by E. C. ALLCARD

[1951]

IT WAS MIDNIGHT, Aug. 9, 1949. The cable rattled out over the stem roller. The anchor bit into New York mud, marking the end of a sail of 4800 miles from Gibraltar, left 80 days before. Once more the feasibility of singlehanded ocean voyaging had been proved.

Although singlehanded sailing is not practiced often, either coastwise or deep sea, many times one must handle a craft with one pair of hands, even if there are others aboard who may be incapacitated through seasickness or injury. Then again, crews are apt to leave in foreign ports, which might entail heavy expense to the owner if he were not confident of handling his boat alone. The lively interest in what constitutes the ideal singlehander has been shown to me by the number of questions on the subject, so I have endeavored to pass on practical advice after the experience gained on my passages.

The questions I am most asked are: "When do you sleep?" and "What happens to the boat in the meantime?" Then again, more stupid ones like "What do you do for water?"

The prize question came from a playwright who said, "Do you anchor nights?"

"No," I replied, "You see, carrying eight miles of chain cable is not really practical."

Singlehanded cruising teaches many lessons in coordination

and seamanship, and is certainly a phase of the sport that all yachtsmen should be familiar with. The study of the longer lone passages is perhaps more important owing to the difficulty in obtaining crews, good or bad, for any length of time. Conor O'Brien once said to me, "If you want a crew, marry one." Good advice probably, but somewhat drastic.

The main aspects of singlehanded ocean cruising can be reduced to the following headings—size, type of hull, type of rig, layout below decks, auxiliary engine, special equipment, sailing routine.

Size. It is an adage that, for the singlehander, the largest size is governed by the weight of ground tackle. I remember several instances in my last boat, a 38-ft. waterline cutter with half-inch diameter anchor cable, when it was necessary to get underway in a blow under headsails until clear water could be reached to hoist the mainsail. I had found it beyond my strength to break the anchor out of the ground, and had to start the engine and motor it out. However, to my mind the important question of ground tackle is not so much the effort of breaking the anchor out (after all a mouse can lift a ton if given time enough) as the time taken to crank it to the surface. Anchorages are so crowded these days that it is rarely feasible for a large craft to be drifting about with no one at the helm and the anchor dangling fathoms below the surface.

It has been repeatedly said that one should choose the larger vessel if finances permit. With this I do not agree, either for coastal or ocean cruising. At first sight the advantages of a large boat seem good. The motion at sea is steadier, less tiring, and provides a better platform for handling gear on deck. The comparative slowness when maneuvering or going about gives more time for trimming sail. There is less reducing sail to be done, owing to increased stability. The larger boat, too, will be faster on all points of sailing, especially to windward. She will be much drier on deck, and be less likely in Trade Wind sailing to allow a wave to souse the helmsman or drop through an open hatch. Several times crossing the Atlantic I was rudely awakened by a cold seawater douche in the face. Then again, there is more space below for accommodation and storage.

I used to agree with the theory that the larger boat was better for singlehanded work, but have changed my mind after the experiences of the last few years. I did 1200 miles' coastal work, then nine days in a series of bitter winter gales in an ineffectual attempt to reach Gibraltar in 1946, in a 38-ft. waterline cutter. I then sold her and bought *Temptress,* nine feet shorter, and sailed over 6000 miles in far greater comfort and safety.

The smaller boat may have a quicker motion at sea, but not unbearably so, and the fact that the sails and gear are smaller and lighter, hence easier to handle, offsets the quickness in stays. She may need more reefing, but dropping staysail or roller reefing the mainsail is child's play, and even if running hard it is not necessary to alter course. The smaller space below is no problem to the lone hand with his 100 days' stores.

It is presumed that the ocean-goer uses his boat as a home also, so he at least should be able to stand up below, and have a permanent bunk to roll quickly in or out of and plenty of room for books, charts, clothes, etc. I consider that the ideal singlehanded ocean sailing craft should be not over 30 ft., nor under 25 ft. on the waterline. My dreamship (when I build some day) will be nearer the latter length.

Another advantage of the small craft is that, should you go aground, there is a good chance of getting off again. One can hardly jump over and push a 40-footer off, and it would be a difficult job to lay out a big kedge singlehanded. Slocum nearly lost his life doing just that.

Type of Hull. Hull form for the singlehander is a bewildering subject. I think I know the perfect hull, but so do many others with totally different ideas. One only has to look at the lines of the three most famous boats chosen by singlehanders to sail round the world. Slocums' *Spray* had shallow draft with immense beam. Gerbault's *Firecrest* was a deep, narrow-gutted hull; Pigeon's *Islander,* a light displacement, hard chine type.

On one thing all seem to agree, the advantages of a long underwater profile. This should give steadiness in steering, which is more important than sensitiveness, and will help in heaving to and self-steering, two "musts" for the one-man crew.

Long overhangs should be avoided forward, as they tend to pound, make the boat range about excessively when hove to, and in certain seas make her difficult to put about. A moderate overhang forward, with good flare and sheer, gives a safer and drier foredeck, and only needs a short bowsprit.

All designers have preferences about sterns, depending on where they are educated, but give me the double-ender every time, either the Scandinavian, Scottish or canoe stern. Having owned boats with every possible type of stern, I am convinced that the pointed stern has some miraculous power of cutting a wave in two without causing enough disturbance to make it break. In my time I have had some hair-raising runs before gales. There is one fault in the canoe stern, surely the prettiest of them all, and that is the necessity of having an inboard rudder. The steering gear is a vital part of a boat, and if the rudder is damaged there is always *something* one can do with an outboard rudder, which of course should be designed to unship with the boat afloat, a great asset, especially in the nontidal waters of the Pacific with slipways few and far between.

For the boat I have in mind, displacement would be more than moderate, beam not less than one-third and draft about onefifth of the waterline length, with a fairly easy midship section. Inside ballast I do not favor. There is always the alarming thought that it might fall out through the skylight in moments of excessive stress. I am alive now only because one boat I had in 1932 was so ripe that the inside ballast was cement and boiler punchings (to hold her together) and did not shift when she was rolled upside down in a gale.

Type of Rig. What can be worse than to be asked suddenly, in company, "What is the best rig?" One hedges and mumbles something about having to ring up someone about a boat, but there is usually no escape. The ketch, yawl, schooner, cutter, sloop, and what-have-you maniacs gather round ready to defend their pet rig to the last.

However, the ocean-going singlehander has several specific

wants in his rig. To begin with, every sail must be capable of being lowered in any sea while heading in any direction relative to the wind. Sails must be easy to reef and trim. He will often want to shift his center of effort forward when off the wind to help with self-steering.

To my mind, the ketch fulfills these wants better than any other rig. The marconi rig lends itself well to the ocean ketch, as the masts can be well stayed. The mizzen should be stout enough to have no spreaders. Then mast hoops can be used so as not to have the danger of a jammed track, and the sail cannot get caught aloft when lowering off the wind. The mainmast need not be a lofty stick such as required in a cutter, and with one set of spreaders one can use hoops up to them with jackstay above, similar to Gerbault's *Firecrest*. With the marconi rig it is also possible to have permanent backstays, which obviate the greatest cause of bad language and lessen the chance of a broken boom in a sudden jibe—by no means a rare occurrence at night when the helmsman nods at the tiller.

For deep sea work it is far better to have the headsails split up into two with the forestay led to the stemhead. A bowsprit is a great help when the boat is sailing herself, and generally it is better to spread out the canvas fore and aft as much as possible, keeping the sails low, as with the heavy canvas necessary it is less likely to roll the wind out.

The English practice is to have jibs of three sizes set by means of a traveler on the bowsprit. However shifting jibs can be a difficult and sometimes dangerous practice. It is better for the singlehander to have a strong working jib only, cut so that it does not foul the forestay, and either hanked to a wire stay attached to the traveler, or set flying with the Wykeham-Martin roller furling gear. This gear works in all weathers but it is essential to have a really stout luffrope of rigging wire. Otherwise it is difficult to furl in a strong breeze, as the luffrope will twist and only the bottom of the sail will roll up. Double forestays can be very handy, enabling the reaching and working staysails to be set easily.

With a rig as described above, the lone hand can view the

increase of wind with equanimity, and in the usual daily occurrence of a tropical squall all he need do is to let the mizzen run down without leaving the cockpit.

If possible all rigging should be wire or chain, and all attachments metal to metal, for even seizing wire lashings chafe through. Simplicity and long life should be the watchword of rigging, with special attention given to the strength of metal fittings. The average "yacht" fitting sold may be very well for Long Island Sound and the Solent, but is not usually strong enough to stand up to the terrible snatching in a heavy swell and no wind. Off the Portuguese coast my complete mainsheet fitting sheared off in such conditions, and the boom took charge, swinging broadside off one way, then the other as the vessel rolled heavily, and was secured only after taking a serious risk. And making repairs with hacksaw and riveting hammer in the sweltering heat was not very amusing, either.

Other rigs have their good points, but it is significant that almost all the long trips have been done with two-stickers. I have had no experience with the schooner rig, perhaps the most graceful of the lot, but it seems bad to have one's main driving sail aft when in ocean work most of the voyaging will be in winds abaft the beam. Special sails for running are of particular importance and will be discussed later.

Layout Below Decks. Before the war I drew an accommodation plan of my "dreamship," and in the light of experience I have seen no reason to modify it. In fact several designing competitions have been won since with such a layout. The important thing is accessibility. Let us imagine the singlehander at the tiller or wheel. He stands in the small, self-bailing cockpit. Immediately in front of him there is a doghouse, just big enough to hold all his ready use gear, such as logbook, flashlight, binoculars, hand bearing compass, and when necessary a board for his chart. A hatch to one side leads below to the galley where it should be possible to sit clear of the gangway, so chocked in that hands are free to minister to the stoves (I use two Swedish kerosene Primuses slung in gimbals) and be in reach of the sink. This should have sea as well as fresh water pumps, and the waste should be pumped out. How many boats one sees with gravity outlets which prevent the sink being used in any breeze!

Opposite the galley is the permanent quarter berth, shielded from spray coming down the hatch, in which one can turn in or out with equal facility. By the hatch is provision for wet oilskins with grating on the deck. Thus one can sleep and cook where there is the easiest motion, and can actually watch his food cooking while at the helm.

Going forward through a bulkhead there is the saloon with settee each side with provision for bunkboards, and lockers behind. Hinged-up Pullman berths are too much of a space waster. A properly designed swing table with ballast at the ends and not where it can catch one's shins is offset to allow a reasonable passageway forward. Above the settee backs are shelves for at least 50 books. Elsewhere there are lockers and small drawers.

Passing through another strength bulkhead near the mainmast one enters the fo'c'sle in which there is room for a bunk on either side, which are used at sea as sail lockers and food storage. The "head" is right in the eyes of the boat.

If necessary one can sleep five people in such an accommodation, which can be worked in for a boat only about 26 feet on the waterline in such a hull as under review. Yet the singlehander has great accessibility and storage space for ocean voyaging. There is room for an auxiliary engine abaft the main hatch ladder.

Auxiliary Engine. Often one is far better off without an engine, but I consider it bad seamanship not to have such insurance. The reliability and easy starting of the small diesels now on the market, especially in England, has to be experienced to be believed, and I consider this type of engine the best for the singlehander. There is little fire risk, no warming-up period in an emergency, and push-button starting from deck. And of course the range is nearly double, per gallon of fuel, that of a gasoline or kerosene motor. Naturally the usual precautions as regards accessibility, etc., apply for an engine, and all controls should lead to the cockpit.

Any engine must be capable of running in any weather, which

means careful design of the exhaust pipe system. Many yachts have auxiliaries which are installed so as to be incapable of running in bad weather. This is even so in my present boat and a modification tops the list of jobs to be done. Coming over, I had the devil's own job finding a quiet spot in the ocean every two or three weeks to charge batteries. I also had a hair-raising time off the entrance of the Tagus, in a gigantic swell with no wind, while being carried towards the sandbar, and could barely keep the engine running. Incidentally, I consider electricity a great boon. There is enough to do without messing about filling kerosene lamps.

Special Equipment. For the westward Atlantic passage *Temptress* had just her working canvas, with no special running gear. Like most sailing boats she could be made to sail herself with wind anywhere forward of the beam, but needed a hand on the tiller for a fair wind with all sails set. And as I had a fair wind for the first two months it meant quite a lot of steering. In fact I would not attempt the trip again without some sort of running gear. It is not that I want to do a voyage any faster (the Atlantic run was not long enough for me) but that I do not want to spend such long hours at the helm when one could be doing more constructive work.

The best and cheapest gear I know is that used by my friend Marin-Marie and described in his book "Wind Aloft, Wind Alow." This consists of twin staysails held out by booms connected to twin forestays, and the sheets led to the tiller.

If one has a fairly large mainsail which has to be reefed for a squall, I recommend roller reefing, for the joy of being able to reef in comfort while running hard and without altering course. Like everything else, it has to be properly installed. Sheet winches and other labor-saving gadgets apply equally whatever the number of crew.

Sailing Routine. The answer to the question "When do you sleep?" pretty well sums up this matter, and this depends directly on whether there is shipping about or not. My run from Gibraltar to the States by the Trade Wind route was mostly in the area of strong fair winds with little shipping and my sleeping was done at night. I used to get up at dawn, cook a large quantity of oatmeal for breakfast, then go on deck to hoist the mainsail and mizzen and take the tiller for 10 or 12 hours.

At sunset these two sails would be stowed and the boat left to run through the hours of darkness under headsails alone with helm lashed near amidships. I would prepare a large meal, work out navigation sights taken during the day, check wristwatch with the radio, do a bit of reading and turn in, while the boat kept remarkably well on her course, although rolling abominably. A powerful electric light in the rigging was usually lit when I slept. If I was near steamer tracks sleep was taken by short catnaps, but I would not actually steer at night, as steering during the blazing day was enough for me.

I do not advise crossing the oceans without some patent running gear. It brings extra hardship to the singlehander. I had to do it for financial reasons. Finally, I doubt if there can be greater mental satisfaction than completing an ocean crossing by one's own unaided effort.

37

Passage Sails

by ERNEST RATSEY and W. H. DE FONTAINE

[1948]

NOW THAT THE URGE to take to the sea and cruise to the ends of the earth seems to be almost universal, it seems appropriate to set forth some thoughts on the subject of perhaps the most useful sails in the locker to the deep sea cruiser.

Generally speaking, this group of sails can be used to advantage only when the wind is well aft, although sometimes square sails and raffees may be trimmed to take advantage of winds which are forward of the beam. A great deal depends upon the cut of the sail and the arrangement of the standing and running rigging. If the sail is cut too full or the shrouds are so led that the yard cannot be braced sharp up, it will be impossible to carry these sails efficiently except with the wind aft.

SQUARE SAILS

Square sails date back about 5000 years to the Minoans and they have been in use ever since with little change in their handling. The term "square" is used to distinguish these sails from "fore and aft" sails, not necessarily as an indication of the shape of the sail. A sail of this kind is hung from a yard which is usually supported by slings or halyards and lifts and is controlled in a fore-and-aft direction by braces. The length of the spar is usually twice the beam of the yacht. The sail is secured to the yard by various methods and is in turn controlled by lines at the clews. If properly rigged, square sails sometimes may be carried with the wind somewhat forward of the beam. To make this possible, however, there must be two lines (in large

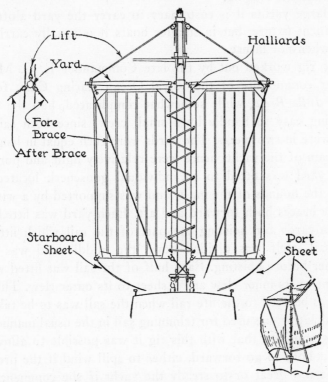

Looking aft, showing arrangement of the double square sail on *Jolie Brise*. The inset shows how half the sail can be set opposite the mainsail.

sails—two tackles) rigged to each lower corner of the sail. One line, called the tack, leads forward and the other, the sheet, leads aft.

With the wind on the beam, or forward of the beam, the tack is carried forward, hauled taut and belayed, and the sheet is trimmed aft and belayed, in much the same manner as the sheet of a loose-footed jib. When running free only the sheets need be used. The degree to which the yacht will be able to point to windward under a square sail will depend largely upon how sharply her yard can be braced up. The manner in which the yard is hung and its relation to the shrouds will determine this. To make this sail efficient on the wind requires much care and thought in its rigging.

In large yachts it is customary to carry the yard aloft as a permanent fixture, but in smaller boats it is usually carried on deck when not in use.

The rig worked out by the late Commander E. G. Martin, former commodore of the Royal Ocean Racing Club, for his cutter *Jolie Brise,* while somewhat complicated, had the virtue of being easy to handle by a small crew, since both sail and yard were in two pieces. The yards were each equal in length to the beam of the yacht, hence were relatively light and portable. Each yard was fitted to an individual gooseneck located just below the hounds of the mast, and was supported by a wire lift and by braces both forward and aft. Each yard was fitted with two halyards for hoisting the part of the sail which fitted it. The sail itself was divided down the middle and was laced together before hoisting. Each half of the sail was fitted with a clewline at its inner clew and a sheet to its outer clew. The former was belayed to the fife rail when the sail was to be taken in and the latter was used for trimming sail in the usual manner.

It is apparent that with this rig it was possible to allow one yard or both to go forward, either to spill wind if the pressure became too great or to steady the yacht if she commenced to roll too violently. Also, one half of the sail could be set with the mainsail carried on the opposite side. For long passages in the Trades there seems to be much to recommend this rig.

THE RAFFEE

One of the best known exponents of the raffee is Captain Irving Johnson, who sailed three times around the world in his old schooner *Yankee,* using one of these sails on his foretopmast. His sail takes the form of a truncated triangle with a short yard, or club, at the head and its clews sheeted to the foreyardarms in the usual manner. This is a light sail and would not be carried in strong breezes. It should be fitted with clewlines and a buntline or two to facilitate handling. The jib topsail halyard will be used also as a halyard for the raffee, since the two sails will not be carried simultaneously.

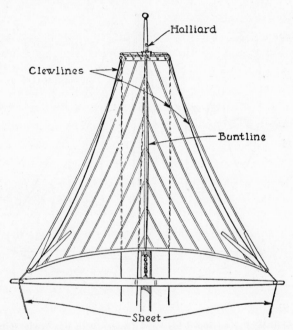

The raffee as used aboard the schooner *Yankee* on three world-girdling voyages proved a fine pulling sail and could be carried when fairly close hauled.

Conor O'Brien, in his book ON GOING TO SEA IN YACHTS says: "I can't praise the raffee too highly. It is easy to hoist—it comes down with certainty in any conditions; it pulls nobly four points off the wind—and goes on pulling when you've rolled all the wind out of the fore and afters." In setting the raffee, it should first be sheeted home to the yardarms and then hoisted to the masthead. When dousing the sail, the sheets will first be slacked off, the clewlines and buntlines will be hauled up and then the halyard will be slacked away and the whole sail lowered to the deck.

CAPTAIN WALLER'S TWIN SPINNAKERS

Another rig which seems to have a good deal to recommend it for long ocean passages is one developed by Captain Otway Waller in 1930. Using this rig as an important part of his inventory of sails, he made the passage from Limerick, Ireland, to

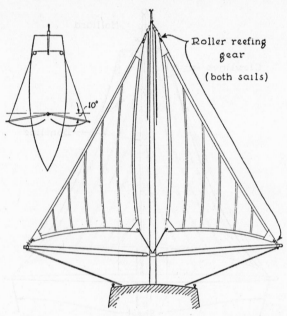

Captain Otway Waller equipped his yawl *Imogen* with this "twin spinnaker" rig.

Las Palmas singlehanded in the yawl *Imogen* of only 22 feet 6 inches waterline. The rig is called twin spinnakers. Briefly, it consists of a pair of triangular sails, almost equilateral in proportions, which were carried on two stays slightly forward of and on either side of the mainmast. These stays were equipped with Wykeham-Martin roller reefing gear so that the sails could be taken in by simply rolling them around the stay. The spinnakers were rigged with individual poles and were normally trimmed so that the latter were about 10° forward of athwartships. Sheets or guys leading from the ends of these poles were rove through a pair of quarter blocks located outboard of the tiller head and thence to the tiller. Forward guys were carried slack to act as preventers in case of an unexpected backwinding. When they were set the mainsail was taken in. The slightest deviation of the boat from her course, when dead before the wind, would increase the wind pressure on the weather spinnaker and decrease the pressure on the lee one, thus pulling over the tiller and bringing her back to her course. Apparently this rig was quite satisfactory.

THE FENGER TWIN SPINNAKER RIG

In July, 1932, Frederick A. Fenger published in *Yachting* an article describing a further development of Captain Waller's

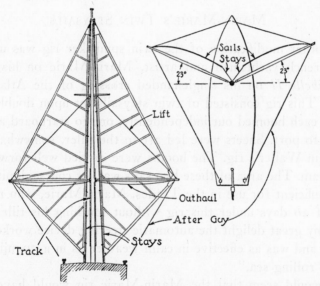

The Fenger rig was an improvement on Captain Waller's.

rig. This was based upon experiments made with a model over a period of about a year. These tests indicated that better performance could be expected from a slight modification of the Waller rig. By spreading the jackstays upon which the spinnakers were carried so that there was the equivalent of three or four feet of space between them at the deck, and also by increasing the boom angles from 10° to 23° forward of the beam, it was found that the model would run dead before the wind without any use of the rudder whatever. The after guys were belayed instead of being led to the tiller and the mainsail was taken in as in the earlier rig.

In both the above rigs the name spinnaker may be somewhat misleading, since it is usually associated with an extremely light sail which is intended primarily for use when racing, whereas these sails were of fairly heavy canvas and had the character more of staysails than of spinnakers. This rig was used by Paul Hammond in his big ketch *Landfall* and later in his 39-foot cutter *Barnswallow*.

MARIN-MARIE'S TWIN STAYSAILS

Another modification of the twin spinnaker rig was used by the French yachtsman and artist, Marin-Marie on his cutter *Winnibelle II* on his singlehanded crossing of the Atlantic in 1933. This rig consisted of twin staysails set upon double forestays, each boomed out independently, one to starboard and the other to port. Sheets were led aft to the tiller, somewhat as in Captain Waller's rig. The booms were carried well forward of the beam. The area of these two sails was, of course, limited but was sufficient for use in the Trades. Marin-Marie, who made a run of 26 days under this rig without touching his tiller said: "To my great delight the automatic steering device worked perfectly and was as effective in calm weather as in a 50-mile wind and a rolling sea."

It would seem that the Marin-Marie rig would have three possible advantages over that of Captain Waller. First, being farther forward on the boat thus placing the center of effort of the sails well ahead of the center of lateral resistance, there should be far less tendency to yaw; second, the angle of the forestays would give the twin staysails a lifting component; and third, being so far forward, there should be less possibility of the ends

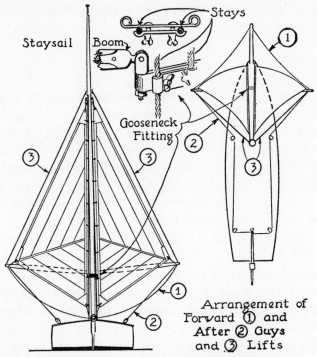

Marin-Marie's twin staysail rig in *Winnibelle II*.

of the booms tripping in the bow wave no matter how far down the boat might roll.

Storm Canvas

To the cruising man, particularly the deep water cruising man, storm canvas can be the most important equipment in his sail locker. When clawing off a lee shore in a gale of wind, when the motor has gone dead, a proper trysail may mean the difference between safety and disaster. And for ordinary 'longshore cruising, too, a trysail can add considerably to the comfort of a passage when the wind blows hard. British yachtsmen use what they call a "passage trysail" for this purpose. It is larger than a real storm trysail, sometimes has a small gaff, and may be of somewhat lighter cloth but it is set in the same manner. Such a sail has much to recommend it.

TRYSAILS

The storm trysail as used by American yachtsmen is usually a triangular sail made of canvas of about the same weight as the yacht's working mainsail. The cloths run parallel to the leach and the sail should be hand sewn and treated to render it mildew-proof. It should be roped on all three sides and the cringles and thimbles at the head, tack and clew—particularly the clew—should be extra strong. In area it should be somewhat smaller than the yacht's close-reefed mainsail.

According to Captain Irving Johnson, whose opinion can be accepted as authoritative, the best way to rig a trysail is to have a lanyard eye-spliced to every other grommet in the luff of the sail, commencing at the top. These lanyards are long enough to lead around the mast to the grommet next below, where they are secured with a figure eight knot. The accompanying sketch will make this clear. No rollers or parrel balls are required with such a rig since the diagonal lead of the lanyard will prevent it from binding.

Captain Johnson says that it is always advisable to hoist a trysail in stops and to have all the lanyards rigged and the tack lashing secure before the sail is broken out. And stand clear as it whips out in the wind, for the flying clew can be dangerous. Sheet the sail home as soon as possible to prevent it from flogging itself to ribbons.

The cut of a trysail is largely a matter of personal preference, but the usual arrangement is to have it cut high enough at the tack so that it may be set over the lowered mainsail, and the clew is generally cut somewhat lower than the tack. The sail is sheeted to the yacht's quarters, well aft and near the rail. The number of parts in the sheet will, of course, depend upon the area of the trysail. If the lead of the trysail sheet would cause chafe on the lowered mainsail, be sure to parcel the latter with

several thicknesses of chafing gear of some kind. Almost anything that will prevent chafe will serve.

Do not use a single lacing line to secure the sail to the mast as,
if such a line should part, the whole luff of the sail would come
adrift and would be extremely difficult to handle in the wind and
sea which prevail when a trysail is called for. Do not use a

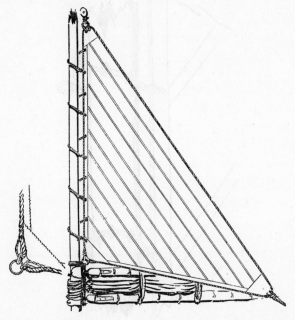

How Irving Johnson rigged a trysail aboard the schooner *Yankee*.

sheet which is hooked to the clew since a hook may open up
under stress; use a shackle. If the yacht is not equipped with a
gallows frame for the main boom, the best rig will be to have
a wire topping lift and use boom tackles. The weight of the boom
and sail are taken by the lift and its lateral movement is curbed
by the tackles. Do not depend upon an ordinary boom crutch for
holding the boom under storm conditions for it will almost
certainly carry away and permit the boom to take charge. And a
rampaging boom is a dangerous shipmate.

Some sailmakers prefer to secure the trysail to the mast with
lanyards which lead directly around the mast. They are usually

seized to the luff of the sail at about their middle point and meet
on the foreside of the mast, having an eye splice in one end and
a wooden toggle in the other, which slips into the eye splice.
Such lanyards will require parrel balls to prevent them from
binding.

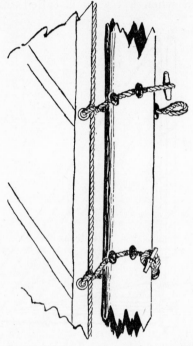

Another way to rig lanyards for a storm trysail. Note the use of parrel balls.

Some modern yachts, particularly ocean-racing yachts, with
jib-headed mainsails which slide on a track secured to the mast,
have been equipped with a switch in this track just above the
top slide of the lowered mainsail. This switch leads to a short
piece of track which is run down one side of the mast, parallel
to the main track. With this rig it is possible to get the trysail
all ready to hoist before the mainsail is lowered. The trysail is
fitted with slides which are slipped onto the switch track all ready
to be hoisted, the sheets are made ready and rove through their
proper blocks. Then the mainsail is lowered away, the halyard

is shackled to the trysail, the switch is thrown and the sail is hoisted promptly. Thus little time or headway need be lost. Many people, however, do not feel that track and slides are strong enough to take the stresses to which a trysail is subjected under extreme conditions. They prefer to rely upon the lanyards described above.

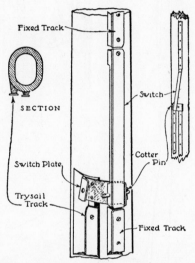

One type of switch to make sail changing easier.

An emergency trysail may be improvised by using a working jib (preferably one equipped with a wire luff rope). Secure the tack of the jib at the point where the tack of the mainsail usually lies; bend on the main halyard to the head of the jib, shackle a strong piece of line to the jib clew to act as the trysail sheet and you are ready to hoist away. After hoisting the sail, carry the sheet aft and make it fast to the main boom at a point where the lead is satisfactory. You may then control your sail by trimming the main sheet in the usual manner. If your mast is equipped with a track it is advisable to carry slides to which strong wrought iron rings have been lashed—one for each hank on the luff of the jib. By putting these slides on the track and hooking the luff of the jib to them the sail will be held more closely to the mast, without excessive strain on the halyards.

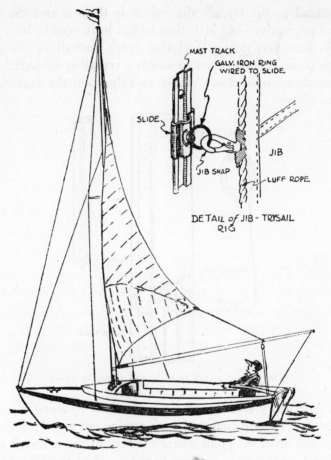

MAST TRACK

GALV. IRON RING
WIRED TO SLIDE.

SLIDE

JIB

JIB SNAP

LUFF ROPE

DETAIL of JIB - TRYSAIL
RIG

An emergency trysail rig is useful now and then.

"Spitfire" or Storm Jib

Along with the trysail the "spitfire" jib is the sail upon which the cruising and long-distance-racing man will depend when the going really gets tough. It will be the smallest sail in the locker and one of the most important. It should be at least as heavy as the trysail. Since a spitfire jib may be unused for seasons at a time, and as it is of such vital importance, it is always advisable that it be hand stitched and well treated to make it mildewproof.

A properly made spitfire will have a wire luff rope and both its leach and foot will be roped. Cloths will be diagonal and cringles and thimbles will be extra strong. Care should be taken not to leave your storm jib in a locker where it may be exposed to dampness and it should be brought out and aired on sunny days at least several times a season. You may need this sail seldom but when you do you will probably need it badly, so take good care of it.

Since the spitfire will usually be rigged on the jibstay and will be trimmed with the working jib sheets, it is advisable to provide a short pennant rigged from the tack of the sail to the fitting on the bowsprit or stem head (wherever the jibstay leads). This pennant may be of either manila or wire rope. The length of the pennant will depend upon the location on deck of the jib sheet lead blocks. The lead of the sheet should be such that if it were continued to the jibstay it would intersect that stay at a point slightly above the miter of the jib. An angle of about five degrees above the miter would be about right in most cases. In determining the proper length for the tack pennant, therefore, rig the sheet and hoist the sail until the desired relationship is established. This will give you the proper length, which will also serve to keep the foot of the sail out of the water when the yacht is plunging into a head sea and taking it green over the bow. It is hardly necessary to add that this adjustment should be made during fine weather, not in the stress of a storm at sea.

38

Prelude to Deep Water Cruising

by FREDERIC M. GARDINER

[1938]

A WELL-KNOWN DEEP WATER SAILOR naïvely describes how he started across the Atlantic in his yacht, only to find confusion below in the form of gear adrift and gallons of oil in the bilges. Being a good sport he lays the blame nowhere, leaving, rather, the impression that that was just one of those things. A competitor in a Miami-Nassau race turned back because his storage batteries had gone adrift and nearly asphyxiated the crew. That was another of those things. And I shall never forget the day I myself proudly launched a fine, able schooner, with all the seacocks open!

We have all gone on cruises on which things went adrift below (with an awful racket); when the cook got seasick and we had to eat cold grub; when water went bad; when the headstay carried away; when somebody forgot to make fast the bitter end on a new hawser; or when the kerosene can capsized into the Irish stew! And we probably all thought "it's all in the game."

Which is a good sporting way to take it, if we have to take it, but why take it? We won't have to take it if we go about things systematically.

There is no unsurmountable obstacle to good behavior alow and aloft, on deck and in the bilges, regardless of the heeling, pitching, wallowing or other motion of the yacht, within reason, of course. I do not maintain that you can go through a hurricane, or emulate Captain Voss's upside down tactics in a typhoon, without the likelihood of some of the gear taking chips out of the carlins. Nor is it possible, at the last moment, to guard against slipshod structural work which is already well covered up; that must be avoided in the building of the ship and in the supervision of work at fitting out time.

Successful preparation for deep water cruising, or racing, is a matter of experience, study, care, and system. The great difference between deep water work and ordinary cruising is that once at sea with no harbors of refuge under your lee, your vessel becomes a world of its own, dependent on her own strength, equipment, and crew for everything. As an old salt said, "There ain't no back door at sea you kin slide out an' get things!"

The weakest link in the chain of operations which prepares a yacht for deep water work, is very apt to be *system*. There are excellent books and articles of references to which you can turn to supplement your own knowledge, and there are plenty of men with whom to discuss your problems. But unless you lay out the work logically, unless you prepare lists, and lists, and more lists, and then follow and check them meticulously, important details which you are fully aware should be taken care of are almost sure to be forgotten. Of course you will say, "Anybody knows that!" Admitted; but while everybody knows it, only about 10 per cent do it thoroughly. The open seacocks over which I blushed were the only things, in that instance, that I can remember which were not taken care of, and *they were not on the list!* They were not on the list because who would ever think that somebody wouldn't remember to close seacocks? So leave out *nothing* from the lists which should be done.

As a first step, divide your yacht into departments:

1. *Deck Department:* Navigation; Boatswain (lamps, paint, sails, etc.) ; Safety appliances.
2. *Engineroom:* Mechanical equipment (include fuel and lubrication) ; Tools and spare parts; Electrical equipment; Fire protection.

3. *Steward's Department:* Galley; Stores; Medical equipment.

There is not space here to attempt to make complete lists of what should be done, or what supplies should be carried for ordinary cruising. Most of you have your own lists from previous seasons; THE GALLEY GUIDE, by Alex W. Moffat, has excellent lists of supplies, spare parts, etc., and DEEP WATER CRUISING, by E. G. Martin, is a book well worth the attention of anyone contemplating that sort of enterprise—well worth, as a matter of fact, rereading before each such cruise.

In the deck department, bearing in mind that you won't be able to run to the corner store to replenish, in addition to the ordinary navigation and other equipment, you must carry all the equipment for celestial navigation, instruments, books, and tables (see catalogs of nautical instrument shops); and if equipped with radio and/or direction finder, charts and instructions to go with them. You must have spare canvas of proper weights to repair both light and working sails, and plenty of it; manila and wire rope to replace running rigging; spare blocks, shackles, and jigs; extra rotators and lines for the patent log; strong canvas covers for hatches and skylights; deadlights for portholes; lumber for fishing broken spars, and wire to go with it; spare slides (for jib-headed rig) or mast hoops (for gaff rig); you should have put baggy wrinkle in the proper places to prevent chafe, but it is a good idea to have some extra made up; candles and candle lanterns; rockets and/or Very pistol and cartridges; and oil (preferably fish oil) for heavy weather, and a pump for *sea work,* not for river cruising!

The carrying of a sea anchor is a controversial subject, but I think every small yacht should carry one in the open sea. Even though the boat may take care of herself in a storm, without a sea anchor she may drift far off her course, or be endangered for lack of sea room. An approximate formula for size of sea anchor is one foot diameter of opening for each 10 feet of waterline length; with a small opening at the peak of the cone, and the length of the anchor one and one-half times the diameter of the large opening.

If you have room, carry a fisherman type dory for a lifeboat; they are by far the most seaworthy. The ordinary "dinghy" is of little value in the open sea. If you can't carry a dory a life raft is the next best bet.

Carry lines to secure the men on watch in heavy weather, with sufficient length of line to give the men freedom of movement, and with sufficient strength so that, if a man is swept overboard the line will hold the strain. Special belts, made for this purpose, are on the market.

As deep water cruising will be almost wholly under sail, the main problem in the engineroom is to see that everything is secured so that you can forget about it. You should, however, be equipped with spare parts of the kind which can be installed without the services of a mechanic (spark plugs, distributor points, etc.), and of course with a complete set of tools. You should also be sure that your exhaust line is arranged, or equipped, so that water cannot get back into the cylinders when following seas boil up to your counter.

Fire is usually thought of in connection with the engineroom, so we may as well speak of it here. Again I assume that those contemplating deep water cruising have sufficient experience to be familiar with the ordinary precautions against fire, and with the types of fire-fighting apparatus applicable to small yachts. If not, they had better familiarize themselves at once, before they start off again on *any* sort of a cruise. One cause of fire, however, which does not seem to be given the consideration it deserves, is spontaneous combustion. Oily rags in a confined space, damp coal—particularly coal dust or soft coal—wet oilskins, and other material of like composition, may yield to heat generated within and burst into flame. Anything of this sort should be kept well ventilated, never put into tight lockers or other unventilated compartments, or in a locker near a stove.

While the food you eat, the water you drink, the fuel with which you cook, may not compare in importance with soundness of hull or adequacy of fire protection, it is far more important than the average yachtsman seems to think. On deep water cruises, particularly, when a five-day offshore cruise may develop into a three weeks' endurance test, they deserve serious consideration.

Too much water, too much food, too much fuel means not only wasteful use of valuable space, but may bring your yacht dangerously low in the water.

In considering supplies for a deep water cruise, or race, you may expect to be at sea for five days, but any of a number of things may happen to prolong that five days considerably. The Bermuda Race normally takes in the neighborhood of four days, but the rules committee requires every competitor to carry "stores sufficient for the crew for three weeks." A good rule of thumb is: take full rations for twice the estimated time, and *add* emergency rations (discussed later) for twice the estimated time.

Suppose, for instance, you plan a five-day cruise with a crew of ten. You allow 10 days' full rations, and 10 days' emergency rations. The following table, for greater elasticity, is based on ounces per man per day.

FULL RATIONS

Water: British Board of Trade allowance, 1 gallon per man per day, 10 days, 100 gallons. Storage of water is discussed later.

Food: 10 men, 10 days; as follows:

	Ounces per Man per Day	Total in Ounces	Total in Pounds
Meats, Poultry, Fish			
* Fresh	2.4	240	15.00
Canned	4.2	420	26.25
Salt (bacon, ham, etc.)	8.0	800	50.00
			91.25
Drinks			
Coffee	2.0	200	12.50
Tea	1.0	100	6.25
Cocoa	1.0	100	6.25
			25.00

	Ounces per Man per Day	Total in Ounces	Total in Pounds
Dairy			
* Milk (fresh) (½ pint)	8.0	800	50.00
Milk (evaporated)	4.0	400	25.00
* Butter (fresh)	2.0	200	12.50
Butter (tinned)	2.0	200	12.50
Eggs (3)	4.0	400	25.00
Cheese	2.0	200	12.50
			137.50
Cereals and Bread			
Dry cereal	1.0	100	6.25
Cereal to be cooked	1.0	100	6.25
* Bread	2.4	240	15.00
Flour	5.6	560	35.00
Pilot bread, crackers	2.0	200	12.50
Cornmeal	1.0	100	6.25
			81.25
Fruits			
Fresh	3.0	300	18.75
Canned	4.0	400	25.00
Dried	1.0	100	6.25
			50.00
Vegetables			
Potatoes	6.0	600	37.50
Onions	1.0	100	6.25
Fresh (green)	2.0	200	12.50
Canned	2.0	200	12.50
			67.75
Soups			
Dried	1.0	100	6.25
Canned	2.0	200	12.50
			18.75
Sweets			
Sugar	6.0	600	37.50
Maple syrup	0.5	50	3.13
Sweet chocolate	2.0	200	12.50
Preserves, jams	4.0	400	25.00
			78.13

Items marked * are expected to be used for the first few days only, while ice supply lasts, *e.g.*, fresh milk supply is equivalent to 1 pint (16 oz.) per man per day, for *5 days,* etc.

In addition, the following seasonings, etc., for the ten days, amount to about 10 pounds total, quantities of each being too small to bother to figure on the "constant" basis.

Salt 2 lbs. (a good deal of cooking of vegetables, cereal, etc., can be done with sea water, either entirely or with part fresh water to suit the taste, thereby saving both fresh water and dry salt); peanut butter 2 lbs.; baking powder 2 lbs.; bay leaf 1 pkg.; Worcestershire sauce 1 btl.; A-1 sauce 1 btl.; tomato catsup 1 btl.; vanilla extract 1 btl.; cloves 1 pkg.; poultry seasoning 2 pkgs.; curry powder 1 can; mustard 1 can; pepper 1 can; lemon extract 2 btls.

The above all comes to 559.8 pounds, or about 5½ pounds per man per day, of unprepared food, equivalent to about 8 pounds of prepared food. From a study of portions, menus, etc., people eat between 6 and 10 pounds of prepared food (4 to 7 pounds of unprepared) per day, and our allowance is about halfway between. On short cruises you can afford to increase the amount, but on very long cruises it will be wise to stay near the minimum, using concentrated foods to make up any apparent deficiency.

Each skipper knows, or should know, the fuel consumption rate of his cooking apparatus, be it for coal, alcohol, bottled gas, kerosene, or what have you. He should, therefore, be able to figure out what supply he should carry.

In stowing coal, kerosene or other liquid fuel, it is not necessary nor advisable to carry the entire supply in or near the galley. A supply for a few days should be in the galley, and the remainder stowed conveniently about the ship, but *handy to get at,* and in dry places.

EMERGENCY RATIONS

Asked to check over the food lists of a friend who was planning an ocean passage, I found supplies adequate for eight weeks for a run which should not take over a week. I finally persuaded him that, when he got his boat loaded she would be so low in the water that he would be taking plenty of chances if he struck heavy weather. By substituting concentrated foods and cutting his time allowance from eight weeks to five, he saved nearly 1000 lbs. in weight in fuel, food, and water and a good deal of valuable space.

The term "emergency rations" means rations on which you can sustain life; they are not intended to supply you with daily banquets. In the following list, if you multiply the figures shown, which represent ounces per man per day, by our constant of 100 man-days, you will get a total weight of 197.51 pounds, but you will have a food value of about 70 per cent of the "full ration" list, due to the highly concentrated character of the food. Water allowance should be ½ gallon per man per day, and should be used for nothing but drinking and cooking, with sea water used for cooking as much as possible. Salt and other condiments take up little room, and the weight is negligible, so use your own judgment in referring to those recommended under "full rations."

Canned meats	2.0	Flour	2.0
Bacon	2.0	Pilot bread	3.0
Dried beef (jars)	1.0	Dried fruit	4.0
Coffee	1.0	Desiccated vegetables	0.5
Tea	2.0	Desiccated potatoes	0.5
Powdered milk (Klim)	1.6	Rice	1.0
Eggs, desiccated	2.0	Sugar	4.0
Cheese	3.0	Sweet chocolate	2.0

Several medical supply houses put up adequate first aid kits, varying in size for duration and crew. In addition to such a kit, or kits, it is wise to take extra "Band-aid," bandages, adhesive tape, sterile gauze, mercurochrome or iodine, castor oil, laxatives, aspirin, bicarbonate of soda, oil of cloves, safety pins, and a goodly supply of brandy (as medicine, not as a beverage).

The selection of crew is of paramount importance; you want some beef, the ability to "take it," and plenty of congeniality! In addition, it is a good idea to check up on tendencies toward *mal de mer* before signing anybody on. I can put up with a deckhand or two who gets seasick, provided they can, and will, do their work; but I rise with a loud and eloquent protest at the thought of a seasick cook!

Finally, a word about stowage. Gear is sure to go adrift when the boat starts to kick up in a rough sea, unless everything is properly secured, and there is nothing more discouraging than a cabin full of loose gear, half of it probably wet. For ocean work additional hooks should be put around in convenient places; you can't have too many! Every drawer, locker door, and compartment should be equipped so that, when you close it it will *stay closed* until you want to open it. The lips on shelves should be raised or, better yet, battens be placed above the shelves to prevent things from sliding out, and down underfoot!

In stowing expendable stores—water, food, fuel, etc.—thought must be given to the trim of the boat. Otherwise, as they are used up, it may spoil the trim of your boat and hurt her sailing qualities. It is difficult to judge the trim of your boat out at sea, unless you get a break of calm weather. It is wise, therefore, to distribute your weights as much as possible. Canned goods, and goods in jars, can be stowed in the turn of the bilge if room is needed, but in this case it is a good idea to use them as early as possible.

One of your heaviest weights is water. It is probable that your regular water tanks will not hold all the water you need to carry. A good solution is 5-gallon gasoline (or other) tins, with a thin coating of paraffin inside. These are easy to handle, and can be stowed at will about the ship, thereby avoiding disturbance of trim and when empty you can give them "the deep six." To paraffin the cans, melt the paraffin in a large pot, getting it good and hot (not boiling). Insert a funnel in the opening of the can (cans should have screw tops), pour the paraffin in, slosh it around quickly, and pour what doesn't stick to the inside of the can back into the pot.

The foregoing professedly covers only the high spots—I might say the pinnacles—of preparation for deep water cruising. But I hope that it will be found to contain useful suggestions.

39

Working Ship—Handling of Square Rigged Vessels

by CAPT. E. I. MORTON

[1936]

IN THE SUMMER OF 1922, moving pictures were taken, south of Noman's Land, of the old New Bedford whaling bark *Wanderer* going through the maneuvers, with her boats, of catching a whale. When these pictures were exhibited, men acquainted with the sea wondered why, with such an opportunity, she was not shown tacking ship. This is a sight now rarely seen and will soon be only a memory to old sailormen, revived, perhaps, when reading tales of the sea.

My first voyages were made in schooners. When I first boarded a square rigger I wondered at the maze of spars and rigging, some of which appeared unnecessary. Yet, after some years' experience in square riggers, I found them more comfortable and much to be preferred for deep water voyages. Sail can be quickly reduced without reefing big sails and can be furled aloft on the yards where it is dry instead of below, with a deck full of water. Besides this, in calm weather, they will roll more easily when broadside to a swell at a time when schooners would find it necessary to lower their sails to prevent ruining both sails and gear by slatting.

Some modern yachts have been rigged as ships, barks and brigantines, and many yachtsmen are interested in the art of handling them. A bark is, perhaps, the best rig for illustrating the method of getting under way from an anchorage, tacking ship, wearing round, and similar maneuvers. A bark is square rigged on both foremast and mainmast, but fore-and-aft rigged on the mizzen-mast, therefore not greatly different from either a ship or a brigantine.

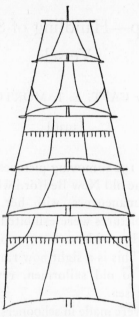

The square sails on mainmast, or foremast- mainsail, lower topsail, upper topsail, topgallantsail and royal. The forward side, showing buntlines and leech lines.

Lying at anchor, head to the wind, with yards square and ready to get under way, all hands "man the windlass." The chain cable is hove short, when the mate gives the order: "Avast heaving"; then, if the pawl is not in place, "Heave in pawl," and the windlass is moved enough for the pawl on the after side of the pawl bitts to drop into its notch on the windlass.

The men are now ordered to loose all the sails, alow and aloft, if the wind is light or moderate; the port watch goes to the foremast and jibboom, while the men of the starboard watch hurry aft to the main and mizzen. The spanker and mizzen stay-sail can be hoisted when ready.

The jibs and staysails are now loose and ready for hoisting and the square sails are held by the bunt gaskets only, ready to be dropped from the yards at the order, by men stationed aloft at both the fore and maintops. As the sails drop from the yards the first mate, forward, and the second mate, at the main, let go clewlines and buntlines and the lower topsails are sheeted home. Then upper topsails are hoisted up, while the foresail and mainsail (called the courses) are left hanging in the gear with the bunt gaskets still fast.

The yards are braced according to the course desired to be made at the start. If to make a reach on the starboard tack, the mainyard is trimmed by slacking away on the starboard and haul-ing in on the port braces, while the foreyard is trimmed aback by hauling in on the starboard braces. The windlass is again manned and, as the anchor breaks away, the bow pays off to port and the jibs and staysails are hoisted and trimmed. As soon as the maintopsails are rap full, the foreyard is swung by hauling on the port braces until the sails fill on the starboard tack.

The foresail is next set. The man aloft at the fore lets go the bunt gasket and pushes the sail off the yard, while the men on deck tail on to the foretack and foresheet as the clew garnets, buntlines and leechlines are cast off their pins, allowing the sail to spread. If the gear is wet or foul, the man aloft can assist by overhauling the ropes through the lead blocks. The foretack is passed through the leader on the weather side of the forecastle-head and hove down by the capstan. If sailing "full and by," the fore bowline is rove and hauled taut forward to allow the sail to fill close-hauled, while the lee sheet is hauled aft.

The bark is now under way with sail enough to handle her; the topgallantsails and royals are to be set whenever desired. If making short tacks, the mainsail can be left hanging in the gear, but if on a long reach, it can be dropped and trimmed as was done with the foresail, trimming tack and sheet and haul-ing out the main bowline. If leaving an anchorage with a fair wind, the spanker and mizzen staysails should not be set until the ship is off on her course.

When sailing "full and by" and about to tack ship, the helmsman is ordered to keep her "full for stays." With a good rap full, increased headway is gathered for coming about. The master

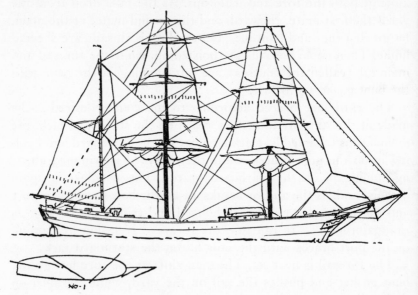

A bark just leaving her anchorage with mainyard, spanker and mizzen staysails trimmed on the starboard tack, while the foreyard is aback to pay her head off as the anchor breaks out. The courses are still hanging in the gear for easy swinging of the yards and giving better view on deck.

takes position on top of the house on the poop and shouts the order: "Stand by for stays!" The second mate and the afterguard take their stations near the mainmast, and the lee braces, fore and main, are coiled down on deck in flakes so as to run easily and without fouling when the yards are swung. The first mate is stationed on the forecastlehead with a few men.

The captain now shouts the order: "Ready about!" and, to the second mate: "Clew up the mainsail!" The main tack and sheet are slacked away while the crew haul up on the clew garnets. The buntlines and leechlines are hauled up enough to be out of the way and give the master a clear view to the forecastlehead from his station. At the same time, the first mate unhooks the fore tack and lets the forward leech of the foresail hang on the fore bowline. The weather foresheet is thrown out of the beckets in the fore rigging and the cook jumps out of the galley to haul it in when the yards swing.

The captain now shouts the order: "Hard-a-lee!" and, to the helmsman: "Down helm, hard down!" The wheel is put hard down and the men forward ease up the jib sheets as she comes up into the wind. The second mate stands by the lee main braces; the crew by the weather main braces. All must be ready for quick work. As she heads up into the wind, the weather side of the maintopsails are caught aback, while the lee side is becalmed by the sails on the foremast. At this moment the captain shouts: "Maintopsail haul!" The second mate throws off the lee braces (which he has prepared for instant release) and the crew round in the slack on the other side. If the move is made at the right moment, the yards will swing around of themselves. The yards on the mainmast are hastily trimmed, staysails and jibs are shifted over and second mate and crew rush to the fore braces.

As she pays off, with the foreyard aback, the sails on the mainmast fill on the other tack and the captain shouts the last orders: "Fore bowline!" and, as the first mate slips the bowline: "Let go and haul!" The second mate lets go the fore braces and the crew pull on the other side, while the cook gathers in the foresheet. At the same time the men on the forecastlehead pull forward and heave down the foretack and haul out the forebowline on the new tack. In tacking a full-rigged ship, the yards on the mizzen are swung at the same time as the mainyard.

When close-hauled on the wind, the fore, main and crossjack (mizzen course) yards are jammed up against the swifter shrouds and backstays by hauling on the lee braces all possible, after which the weather braces are hauled taut to take part of the strain. The upper yards are checked in at a slightly lesser angle so that when steering "full and by" the man at the wheel keeps his eye on the royals to see when the weather leeches begin to lift.

When making short tacks, the weather braces are hitched on the belaying pins when on each tack and kept so until finished. In this way, the second mate can throw off the lee braces and let them run until they fetch up on the hitches. This precaution avoids any danger, in a strong wind, of springing a yard or mast by the yards swinging too far forward. If wind and sea increase

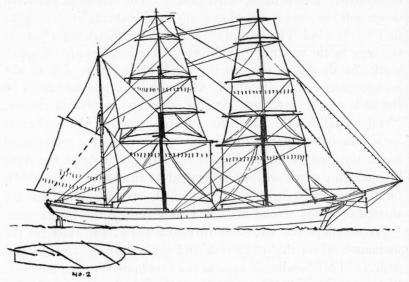

With foreyard braced around, courses set with fore and main bowlines hauled out, the bark is now sailing close-hauled on the starboard tack.

while sailing by the wind, the lee braces should be slackened (to ease the yards off the backstays) and the weather braces tautened, thereby lessening the strain on both hull and spars.

I am reminded of a day long ago when I was second mate of the British bark *Talisman*. She was originally an American vessel in the coffee trade between Brazil and Baltimore but had been put under the British flag during the Civil War to prevent capture by the *Alabama*. We arrived off Sandy Hook on the morning of Dec. 23, 1889, just 23 days from Georgetown, Demerara, with a cargo of bag sugar. Pilot John Wolfe, of the pilot schooner *Mary A. Williams,* had taken us in and out of New York for several voyages and by good luck he came aboard again this morning. Captain Delano remarked: "I do not see any towboats around," to which Pilot Wolfe replied: "What do we want of a towboat; let's sail her up." And so it was agreed. This meant following the old main ship channel down around Southwest Spit, as there was no Ambrose Channel at that time.

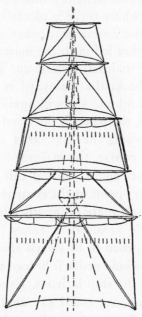

The after side of the same sails, showing clew garnets and clewlines. Also the downhauls on the upper topsail yard and the footropes on the yards.

The wind was fresh NW, just a good, cracking, whole sail breeze, but a dead beat nearly all the way up. Pilot Wolfe took his station on top of the house aft and took charge as if he enjoyed it, while the crew, all young fellows like myself, seemed to share his enthusiasm and worked with a will. As second mate, it was my duty to handle the braces as we continued tack and tack up the bay and through the Narrows. Arriving off Quarantine Station, we did not anchor but simply laid the mainyard aback, stopping her way while the doctor boarded us and granted pratique. Then we filled away and continued up to Red Hook, gradually shortening sail until we anchored there. "Up aloft, boys, and roll 'em up!" shouted Pilot Wolfe before he left his station. *Talisman* was a small vessel and easy to handle, but only one other time did I ever beat a square rigger into New York, pass Quarantine and reach an anchorage under sail.

A square rigger is sometimes caught aback, either by carelessness of the helmsman, an unsteady wind, or a shift of wind. In such a case, if at sea where there is plenty of room, the simplest way to get back on the course is to wear around. The spanker should be lowered or brailed in to the mast, the mizzen staysails hauled down and the mainsail clewed up. Then, as she pays off with the headsails aback, the mainyard is squared so that the sails on the main will fill and she will again gather headway. As steerageway is gained, the wheel is put hard up and she will come around without disturbing the headyards and headsails. As she again luffs up on her course, the mainyard is braced up and the sails on the mizzen set again. During this maneuver the ship's head goes around every point of the compass.

While serving as first mate on another bark on a deep water voyage, I was greatly annoyed at times by the action of the master when she happened to be struck aback. Instead of squaring the mainyard, he would order it braced up sharp on the other tack, thereby putting the ship in irons. Even the sailors saw the absurdity of it, yet no one could say anything for those were the captain's orders. As may be easily understood, the forward sails were forcing her astern and holding her head off, while the sails on the main were forcing her ahead and her head up, causing her to lie there broadside to the wind. Of course, she would eventually gather headway enough to get her around but much time and patience was lost by this lack of skill. If the captain went below for a minute, I grasped the opportunity to square the mainyard and the sailors would jump to the task, grinning.

In wearing ship, the performance is much the same except that the ship is changing her tack and the maneuver is usually made in heavy weather, under short sail, when tacking is not feasible. As before, the spanker is lowered or brailed up and the mizzen staysails hauled down. The helm is put up and, as she pays off, the mainsail is hauled up and the mainyard squared. While before the wind, the jibs and staysails can be shifted over, then the foreyard is braced around on the other tack and properly trimmed. As she luffs up on the new tack, the mainyard is braced forward and the after sails reset. Wearing ship may be necessary when entering a port, sailing up a river, or making turns in following a channel.

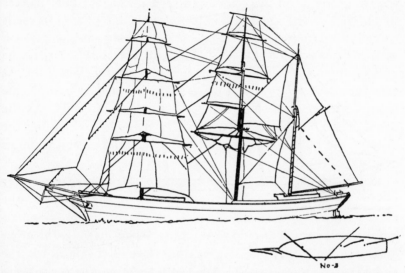

Tacking ship. The mainsail has been hauled up, the mainyard swung and braced up on the port tack. The foreyard is aback, while the foresail is hanging on the fore bowline waiting for the order: "Fore bowline" and "Let go and haul!"

Many years ago, a Maine shipping firm sent a schooner captain to San Francisco to take command of a full-rigged ship. Another shipmaster (a personal friend) took him to task about it, asking how he dared take charge of a square rigger without previous experience in one. His reply was, "Oh, that was all right. I towed to sea and ordered the mate to make sail. Then, when offshore, I told the mate to put her around to see how she worked. I watched what he did and soon got on to it." At that time no government licenses were necessary, but one wonders whether the underwriters were notified.

In the 1880's many Nova Scotia brigantines traded between

Halifax and other home ports and the West Indies with dried
salt fish and potatoes, southbound, sugar and molasses, north-
bound. Many of them came into Port of Spain, Trinidad, where
a large fleet of sailing ships was always anchored. These small
craft anchored inside the larger vessels, not far from the jetty.
The regular Trade Wind blows directly offshore so that they

No-4

Now the foreyard has been swung and the bark is braced up on the port tack, with
mainsail again set and fore and main bowlines hauled out.

laid head on to the shore when anchored. It was a pretty sight
to see them taking their departure. The topsails, topgallantsail
and royal were sheeted home and hoisted, while the foresail was
left hanging in the gear. The foreyard was braced up sharp and,
as the anchor broke away, the jibs were hoisted, causing the
vessel to spin around on her heel within a short compass. The
yards were then squared and they would glide out between the
other ships like living things, a really beautiful sight to a sailor's
eye as they were kept clean and trim as yachts.

A ship or bark running nearly before the wind will make better
speed and steer better with part of the after sail taken in. If the
wind is quartering enough for all sail to draw, it is customary

to haul up the weather clews of the mainsail and crossjack to allow the forward sails to draw better.

The old ships had the clewlines led into the bunt, or amidships on the yard, but in later years many changed them to the yard-arms, especially on topgallants and royals. On the courses it is preferable to have the sail clewed up inboard rather than have the heavy sheets and tacks dangling from the extreme yardarm, outside of the ship's rail. The buntlines are rove through lead blocks on the tops and yards and made fast to large grommets or cringles in the foot of the sails, one on each side. The leechlines lead through blocks well out on the yards and are made fast about halfway down the leeches of the sails. Sometimes spilling lines are used for buntlines and leechlines, in which case the lines are rove through bull's eyes or cringles in foot and leeches of the sails, then brought up and made fast on the under side of the yards near their respective lead blocks. In this way the sails are pulled more snugly up to the yards before furling, but they need more overhauling aloft when setting the sails.

At sea it is customary to overhaul the buntlines and leechlines so as to hang slack on the fore part of the sails, the standing and running parts being stopped, that is, tied together just below the lead blocks with two parts of twine. This is done to prevent continual chafing of the ropes on the sails. On large ships, a double set, inner and outer buntlines, were used on upper top-sails and courses, with bull's eyes fitted on the fore part of the sails through which the buntlines were rove to act as fairleaders in snugging up the big sails. Buntlines on topgallantsails were often rove through lizards in the foot of the sails and carried out and fastened in the leeches.

Square riggers need more room to get under way than fore-and-aft rigged vessels, as they make some sternway in filling away from an anchorage. They have an advantage over schooners, however, in being able to stop quickly by backing the yards.

At Grand Turk, vessels anchor on the edge of the reef, on the lee side of the island. It is safe anchorage in good weather as long as the Trade Wind blows. I was there as first mate of a brigantine when the Trades became light and squalls made up to the westward, so hove up anchor and put to sea, leaving the captain ashore. We returned the next day, when the Trade Wind again prevailed, anchoring safely on the edge of the reef. A pilot was on board but the captain was anxiously pacing the beach as we approached the reef, backed the yards, and let go anchor.

Perhaps enough has been written for the purpose of this article for, as a sea yarn is never-ending, so recollections of past experiences follow without pause when drawing from the storehouse of the memory.

40

Easy Does It

by ALEXANDER W. MOFFAT

[1949]

HERB STONE AND I had a provocative conversation at a Cruising Club dinner about the problems of the man and his wife who want to keep afloat but who, on account of increasing years, want to take things a little easier. At the moment it seemed like an easy point of view to present. My wife and I have cruised amicably together in all sorts and sizes of craft for 35 years, barring of course those periods when babies arrived during the cruising season or when a couple of wars intervened. We look forward to many more years afloat.

The actual analysis of the factors involved proved to be like shooting coot from a dory—there are too many misses. The subject cannot be dismissed by saying that for one couple the solution is adding a paid hand or, for another, switching to a smaller craft or, in the case of the sailing man, going motorsailer. The common denominator is not just a desire to take things a little easier. That can be done, in most instances, by staying at the mooring and playing house until the weather is just right. That is not good enough. Nor is the addition of a paid hand, even assuming there is room for one, a happy solution for a couple to whom their ship is an escape to a privacy which is a very special part of the appeal of living afloat.

Let us consider the case of a man and his wife, both healthy and experienced in living together afloat, who want to continue to be aboard as much of the time as his job permits. They are sixtyish.

Their children have grown up and scattered. These oldsters are competent to handle their present ship in any circumstance within their physical limitations. Aye, there's the rub! Neither is as able-bodied as each was. The wife finds that balancing in the galley, climbing in and out of dinghies, hanging on in a squall, are unexpectedly tiring. The husband finds that it takes longer to go forward and that the gear is heavier than he remembered. His back is likely to ache. Being overtired is not conducive to sleep. He finds that on deck he is single-handing it most of the time, and he has had one or two bad scares which he has not admitted to his wife.

There is no blueprint for the size or type of vessel for this situation, but there is one axiom that fits: the smallest vessel that will meet one's needs will be the safest and the most fun. The factors involved must be considered in relation to the size and type of boat that is currently proving to be a little too much of a handful. Some are factors to be increased; some to be decreased. They are, however, universal of application whatever the craft.

Reduce	*Increase*
Hurry	Stability
Ambition	Labor-saving gadgets
Physical labor	Comfort on deck and below
Size of vessel	Relative size of ground tackle
Speed of vessel	Tank capacities
Sail area	Electrical supply
Bright work	Size of boarding ladder
Unnecessary hazards	Size of dinghy
	Stowage capacity
	Forelaying

First, let's scrutinize the whys and wherefores of the factors to be reduced. Try to take more time to do everything, from loading the dinghy to getting the anchor. Hurry is usually caused by a state of mind or nervous tension, rather than by necessity. Move as slowly as the job in hand will permit. A relaxed mind saves the muscles a lot of fatigue. Easy does it.

As you get older you have to reduce your ambition. Plan shorter day's runs, so that you can make a comfortable start in the morning and be all secured in your port of destination before dark. When you fall in with another vessel going your way at about the same speed, resist the temptation to try to beat her. Save that extra work of breaking out a light sail just because you always have. Remember? This is a practical old age for which you are conditioning yourself. Reduction in physical labor requires study for any man habituated to a routine. More of this when we get to labor-saving gadgets. There have been no gadgets invented, however, for moving stores aboard.

Try taking the ice aboard in smaller pieces. Divide up the groceries into smaller, more easily lifted cartons. Every one of those cartons which can be so easily lowered into the dinghy must be lifted over the rail when you get alongside. Don't try to lift anything you can't stand over; use your leg muscles as well as your back.

Then there is the matter of purchase. The International Marine Dictionary, that invaluable volume, defines purchase as "A general term for any mechanical arrangement or tackle which increases the force applied by a combination of pulleys." This means, to you, that if your vessel is not equipped with wire halyards and modern winches it behooves you to multiply your "pulleys." If you have a gaff rig, for instance, substitute a triple and a double block for a double and a single on the throat. Also, a handy billy is handy indeed wherever an extra strain is needed. The usual handy billy is a single block and a double block with a hook on each, rove with light manila. All that is needed is a couple of grommets about three feet long spliced up for throwing a stopper on any standing part.

The size of a vessel, in considering this subject, is so relative to past experience and to her gear that no generalizations can be made. For a couple of oldsters their ship should be big enough only for headroom, elbow room and a reasonable degree of dryness; small enough to be comfortably within their capacity to keep up according to their standards. It has been truly said that it does not take much money to keep a boat—it only takes all you have. Be that as it may, the smaller the vessel, the less the financial worry entailed.

Speed is definitely a factor which should be reduced. Whether straight power or auxiliary, there is nothing more wearing than the sounds which accompany vibration. Ask your wife. Running always on less than half throttle is more conducive to relaxation than you would believe. If you are weak-minded, a screw stop in your throttle quadrant accomplishes the result. Another important aspect of reduced speed is that it permits the navigator to be unhurried in his calculations and to run out his courses in fog at a speed both safe and constant. This contributes to his confidence in the safety of his vessel. Lack of confidence on his part is a communicable disease, as far as his wife is concerned.

Carry less sail to avoid, as often as possible, the exertion of shortening sail. When you think you may have to shorten, get at it before you are forced to hurry. In considering a new rig, plan to have one that is all inboard. Fighting a jib on a bowsprit or passing a gasket hanging out over the stern is as good a way as any to strain a gizzard. Balancing is not as easy as it used to be. You can do it, but your wife may be apprehensive about your losing your hold or straining yourself. If she is a good shipmate she may not say so, but she will be much happier if you give her the fewest possible causes to worry about your welfare.

Bright work requires continuous attention. Varnish and brass, if kept up to standard, require time that could otherwise be devoted to doing other necessary tasks more slowly, with an overall gain in rest and relaxation. Trim and brass can both be painted appropriately and your ship still kept smart.

For peace of mind, unnecessary hazards must be reduced. The greatest of these is fire. Fire is most likely to originate in the engine space or in the galley. The former can be taken care of by an automatic system of piped CO_2 which will smother almost any fire at its inception. In most galleys, however, the space is not sufficiently confined for effective employment of a piped system. Flooding a whole cabin with any unbreathable vapor may be more hazardous than would be a fire attacked with hand-directed equipment. Whatever the equipment installed, it should be augmented by portable instruments for fighting fire, particularly in the galley. Avoid any extinguisher of a type whose fumes can cause serious injury to the lungs.

If a gas stove is used, the supply tank should be located on deck, well secured, and all pipe fittings should be oversize. Piping should be attached to the structure of the vessel to prevent vibration.

Drip pans under engine as well as under carburetor should be provided to prevent any fuel reaching the bilges. Fuel tanks should be installed above a watertight, self-draining deck in case of overflow in filling. Air vents should be led outboard, away from any position where cigarettes are likely to be flipped near them.

Another contribution to peace of mind is to take all precautions against the possibility of falling overboard while under way, particularly at night. When two persons are cruising together and only one is on deck, it is a constant source of anxiety to the other that the one on deck might fall and go overboard while unconscious from a crack on the head or even slip overboard, without being heard.

The first precaution is always to use shoes with soles that really grip; the second is to use lifelines and follow the adage "one hand for the ship and one for yourself." In the case of older persons, whose balance and reflexes are not as rapid as they used to be, it should not seem an extreme precaution always to wear a kapok or air-filled jacket while on deck at night. It should be equipped with a small waterproof battery light. Other precautions which should be taken at night are to tow a dinghy on a long painter and have a ring buoy with a water light located where it can be most quickly released.

Nothing takes the fun out of cruising as much as a situation which causes apprehension to one or the other of the couple. Quit being a viking and don't be ashamed to take precautions to offset your increasing physical handicaps. There ought to be engraved on the main beam of every ship what a very old sailing ship captain once said, "If you are going to sea, and going in safety, you got to be particular."

Now for the factors which should be increased. First comes stability. Entirely aside from the factor of safety in case of a sudden knockdown, it is easier to cook, to eat, to sleep, and safer to move around, on a vessel at a reasonable angle of heel. Shelf stowage becomes more practicable. Plenty of beam is likely to make for a dryer vessel.

Use all the labor-saving gadgets you can apply to your particular ship. Halyard winches should be located at the right height on the mast for you to handle in an erect position, sheet winches where you can operate them close to your body instead of at arm's length.

The job most conducive to strain is getting the anchor. If you have an engine, the recommended procedure is to come ahead until you have taken in all slack, make fast and break out the anchor with the engine. Raising it and getting it aboard single-handed after it is broken out is likely to cause over-exertion because of the frequent necessity for haste. The ideal solution for older people is an electric windlass whelped for chain, the chain led over a roller chock on the bowsprit at a point more than the length of the shank from the stem. This applies to any type of kedge or patent anchor. If your vessel has no bowsprit, install a flat bowsprit of suitable length for your anchor, to be used just for carrying the bower anchor. Such a bowsprit can be supported by a rod in place of a bobstay.

The electric windlass can be wired to control from the cockpit as well as from forward. Without going forward you can raise the anchor two-block to the bowsprit and let it hang there until you have your vessel in the clear. When you can conveniently go forward, with the boathook pick up a line which is always trailing from the anchor, take a turn around the capstan head of the windlass and swing the anchor up under the bowsprit where it may be secured. No mud comes aboard, nothing is scratched, your anchor is always ready for quick release and there's no exertion.

Increase, also for peace of mind, the weight of your ground tackle. With an electric windlass you can use an anchor a good deal heavier than you would care to manhandle, particularly if you do not attempt to stow it inboard. You will sleep better, knowing that your chain is chafe-proof and your anchor adequate.

Instead of rowing, use the lightest, smallest outboard you can find. Lift it aboard, or lower it to the dinghy by a whip on the rigging which can also be used on the ice tongs and on a miniature cargo net for bringing stores aboard.

Give up the idea of taking the dinghy aboard. Own a long guinea pump, long enough so that you can stand on your deck and clear the dinghy of water alongside. Use two painters, a long one for towing and a short one equipped with a few cork floats to use when maneuvering. You can thus avoid, someday, the hard work of having to clear a line from your propeller.

Rig a becket so that it is always handy to take a turn on your steering wheel in case you want to go forward without disturbing your partner.

The older you get, the more comfort counts. Use the modern foam rubber mattresses instead of the stuffed variety, which absorb moisture and mat down from sitting on the inboard edges of bunks. Arrange cabin and cockpit so that there are sloping surfaces to lean back against for relaxation.

Provide hand rails on the deck house and under the carlines in the cabin, for ease in moving around the ship.

Have an awning that rigs high enough to provide headroom, wide enough to shed water overboard instead of into the cockpit. A full width forward curtain to button on makes the cockpit livable at anchor in wet weather.

In planning revisions for old age, increase tank capacities. Have more than one fuel tank, with double strainers on each line. Two people are twice as comfortable with 100 gallons of fresh water as with 50. Increase battery capacity. Whether you use a separate charging unit or an extra oversize generator on your propulsion engine, be able to throw plenty of juice into your batteries. Also, always keep one spare battery, fully charged, that can be cut in if emergency arises, to be considered in the same category as emergency rations. It is pleasant to be able to read as late as you choose with a good reading light. It is even pleasanter to know that if you have to turn out to handle the anchor, an electric windlass will do the dirty work.

Two other items which should be increased for more comfortable use are the size of the dinghy and the size of the boarding ladder. The ladder should be a hinged affair so that when dropped there will be at least three steps under water so mother can get aboard easily after swimming. I have found a Dyer dhow to be a high-sided, stable, incredibly dry dinghy weighing only 100 pounds. It tows level and is generally as satisfactory a piece of floating equipment as two elderly persons could ask for.

As a couple become accustomed to living afloat together, they learn to utilize all possible stowage space. However, they also seem to keep acquiring more and more gear for which space must be found. In a four-berth ship, one berth can advantageously be sacrificed for the construction of additional locker space, and an air mattress on the deck used for the second occasional extra guest.

As people get older there must be more "forelaying" in everything they do afloat, more careful consideration of the weather, more planning of each operation in advance, more precautions against hazards due to physical deficiencies. In spite of these limitations the older people who love boats and cruising get even more satisfaction from their life afloat than most of the restless young.

WIND IN THE WILLOWS, by Kenneth Grahame, describes the appeal of cruising in these gifted words: "Believe me, my young friend, there is *nothing*—absolutely nothing—half as much worth doing as simply messing about in boats. Simply messing about in boats—or *with* boats. In or out of 'em, it doesn't matter. Nothing seems really to matter, that's the charm of it. Whether you get away, or whether you don't; whether you arrive at your destination or whether you reach somewhere else, or whether you never get anywhere at all, you're always busy, and you never do anything in particular; and when you've done it there's always something else to do, and you can do it if you like, but you'd much better not. . . ."

41

Why Not Retire Afloat?

by WILLIAM H. TAYLOR

[1949]

THIS ARTICLE isn't for the man who can maintain summer and winter homes and a yacht when he's no longer active in his business or profession. It's for the mellowing citizen who wants to enjoy his declining years, who's never been able to do all the cruising he'd like, and who plans sooner or later to retire on an income of which he will have to count the dimes and stretch the dollars to live pleasantly. An increasing number of individuals and couples have such plans, and among them must be many who would like to live afloat, for a few years at least. In fact, many already do.

It can be done very practically provided the man has, in addition to the inclination, three qualifications. He should have, or acquire before retirement, some experience in the maintenance and handling of boats. He should be in normally sound health for his age. And he must have a few thousand dollars he can invest in a suitable boat (unless he already has one) on the premise that he can get all or most of his investment back if and when he later decides to swallow the anchor. Obviously, if he has a wife, she must also enjoy life afloat, or at least be game to give it a fair try.

The economic principle is that, during the years you live afloat, your boat is your home and your transportation, thereby eliminating certain major shore expenses. You pay no rent or

operating cost on a home ashore; you eliminate heavy winter
fuel bills and some clothing expense; you need no automobile;
you pay no home real estate taxes and may, by judicious maneuvering, avoid some others. If you own a home you want to keep,
you can lease it until you're ready to come ashore again. If you
contemplate eventually acquiring a smaller house, or one in a
different climate, you can sell your present home and there's
the money for your boat, plus probably some thousands left
over. If you don't own a home, what you'll save in rent should
run your boat. And as you cruise up and down the coast you
can keep a weather eye open for the place you might some day
want to settle down in.

We'll take up some financial details later, but first let's choose
a boat. And here let me commend to any reader interested in
this project Sandy Moffat's article, "Easy Does It," in this
volume, which is directly applicable to this subject.

Requirements will be somewhat different than for a boat
used for summer weekends and an annual vacation cruise. You'll
want full headroom and good floor space; more than normal
locker and stowage room; a couple of really comfortable chairs;
berths as comfortable as your beds at home; lighting equipment
you can read by on long evenings. An enclosed bridge or cockpit
will make life pleasanter in bad weather, and an adequate cabin
heater is a must, for though you'll doubtless follow the sun
south there will be cold, damp days. She should be a strongly
built boat, with guard rails for lying alongside docks, and of
moderate draft for anchoring up in the little creeks and gunkholes.

Among the things you won't need are high speed, which is
extravagant in either power or sail, for you'll have all the time
there is; fancy finish, which takes money or work, or both, to
maintain; and extreme seakeeping qualities. Seaworthiness is
essential, but most of your running will be along the coast, where
harbors are a few hours apart, or on inland waters. Having
lots of time, you can lie snug in port when it looks nasty, and
make your outside runs when the weather indications are good.

Most people planning this kind of life will choose a powerboat, even those who are windjammers at heart, because the power cruiser usually has more accommodations for her tonnage and cost, good headroom and above-deck shelter. A good sailing dinghy can provide the sailing. If you still prefer sail on your cruising home, an auxiliary with plenty of beam and short ends is recommended, as is a divided rig for ease of handling.

The smallest boat in which you can live comfortably will be the best, for both economy and ease of handling and maintenance, but she'll still be larger than you'd need for weekend and vacation cruising. A man alone, used to small boats, may be snug and happy in a 30-footer. For a couple, 35 feet would be about the minimum and 40 feet better for year-round living. If this sounds a bit heavy for one of retirement age, there are ways to make the work easier—again we refer you to the Moffat article. If it were me, I'd install a gipsy winch such as the lobstermen use to haul their pots, run through a power take-off from the main engine. With that and a couple of snatchblocks you can stand in your cockpit and heave in your anchor or put a real strain on any line in the ship.

Bearing the essentials in mind, you'll buy the type of boat that appeals to you. This is a long range proposition. Take your time, scour the boatyards, bedevil the yacht brokers sufficiently, and sooner or later you'll find *your* boat at a price you can pay. She must be roomy and sturdy, in sound structural condition, and not one of the light, high-speed floating greenhouses that will roll your head off every time an outboard skiff goes by. She may be something of the motor houseboat type, at one extreme, or the motor sailer type at the other. A converted Navy, fishing or workboat hull may suit you better than a fancier yacht type. You must decide for yourself how far you can and should go in rehabilitating a superficially run-down craft, but don't fool with basically unsound tubs.

The time to buy your boat is at least a couple of years before you retire. Money for purchase and outfitting will be easier to come by while you're still on the active earning list. Spend as much time aboard as conditions permit, not so much to get used to life afloat as to find out and accomplish improvements to fit the

boat for 365-days-a-year living. You may want new berth cushions, or wider berths. You may knock out a berth and install a big
full length locker in its place, and perhaps enlarge the head.
Perhaps you'll need to increase her fuel, water or ice capacity,
or, if an auxiliary, trim down her working sail area a bit. She
may need a new engine or a thorough overhauling of the old
one. The cook may demand a different stove, better utensil and
dry stores stowage, or a galley ventilator. The skipper may
want an adequate chart table, a comfortable helmsman's seat,
an engineroom work bench or a lighter or heavier anchor. No
boat is finished until she's sunk, but if you spread these preparatory costs and jobs over a pre-retirement period, when the time
comes to shut up your desk ashore you'll be ready to cast off
the dock lines and shove off.

Most cruisers have more berths and less locker space than
the permanent boat dweller needs. You want enough berths so
that children and friends can visit aboard by ones and twos,
but not enough so they will settle down en masse for indefinite
periods. On the other hand, don't have so much stowage space
that you'll be tempted to haul tons of unnecessary possessions
along with you. If you're closing a home ashore, a storage ware-
house will take care of the family heirlooms at little cost and
no trouble to you.

Coming back to the universally unpopular subject of expenses,
we won't try to quote actual figures. They won't be the same
for any two people, or couples. Your income, habits, tastes,
and your outfit will determine what you spend, just as they
would if you were living ashore. You can get along on very
little, or you can spend as much as you can afford. We are trying
merely to compare living costs ashore and afloat.

As against the annual cost of maintaining a home ashore,
either as its owner or in rent, you will have the cost of maintaining your boat, which needn't be large. When business took
most of your time, you had to pay a shipyard to do most of
the work on your boat. Now, instead of a few hectic spring
weekends (on half of which it rained) you can spend as much
time as you like working on the boat, and pick suitable weather.

Unlike the usual spring fitting out rush, year-round maintenance of a boat can be done at leisure, a bit at a time, by an owner living aboard. The equivalent of an hour's work a day should keep a 40-footer in apple pie order year in and year out. For the jobs that are beyond your skill or strength—you'll be surprised how few there are when you have the time to plan and work on them—you are free to shop around the yards that are out of the high-rent-and-wages areas near the big cities and find one that will do the work satisfactorily and cheaply. If your boat is the right model, not too deep and with a straight keel, you can even save some hauling charges by laying her ashore over a tide or two, in a sheltered cove with a hard, sloping beach, to paint the bottom, work on the propeller or rudder, or caulk a seam.

If your hull is sound to start with—and you should have a qualified surveyor determine that before buying—your boat should last as long as you'll want her and have a good resale value when you're through; perhaps higher than you paid, if you've treated her right. A yacht that is used and cared for continuously will outlast one that is stored ashore for half the year.

Much of the above applies to engines as well as hulls. Most yacht engines don't wear out, they rust out. Even if you cruise from the Great Lakes to the Bahamas and back every year, your engineroom log will show only a fraction of the running hours of a fishing or work boat. Frequent but moderate use, with constant good care, is better for an engine than long winter lay-ups. A simple, well built marine engine, not necessarily the cheapest to buy, will be the most economical in the end. Any estimate of expenses should include depreciation to cover replacement in five or 10 or more years, depending on how good an engine it is and how you use and take care of it. Carry a full set of spare parts, learn to do at least the simpler repair and maintenance jobs, and your engine should cost you less than you used to spend on the cars you no longer need. (If you want a shore cruise now and then, drive-yourself cars are reasonable in most big ports.) Fuel, of course, will run several times as much per mile as it would in a car, but you won't travel as many miles. Which brings up the point that, since time is what you're going to have plenty of, you'd be silly to have a lot of power in your retirement yacht. You can go a long way in a day at eight or nine knots, and cruise from Florida to Maine or the Lakes and back without spending too many days under way.

Sails, if you have them, are another depreciation item. But you won't need costly racing sails; you won't often carry them through hard blows, and you'll be aboard to keep them aired and dried. Well made, of heavy material but not necessarily of expensive imported canvas, and treated with a good preservative, a suit will last many years—especially up-and-down cut gaff sails, if speed is no object.

Yacht insurance is expensive and there's not much you can do to save on it, unless you're willing to omit it altogether—too risky a gamble for a man with a sizable slice of his capital tied up in his boat. Otherwise, go to a good broker, tell him your plans, and make the best deal you can.

Food costs about the same afloat as ashore. You can shop as cannily in the ports you visit as you could anywhere; you can dig clams, catch fish and even shoot ducks (beware the game warden in states where you have no license) and you can often buy fish and lobsters, and sometimes farm products, cheaply in the out-of-the-way places. But staples and canned goods cost pretty much the same anywhere and some things, like fresh meat, come high in the small coast towns. Liquor and entertainment bills are what you make them, afloat or ashore, so let your income and tastes be your guides. This also goes for any shore-going or off-the-boat activities.

The tax picture is worth looking into. A yacht is subject to taxation as personal property in some states, and in some towns the assessor covers the waterfront on a certain date and tries—repeat, tries—to collect taxes on every boat he finds, transient as well as local. In other places you may keep a boat for years without hearing from the tax collector. Some seaboard states have income taxes and some don't. It would pay to look fully into the tax possibilities before selecting a home port for your boat and yourself; also into the local tax laws of any port where you lie for an extended period. Let your conscience, if any, be your guide. Roving yachts, and the people who live aboard them, can be hard to catch, but don't play games with the Federal authorities, who can put a plaster on your ship anywhere in American waters.

You will have no furnace to feed, and a little coal heater will keep a cabin warm unless you insist on wintering in icy waters, for which we can see no sensible reason applying to anyone who is footloose and has a boat under him. Cooking aboard more or less continuously, the more expensive stove fuels become an item, and some of them are hard to get, especially in the small southern towns. The most practical combination is a range that will burn anything from hard coal to driftwood, supplemented for hot weather by a pressure stove burning kerosene, which is cheap and obtainable almost anywhere.

Clothing—men's clothing that is, I wouldn't try to tell the ladies what to wear—is an economy item. Dungarees, khakis, sweaters, shorts, sneakers, flannel or tee shirts will take most of the wear on board. A suit of long-handled underwear, a pair of iceman's pants and a warm jacket or windbreaker will be handy, in case winter catches up with you on the way south, and even for an occasional chilly night run in summer up north. Really waterproof gear is a necessity—black rubber suit and boots for serious work and something light and reasonably waterproof for hot weather. None of this is expensive, and for shore-going clothes a decent suit, some gray flannels and a tweed jacket will take care of all occasions, assuming you've outgrown the compulsion to get done up in evening clothes and paint the town every so often. In any event, you'll spend less on clothes than when you had to go to business every day, summer and winter.

So, from the purely practical and mercenary side, year-round living afloat is within many people's reach as a retirement program. It is unnecessary to point out its advantages—either you like it or you don't. A surprising number of families live aboard

their boats in the summer even when the breadwinning member
or members have to commute to business daily, an arrangement
not always either convenient or economical, but obviously enjoyable enough to make it worth doing. Many active men shy away
from retirement for fear of being bored to death with nothing
to do, but the yachtsman need have no such fear. With his boat
and all the things he can do with her, he'll keep busy enough.
He can choose his climate and move up and down the coast
with it. He can moor his home wherever the fishing, the shooting, or the golf calls him. He can loaf away lazy days in the
snug little harbors where life is quiet and pleasant, either alone
or in company with kindred souls in other boats, and when that
palls he can up-killick and move to some port where he has
friends ashore or to some yacht club anchorage where he is
a member or a welcome visitor. When the mood is on him he
can take a fling at the fleshpots in one of the bigger cities or
seasonal resorts. If he gets tired of water all around him, he
can always tie the boat up for a while, charter a rental car, and
head for the nearest foothills. In fact he can do as he damn well
pleases, which for most of us would be novelty enough.

Bigger-than-average icebox and tank capacity are recommended because they make you independent of supply ports for
long periods, in case you want to spend a lot of time up the eel
ruts and in the out islands. But as a change from that sort of
life you can have all the conveniences of modern civilization by
mooring for a while at one of the marinas which are increasing
in number and facilities. There, tied up to a pier for a day or
a month, you can hook into city water, electric current, even
telephone service. You can enjoy dockside store delivery, garbage disposal, hot showers, laundromats, restaurants and movies
within walking distance, and in fact all the conveniences of urban
life. They aren't, of course, free, but neither would they be if
you lived ashore. And with a boat, you can always shove off
and cruise down the bay if the neighbors get too noisy.

One more thought on finances: Most people who have thought
they were going to make a living out of life afloat, by writing
about it, for instance, have learned better. The pickings are

pretty thin. But if, as this article assumes, you have a steady if modest income you may augment it in one way or another. Some boat dwellers write, or paint, or take salable photographs. A couple of men we know of pick up an occasional fee adjusting compasses. Some are itinerant mechanics, carpenters or painters who stop over now and then and take temporary jobs in yacht yards during the rush season. Others, with suitable boats, occasionally take out charter or fishing parties. Such sidelines aren't recommended as producing full-time incomes, but they can help provide the luxuries.

42

Guests Aboard

by EDITH BLISS

[1951]

WE LOVE PEOPLE who hate sailing and readily admit it. Those who say "If it's a flat, calm, sunny day, we'd love to bring our lunch and come sailing tomorrow—but spend a night, or go cruising or on a race? Nothing doing!" That's fine, everyone knows where everyone else stands. But through the years we've learned some painful truths from several of our best friends about the awful times they've had sailing with us.

Having spent my early youth on the water in small boats, sailing with some, let's say "exacting," family skippers, I married what I believed the perfect man afloat. He never raised his voice, never lost his temper, or screamed at me to "Hurry up" when I was obviously doing, as fast as I could, something I didn't have strength for anyhow.

"That's what *you* think," said one of our best non-sailing lady friends one snowy evening last winter. "I'll never forget gnawing my nails all one afternoon in your boat when I was yelled at just for putting the rope around that wench the wrong way a couple of times. You remember," she added, looking at me, "we were racing one of your arch enemies into Edgartown and you got yourself all snarled up in that big Italian sail."

"Italian sail?" There was dead silence and someone said, "Oh, of course. She means the guinea!" "Anyhow," she continued, "no matter how well you think you know anyone on

shore, once they get you afloat they're all dictatorial and smug."
She then told of losing her three best fingernails furling the sail,
and how she had tied up each stop with the greatest neatness,
only to have the skipper say: "Thanks so much, but why don't
you just get out the ice?" while he untied them all and redid
them his way.

How to be the perfect guest afloat? That's the sixty-four
dollar question, and finding the perfect host afloat is probably
just wishful thinking! Everyone's ideals are different, so let's
suppose there are four of us off in a boat about 40 feet overall.
The skipper and his wife are old hands, while our experience
afloat is limited. Here are a few suggestions we feel would help
make for a happier ship.

First, everyone likes to feel useful. We feel helpless watching
other people do all the work, and would be much happier with
some definite job to do, however simple. Most of us aren't such
morons that we can't wash the windshield with fresh water if
we are in a powerboat; or cope with letting the weather runner
or headsail sheet go at the proper time, if we're sailing. One
couple were completely exhausted and discouraged recently by
spending the greater part of the day in a small cutter trying
to dodge their hostess. She was flying around the cockpit trying
to man two winches as well as the tiller while her husband went
forward alone to take the genoa around the mast.

Once shown, we'd like to be trusted. Trusted to produce the
bumpers or boom crotch at the proper moment, to cope with
one of the flags at colors, or to see that the dinghy painter
doesn't get fouled in the propeller while maneuvering. We'd
like to help with the anchor or mooring; or else be briefed not
to. It's no fun rushing forward when the skipper does (because
of some misguided instinct on our part) only to be hit in the
chest by the butt end of the boat-hook which he is frantically
trying to disentangle from a slimy green mooring line, meanwhile screaming at us to let go some halyard whose name and
whereabouts are a complete mystery. Incidentally, if he *should*
miss the mooring it just might be helpful if we had the faintest
idea which was forward and which reverse on the engine.

Next, we'd appreciate being shown the correct and easy way to throw a line. There's nothing more humiliating than standing conspicuously in the bow with a docking line in your hand which falls smartly into the water six feet short of the outstretched hand on the crowded yacht club dock. We'd also like to learn how to cleat it properly and put a half hitch on it that's not backwards. (The skipper will resignedly undo this anyhow if you do.) And we'd like to know one good, simple knot that will really hold, and that the skipper knows he can count on.

Going below, we'd also like to help, yet we don't want to be one of those eager guests who washes the dishes so thoroughly there's no water left in the tanks. If the host would educate us to the water supply it would avoid that dreadful moment when he hears us say "Hey! what's the matter? This thing won't pump any more!" If ten squirts is our ration for the dish-washing, say so, and we'll stick to it.

Next comes the stove. If the guest is to do the cooking, we would love the skipper forever if he would light the stove for us. We are all familiar with the occasional pyrotechnics of even the best pressure stoves. The dreadful, flaring moment when you think this time you'll really have to grab the fire extinguisher, yet somehow just as you reach out your hand, the flames die out and all is well. Stoves are all individualists, and only their owners seem to know and understand their whims and vagaries.

The last thing we ask of the host is clear and positive instructions in the head, framed and hung. Everyone's nerves and tempers will be spared if its operation is explained or, even better, demonstrated. I speak feelingly, having been trapped in one where the water continued to rise and the sliding door had jammed shut. Everyone else had gone ashore and I thought my last hour had surely come.

Skippers are a queer breed of animal, often hard for the layman to understand. Once you solve the formula, you realize they are kind but bloodthirsty. Do not be startled, at the end of a good day's run when you are safely and snugly on your mooring, and comfortably settled on deck with your favorite drink, to see the skipper's eyes suddenly narrow and glitter with

anticipation. You may be sure he has spied some visiting yachtsman, or even better, one of his best friends, coming boiling
down for his mooring. He secretly hopes the new arrival is
going much too fast and, when this is about to prove hilariously
true, frantically signals to his pal Joe, on the next mooring, to
make sure he doesn't miss the show.

Let's leave the skipper for the moment, contentedly basking
on his mooring, and see what the guest's problems are—one
who has never been off overnight before. Foremost comes the
problem of what to bring; more important, what not to bring.
For the man it's easy, except that he does *not* bring those long
fishing rods (unless he's asked to). He does not bring that huge
tackle box or the stiff suitcase, nor all those bulky, delicate
cameras and equipment, when one will do. He *does* bring a soft,
stowable duffle bag, foul weather gear, Topsider sneakers or
their equivalent, blue jeans, or a pair of old flannels—a warm
sweater, shorts and swimming trunks. The guest in the know
carries his town clothes and three clean shirts on a hanger, and
over them he usually puts his slicker. His shirt is flannel so he
has no sweater, but he might be wearing an old tweed jacket.
In his one small sea bag, in addition to his regular necessities,
he carries sun glasses, a visored swordfishing cap, and Dramamine if he thinks he or his wife may feel seasick. Also a carton
of whatever cigarettes he and his wife smoke (which often
saves the lives of all hands on board) and, last but not least,
a bottle of the host's favorite brand of grog.

For the gals it is a bit more complicated. You may have one
small hanging locker, a shelf or hammock, and a hook or two.
Maybe even a shoe bag on the locker door in which to stow
your small items; and you hope a mirror other than the community one in the head. Anyhow, tuck a small hand mirror in
your bag just in case.

Rule One is, keep your things in the space allotted you. Some
of the most seasoned yachtsmen have a dreadful time when there
is room to put anything away. They never by any chance use the
space assigned them. It goes happily empty while you trip over

their shoes and wonder why they insist on keeping their full seabag on the bunk in the main cabin.

You should remember when planning your clothes for the trip that your locker will probably not be full length, so your dress will be crumpled at the bottom unless you fold and pin it carefully over the bar of a hanger. The chances are you won't need a dress other than the one you wear aboard, which should serve for any trip ashore. A girl is fortunate if she lives within motoring distance and has one silk jersey dress carefully rolled in her bag. I carry my clothes on a hanger as the man does. Slacks or blue jeans and shorts go over the bar of the hanger, shirts and dress over the top, covered with my slicker top. Often you will find a hook where this may hang full length; and you will be surprised at how much you can get on an ordinary strong wooden hanger. This leaves your seabag for sweaters, bathing suit, sneakers, toilet articles, pajamas, etc. Incidentally, the best tailored men's pajamas you can find are both smart and becoming; and if you should be suddenly called to lend a hand on deck at night (which *does* occasionally happen), you'll be grateful not to be caught in pleated nylon.

It's a good idea to consult your hostess as to the clothes she's bringing. Once we cruised with a Powers model who brought a mountain of luggage. You can imagine the skipper's expression when he first saw her coming aboard his small ship. She had at least four changes of clothes per day and used them all; always dressing in the head down to the last bitter bobby pin and flick of mascara with complete disregard for everyone else. It soon became apparent that her prime interest in life was a tan and she smelled up and smeared up the whole boat with glop which did irreparable damage to everything she touched, not to mention the emotions of the skipper and his wife.

One of the most important rules in a small boat is always to put things back. This applies particularly to the bottle-opener and ice pick, but is also applicable to most everything aboard. Your safety may depend on keeping all deck equipment in its proper place.

If you are one of those exceptional guests who loves to cook, and find you can produce meals worthy of the best French restaurant even under unfavorable conditions, two points are worthy of mention. Ask first before you bring a huge cold roast as a surprise from home. Your hostess may have one already filling the icebox to the brim. Secondly, don't try to be a perfectionist and wear yourself out below while everyone else is having all the fun on deck.

Once when we were at the boat races in a friend's cutter, a bright gal who writes a famous food column spent most of the sunny afternoon below in the galley, cracking pepper corns with a hammer for some fancy hors d'oeuvres she was concocting. They were gooey and topped with big, beautiful sprigs of fresh green watercress she'd found ashore and dipped in fancy French dressing. I'll never forget the way the wind took that greenery as she triumphantly produced the platter on deck, nor the agonized expression on the skipper's face as he frantically tried to save his beautiful teak deck by retrieving the oily leaves.

If you have any diet problems, discuss them frankly before you go aboard and thus avoid a situation such as this. The ex-commodore of a neighboring yacht club was invited by some new friends to go on an early September cruise to Maine. They spent a happy three days until the skipper went below one evening after a hard, wet sail, to pour a much-needed scotch and soda for all hands. There was no soda. The commodore sheepishly confessed that he had hated to be a bother, but he just couldn't drink tank water.

There are likely to be unforeseen circumstances in the commissary department over a long weekend if you have children aboard. All of us who have teen-agers know they eat what amounts to one meal a day. It starts upon waking up, and finishes at bedtime. No matter how substantially you've fed them, they're always starved. This is where the snack comes in. One loaf of bread, one whole jar of jam or peanut butter, or both, and a quart of milk apiece is wolfed down and disappears before your bewildered eyes at one quick sitting. Many a cruise has had to be cut short because enough food couldn't be carried to fill this bottomless age group. So tell your hostess ahead of time

how much milk they drink if she asks you, and if they are big
eaters don't hesitate to say so. Small children are less of a problem in the food line, but if they are really little, bring their own
miniature life-preservers, as few boats carry them as regular
equipment. Also any contraption you may have that will keep
them in their bunks. And for all ages, *no* potato chips on board!
You wouldn't believe the crumby, greasy havoc they can cause.

A few last general suggestions. In a strange boat getting
under way, sit quietly in one place so the skipper knows where
you are and keep your feet squarely underneath you until given
some specific job. Avoid sitting in the companionway. No matter
what anyone says, you are in the way and there's something
definitely irritating about it. All skippers are familiar with the
guest who lies down. All day you have to step over him and he
can't possibly move quickly should it be necessary. Also, if you
are in a sailboat, don't sit so close to the wheel or tiller that your
knee gets squashed between it and the seat when the boat comes
about.

Try and learn the nomenclature of this strange new life you
are embarking on. Pretty soon when you are asked to "Ease the
main a little," and shouted at to "Make it fast," don't get panicky and let it go entirely like one gal did at a crucial spot in a
race this summer.

Try not to be the gal who "learns so loud" as one of Larch-
mont's saltier gents puts it. We all know her. She's never been
afloat before and is so keen and genuinely anxious both to learn
and to please the boys that she gets all mixed up with well-
meaning actions and nautical phraseology. She usually has a
male opposite number who has had a little more experience and
who never misses an opportunity of saying "Now, when I was
in the *Ranger* we did it this way."

Clean your sneakers with a stiff brush and Bon Ami and it
won't come off on the new navy blue upholstery. Bring your own
bath towels if you can possibly squeeze them in, and tell your
hostess boiling water and cream of tartar will remove the most
stubborn white corrosion spots on aluminum. She'll think you're
wonderful.

How to be the perfect guest afloat! Watch your host and hostess and don't go off anticipating their wants on your own. She may wash all the dishes in what seems to you to be a teacup of hot water; that's her privilege. And as for him; I'm sure you've all sailed in someone else's boat, worked your fingers to the bone, and at the end of the day's run carefully coiled the main sheet and maybe even flemished it! You stand back secretly admiring your handiwork, when the skipper comes along, pipe in mouth, and says "Jeepers! who in the world did this?" And as your masterpiece collapses in his destructive hand, you hear yourself say, "Golly, who could have?"

43

What Every Woman Wants

by RUTH BRINDZE

[1943]

THE TROUBLE with many dream ships—and with some real ones —is that they lack a woman's touch. Whenever the conversation turns to the buying or the building of the perfect ship, it is the men who do the talking. This is a mistake. For women have their dreams, too; as a matter of fact their dreams are apt to be extremely practical. Combine the male and female dreams and you'll really have something.

What a man wants in a boat is a pretty old story. Design, size, rig, motor; these are the things he talks about. Obviously, they are important. But a boat has to have more than a fair turn of speed coupled with sea-kindliness; she has to have more than a well-designed and easily handled rig. To be really perfect, she has to have comfort in the cabin. And this is where the woman comes in. This is the department she knows even though she has never been afloat in her life. She may know nothing about marine interior decorating or design but she can tell if the results are good. So, if you have a mate, Skipper, and hope to sail with her, let her be present and vocal when the dream ship is being conceived or bought.

Builders and designers of stock motorboats were the first to aim at pleasing the ladies, and from this praise-worthy endeavor has flowed many benefits for small boat sailors of both sexes. The motorboat industry went ahead and built cabins that are comfortable to live in and good to look at. Subsequently, designers of auxiliaries followed suit, but it was the motorboat men who proved that modern design can make a small boat a real home on a keel. This is what sold the ladies who went to the motorboat shows. Remember the long lines waiting at the gangways of 30- and 40-footers to get a peep at the cabins? Many a contract was signed because the mate liked the smart little galley or some other similarly important feature. The two-fold result was that the mate took to cruising and the skipper enjoyed his comfort. Maybe there are men who like things rough rather than smooth, but their number is few. I have never yet heard a man complain of too much comfort.

Comfort, of course, means different things to different people at different times. The word is not susceptible of simple definition. But when I mentally step aboard my dream ship (or when I look over a real ship), this is what I mean by comfort.

First of all, I want to be able to stand up straight in the cabin, and I want friends and relatives of the six foot variety to be able to walk upright as the good Lord intended. Modern designers know how this can be done even though occasionally they compromise and provide sailors with headroom only when they are in the doghouse. In a small boat, this two-level arrangement seems ugly to me from the exterior and cruel on the inside. For there are few whose reactions are sufficiently sure and quick so that they will always remember when they must duck and when they can keep their chins up.

Complete privacy in a small boat is achieved only by single-handed sailors. But a cabin can provide the degree of privacy needed for civilized living. There is, for instance, the seemingly trifling detail of privacy when dressing or undressing. Sure, you can play "shut eye" when there are females in the party. "Shut your eyes, Tom," or, "Turn your back, Dick," the mate's about to climb into pajamas or bathing suit. It's been done, and I've done it, but it's handier to have some other arrangement. In a boat sleeping three or more, I would certainly want some means of shutting off the forward stateroom from the main cabin. A curtain would do, or a locker or toilet room door which could be opened out, cutting off the view between the forward and after portions of the cabin. I would not have a fixed door dividing the cabin because of its adverse effect on light and ventilation.

But there must be a full length door and full headroom in the toilet room. The privy, in other words, must not only have privacy, its design must be functionally right. I have seen rooms that looked cute but that apparently were designed for midgets or contortionists. And if this sounds like one lady's nightmare, just look around, mates. You'll see what I mean. In my comfortable cruising ship, the designer must not only allow space enough for the essential fixtures and an average sized human being, but the room should include some of the convenience features of the "powder room" ashore.

On the bulkhead I want a medicine closet for stowing the necessary first aid supplies as well as the toiletries carried by both men and women. I want a mirror door on the medicine chest so that I, and others in the party, can see clearly when our aim is to improve on nature. Below the mirror or within easy reach there must be a shelf so that a woman working with powder and paint, or a man with shaving brush and razor, does not have to juggle equipment.

The bathroom ashore has a closet for clean towels and a hamper for soiled ones and, on my comfortable cruising boat, I'd like similar stowage facilities. This is not an original idea; there are many small cruising boats with such stowage space, but my guess is that it was either a woman who first thought of installing a seagoing clothes hamper, or a man who had his mind set on pleasing the ladies. Another good feature of landlubber construction which has been copied is the use of tile on the toilet room walls. Seagoing tile is of the composition type which is both light in weight and easy to install. I like it, not for its eye appeal but because it is downright practical. Toilet room walls must be washed down more frequently than those in other parts of the ship, and painted surfaces will stand just so much washing before the paint begins to wear away. The right kind of tile stands up better under a soap and water treatment. A good deal of time has already been spent looking over the toilet room but, before leaving this vital section, it should be added that there must be adequate natural light, and good ventilation. And, if an acoustical engineer could devise some method of soundproofing, that would be a real improvement.

Old time cruising men have always done a lot of talking about food but, upon analysis, the epicurean highpoint of the tales frequently turned out to be a clambake, or lobsters cooked in the dishpan on the beach. Ashore, the cook had the scope he needed which he definitely did not have in the galley. Galleys certainly have improved since the days when the stove was set somewhere in the forepeak and the ice box fastened in front of the motor. In a comfortable small ship, it can have the efficiency features of a modern kitchenette, which every cook is entitled to.

Three operations are performed in the galley; mixing drinks, cooking, and washing up, and of these, the first two are not only the more pleasurable but also the more important. With this in mind, therefore, my galley will include a stove set in gimbals, so that a pot of soup will not spill over when the boat is under way or rolling at anchor in the swell of a passing boat. It must also have a good-sized, well-insulated ice chest. I prefer a chest that opens at the top, into which the food is packed, although in some respects it is less convenient than one with a side door. The latter is apt to be dangerous. Even though the lock never slips its mooring, all the food on the shelves crowds against the door when the ship is rolling and woe to the cook who opens it at such a time. It's enough to make even the sweetest mate turn sour. However, if I saw a boat perfect in all respects except for the refrigerator, I'd take her, fasten battens across the shelves to hold the food in place, and then talk of the compensations of ample shelf space.

After eating or drinking comes the wash-up. It is unfair to expect a dishwasher to perform this labor of necessity in a sink of dollhouse proportions. If the galley is so small that an adequate-sized sink cannot be installed, I'd use a dishpan. The old-fashioned dishpan not only has the advantage of being man-sized but it can be set directly on the stove and the dishes washed as the water heats. Besides, it comes in handy for collecting lobsters from the lobster man and for cooking them.

There can't be too much locker space in the galley. You need space for pots and pans, plates and cups, and for such essentials as can opener, ice pick and corkscrew. As for food, even for weekend cruising it bulks up to rather tremendous proportions; for a cruise of a week or two, the amount of food which must be stowed until it is stowed away by the crew, is something to figure. Of course, the food can be tucked away on shelves in the main cabin, or in drawers up forward, but then where will shirts, pants, handkerchiefs and other necessary items find a safe resting place? Or if the pots are stowed in the blanket locker, where do the blankets find boat room? In my comfortable cruising ship, I'd look for adequate stowage space for all gear needed for crew and ship. Sailors have done with less, but more is always better.

One way to decide what locker space is needed is to visualize life afloat, a variety of day dreaming which is next best to the real thing. All right, you are now aboard. Your clothes are freshly pressed and you want to keep them in this condition for the return trip home, for a dance at the club or for some other gathering where fresh pressing is expected. A locker is needed in which to stow shore clothes and this locker should be tall enough so that slacks or dresses need not be folded half a dozen times before they are hung. Clothes used on the boat can be folded so a small locker or drawer will do. And how about the wet weather clothes? Stowage space is needed for these too, and the best place is near the entrance to the cabin. It is a tough enough job to keep a cabin dry on a wet day without carrying dripping clothes through it to a forward locker. Bulky items like blankets must also be stowed and these require space. But there are half a dozen ways of providing it.

And now to bed. First of all, how many bunks should there be? Unless the family adds up to an odd number and guests are never invited, I'd want a boat with two, four or six bunks. An extra bunk is liable to cause trouble unless there is a single man or woman for whom it is especially reserved, for it encourages an invitation to another couple—the lady will sleep inside and her companion of the stronger sex in the cockpit. Theoretically, outdoor sleeping sounds all right but, practically, only a few can take it and it seldom happens that they are the guests. The dew gets into their hair, the rising sun into their eyes and a gremlin acidifies their dispositions. In my comfortable ship, there must be inside accommodations for everyone in the party; if anyone decides to sleep above deck, that's all right, but there will be a bunk waiting for him inside so that when the rain comes he can duck below.

It is easy enough to dream of a perfect ship but it's a harder job to make the dream come true. Then it is a question of compromising the ideal for the real—but I wouldn't compromise too far. A handyman or a handywoman can work marvels in the cabin of a small boat but neither one of them can perform miracles.

Start out to buy the perfect boat, then, with dreamy eyes and a practical mind. Climb on board; you can't get the feel of her until you step into the cabin. Walk around, open doors and pull out drawers, try the elbow space and the foot space. And, while you do this, visualize what the cabin will look like and be like when the ship is in commission. A boat seen on a winter day, with nothing in place and a layer of dust dulling brightwork and paint, has to be viewed with imaginative eyes. When boats are displayed in a showroom, they're polished up to shine, and they're furnished even unto nautical ashtrays and pillows, but most boats laid up in the shipyard have a grimy, out-of-commission look. It's up to the prospective skipper and his mate to see through the dust and to visualize what she will look like when she's clean and pretty. And, if the cabin did not fit into the pattern of the dream, I wouldn't look further. Even though the hull were a beauty, and rig and motor were right, I wouldn't want her unless the cabin was cut from the same piece as my dream. A good ship and a comfortable one—that's what I want, to which all honest women (and men) say "aye."

44

Powerboat Handling

by ROBERT N. BAVIER, JR.

[1946]

"FINE LANDING, skipper!" exclaimed the gas dock operator to the owner of the small power cruiser which had just pulled in. A quick smile spread over the helmsman's face. He had a right to be pleased. It was blowing hard, the tide was sweeping past at a full two knots and there was precious little room to get lined up for an approach. But he had brought her unerringly through the crowded anchorage, turned sharply to leeward of the dock, maintained way until almost upon it and then, at the last moment, spun his rudder and backed down fast so that the stern swung in parallel to the dock and not six inches away.

We had seen several boats come in earlier and all had made hard work of it, but this skipper made it seem easy. Timing, judgment, an eye for distance and considerable practice had all contributed. These things can be acquired only by getting in a boat and experimenting, first by approaching some floating object in open water, where mistakes damage only your self-esteem, and later by coming alongside a real dock. But it takes more than practice to become adept at handling a powerboat. Certain fundamentals must be understood and observed. Perhaps we can save ourselves and our boat many hard knocks by a brief discussion of the fundamentals of boat handling.

Certain characteristics apply to all single-screw power boats, an understanding of which can be of real help in maneuvering. It is more than custom or etiquette, for instance, which prompts the launchman always to make your starboard side. He has found that, with a single-screw boat with a right-hand propeller, the stern will always swing to port when he backs down. This feature can make his landings easier, providing he approaches with the launch's port side next to the dock or boat alongside of which he is landing. Since the stern tends to swing more than the bow, the bow will remain close to the dock and the stern will swing in toward it as the engine is backed.

Single-screw boats behave in this fashion because the lower part of the propeller, being in denser water than the upper part, tends to thrust the stern sidewise. With the propeller revolving counterclockwise when backing (as does a right-hand screw) the lower part, rotating to starboard, exerts a thrust on the stern in the opposite direction, to port. The reverse is true when going ahead. Then the stern tends to swing to starboard but, since a slight bit of rudder can counteract this, its effect is negligible. This tendency of the stern to swing to port when backing and to starboard when going ahead applies only to boats having right-hand propellers. A left-hand screw will swing the stern to starboard when the engine is reversed and to port when going ahead. Since virtually all single-engined boats have right-hand screws we have used that type in our illustrations.

This characteristic may also be used to advantage when making a U turn in a slip or other waters so confined that it is necessary to back down, making the turn in stages instead of in one sweep. If possible, the turn should be made to the right. Then when the boat is backed her stern will swing to port, thus contributing to the turn rather than fighting it as would have been the case had a turn to the left been attempted.

Another feature common to single-screw boats is the need of considerable sternway before they can be steered when backing. It is fatal, therefore, to "play it safe" by backing slowly. Even when backing in close quarters, it is usually safer to give her the gun to gain steering control.

Aside from the generalities stated above, not all single-screw boats should be handled alike. Basically, there are two distinct types; the broad, shoal draft hull and the narrow, displacement hull type. The former is the outgrowth of the desire for more room in a boat of a given length and also reflects the increase in the power of today's engines. Given sufficient power, such a hull will plane, and so attain high speed. As the boat's size increases, power must be proportionately greater to make this possible. Hulls of this type can be seaworthy and not difficult to handle, providing their peculiarities are understood. They will steer well as long as plenty of power is used, but as soon as they are slowed down they respond to their rudders sluggishly and are carried off course easily by a strong wind or heavy sea. When the power is cut, they lose way rapidly.

Obviously, then to maintain control of a boat of this type it is best to hold considerable speed and use enough power to keep her manageable. If you do, she will spin like the proverbial top. This applies even when approaching a dock, because their capacity to lose headway rapidly once the power is cut acts as a real safety factor in boats of this type. When backing, a broad, shoal hull is hard to steer. Only if backed fast will she respond well and this is not always practicable. Whenever possible, then, in a boat of this type one should try to avoid having to back in a crowded anchorage.

The narrow, deep, displacement type of power boat handles quite differently. As a rule, at high speed she will require much more space to turn in than a shoal draft hull. Also, since the hull is more easily driven (until she gets up close to her maximum speed), headway is maintained for considerable distance when the power is cut. On the credit side we have the fact that these boats can be steered easily at slow speeds. Also, wind and sea affect them less when they are slowed down—they maintain a course more easily than a shallow draft hull and make less leeway. It follows, then, that when docking or maneuvering in close quarters with a boat of this type, it is best to keep her speed low, use less power and remember that she carries her way easily and must be backed in plenty of time. Since a boat of this type can usually be steered fairly well when backing, it is not so necessary to avoid going stern first in close quarters.

If you have just bought a new boat, decide what general type she falls under and you will then have a partial preview of her maneuvering characteristics and can handle her accordingly.

At this point it might prove helpful to review, step by step, the more common maneuvers you will be confronted with in handling a power boat. Approaching a dock will be one of the more frequent, and one which will require the greatest amount of skill. Let's assume, as a starter, that there is little or no wind or current to bother us. We should get on our approach course as far from the dock as possible to insure that the boat is properly lined up. This course should converge at about a 15° angle with the face of the dock, the bow heading for the point on the dock alongside of which it will eventually come to rest. Then, when about five lengths from this spot, slow down radically (even with a broad, flat hull) possibly even to the point of disengaging the clutch.

With the narrow hull we will then proceed with the screw just barely turning over. With a broad, shallow hull, as soon as she has lost some headway (but before she loses steerageway) kick her ahead again at medium speed. She will not have time to gather much additional headway but, assisted by the slipstream of the screw current against the rudder, she will remain maneuverable. It is best, in both type hulls, to keep the screw turning ahead right up to the time the engine is reversed. No hard and fast rule can be laid down on when to reverse. It depends not only on the type of boat but also her size, weight and power. Practice will tell, but it is obviously better to back too soon rather than too late. One boat length is about the average distance required to bring her to a stop.

As the engine is reversed, spin the steering wheel to head the bow away from the dock. For example, if making a port side landing, spin the wheel to starboard; if making a starboard side landing, spin the wheel to port. When making a port side landing, the wheel need not be spun until after the engine is reversed, because the screw will swing the stern in. (See Fig. 1, port side landing.) Continue backing until the boat is dead in the water, get the lines over and, if she is not in just the right spot, give a short kick ahead or astern as required.

Making a starboard side landing is more difficult. To prevent the stern from swinging away from the dock, the following procedure is recommended. Head in as before. When about one boat length from the spot where you will back, swing the rudder hard over to port, with the screw still going ahead. This will cause

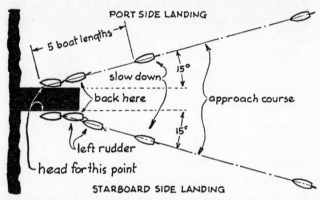

FIG. 1. Note particularly the difference in course and rudder angle during the later stages of port and starboard landings.

the bow to swing away from the dock and the stern toward it. When the boat is swinging fast, and just before the stern sideswipes the dock, back hard. (See Fig. 1, starboard side landing.) This will stop the boat and will also stop the stern from swinging into the dock. Providing the stern was already swinging toward the dock before the engine was reversed, its momentum will prevent it from going away when the boat is backed. If timed properly, the boat will end up parallel to the dock when all headway is lost.

Suppose, however, that in making a landing we wind up about ten feet or more away from the dock. Until we have become accustomed to handling our boat, we will find ourselves in this position often, and rightly so, because it is far better to be too far off than to crash the dock. Actually, it is easy to bring her in. All boats carry bow and stern lines to tie up alongside with. While these are necessary, they are of little value for getting the boat

alongside. Far better for this purpose will be a line attached to a
cleat on the pivot point (the point about which the boat pivots
when making a turn. It is usually about one third of the boat's
length from the bow.). Throw a line to someone on the dock, belay your end of it to the cleat on the pivot point and have the dock
hand make his end fast on the dock. We then have a spring line.

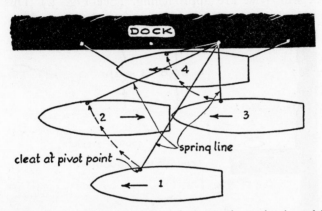

FIG. 2. A spring line, attached to a cleat at the boat's pivot point, is useful in pulling a boat sidewise into her berth. From position 1, with spring line made fast,
engine going ahead slow, boat will follow dotted course to position 2. Here, engine
is reversed and slack in line is taken in. When boat reaches position 3, spring line
is again made fast, engine is kicked ahead and she slides into her berth, position 4.

When we go ahead on the engine, this line pulls the boat broadside in toward the dock. If we had used a bow line, only the bow
would come in; if a stern line, then the bow would remain out. But
with the spring line the whole boat is pulled sidewise through the
water. (See Fig. 2.) Just before she reaches the dock, cut the
power, throw out and secure bow and stern lines and make
sure that fenders are over the side. The use of a spring line is
especially helpful when making a starboard side landing. If the
stern is far out, and the bow alongside the dock, put a fender
over the bow, secure the spring line, swing the rudder hard left
and go ahead on the engine. The spring keeps the boat from going
ahead, the stern swings in parallel to the dock and one need only
belay the lines to keep her there.

Wind and current can make docking more of a problem but

these difficulties are far from insurmountable. Suppose, for example, that we are making a starboard side landing and that both
wind and current are setting our boat to port (away from the
dock) as she approaches. Under these conditions we have found it
advisable to approach at a sharper angle, about 25° to 30°,
and to head for a spot to the right of or inside of the edge of
the dock which we are approaching. (See Fig. 3.) This latter

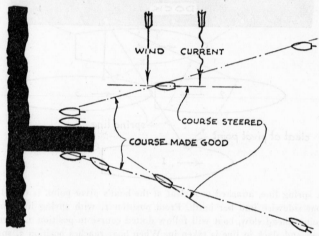

FIG. 3. With wind and current causing leeway, docking becomes more difficult.
Note difference between courses steered and those made good.

point is important, being necessary to counteract the leeway imparted by wind and current and which in this instance was setting
us to the left. By so heading, the boat *makes good* a course to the
proper location alongside the dock, arriving there somewhat in
the fashion of a crab. If one headed for the berth alongside the
dock, by the time it was reached the boat would be far off to
leeward and a new approach would be necessary.

When the boat is in heaving distance from the dock get a
spring line over, attach it as outlined above, swing the rudder
away from the dock and go ahead with the engine. The force of
wind and current will keep her from coming in too fast but, no
matter how strong they are, the use of the spring line and plenty
of power will bring the boat in. Under these conditions, it is im-

portant to get the bow and stern lines over smartly to keep her alongside once she is in.

With wind and current setting on the dock, it is advisable to approach a position well off the dock (as much as two boat lengths) on a course approximately parallel to its face. Then, when you are abreast of the desired location, back down, put the fenders over and let the wind and current bring you in. During this time the engine and rudder may be used sparingly to keep the boat lined up properly as she crabs into her berth.

While presenting fewer problems than docking, certain fundamentals must be observed when leaving a dock. If there is clear water up ahead, one will often prefer leaving bow first. Unless wind and current are setting hard against the dock, this is the easiest way. Cast off the bow line first, push the bow as far off as possible with a boat hook and then cast off the stern line. Go ahead with the rudder amidships and *watch the stern*. If it is about to hit the dock, a bit of rudder toward the dock will keep it clear. The important point to remember is never to turn away from the dock until sufficient water has opened up to permit the stern to swing without crashing into it. The stern always bears watching when going out head first.

With wind and current setting on the dock, making it impossible to push the bow out, or if there isn't room to go out head first, backing out is necessary. For the sake of illustration, imagine our boat tied up starboard side to a dock with wind and current pushing her against it. The stern can be gotten out easily. Merely secure the bow spring line as outlined previously. Then put fenders over the starboard bow, swing the rudder right, *toward* the dock, and go *ahead* on the engine. This will cause the stern to swing out. When the stern is out at an angle of about 25°, disengage the clutch, cast off the bow line, put rudder right and back down swiftly before the stern has had time to swing in to the dock. (See Fig. 4.) At first glance, one might wonder why we put the rudder right. We do so in order to keep the bow from scraping the dock as we back out. With the boat's natural tendency to back to port, the bow will swing to starboard (though not as far as the stern swings to port). To combat this swing, and to save our paintwork on the starboard bow, the rudder is put right and we then have a better chance of backing clear.

The last maneuver we will consider is making a 180° turn in waters so confined that the turn can not be completed without backing. We have already pointed out that it is preferable to turn to the right so that the stern will swing to port when backing, and thus contribute to the turn. It can be accomplished either

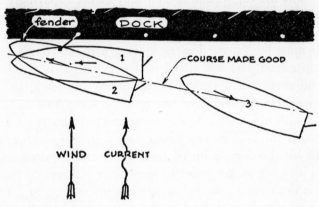

FIG. 4. Stages in backing away from a dock with wind and current setting against it. Rudder angle, fender and spring line are important.

way but for the sake of our illustration let's assume we are turning to the right in a narrow slip. We will approach up the left hand side of the slip at slow speed. Next, put the rudder hard right and speed the engine. After a few seconds of this, we will reverse the engine and also the rudder, putting it left, since we are about to go astern. After we have gained sternway and are again near the side of the slip where we commenced our turn, throw out the clutch and swing the rudder full right *before* the engine is kicked ahead. This last point is important because the slip stream against the rudder, before the boat has gained headway, is especially effective in turning her. When you do go ahead, do so with plenty of power. The slipstream will swing the stern rapidly left and the bow right before much headway is gained. (See Fig. 5.) Once she has gained headway, it is prudent to slow down a bit. If the turn is not completed, repeat the above process until it is. It is of the utmost importance to remember to put the rudder over *before* you go ahead on the engine and to use plenty of power when you do go ahead, especially at first.

The effects of tide, wind or both, present some of the greatest stumbling blocks to the successful completion of all maneuvers. Although specific conditions will require special solutions, certain

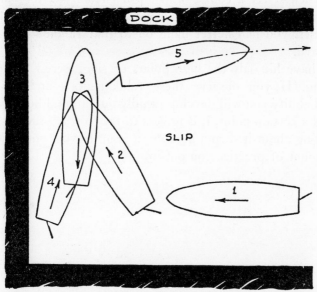

FIG. 5. During all stages of making a turn in a narrow slip, the correct rudder angle before power is applied is essential.

generalities can be applied to all cases. A shoal draft, beamy hull, with high freeboard and large deckhouse will be especially affected by wind. To minimize this effect, it is best to maintain good headway. Doing so keeps the boat maneuverable and lessens the amount of leeway she will make.

Leeway is also imparted by tide and this affects all boats about equally. Again, one solution is as high a rate of speed as is consistent with safety. But that's not the whole story. When a boat is making leeway, because of either wind or tide, she can not head directly for a mooring or dock if she hopes to get there. She must, instead, head to windward of it, or up-tide of it, to compensate for the set. The boat will then crab into the desired berth. Wind and tide in opposite directions will tend to balance each other.

In any event, whenever you encounter wind and current, decide what effect they will have before commencing a landing or other maneuver. It is wise to lay off for a few moments until you are sure. Then select a course which will enable you to remain on the approach line and use a fair amount of speed. And the first few times, you had better hang on to that rabbit's foot pretty darn hard.

We have hit only the high points of single-screw power-boat handling. If you observe these fundamentals and have fair natural ability you will develop rapidly into a good boat handler. Beyond a certain point, it is useless to try to teach such a subject by writing about it. From here on, it is up to you, your boat and the amount of practice you put in.

45

Why the Engine Stopped

by W. MELVIN CROOK

[1950]

YOURS IS THE BEST ENGINE money could buy. Each autumn you religiously bestow on your little jewel a methodical lay-up routine memorized from the boating magazines. With the coming of spring your pampered power plant receives the full treatment recommended for removing it from hibernation. At regular and frequent intervals during the boating season you check and service everything called for in the instruction manual. And then—inexplicably, perversely, and at the worst possible moment—the engine stops.

It may make good hot-stove conversation during the next winter to philosophize about which of your routines you flubbed, causing the stoppage. But until you get that chunk of machinery percolating again, such rumination is about as helpful as mid-sneeze curiosity over how you caught cold.

Engines stop for more reasons than anyone was ever able to list on paper. Most of those reasons are so unlikely to come your way that you can forget about them. The more involved causes will require the services of a professional mechanic. Fortunately, a very high percentage of engine illnesses and deaths arise from two types of failure—ignition and fuel. And many of these fuel and ignition difficulties can be cured—at least temporarily—right on the spot, with the tools, supplies and skill available aboard.

427

Fuel System Troubles

Fuel woes will almost always cause a gradual slowing down of the engine, rather than an abrupt cessation of combustion. When operation becomes erratic, with coughing through the carburetor, you should suspect that you are getting *too little* fuel to the engine. If the engine slows down with an overloaded, lazy, sort of action—particularly if it emits black smoke from the exhaust—you are probably feeding it *too much* fuel.

Too little fuel—a starving, or lean mixture condition—is the one you are more likely to encounter. Unless the characteristic loss of power, ragged running and coughing stop at once, you had better shut off the switch and investigate before the engine coughs off its flame arrestor and sets fire to the boat.

Then, in this order, go about locating the source of trouble. (a) Out of gas (you'll pardon the effrontery; maybe it all evaporated). (b) Plugged air breather vent in top of the tank. (c) Water or dirt in the fuel system between tank filler and carburetor. It may have come in with the last fuel you put aboard, something you could have avoided by using a good funnel that passes the fuel through a chamois skin. It may be the result of a fuel tank that is sludged up or flaking off scale to mix with the fuel. Either of these primary factors is beyond permanent cure on the spur of the moment and will have to wait for future attention. Right now you must try to get a clear flow of fuel to that carburetor. So—Clean all strainers in the fuel line and carburetor. This requires the use of a container or ample wad of cloth to catch the fuel you are sure to spill. This spillage must be removed to a safe spot as quickly as possible. After cleaning the strainers, allow time for the fuel you spilled to be replaced by gravity or your fuel pump. Then go through your usual starting procedure.

If cleaning the strainers didn't turn the trick, you must start a systematic check of the lines from tank to engine. Throughout this procedure, exercise the same care in regard to spilled fuel. Shut off the valve, if any, at the tank. Disconnect the line that runs from this valve toward the engine. With the line disconnected, open the valve to determine whether fuel can flow to this point at a normal rate. If you have no valve at the tank, and the outlet is from the top, disconnect the line at the outlet and blow back into the tank to make sure the riser pipe is clear. In the incredibly dangerous instance of having a bottom outlet and no valve, be ready to plug the outlet the instant the line is disconnected.

Disconnect the other end of the fuel line at the spot where it first reaches the engine (at fuel pump or carburetor). Now blow through the line from either tank or engine end until you have freed it of all traces of water or other foreign matter. Reconnect the line at both ends. This time it will require a bit of time to refill the emptied lines and get fuel to the carburetor, but do not assume that you are still in trouble until you are sure that the carburetor is filled again.

When you are convinced that the fuel has a clear path from tank to engine, and your power plant still plays dead, your next object of suspicion should be the fuel pump. Those of you with gravity feed can, of course, skip this procedure.

Disconnect the carburetor end of the fuel pump-to-carburetor line. With a container placed so as to catch any fuel you can coax out, without turning on the ignition switch, wind the engine over with the starter for 10 seconds. If the fuel pump is in good shape, you should force a substantial stream of fuel from the open end of the line. If the flow is lacking, or insufficient, the pump is the villain. A defective fuel pump is best cured by replacing it. Some owners carry fuel pump repair kits with them, permitting the repair of most of the possible fuel pump troubles.

If the fuel pump delivered enough fuel, reconnect the pump-to-carburetor line and direct your attentions to the carburetor. Please note that the carburetor is the *last* of the fuel system components to check, and this for the simple reason that it is the least likely to give you a starvation condition. Most carburetors have just one adjustment, a needle valve that regulates the mixture at low speed. It is almost incredible that this adjustment could have been disturbed, so leave it alone. Carburetor adjustments should be made only as a step in a motor tune-up, never to restart a suddenly ill engine.

Trouble narrowed down to the carburetor is something that calls for the skill and equipment of the professional. Such repairs should be attempted as an emergency, on-board measure only as a last resort. *If you must,* remove the carburetor from the engine. Set it up in a clean, well-lighted spot and make provision to prevent the droppage or loss of any of the minute screws or gismos that make up the device.

There are only three things that could have gone wrong with the carburetor which you can hope to repair on the spot. (a) A gasket may require replacement. (b) One of the internal passages, or a jet, may have become clogged and require freeing. A little dry-cleaning fluid, some soft copper wire and your own ability to simulate a compressed air jet will be the tools to use. (c) The float may have become gasoline-logged and ceased to function.

A submerged float causes excessive amounts of fuel to feed to the engine and will produce the characteristic symptoms of this condition. The spotting of the lazy engine and black smoke would provide the only justification for attacking the carburetor first in your fuel system check.

The logical cure for a float that has lost its buoyancy is a new float. Lacking a replacement, you can repair the hollow metal type as follows: Dry the outside of the float and watch for a spreading dampness to betray the spot of the leak. Drill or punch a small hole at this spot and shake all the gasoline out through this hole. Then submerge the float in carbon tetrachloride, with the hole up, and wait until the bubbles cease pouring from the hole. Now shake out the carbon tet and solder the leaky spot.

There are several ailments related to the fuel system which are likely to prove as baffling as they are annoying. They will seldom cause the engine to stop altogether, but they are likely to be recurrent under similar weather and operating conditions. The first of these is vapor lock.

Vapor lock is caused by a bubble of vapor in the fuel line blocking the passage of liquid fuel. To appreciate just how this can happen, you must remember that gasoline starts to boil (turn into vapor) at ordinary room temperatures. So, if your fuel line runs in an area of heat concentration, you are asking for it. As you who have attempted to boil any food in the low-pressure atmosphere of a high altitude realize, the boiling point of a liquid drops as the pressure on that liquid decreases. Thus, in the usual case where fuel is sucked from the fuel tank by a pump, the gasoline in the line is under a pressure less than atmospheric and its boiling point is thereby dropped even lower. Hence, the fuel line from tank to pump must be kept cool and even the line from pump to carburetor cannot be allowed to run warm.

Fuel vaporizing (boiling) in the line forms a bubble of gas vapor which, under the influence of heat, expands. It will seek a high spot in the line, throughout which it will expand until it blocks off the liquid gasoline flow and your engine strangles. Vapor lock can therefore be discouraged by running your fuel lines constantly upward from tank to fuel pump and, if possible, constantly upward from pump to carburetor. Avoid local high spots in the line. Avoid all local warm areas with your fuel line. If necessary, shield it from hot spots such as exhaust pipes.

As an emergency measure, vapor lock can be attacked by (1) shutting down the engine, (2) getting fresh cool air into the hull, (3) cooling warm portions of the fuel pipe with water or damp cloths and (4) insulating or shielding parts of the line near hot elements.

Another recurrent type of ailment you may experience is caused by a lack of fresh air to the carburetor. The average 100 hp. engine will require about 250 cubic feet of air per minute at full speed. If the air vents to your engine space tend to restrict the flow of air so that the carburetor cannot inhale as much oxygen as it requires, you will lose power.

A third trouble related to your fuel system occurs in that part of the engine which heats the fuel mixture before it is admitted through the intake valves. Generally this heating takes place in the intake manifold immediately adjacent to the carburetor and is applied by a jacket around the manifold, through which hot exhaust gases are circulated. You will find that many engines are so carbureted, manifolded and timed that this heating of the mixture is essential to proper performance.

If, for any reason, the flow of exhaust gases should be cut off from circulating around the intake manifold, the fuel mixture will not vaporize properly and the engine will give forth symptoms similar to those of an incorrect mixture. The condition can best be identified by the fact that the engine generally is reluctant to accelerate plus the fact that your troubles seem to lessen or vanish when the engine has warmed up. Whenever you meet up with this combination, check to see that your heat passages are clear.

Ignition System Troubles

The symptoms of ignition trouble are many and diverse for the simple reason that there are so many different parts of the spark-making equipment that can go off the beam.

If the engine stops suddenly and completely—look for a disconnected wire:

(a) In the low tension system connecting battery, switch, ammeter, coil, condenser and distributor. Remove the distributor cap, turn the engine over until the points close, turn on the switch and separate the points manually. If you detect a spark as the points separate, you will know that the primary (low tension) wiring is intact.

(b) In the high tension wiring from distributor to coil. Disconnect the wire from one of the spark plugs and tape it in a position so that the terminal rests about ⅜″ from some metal part of the engine. Turn the engine over with the ignition switch on. A spark will show that the ignition wiring is o.k.

Sometimes everything will appear to be in order with the wiring and, after the usual tugging and shaking involved in an inspection, the engine will start and run properly—only to die completely some time later. This sort of subversion can come from a wire that has broken inside the insulation or inside a wad of tape. Your shaking pushes the ends together, but they will separate again under vibration. A similar practical joke can be played by a wire wearing through its insulation until the bare wire contacts a metal conduit or some other grounded metal, giving you a short circuit. Here too your tugging at the wiring can clear the "short," but it will come back to haunt you.

In rare cases a battery will go dead while the engine is operating. The engine can go on running with the ignition drawing its juice from the generator—as long as the generator is charging. But once you slow down to the point where the charge is cut off, the engine will die. This predicament can be spotted by testing to see whether the battery will operate the starter or other electrical units.

If the engine misses in a more or less regular cadence—this can be distinguished from fuel system worries by the fact that there is no tendency to backfire, nor to lay a smoke screen. Rather, the engine lacks power and operates with a vibration that indicates one or more dead cylinders.

Stoppage in these circumstances can usually be traced to inoperative spark plugs. Locate the culprits by the familiar screw driver test where you short out each plug in turn by touching the blade of an insulated-handle screw driver simultaneously to plug terminal and engine. When you reach a plug that, when shorted, causes no additional skip or decrease in power, there is your villain.

Remove the dead plug or plugs for inspection. Any plug with a cracked or broken insulator should be discarded. Where the electrodes appear badly burned away, the plug should also be given the heave-ho (slightly burned electrodes might be moved together enough to provide an emergency, temporary cure). If the plug is dirty and damp inside, and you have no replacement, slosh it well in carbon tet and blow it out until dry.

Rough, generally sporadic engine operation with loss of power, *i.e.,* irregular engine performance that doesn't fall into the fuel failure symptom bracket because it yields neither backfires nor smoke-screens, and cannot be traced to plugs, leaves three probabilities: (1) distributor, (2) coil and (3) condenser.

Check the distributor first. Remove the cap and examine it for signs of dampness or cracks. Pull the points apart and see whether they are badly burned or pitted. Burned or pitted points cast a suspicion on the condenser, but themselves require (a) cleaning up with a point file and (b) resetting.

Neither coil nor condenser can be readily checked on board. If you have traced trouble to the door-step of either, try replacing first the condenser and then the coil. Obviously you will try the engine after making the first replacement and will not change the second unit if the first switch stopped the trouble.

WHEN THE OUTBOARD STOPS

Fuel system troubles—If your engine commences to ail, you will undoubtedly try adjusting the carburetor mixture control first thing. When, despite your adjustment, the engine slows down gradually, with a tendency to sputter, look for insufficient fuel to the carburetor. Such a slowing down accompanied by exhaust smoke usually indicates a mixture with too much oil, or oil improperly mixed.

A logical order of checking is: (1) Fuel in the tank? (2) Is the tank air vent open? (3) Depress the choke control and note whether you feel the squoosh of fuel in the carburetor and whether fuel overflows as you continue to choke. If the carburetor feels dry, or fuel fails to overflow, or the engine still won't start—(4) (a) Shut off the fuel valve. (b) Remove and clean the fuel strainer. (c) Drain the fuel from the carburetor, catching some in your hand to note whether it contains water or is too oily. (d) Remove and blow out the fuel line. (e) Open shut-off valve momentarily to see whether fuel flows at this point—and whether it contains water or unmixed oil. (f) If water or excess oil is detected at the fuel tank, it may be necessary to drain the tank and refill with fuel that has been properly mixed and contains no water. (g) Connect the fuel line, reinstall the strainer and open the fuel valve. (h) Choke to be sure that fuel has reached the carburetor. (5) If the carburetor fills properly, but the engine still will not run, you may have a clogged jet or internal passage in the carburetor. In an emergency you may try freeing this device by opening it up and blowing through all passages.

Ignition system troubles—Ills of the spark-making machinery generally produce symptoms much different from those indicating fuel system worries. If the engine slows down to a more or less steady pace and operates with the roughness indicative of a dead cylinder (1) Make sure that wires to the spark plugs are connected (2) Check these wires for excessive dampness or broken insulation that might cause a short circuit (3) Remove the plugs and inspect them. Discard any with cracked or broken insulators. If the plugs are wet and fouled, clean them well with gasoline and blow them dry.

Those difficulties which you stand a fighting chance of clearing on the spot are generally the fuel and ignition system aberrations we have discussed. In most cases, a thoughtful, analytical approach will permit you to get her running in a short time.

46

Tools and Engine Spare Parts

by W. MELVIN CROOK

[1950]

ANY STRANGER attempting to prescribe a list of tools and spare parts for you to carry aboard your boat must lay claim to the wisdom of many Solomons. After all, how can he tell whether you are about to leave on a non-stop cruise around the world or will never venture beyond hailing distance of a boatyard? The contents of such a mechanical hope chest must vary widely according to the type of boat it is to grace and the sort of service that boat is going to have. For your offshore cruise to far-away places there is good reason to take spares for everything in your inventory—including a spare hull hung in davits. From this extreme of arduous boating to the confining service of a yacht club launch, the completeness of the on-board kit of magic will vary in proportion.

This list was prepared with no pretense of supernatural wisdom. Nor is it aimed at the mythical "average boatman." It is merely a suggested assortment for you to mull over. You will undoubtedly reject some of the items as unnecessary in your case. You will add others—some peculiar to your craft; some indicated by the sort of boating you plan; and still others because they happen to strike your gadget streak.

Whatever you decide to include, please be sure that you can provide it with suitable storage space. The natural desire to get such mechanical components out from under foot frequently leads to their being either (1) buried in a spot that all but defies access, or (2) stuffed into some cranny in the bilge where they quickly rust into uselessness.

Spare parts should be treated and packaged in the way that similar things are processed and wrapped for export to a tropical climate. This generally consists of coating them thoroughly with a grease-like rust preventive compound, wrapping them in waterproof paper and sealing the joints of the wrapping tightly.

Tools would certainly last much longer than they generally do on board a boat if they were given the same treatment as the spare parts. Unfortunately tools would be pretty useless in an emergency if they were all wrapped up and smeared with anti-rust guck. You can, however, do a satisfactory job of keeping them in shape by the use of an anti-rust oil. This oil can be obtained from the same source that supplies your lubricating oil and resembles lube oil in appearance and consistency. All you need to do is be sure that each tool is well coated with the anti-rust oil before it is put away after each use. The oil can easily be wiped off whenever the tool is to be used.

Here is a word of detail about some of the tools listed. The slip-joint pliers are the common garden variety found in most auto tool kits and are sometimes called "gas pliers." What we have shown as water pump pliers are another slip-joint tool with the jaw opening at an angle to the handles and a capacity—with approximately parallel jaws—of an inch or more.

Open-end wrenches are essential since they are the only kind that can reach certain jobs. You may have one or more spots so diabolically located that you will have to start with a standard end wrench and grind or cut parts of it away to reach the particular gimmick.

Box wrenches are a handy but not essential addition to the wrench complement. The sockets will be found absolutely indispensable only for nuts that are so recessed or buried that end type wrenches cannot reach them. If you need one socket, you might as well get a set of them. The spark plug deep socket is a "must" on some engines and the best spark plug wrench for all engines. The ignition set consists of small open-end wrenches in a range between about ⅛″ and ⁷⁄₁₆″, which in the more expensive sets are accompanied by tiny sockets in the same size range. Tappet wrenches are super-thin open-enders in the sizes needed to fit valve tappets.

A spark plug gap gauge measures by means of a wire of appropriate diameter. This gives a much more accurate estimate of the plug gap than you can hope to get with a flat thickness gauge. The ground wire on the funnel is used to make an electrical connection from the metal of the funnel to the metal of the gas tank and drain off that static electricity that might otherwise light off the whole fuel load.

In selecting spare coil, plugs, condenser, points, rotor and cap, better be triply sure that you are getting the size and type used on your particular power plant. They all look so much alike that you can easily invest in, and rely on, some piece that won't do the job any better than the one needing replacement.

In connection with the starter drive spring, watch that you get not only the right size but the right rotation. These things generally come in both right and left hand styles and they are not at all interchangeably useful.

The propeller may be a brand new or a rebuilt job. In either case, it is helpful to store with it a key that has been fitted to both the shaft and the propeller keyways.

The gasket material should be the kind that looks, from a distance, like extra heavy brown wrapping paper. You can make replacement gaskets with a ball peen hammer and a sharp knife, but a set of gasket punches is a big help in cutting clean round holes for studs and the like. The gasket compound is the familiar paste that can be smeared on the mating surfaces to form a gasket as those surfaces are pulled together. Non-hardening paste is the more generally used type. Gasket shellac is actually used for a thread seal on small pipe and tubing fittings and to smear in rubber-hose-to-metal joints. It should only be used on gaskets where the engine manufacturer specifically recommends it.

Your safety wire may be ordinary galvanized baling wire, copper, brass or Monel, depending on how rugged a use you are going to give it. The ammonia is handy for cleaning corroded battery terminals and the vaseline can be smeared on clean terminals as a protective coating.

Take a look at the tools and spare parts carried by your boating pals. You can all gain by swapping some of your pet ideas.

INBOARDS

Tools	Spare Parts and Supplies
1 pair slip-joint pliers	1 ignition coil
1 pair side-cutting pliers	1 set spark plugs
1 pair vise-jaw pliers	1 condenser
1 pair water pump pliers	1 set of points
Assorted screw drivers	1 distributor rotor and cap
2 pipe wrenches	1 starter drive spring
1 adjustable end wrench	1 fuel pump
1 monkey wrench	1 vee belt of each size used
Open-end wrenches ⅜" to 1"	Lengths of packing
Box wrenches ⅜" to ¾"	1 propeller
Socket wrenches with ½" drive	Assorted bolts and nuts
Spark plug socket wrench	Assorted flat and lock washers
Torque handle for sockets	Assorted cotter pins, tubing fittings
1 set ignition wrenches	and pipe fittings
1 set tappet wrenches	Lengths of tubing
1 set thickness gauges	25' low tension wire
1 spark plug gap gauge	10' high tension wire
Hacksaw with spare blades	Assorted electrical terminals
1 ball peen hammer	Gasket material ¹⁄₁₆" and ¹⁄₃₂"
1 knife	Tube of gasket compound
1 cold chisel	Bottle of gasket shellac
1 oil squirt can	Soft brass safety wire
1 grease gun	Household ammonia, vaseline
1 battery hydrometer	Fireproof cleaning fluid
1 fuel funnel with strainer and ground	Lubricating oil
wire	Grease
1 flashlight	Penetrating oil
Files	Distilled water
Tubing flaring tool	Friction tape

OUTBOARDS

Tools	Spare Parts and Supplies
1 screwdriver	1 set spark plugs
1 pair slip-joint pliers	Several shear pins
1 monkey wrench	1 propeller and nut
1 adjustable open-end wrench	Soft brass safety wire
	2 starting ropes

47

What If You Lose Your Navigator?

by ROBERT N. BAVIER, Jr.

[1947]

IMAGINE YOURSELF hundreds of miles at sea bound for a tiny island, without sufficient food or water to reach any other land and with the boat's only navigator seriously ill or lost overboard. A tough spot, but such a situation could arise in a yacht racing to Honolulu, Bermuda, or elsewhere, or on a deep sea cruise with but one navigator on board.

Many racing skippers go offshore so seldom that they don't consider it worth while learning to navigate, so long as one member of the crew can. In spite of the simplification of celestial navigation today, their point is understandable. It still takes quite a bit of study to get navigation under one's hat. But why not learn *in an hour or two* enough about taking and computing one type of sun sight to enable anyone to make a landfall on the smallest island—not a swift landfall, not one suitable for racing, but one which is sure.

The method we are about to present was used in less simple form by Columbus, Magellan and the other ocean trail blazers. Many a whaling master knew no other means to make his landfall. In fact, until the present century, the majority of the ships that sailed the seas found their way by dead reckoning and this one type of sight. In brief, it amounts to taking a sight of the sun at noon, at which time it is either due north or due south, and thereby determining the ship's latitude. It is the easiest, quickest and most readily comprehensible sight of them all and yet, with it, you can find the smallest island.

Suppose, for example, one were 300 miles from Bermuda when the navigator was lost. To get there one would need only to observe the following procedures: 1. Lay a course by dead reckoning for a point 40 to 60 miles due east or west of the island (whichever the prevailing wind made more desirable). 2. Take simple noon sights to determine when you arrive either due west or east of the island (or, in other words, when your latitude is that of the island). 3. Then sail either due east or west, depending on which side of the island you are, checking your latitude by a sun sight each noon, and continuing until the landfall is made. The purpose of steering originally well to one side of the island instead of directly for it is to insure that when you reach its latitude you know on which side you are and will not run the risk of sailing away from it.

Let's find out how this sight is made. Henceforth, our sight will be called an LAN (local apparent noon) sight because it is taken exactly at noon for the longitude of our vessel's position. At this instant the sun will bear either due north or due south of us. A table of declination in the *Nautical Almanac* tells us by inspection in degrees how far north or south of the equator the sun is (one degree of latitude being equal to 60 nautical miles). In other words, it gives the sun's latitude in the celestial sphere, for which there is a corresponding position on the earth, called the sun's geographical position. Declination, therefore, can be thought of as the latitude of the sun. Next, our sextant tells us how many degrees (again one degree equals 60 nautical miles) we are north or south of the sun's geographical position on earth. Since declination shows the sun's latitude and our sextant shows our position relative to the sun's geographical position, by combining the two values we can find our position relative to the equator, said position being our latitude. That's all there is to it. See Fig. 1.

First we must determine when it is local apparent noon at our longitude so that we will know when to take our LAN sight. Refer to Fig. 2 while reading this paragraph. Let's assume the time to be 1100, June 1, 1947, and our dead reckoning (D.R.) longitude at this time to be 70° 15′ W. Although in the +5 Standard Time Zone, we are keeping +4 time (eastern daylight saving time) which means that our clocks are 4 hours *behind* Greenwich time. Stated otherwise, our clock is set to a zone time of 60° W longitude, since each hour of time equals 15° of

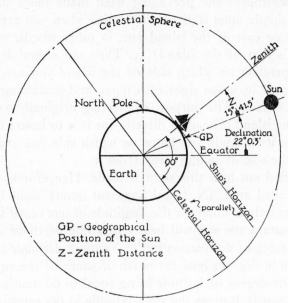

FIG. 1. Ship's latitude equals declination plus Z. See Fig. 5.

longitude. Therefore, the mean sun (the sun with a theoretical uniform rate of apparent advance) will be 10° 15′ east of us, since it will be directly over 60° W longitude, when our clocks read 1200 or noon.

In other words, it will be noon *at our longitude* 10° 15′ later than our clocks show. Converting 10° 15′ into time (by the table in the *Nautical Almanac*) we get 41 minutes of time. Adding this value to 1200, we get 1241. Therefore, if the sun travelled at a regular rate, this would give us the time to take our sight. Unfortunately, however, the sun travels irregularly and it is necessary to apply the so-called "equation of time" to 1241 to get our LAN. We can do this easily in the *Nautical*

Almanac under the date June 1 (Fig. 3). Remember, in entering these tables, to use GCT (Greenwich Civil Time) which in this case is 4 hours *later* than our time of 1241, or 1641. The tables under June 1 at this time show us that the equation of time is +2 minutes 23.3 seconds. We apply this to 1241, *reversing* the

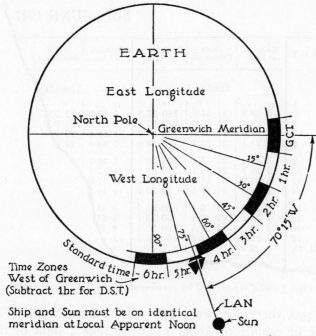

FIG. 2. Fifteen degrees of longitude equals one hour.

sign. Never mind why the sign is reversed but remember that it always is in making this step. Subtracting 2 minutes 23 seconds from 1241 we get $12^h 38^m 37^s$. This, then, is the time of LAN for longitude 70° 15′ W on June 1, 1947. It is the time to take a noon sight.

If, however, we have changed our longitude by advancing on our course line between 1100 and 1238, the amount we have changed longitude should be reckoned and converted into time to give a truly accurate figure. Assume that in plotting the D.R. we find our longitude at 1238 will be 70° 07′ W instead of 70° 15′ W. Turning again to the *Nautical Almanac*, we convert

the 8' difference of longitude between the above figures into
32 seconds of time. Since we have moved to the eastward it
will be noon 32 seconds *earlier* and therefore we *subtract* 32
seconds from 12:38:37 and arrive at 12:38:05 as the time of
LAN. This is the time to take our sight.

SUN, JUNE 1947

G.·C.T.	Equation of Time	Sun's Declination	Sun's G. H. A.	Equation of Time	Sun's Declination
		Sunday 1			Thursday
h	m s	° '	°	m s	° '
0	+2 29.3	+21 54.5	180 37 3	+1 52.1	+22 25
2	2 28.6	21 55.2	210 37 1	1 51.2	22 26
4	2 27.8	21 55.9	240 37.0	1 50.4	22 2
6	2 27.1	21 56.7	270 36.8	1 49.6	22
8	2 26.4	21 57.4	300 36.6	1 48.7	
10	2 25.7	21 58.1	330 36 4	1 47.9	
12	2 25.0	21 58.8	0 36 2	1 47 0	
14	2 24.2	21 59.5	30 36 1	1 46	
16	2 23.5	22 0.1	60 35 9	1 45	
18	2 22.8	22 0.8	90 35.7	1 44	
20	2 22.0	22 1.5	120 35.5	1 43	
22	+2 21.3	+22 2.2	150 35 3	+1 4	
H. D.	0.4	0.3	... ...		

FIG. 3. Figs. 3 and 4 reproduced by permission of the U.S. Naval Observatory.

At 1230, therefore, we break out the sextant and head for
the deck or cabin top. About 1232, we take a sight of the sun
and a minute later try another to satisfy ourselves that it is
still rising. Then, about every 30 seconds or so we check again
to see that it continues to rise. From 1237 on, *until it begins
to fall,* we take shots every 15 seconds, making sure to take
one at 12:38:05, at which time the sun should be at its highest
point, *providing* our D.R. longitude is correct. Incidentally, by
noting the actual time the sun is at its highest point, we can
get a rough check on our longitude (within 30 to 60 miles).
We use the highest altitude obtained from the series of sun
sights taken, even though it is observed at a time slightly different from our predetermined time of LAN. However, if one
sight shows a *greatly* higher value than all the others it should

be viewed with suspicion and considered a wild shot, since the sun changes its altitude slowly at this time. An average of the three highest sights, if they are taken within a few seconds of each other, should result in an accurate figure. A logical progression of sights, taken every 15 seconds during the minute the sun was at its highest, might be 74° 5.'7, 74° 6.'0, 74° 6.'1, 74° 5.'8. In this case, there are no wild shots and we would use either 74° 6.'1 or 74° 6.'0, the difference between them being negligible (⅒ of a mile).

The alert reader may have noticed that we could have made a poor estimate of watch time of LAN and still, by starting to shoot the sun well before it appeared to be reaching its highest point (and well before it bore due north or due south) and continuing to take sights at frequent intervals (the most frequent as its rate of climb started to slow), we could still find our latitude. We would merely use the highest sextant altitude (H$_s$) recorded in the above manner and our results would still be accurate. Actually, even if we had no watch and did not know how to figure the time of LAN, we could still get our latitude in this way. It would be tedious and therefore we use the other method, but in an emergency it could be done.

We will not review the mechanics of using a sextant, because a few minutes with the instrument, under instruction by a competent navigator, followed by practice on your own, is worth a volume of written words on the subject.

Having obtained our sextant altitude (H$_s$) of 74° 6.'0, we need to correct it for refraction, time of the year and height of eye above sea level to get its true observed altitude (H$_o$). The *Nautical Almanac* sextant correction tables A, B and C (Fig. 4) do this for us in short order:

Table A corr.:   +15.'8

Table B corr.:   − 0.'2

Table C corr.:   − 3.'1

(Our height of eye
being 10 ft.)
_____

Total corr.:   +12.'5

There is a rule of thumb which calls for a 12.′0 correction at this point without reference to the tables. This is almost always within 1′ of the figure the tables give and results in simplification at a small sacrifice in accuracy. In this case, however, we will

ALTITUDE CORRECTIONS

TABLE A			TABLE B	TABLE C			
FROM SEA HORIZON			☉	Corr. for **D I P** Ht. of Eye			
Alt.	☉	★	Seasonal	Ft.	Corr.	Ft.	Corr.
° ′	′	′			′		′
6 00	+ 7.7	−8.5	Jan +.′3	0	0.0	100	− 9.8
20	+ 8.1	−8.1					
40	+ 8.4	−7.7	Feb +.′3	5	−2.2	150	−12.0
7 00	+ 8.7	−7.4	+.′2	6	−2.4	200	−13.9
20	+ 9.0	−7.1		7	−2.6	250	−15.5
40	+ 9.3	−6.8		8	−2.8	300	−17.0
				9	−2.9	350	−18.3
40°	+15.0	−1.2	√June −.′2	√10	−3.1	400	−19.6
45	+15.1	−1.0	July −.′2	11	−3.2	450	−20.8
50	+15.3	−0.8	Aug −.′2	12	−3.4	500	
55	+15.4	−0.7		13	−3.5		
60	+15.5	−0.6	Sep −.′1				
65	+15.6	−0.5				5500	−58.0
70°	+15.7	−0.4	Oct .′0	60	−7.6	3600	−58.8
√75	+15.8	−0.3	+.′1	70	−8.2	3700	−59.6
80	+15.8	−0.2	Nov +.′2	80	−8.8	3800	−60.4
85	+15.9	−0.1		90	−9.3	3900	−61.2
90	+16.0	−0.0	Dec +.′3	100	−9.8	4000	−62.0

FIG. 4. Corrections to be applied to the observed altitude of a star or of the sun's lower limb, to find the true altitude.

use a +12.′5 correction. When added to our H$_s$ of 74° 6.′0, this gives us a true observed altitude (H$_o$) of 74° 18.′5.

It is now necessary to subtract this value from 90°. We do this because we want to find our distance in degrees north or south of the sun (Z), not only the sun's altitude (Fig. 5). For example, if we were at the North Pole and the sun was directly over the Equator (declination 0°) its altitude would read 0°, and it would appear to be right on the horizon. But the latitude of the North Pole is 90°, not 0°. Subtracting the altitude (in this case 0°) from 90° still gives 90°. Another example: If we were on the Equator and the sun was directly overhead at noon (again declination 0°) its altitude at noon would be 90°. Subtracting 90° from 90° would give us 0° which, since we are on the Equator, is indeed our latitude.

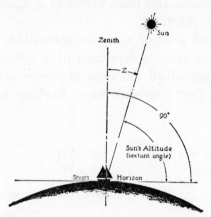

FIG. 5. Z equals 90° minus sun's altitude.

Subtracting then:

$$89°\ 60'\quad \text{(Equivalent of } 90°\text{)}$$
$$74°\ 18.'5\quad \text{(Sun's corrected alt.)}$$

$$Z = 15°\ 41.'5 = \text{the amount in degrees}$$

we are *north* of the sun (since the sun bore due south at LAN).

Continuing with our example, we find in the *Nautical Almanac* (Fig. 3) under Sunday, June 1, at 1638 GCT (we always enter the tables for GCT, *not* our local time) that the sun's declination is listed as +22° 0.'3, the plus sign meaning north. At this instant, then, the sun was 22° 0.'3 north of the Equator. We have already found that we are north of the sun by 15° 41.'5. To find our relation to the Equator, then we *add* 22° 0.'3 and 15° 41.'5 and get 37° 41.'8. This is our latitude. If the sun had been south of the Equator (declination minus or south as in the winter) we would have *subtracted* the declination to get latitude. If the sun was north of us and we were in north latitude, we would have subtracted our Z figure from declination to get latitude. It is not necessary to memorize the above rules, because when it comes to working the final computation it will become obvious what to do, because you already know your *approximate* latitude and must arrive at a figure within a few degrees of it, at most.

The above took a lot of space in explanation. Once you have the hang of it, it takes a maximum of 5 minutes to perform. Below, are presented all the steps necessary in the form they should take in your notebook when working a noon sight to obtain latitude.

June 1, 1947

DR Long. at 1100 + 4 time:	70° 15′ W	
+4 time is for Long.	60° 00′ W	

Difference: 10° 15′ W = 41 minutes of time

Equation of time: +2^m 23.3^s (reverse sign)

Correction to be applied to noon: +38^m 36.7^s = 38^m 37^s
                                            +12^h 00   00

Time of LAN for Long.	70° 15′ W =	12^h 38^m 37^s
Long. at 1238:	70° 07′ W	

Difference: 8′   =   − 32^s

Watch time of LAN (time to take or sight): 12^h 38^m 05^s

Sun sight at 12 38 06:

$$H_s = 74°\ 6.′0$$
$$\text{Correction A} = +15.′8$$
$$\text{Correction B} = -\ 0.′2$$
$$\text{Correction C} = -\ 3.′1$$
$$H_o = 74°\ 18.′5$$

$$90° = 89°\ 60′$$
$$H_o = 74°\ 18.′5\ \text{(subtract)}$$
$$Z = 15°\ 41.′5$$
$$\text{Dec.} = +22°\ 0.′3$$
$$\text{Latitude:}\quad 37°\ 41.′8\ \text{N}$$

All problems follow the same pattern as the example above. With this example as a guide and a *Nautical Almanac* at your side to give the necessary tabular information, you should, after a few hours study, be able to determine your latitude for any day of the year and any location. Spend several days practicing with a sextant before you head to sea, receiving instruction in its operation from someone who knows how, and you should be able to make an emergency landfall on your own.

Here's hoping that the need will never arise and that the main contribution of this article will be a greater peace of mind for you when you go to sea with only one navigator on board, but with the realization that you could get her home yourself if the need arose.

48

Coastal Winds

by GARDNER EMMONS

[1950]

To the race committee faced with the problem of selecting a suitable course for the afternoon regatta, it is common experience that the official forecasts of wind direction and force issued by the Weather Bureau are not of much help. Likewise, the owner of a cruising boat seldom finds that he can successfully plan his day's sail on the basis of the early morning weather bulletin broadcast over the radio.

This situation is not an indication that the government weatherman is lacking in skill. The official predictions disseminated through the press, the radio, and the local telephone company are meant to serve the residents of a rather wide territory, so that the wind forecast perforce specifies only the *general* conditions that are expected to prevail over *most* of the area. The forecaster formulates his wind prediction from the major features of the air flow ("general wind") revealed by his weather map. Furthermore, the scale of the standard meteorological chart is about 150 miles to the inch, so that in any case minor, local irregularities in the wind pattern are obscured.

Forecasting the behavior of the wind in any restricted coastal region is especially difficult in summer, when the "general wind" is usually light and may easily be superseded by local air motions. Successful local prediction requires long experience in the area, combined with an on-the-spot diagnosis of the existing condi-

tions exceeding in completeness anything that can be achieved
through an analysis of the standard, routine weather observations. Thus, it is little wonder that the meteorologist, in the
confinement of his office ashore, rarely produces a wind forecast
adequate, from a yachting standpoint, in detail and accuracy,
even on special request.

The deviations of the actual local wind from the general
wind indicated by the trend and spacing of the isobars on the
weather map are determined by several factors; notably the
contrast between the temperature of the air over the water and
that of the air over the land, the general orientation of the coast
line, and the configuration of peninsulas, islands, bays, and
sounds. Peculiarities in the behavior of the wind are particularly
noticeable where the waters are quite cool relative to the land,
as is the case along the Atlantic Coast from Nova Scotia to the
Delaware Capes and along the entire Pacific Coast of the United
States during the summer.

On sunny summer days, in the areas mentioned, there is
always a tendency for the cool air over the water to flow landward, giving rise to the so-called "sea breeze." A similar tendency occurs along the shores of the Great Lakes, where it is
referred to as the "lake breeze." The strength and steadiness
of the sea breeze depend largely upon the orientation of the
coast line with respect to the direction of the general wind.
Thus, if the trend of the coast is such that the resulting normal
direction of the sea breeze is the same, or nearly so, as the direction of the general wind, the sea breeze will blow with fresh
velocity and from practically the same point of the compass
throughout the afternoon. On the other hand, if the general
wind (the direction of which can be gauged from the motion of
the cumulus clouds over the land) happens to be blowing more
or less directly offshore, the sea breeze, if it develops at all,
will be comparatively light and fluky.

Once the sea breeze has become well established, it blows
not perpendicularly onshore but nearly parallel to the coast line
in the direction such that the land lies to the right of an observer
facing the wind. This rule, together with the facts mentioned

in the preceding paragraph, provides the explanation of the variation in average wind conditions along the Atlantic Coast. The prevailing (*i.e.,* the most frequently occurring) direction of the general wind over the eastern United States in summer is SW. Along the south shore of Long Island and from southwestern Connecticut to Nantucket, the normal direction of the sea breeze also is SW. Consequently, these parts of the coast enjoy steady southwesterly breezes during the majority of summer afternoons.

From Cape Cod to the vicinity of Portland, Me., however, the usual direction of the general wind (which, owing to the local trend of the coast line, is offshore) is in conflict with the normal direction of the sea breeze. Thus the winds over Massachusetts Bay are decidedly fickle in comparison with conditions south and west of Cape Cod. East of Portland the coast line again assumes a favorable trend with respect to the prevailing general air flow, and a southwesterly breeze can usually be relied upon to spring up around noon if the morning is a calm one.

The Pacific coast has quite uniformly advantageous conditions. The constancy of the general wind there in summer is greater than on the Atlantic coast. Its predominating direction (NW) is within a couple of points of the normal direction of the sea breeze at most places, so that practically never is there a lack of wind in the afternoon.

In addition to the deviations from the general wind that are caused by the sea breeze there are aberrations of smaller scale that occur typically within bays or sounds. Because the air over a bay or sound is cooled by contact with the water, it becomes heavier than the air over the surrounding land. For the same reason, it acquires considerable "vertical stability." By this we mean that the increase of air density downwards is considerably greater than normal. Accordingly, the natural eddies in the wind tend to be suppressed, with the result that there is less mixing between the air at sea level and the air aloft. This condition is visibly manifested by the way smoke from steamers forms long, flat, persistent trails whenever the air has considerable vertical stability. It permits the horizontal motion of the air at sea level to be more easily retarded by friction with the surface of the water.

This effect is particularly pronounced at the western end of Long Island Sound, where the surrounding land areas are strongly heated during nearly every day in summer. On sunny days, with the general wind from a westerly direction, these waters form a pocket where cool air collects and becomes virtually stagnant. The resulting light, variable airs and calms are well known. This annoying situation is usually rectified sometime after the middle of the afternoon. By then the normal southerly sea breeze on the south shore of Long Island has developed sufficient strength to cross the land without becoming so heated en route that it rides over the air blanketing the Sound, and so is compelled to move aloft just out of masthead reach. The moment at which the southerly first sets in at the surface coincides with the time when the sea breeze, from the ocean south of Long Island, manages to arrive at the north shore of the Island with a temperature about the same as that of the stagnant air over the Sound.

There are, of course, many other waterways similar in shape to Long Island Sound, but no two of these exhibit identical peculiarities of wind behavior. However, the following general principles can be applied to any elongated body of water. When the direction of the general wind has a component across the axis of the elongated bay, the breeze tends to be weaker in the middle, and near the leeward side, of the bay, as compared to the windward shore, where the air blowing from the land has not had an opportunity to be cooled off (cf. the phenomenon of "hot puffs" off the land). Many sailors have learned from experience that a stronger breeze can usually be expected "under the beach." Furthermore, the cooled air over the middle of the bay tends to follow the path of least topographic interference, and assumes a direction of flow more nearly parallel to the axis of the bay, as compared to the flow of the air coming off the land. This explains why, when beating to windward through a bay or sound, a boat that stands in toward the windward shore is usually "let up" on the subsequent offshore tack and, therefore, is able to make a better heading toward her destination than another boat out in the middle of the bay.

If you are becalmed in the middle of a bay, it is discouraging to see a competitor holding a good breeze under the shore. Your temper probably will not be improved by the realization that in such a case there may well be a 10-knot wind 300 to 400 feet above you. Yet this is a typical situation wherever and whenever the water is considerably cooler than the air. The air then develops a high degree of stability, vertical exchange of momentum through the medium of eddies practically stops, and the motion of the air close to the water is slowed down. This action creates a large vertical gradient of wind speed; that is to say, if we measure the air motion at successive heights above the water, we find that the wind speed increases rapidly with altitude.

The existence of a high degree of vertical stability does not mean that there must be an almost complete absence of wind at the surface. The air composing the prevailing afternoon southwesterly breezes along the south shore of Long Island and the coast of southern New England sometimes shows a temperature difference amounting to as much as 10° F between deck level and a height of 500 feet, the air being warmer at the upper level. Yet these winds usually have sufficient strength to provide ideal sailing conditions, because the cool air over the ocean moves landward in response to the normal sea-breeze tendency. But, as a result of the upward increase of temperature, the velocity at the surface, adequate though it may be, is still considerably less than the velocity a few hundred feet aloft.

Large vertical gradients of wind speed are not peculiar to coastal waters alone. They exist whenever the air has considerable vertical stability, whether this stability occurs in air over land or in air over the open sea. For example, readings of vertical distribution taken at sea by an oceanographic expedition show (1) a five-kn. surface wind blowing 13 kn. at 200 ft. elevation and 40 at 600; (2) a 13-kn. surface wind blowing 18 kn.

at 200 and 24 at 500; and a 15-kn. surface wind blowing 17 kn. at 200 and 31 kn. at 600.

This explains why a racing yacht with a tall rig has a distinct advantage over its competitors in most light weather situations. Some readers will no doubt recall the sight of the J Class yachts working to windward in a faint southerly off Newport. The breeze might be only Force 1, barely strong enough to ruffle the surface of the sea, yet the Js, close-hauled, would be traveling through the water at five or six knots. One heard it said that they were "making their own wind." The idea behind this expression was that once the Js had acquired steerageway they created an apparent wind which was a little stronger than the real or observable wind. This caused the yachts to increase their speed slightly. In turn the apparent wind was increased, and so on, until a balance was reached between the driving force of the apparent wind and the resistance offered to the hull by the water. The true explanation, which very few of the spectators understood, was, of course, that the upper portions of the sails projected into a layer of air that was moving much more rapidly than the air at deck level. Thus, the character of the wind close to the water gave rise to an entirely misleading impression of the total pressure of the real wind on the lofty sails of those yachts.

Another noteworthy characteristic of a stable condition of the atmosphere is the steadiness of the wind. Whenever an upward increase of air temperature exists, the wind is relatively free of fluctuations in direction and velocity because under these circumstances the formation of eddies is checked. Since this kind of thermal arrangement usually develops in the air over coastal waters in summer, we find that onshore breezes rarely are gusty and seldom contain "soft spots."

In contrast to the steadiness of onshore winds is the fickle, puffy character of offshore winds. Take, for example, the occasional summer northwester along the Atlantic Coast. In this case the air has been heated over the land and has become vertically unstable, so that the natural eddies created by passage of the wind over rough ground are greatly intensified by thermally-induced overturning and stirring of the air. Consequently, the wind direction may fluctuate as much as 30° and the wind speed may almost be doubled or halved within a period of a few seconds. As soon as the air leaves the shore, it commences to be cooled from below, and a stabilizing process sets in, but some time is required for the dissipation of the eddies, so that even at a distance of 10 miles from land a summer northwester may still be fairly fluky and gusty. Typically, however, the strongest puffs are encountered right under the shore.

The reason that an offshore wind dies down very quickly and loses its gusty character around sunset is that the surface of the ground begins to cool rapidly in the later afternoon. The land then reverses the effect it had on the air during midday and commences to exert a stabilizing influence. Although the wind aloft (at a height of one thousand feet, say) continues to blow with about the same velocity that it had in the middle of the day, the suppression of turbulent motion by cooling from below permits the air near the ground to be slowed down by friction.

Up to this point we have laid considerable emphasis on the vertical variation of wind velocity that occurs in thermally stable air. We should, therefore, not neglect to stress equally the fact that there is very little change of wind velocity with height in air that has been moving over a land or water surface having a higher temperature than the air. The northwester discussed in the preceding paragraphs is only one example of the general case in which air that has been heated from below becomes thermally unstable and develops turbulent motion. The resulting stirring-up of the air tends to equalize the wind velocities at the surface and aloft by slowing down the upper strata and speeding up the lower ones. Therefore, in winter, when the temperature of the sea is usually higher than that of the air, we seldom find the large vertical variations of wind velocity that occur so frequently over our coastal waters in summer. Winter winds are usually just about as strong close to sea level as at an elevation of several hundred feet, and they are more often gusty than not.

This difference between the wind structures in stable and

unstable air sometimes produces an interesting, if quite local, phenomenon off the lee side of an island. Let us imagine a sunny summer day. The sea is cooler than the air, so that the wind velocity increases upwards at an appreciable rate. We are sailing in open water with a steady breeze of 10-knot velocity at deck level. We do not realize that the wind is blowing at 20 knots about 300 feet aloft. As we pass close to leeward of an island, the wind becomes puffy, and the average velocity at deck level jumps to 15 knots. (The increase of velocity from 10 to 15 knots corresponds to a doubling of the wind pressure.) After we clear the island, the wind drops back to its previous velocity.

This is explained in the following way. The lower strata of air approach the windward side of the island at a speed of 10 knots. As this air crosses the island, it travels over ground that has been strongly heated by the sun. The vertical stability that it possessed over the water is destroyed, overturning sets in, and the faster moving upper strata mixes with the lower strata, thereby eliminating the velocity difference between the two. In consequence, the wind at the surface increases and becomes gusty. This condition is transported offshore on the lee side of the island; it eventually disappears at some distance downwind.

Another very much localized influence on the wind is that exerted by strong tidal currents. Over a tide rip the wind often is weaker than elsewhere. Of course, the water is rougher there than in the surrounding area, and this fact alone makes the wind *seem* less, because not only does the chop interfere with a boat's progress but the increased pitching and rolling disturbs the aerodynamic balance around the sails. However, there are two additional factors which tend to "kill" the wind. Firstly, the greater roughness of the sea causes a greater frictional force to act on the wind, thereby slowing it down. Secondly, the temperature of the water is apt to be lower in a tide rip than in the surroundings, because the stirring action of the current churns up colder water from near the bottom and brings it to the surface. The presence of this colder water increases the vertical stability of the air and so reduces the wind velocity, as explained previously.

The aforesaid effects have no relation to the popular theory that changes in the direction and strength of the wind often coincide with, and, therefore, must in some way be caused by, the turn of the tide. This theory has never been proven or, for that matter, definitely disproven, because there are very great difficulties involved in the testing of it. For example, in order to verify the existence of winds produced solely by tidal changes, such winds would have to be distinguished not only from the general wind prevailing over a large area but also from local winds of the kind we have been considering elsewhere in this article.

There is the possibility that lunar tides in the atmosphere might exert some influence on the wind. (Note that the period of these tides would correspond in length of time with that of ocean tides.) Actually, the lunar atmospheric tide has been studied and has been found to be far too insignificant to bring about perceptible changes in the wind. Furthermore, it is impossible to explain, in terms of frictional drag, how a change in the direction of movement of the water accompanying a turn of the tide can have any important widespread effect on the movement of the air when the velocity of the current is of the order of one or two knots, or less.

There is absolutely no scientific evidence to substantiate the belief that tidal changes exert appreciable control over the wind. The persistence of this belief can be explained by the fact that tidal phenomena are most noticeable along the coast, especially in bays and sounds—just the regions that are most favorable to the development of sea breezes and other localized winds. Consequently, such winds may easily be incorrectly ascribed to a turn of the tide. (To quote the "British Meteorological Glossary.") "There is always the risk that meteorological events may be related in the popular mind with tidal changes, simply because the latter afford a convenient subdivision of the 24-hour day with which to associate changes that may really have been distributed over periods of several hours."

IN THE MIDDLE of a combination brain and stomach wave which

49

Pity the Poor Navigator!

by ALFRED F. LOOMIS

[1933]

IN THE MIDDLE of a combination brain and stomach wave which
assailed me in the last Bermuda Race I hit upon the only exact
definition of the art of small boat navigation. This is it, with the
customary apologies for a didactic assertion.

"The art of navigation is the immediate recognition and correction of mistakes made in ascertaining a position at sea."

Let me prove the definition by citing the imaginary example
of a poor dog of a navigator who was last seen skulking in
doorways, shunned by his late shipmates. He was a good navigator, but he failed to recognize his mistakes in time. Navigating the scratch entry in whatever race it was, he made allowance for steering error, leeway, current, or something else that
didn't happen to exist. Consequently, he brought his ship to the
finish line just 15 minutes later than she should have been there.
The delay cost his owner the mug and lost him four places
besides.

Here is how it happened: There was a lightship to be rounded,
and our navigator picked it up on his starboard bow instead of
dead ahead. At first this didn't seem a matter for recrimination
or *hara-kiri*. The navigator's owner and shipmates clapped him
on the back and exclaimed, "Snappy work, Oldtimer. That's
knocking 'em for a row of steam gauges!" and he allowed that
the landfall wasn't bad considering the conditions. When they

crossed the finish line and found that they were the first in, his friends' elation was unbounded, although the navigator's part was somewhat overlooked in the general satisfaction with their own prowess as seamen.

The first tincture of disappointment clouded the navigator's reputation three hours later when the second boat to finish saved her time by four minutes. Owner and crew of the scratch boat thought bitterly of a number of occasions during the race when they could have saved four minutes, but fixed their attention principally on that starboard-bow landfall. If only the navigator hadn't allowed for a current that wasn't there. Subsequently, four other boats finished within their time and shoved the scratch boat back to fifth place by 14 minutes. After that it was just too bad.

All hands went ashore to make the best of a bad job, but the navigator took his roll of bedding with him. His ex-shipmates mingled with old friends, and this was the nature of their alibi: "We sailed a fine race and everything would have been jake if (sh-sh) it hadn't been for our damned navigator. We told him he was steering wide of the lightship but the poor fish made allowance for a current that wasn't there, and we lost fifteen minutes beating up to the mark. That's what cooked us. Next time we're going to get a *good* navigator."

How about the poor navigator? Was he paid for his thankless task, or did he take it on because he loved the sport? Did he have the benefit of radio bearings and enjoy the other luxuries of steamboat navigation, or did he stand day and night watches as ordinary seaman in addition to his regular work? Did he sleep in a dry bunk and soothe his nerves with hot food at regular intervals, or was he racing in a small boat? Would anybody have given him credit for winning the race if he hadn't lost 15 minutes in a clever miscalculation? You know the answer to these questions. The sailboat navigator's life is not a happy one.

Too often he goes aboard an ocean racer in an anomalous status. Unless he is an experienced man with a reputation he doesn't know whether he is to stand a navigator's watch or will be required to turn out, four and four, for deck duty. He doesn't know whether he is to be a mechanical position-plotter or is expected by the owner to be the strategist who directs the course, foretells the weather, and conducts the campaign in opposition to any competitors that may be in sight. Least of all does this inexperienced navigator know the extent of his authority in the most essential matter of helmsmanship.

For the sake of harmony and racing efficiency these uncertainties should be definitely removed before the start of a race. If the navigator is to be a low private in the rear rank he should be publicly exonerated of all blame when a race is lost. But if he is to be the mastermind directing the destiny of the vessel in which he sails he should have the heartiest support of owner and crew. If he is to have authority over helmsmen his power should extend to the owner, mate, and all other dignitaries on board.

There are various excellent reasons why the navigator should have authority to order this man or that, including the owner, away from the wheel. The first is that he is the detached, philosophic member of the crew, able to see the whole race in perspective despite the prominence of nearby details. The second reason is that helmsmanship is about the most vital element in the sailing of a race. This fact is generally conceded when two boats are in sight fighting a ding-dong battle. At such a time only the best men are allowed at the helm, and differences of steering are quickly noted in the relative positions of the two competitors. But let one boat draw far away from the other, or let night intervene (as it will whether you let it or not), and interest in steering falls off. Every man is permitted to take the helm in regular rotation.

It is traditional for the owner to steer when any important shift of canvas is to be undertaken. This is just the time when the navigator should have authority to order him below to smoke a pipe, or forward to take a ducking on the bowsprit. I speak now as an owner rather than as a navigator, and I speak truth. As an owner there's nothing I like better than squatting on a soft cushion by *Hotspur's* tiller and saying, "All right, boys. Get in the ballooner and set the jib." Not only do I like steering and giving orders, but I know that steering is my prerogative and that I, better acquainted with my boat than anybody in the crew, am theoretically best qualified to take the job.

This is only theory. As owner and responsible party, I am the least qualified to steer the boat. I find myself wondering whether the balloon jib is going to be dragged in the water, and the next thing I know *Hotspur* is three points wide of her course. I wonder if somebody is going to forget that the working jib is liable to tear on the bowsprit roller chocks, and by the time I've mentioned that liability in a loud tone of voice I've got the boat in irons. I curse myself out, a process which involves steering a serpentine course for two minutes, and then notice that there is a half foul in the jib halyard. So it goes. Because I "rate" the helm I lose the boat a couple of hundred yards that are lost forever.

But I don't do that any longer. Avoiding the helm is one of the best things I do aboard ship. It is not even a point of pride with me to take the tiller in crossing the finish line. I've seen valuable minutes lost in the maintenance of that hoary tradition, and I now believe that this post should be not one of honor but of racing efficiency.

Shifting the angle of view a bit, let us now see what an owner should expect of the navigator in whom he reposes the responsible task of finding the finish line. But in what follows for a paragraph or two, be it understood that I speak largely from vicarious experience. I have only once been shipmates with another navigator and so only know the good ones from my own sort by what I hear when keeping an ear close to the bar at the conclusion of races.

First, I am told, an owner should find out whether his sun-shooter is a steamboat or a sailboat navigator. If of the former persuasion, the navigator won't know that his prime duty is to keep the boat moving as fast as possible as close to the ideal course as the elements allow. A steamboat navigator will set a course of, say, 106° and fight to the death to maintain that course even though the boat is starving to death and shrivelling up. A sailboat navigator, on the other hand, will watch the boat's performance on the ideal course (which, if it is 106°, he will call east by south a half south) and then if he sees that she is not footing properly will order the boat sailed by the wind.

Or, if the wind is free, a good navigator, they tell me, will set courses in points, half-points, or quarter-points. A helmsman must have something definite to think about. There is nothing definite about an eighth-point, which is unmarked on some compasses and illegible on most. Given such a course, for instance, as east seven-eighths south, the helmsman will mentally translate it as "somewhere between east by south and east three-quarters south." Part of the time he will sail as close to east by south as the sea lets him and part of the time he will try to average east three-quarters south. But a good share of the helmsman's time will be spent trying to recall what course it was the navigator gave him.

The same indecision and the same resulting loss in steering efficiency obtain when courses are given in degrees. Many navigators received their training in the Navy and do their compass thinking in degrees. But a majority of the ocean-racing scoundrels think in points. A 222° course might be the shortest to a vessel's destination, but no windjammer will steer it.

To be an asset to his ship, therefore, a navigator must bear constantly in mind that his job is an adjunct of ocean racing and not an individual, privileged science. A man who will not bring his sextant on deck when there is spray flying should either give up the navigation of ocean racers or borrow the owner's sextant. I have frequently been told of navigators who knock a close-hauled boat off her course every time they take a sight, their idea being to obtain a steady platform and an atmosphere free from flying particles of water. This may be excellent navigation, but it is execrable racing. The boat must be kept sailing on the course closest to her objective; the navigator must keep track of her position despite the difficulties which racing imposes. If, at any given time, there is too much spray for sights, their taking should be postponed. If, however, clouds threaten to obscure the sun or if the imminence of a landfall makes a sight imperative, then, and then only, should the course be altered for the convenience of the navigator.

If this sounds like too positive a statement let me illustrate it with a specific case. In navigating the *Brilliant* in a Bermuda Race I took and worked 30 sights. My sextant (or, rather, the owner's) was frequently drenched, and there were many times when I was on deck with it for ten-minute intervals. Assuming, however, that each string occupied me for not more than five minutes, it may be stated that the taking of sights totaled 150 minutes—two hours and a half of dodging shadows, cursing clouds, waiting for the *Brilliant* to rise to the top of a wave without throwing me off my balance, hoping that the spray would not mist the mirrors.

We were sailing with sheets started, averaging eight knots. Now, if I had asked the helmsman to knock *Brilliant* off three points to smooth the platform and drop the spray, she would have sailed, in two and a half hours, ten miles to leeward of her course. Assuming, again, that by hardening our sheets we could have sailed a point high of our desired course, we would have regained our windward position in eight hours of sailing at a reduced speed of seven and a half knots. As I work it out on a plotting sheet, the net time lost in these ridiculous maneuvers would have been 54 minutes. If we had dropped only 33 minutes in the interest of scientific navigation we would have lost two places in the finish order.

As it happened, I altered course but once in the 30 strings of sights. The sun on this occasion was swinging quickly from southeast into south and I wanted a check for longitude on the last morning of the race. As the orb bore half a point on our lee bow and couldn't be seen through the sextant from any spot on deck, I gave the fateful order to bear away two points for three minutes while I snapped my sights. . . . We lost fifth place to *Highland Light* by one minute and forty-six seconds. That is what steamboat navigation does for the hopes of owners.

By giving this personal example I have worked myself back into a state of sympathy for the imaginary navigator seen lurking in doorways at the beginning of this article. Not that I have

anything with which to reproach myself. On the morning of the
last day of the Bermuda Race four competitors appeared in
sight dead ahead, and it is only a wilfully mistaken navigator
who cannot follow his leaders across the finish line. Our landfall, in short, was perfect.

Let us, however, inquire into the anxieties and the hazards of
a navigator's position. There is nothing tangible about his job,
as there is, for the sake of a comparison, about the mate's. The
owner looks to weather and says to his mate, "There's more
wind up there and we'll do better without the foresail. What
do you think?" The mate either agrees or advises carrying on
for a while longer. In either case the decision is one of the
moment—the exigency is soon past. Each problem of sailing
is tangible and present. The future belongs to the navigator and
the past is soon forgotten.

But suppose the owner says to the navigator, "The glass has
risen, and the sky shows signs of breaking away to the northwest. What do you say to starting the sheets and making knots?
When the wind does haul abaft the beam we can quickly work
back to our base line." What answer can the navigator give?
If he alters course to leeward and the expected lift doesn't come,
he is sunk. If he holds the course, hammering into it for several
hours, and the wind then frees, he is sunk deeper still.

Or take a complex case more directly related to his official
responsibilities. His boat is reaching southeast on the starboard
tack. Three star sights at morning twilight give him a fix ten
miles west from his D.R. position. Sun sights the same morning
throw him ten miles farther west. He is near enough his expected
landfall to render a change of course imperative if the sun
sights are correct. So he balances the probabilities, past, present,
and future—which are:

One, westerly current. If it has set him ten miles in five hours
must he allow for the same set to the finish? A two-knot current
in the ocean seems excessive. It is better, therefore, to account
for the discrepancy elsewhere. Nevertheless, doubt remains.

Two, steering error. The sheets have been eased, the sea runs
high and there is the strong probability that the ship has worked

out to weather. But not ten miles in five hours. Still, there may
be a small steering error in conjunction with other uncertainties
and the navigator will be a fool if he doesn't include it in his
calculations for a perfect landfall. However—

Three, the star fix may have been wrong. Bad stellar fixes
have cost more than one ocean racer her chance of finishing
within the money. They may not at the time have been recognized as bad fixes, the bad landfalls which resulted have generally
been ascribed to current. The fact remains that star work from
the galloping deck of a small sailboat is open to suspicion. Yet—

Four, the sun fix may have been imperfect. The sights were
taken from the lee side, spray threatening the instrument, the rigging getting in the way, the mainsail pressing against the navigator's back, as, supported by a shipmate, he attempted to keep
a footing on the slippery cabin house. Perhaps the height of eye
was too low. Perhaps he did not level his sextant on the horizon,
but canted it up to the deceptive crest of an intervening wave.
Yet the navigator's work with the sun has generally been satisfactory and his landfalls on past occasions, entirely by benefit
of solar observations, have been good.

As if this four-horned dilemma weren't uncomfortable enough,
there is a fifth uncertainty to be reckoned with before the poor
navigator comes down to earth. The race, say, has ten hours
to run. The prevailing wind is southwesterly and it has been
blowing so for four days. Latterly it has diminished in strength,
and there is the possibility that it will shift and come in southeasterly. So, even if the accuracy of the solar fix is not entirely
credited, would it not be advisable to change the course a bit
to eastward, just in case?

Well, there is a good example of the intangibles with which
the navigator deals. He can't trust the future, the present, or
the past. He knows by the discrepancy between his two fixes
that he can't always trust himself. He is, if you please, a Dr.
Jekyll and a Mr. Hyde, but he can't decide clearly which of the
two gentlemen it was that committed the outrage on the heavenly
body. Meanwhile, half the crew are asking him how far he is

from his destination and what the course is going to be, while the other half are informing him that boats in sight ahead or astern are sailing diverging courses.

Yes, the navigator's lot is a damned unhappy one. Damned if he does and damned if he doesn't. And through all his uncertainty, his mental groping backward and forward over work done and to be done, he is doomed to keep his mouth shut and look sure and cheerful. If he admits his quandary or if he commits himself to a course of action which in these climactic hours of the race proves incorrect, or if he even facetiously asserts (as I once did to a literal-minded skipper) that he is lost, then he is lost indeed.

Which is why I maintain that the dictionary definition of the art of navigation is inexact, and that the true art consists in the immediate recognition and correction of errors made. I would not have had the temerity to enlarge upon this definition if I had not made a good landfall on St. Davids Head in the last Bermuda Race. My star fix the last morning was not ten miles to the westward. I invented that in the foregoing example to make it easy for the reader. My stellar fix was actually ten miles to the eastward of my D.R., indicating an easterly set. And my sun sights for longitude five hours later were, respectively, 12, 24, and 28 miles to the westward. That was pleasant, but when I learned that the man who had taken chronometer time for me was sure of his seconds but unsure of his minutes I took another string of three. These averaged ten miles to the westward—right back to where my D.R. had been before I obtained a three-star fix.

In my dilemma, which bordered on apoplexy, I thought of the currents north of Bermuda and dismissed them because no man has yet proved to my satisfaction that they can flow north, south, east, and west all in the same day—as they seem to do if one takes a poll among navigators at the yacht club bar. I thought of the leaping sea to leeward and the strong probability that I had measured a false horizon. I thought of the three-star fix and that made me think of the Three-Star Hennessy awaiting me at Bermuda. So I crossed out the sun sights and put my faith in the three stars. And *Brilliant* made so perfect a landfall that we did not have to alter a degree to round Kitchen Shoal buoy close aboard. But don't forget the perfect landfalls of those four boats in sight ahead of us.

50

If You're Going Ocean Racing

by T. W. HOWLAND

[1950]

EVERY FEW YEARS it is customary to offer invaluable advice about how to get ready to go ocean (or Great Lakes) racing. So far we've never been able to prove that reading these articles has won a race for anybody, but anyhow, here we go again. Experienced deep water sailors will doubtless complain that we have omitted important points, but at least this may serve as a reminder.

One element is the current rule of measurement under which your races are to be sailed. Most measurement certificates more than two years old are null and void, so if you haven't a new one, get busy and add to the already over-worked measurer's troubles by hounding him for one.

The rule is always worth the owner's close study, maybe with the collaboration of his designer. It just might be that he could find in it a gimmick to get his rating down a tenth of a foot, by putting black bands on his spars, cutting a foot or two off his spinnaker pole, or some such finagling. Or maybe a rule change will allow him to use some new sail to advantage, something he wanted to try before but didn't because the old rule penalized or barred it.

Speaking of measurements, read over the rule and be sure just what you can and can't do. For instance, if your boat was measured with the chain in the locker and the heavy anchor on

469

deck forward, you're liable to disqualification if you decide, just before or during the race, to move them down into the bilge under the cabin floor. Anything other than consummable stores (meaning grub and water and a case or two of beer) rates as ballast if stowed down there. Also, check up on sail limitations. A schooner was once disqualified in an ocean race because, half-way across, her crew got the bright idea that the spinnaker would draw better if hoisted to the main truck, instead of its regular halyard block on the foremast. It never occurred to them that they were breaking a rule until, after the race, some-one saw a picture taken of her from a passing steamer and said "Hey! What goes on here?"

Apropos of sails, even if you don't need any new ones (lucky fellow) it will pay to have your sailmaker give the old ones a going over, renew stitching wherever necessary, reinforce any chafed spots, renew servings, refasten slides and hanks and, in general, put the canvas in seaworthy shape. How about that storm jib and trysail you haven't used for a couple of seasons— have the mice got into 'em? Once you're in commission, of course, you'll try out every sail on the ship to see if any need recutting. How about your sail-mending equipment? And have you a roll of sticky tape for quick temporary repairs and pro-tection against chafe? A small, hand-operated sewing machine might come in handy.

We assume your ship is sound and tight, seams caulked, payed and smoothed, underwater fittings checked and the bottom as smooth as you can get it. If not, get busy. If your masts were out for the winter, of course you went thoroughly over every splice, shackle, tang and fitting of the standing and running rig-ging. If you haven't, get a reliable helper (one who won't forget to hold a turn on the halyard) and a boatswain's chair and spend half a day aloft doing a boatswain's inspection of all gear. A new shackle or two, or a new stay if an old one looks at all doubtful, is cheap insurance. It's sort of lonesome drifting around out there with your rig over the side. This is also a good time to take inventory of spare gear of all kinds, coils of new line of the sizes you use, tools, and gear in general.

The running rigging wants looking over. A few years ago the inspection committee, before a Bermuda Race, noticed a gray, weary-looking mainsheet aboard a yacht. The skipper—a man who should have known better—had a coil of new line aboard, but thought he'd try to make the old one do because it was so soft and easy on the boys' hands. The committee was polite about it, but the new sheet was rove off. A sheet or halyard that parts in a squall can raise a lot more concentrated hell with gear and crew than it's worth to save a few dollars by making the old gear do. While we're on running gear, all winches and blocks ought to be taken apart, inspected for worn parts, and lubricated. Are all your turnbuckle cotterpins taped over to keep them from tearing sails? Rig chafing gear where you know it's needed and make up some spare pieces to put on later.

How are your pumps? No matter what electric or engine-driven pumps you have, a big, husky hand pump that will lift a maximum of water with a minimum of elbow grease is a must. If you want to be comfortable, install a suction line to each bilge, besides the main intake, so when she's heeled down you can pull out those last few gallons of water that otherwise manage to climb into the lee bunks.

If not already installed, put in racks, hooks or other suitable fixed stowage for winch handles, snatch blocks, light sail sheets, guys and other occasionally-used gear, to which they must always —repeat, always—be returned when not in use so the crew can lay hands on them instantly in the dark. Light and storm sail sheets may be made up on the sails and bagged with them. Are your sail bags conspicuously marked, and are the same sails always stowed in the same places, on racks so you can get the one you want without fighting your way through a stack of others?

If you haven't rigged floodlights under your spreaders, give the idea some consideration. And while you're at it, how about a masthead spotlight to show on the fly? A trouble light on a long cord may be worth many times what it costs. A bushel basket full of assorted flashlights is about the right quantity— they're always getting broken or shorted, or the batteries go dead just when you need 'em. And if anybody in your crew can read and send blinker messages, a good blinker light may be the means for passing the time of night with competitors, and just possibly sending a distress signal, God forbid!

While you won't use your engine for making power dashes on calm nights, there are preparations to be made in the engine-room. If you use your main engine to charge batteries, rig some sort of clamp on the propeller shaft so it can't accidentally turn when the engine's running. Disconnecting the coupling will make this doubly sure. See that your feathering propeller really feathers—it may be too rough out at the starting line to send a hand overboard to look at it. If yours is a centerline propeller installation, mark the shaft or coupling—a dab of paint will do —to show when the propeller is up-and-down behind the dead-wood. If you have a separate generator, be sure it's working right. The modern ocean racing yacht has a lot of equipment that is dependent on electric power.

Decide whether you'll carry your fuel tanks full or empty— full is safer; empty saves weight; half-full is dangerous—and either top them off before starting or drain out all but enough gas to get you out to the starting line if it's calm. Prepare plugs or install shut-off valves for the tank vents and fill pipes, to keep gas and vapor out of the boat and water out of the tank in heavy weather. Make a plug, or install a valve, in the exhaust line so water can't run back into the cylinders in a following sea. A petcock at the low point of the exhaust line, left open at sea, further insures against this. If it dribbles water into the bilge, pump it out, but don't shut the petcock—find out why it dribbles and fix it. If you use your engineroom for a sail locker when racing, protect both engine and sails with a tarpaulin over the engine.

Don't overlook safety equipment. Test and fill fire extinguishers. Check your distress signals—the parachute or rocket type that make both fire and smoke are desirable. Check the water lights—electric or chemical—and secure to ring buoys. Get a few packets of the green dye marker which, dumped in the water, makes a fine, big splotch for aircraft to sight, just in case you get in real trouble. The same people who make it also make a shark-inhibiting chemical, which might be comforting to drop in the water in case you're becalmed and want to take a swim. Inspect the lifelines. Provide safety belts with rope tails and snaphooks for the crew.

If you depend on inflatable boats or rafts, see that they're tight and provide cartridges, or a good air pump, to inflate them. Make sure all hands are provided with nonskid footgear, and to make doubly sure, put nonskid paint on all decks, cabin tops, bowsprits and walking surfaces in general. Overhaul and replenish your medicine chest, seeing your own physician for prescriptions that may be needed. And don't overlook Dramamine, a generally dependable cure for what sometimes ails some of the lads. Better yet, test your crew for seasickness and leave the susceptible people at home.

Having taken care of these and a couple hundred other details, the ship may be ready, but how about the crew? Of course you signed them up early in the winter, and lined up a couple of alternates in case some joker finds his grandmother or his business is dying at the last minute. (In an emergency, there'll probably be some hopeful pierhead jumpers, of uncertain value, hanging around— the race committee will know of them.) Get as many of the gang out as many weekends as possible before the race, practicing everything from setting spinnakers to heaving-to and man-overboard drill. If you can, take them on a preliminary overnight race.

Choose your watches carefully. Size up your gang for day and night helmsmanship and divide good helmsmen evenly between the watches. Each watch should contain at least one man thoroughly familiar with the ship, gear, sail and spare equipment stowage, electrical and mechanical equipment and so on —say the owner in one watch and the paid hand or someone who sails with you regularly in the other. If the navigator stands a deck watch, have someone in the other watch on whom he can depend for intelligent dead reckoning and to call him, or not, when conditions are propitious or otherwise for morning and evening star sights. One skipper we know sizes up each crew member's steering habits and makes allowance for divergence above or below the course for the time each man has the helm, in figuring dead reckoning.

Make it clear that watches are to be kept from the start, or at least from dusk the first night. This iron man business of everybody staying up all the time is strictly no good after the first six hours—sooner or later all hands begin to dope off at one time. The off watch should be in their bunks, or at least resting below, unless an all-hands job comes along. This may not apply to the skipper or navigator if they aren't assigned to regular watches but, like the boatswain's monkey, stand no watch and all watches. Nor to the cook, whose hours depend on the crew's appetites, including snacks for the change of watch at midnight. If the boat is small or stowage space limited, instruct each hand what, and particularly what *not,* to bring aboard.

The navigator can do a lot of work in advance. If, like most of us, he's only an occasional navigator, who works at it once every year or two, he'd better dust off his sextant, get out in a boat or at least down to the shore, take a few sights, and go home and work them up for practice. If he can't get sights, he can at least get a book of problems and run through a few of those based on the approximate date and DR positions he'll be working with at sea. He can renew acquaintance with the "Nautical" or "Air Almanac," whichever he uses. And he can make sure that either he or the ship has the requisite books, tables and instruments.

The more actual work he can do in comfort, on the dining table at home, the less he'll have to do, and with less probability of error, on a rolling, pitching, small yacht at sea when he's tired, sleepy, cramped, wet and being trampled on by the watch. He can buy his charts (a complete set, up to date) and plotting sheets and, after reference to the suitable pilot charts, lay out on them the set and drift of known currents, and the base courses (rhumb lines, Great Circles or whatever) that he hopes to sail.

If going to Bermuda, for instance, he can work out how far upstream (God willing) he wants to hit the Gulf Stream's northern limit of influence in order to make a quick crossing under normal wind conditions and come out on the rhumb line on the southern side; also, what compass courses to steer in the Stream, at various sailing speeds, to make good the rhumb line course over the bottom (a Navy maneuvering board is handy for this). He can do his star-finder work in advance and list the approximate altitudes and azimuths of stars for probable rough DR positions each day.

He can check and plot useful radio beacons. In the Bermuda Race, for instance, the Bermuda airport beacon signals are continuous and audible at 200 miles, whereas the marine beacon is intermittent and relatively short-ranged. The chronometer should be professionally rated, if it's been ashore for the winter, and the rate checked for several days after moving it aboard. The direction finder can be checked and a correction card made. The radio receiving set should be tested, and a list of the hours and frequencies of available weather and time broadcasts prepared.

The cook should be making up a list of stores, based on daily menus for a few more days than you hope the race will take, plus a generous allowance of emergency rations—canned, dry and imperishable stores—in case things go extremely wrong. We won't go into sea cookery, on which libraries have been written, but here are a few reminders. Cans to be stowed in the bilge or under bunks should have paper labels removed and the contents identified with paint on the can. Cigarettes, tobacco and matches—lots of matches—should be waterproof-stowed. We remember vividly the crew of miserable nervous wrecks who stumbled ashore from a schooner after an ocean race some years ago, after running out of matches and going without hot food or smokes for three or four days.

Check the condition of the stove, the fuel supply, and the galley exhaust blower, if any. Maybe the cook can hornswoggle the skipper into having a safety belt installed with solid moorings in the galley, so he can stay with his job in rough weather and have both hands free for cooking. If the icebox door opens athwartships (God forbid) install plywood, Plexiglas or similar guards to prevent everything leaping out when she rolls with the door open. Most ships buy and stow canned, salt, dry and bottled stores at their home ports well before the race. Buy your fresh meat, fruit, vegetables and such the day before the start and fetch 'em aboard yourself, no matter how solemnly the grocery clerk may promise to do it. And just before sailing, be sure the water tanks are topped off. Also that valves are closed so that you're pumping water from only one tank at a time. No seagoing yacht should have fresh water under pressure —pump by hand and save water.

Plan to get your boat to the starting port of the race in plenty of time. One of the many headaches of the ocean race committee is the number of owners who, if the instructions call for all yachts to report for inspection three days before the start, ask the special privilege of getting there later. If they all showed up the last day, nobody could inspect them all. And if the weather is exceptionally bad for the last two or three days before the race, the man who cuts it too fine may not make it. Better to get her there, if the race starts a considerable distance from your home port, the weekend before than to find yourself beating hopelessly to windward in a gale, or rolling around becalmed with a stalled auxiliary, as starting time approaches.

Don't count on getting her hauled out for a bottom-polishing job the day before the race, either. The local railways may all be busy. Better get a decent bottom on her before you leave home, maybe a couple of weeks before the race, and for the final spit-and-polish job send a few hands over the side to give her a scrub at anchor just before the start—any fouling will probably be along the waterline rather than deep down on the garboards, and the swim will help cure any sailing-day hangovers that may turn up. Apropos of which, one way to go to sea with a disgruntled crew is to try to keep the convivial souls on the water wagon the night before sailing. Let 'em howl, if they want to.

A few other last minute thoughts, just before you hoist the

dink aboard and stow the heavy anchor below: Have you attended to the formalities of clearance and health papers and crew lists, if going foreign? Did you put fresh batteries in all the flashlights? Have you charged the ship's batteries to full capacity? Did you get the rating and identification lists, special anchorage charts, race instructions and last minute information from the race committee? Have you got the latest weather predictions and the maps for the past few days? If your engine is secured, will some kind friend tow you out to the starting line in case of light weather?

All right. Heave around on the windlass, and good luck!

51

Pointers on Handling Light Sails

by RODERICK STEPHENS, Jr.

[1939]

"PUT A POSTAGE STAMP on it, address it to the Royal Western Yacht Club, and cut it adrift." That was Bill Roos' suggestion for getting the balloon jib off *Skal* as she staggered by Lands End in a southerly gale during the 1931 Fastnet Race. But, on the chance that delivery at destination by this method may be doubtful or that you may want the sail again before you get ashore, other methods of doing the job suggest themselves. Here are some of them.

Basically it is desirable to bear off *away* from the wind when it comes to getting in a ballooner or big genoa. The mainsail will blanket the headsail, while the fore deck remains relatively dry and steady. In a 14-mile breeze, assuming a boat speed of six knots, you'd feel only some eight miles of wind when right off before it, while it would pipe right up to 20 were you to forereach up into it while luffing.

Of course, if there isn't sufficient room to leeward, or if you've parted your sheets or started the sail or some gear so that bearing off is unwise, luffing is second choice. In light weather and smooth water, all is well, but if there's a breeze and the accompanying sea, hang on tight and stay well clear of the clew. Above all, get the sail down quickly so it does not flog itself to destruction and so that you can fill away before all steerageway is gone.

In sailing to windward, except where roughness of sea makes it absolutely imperative, bearing away will be too costly in distance while luffing will lose valuable headway. The alternative is sufficient manpower to overcome the pressure in the sail without change of course.

The first job is to overhaul the halyard thoroughly, flaking it down, starting with the bitter end. This end should be made fast so it won't go aloft, even when the man who is lowering away turns from his work in a fruitless effort to retrieve his hat (or gets a telephone call, as one did in *Blitzen* in a Nassau Race).

Next, get as much of the foot onto the deck and as far up to the weather side as possible. Start from the tack (forward) and work aft. The halyard has to be slacked at the same time to make this possible. Hold the sheet until the foot is well in hand and the sail partially lowered. Slacking the sheet too soon results in unnecessary flogging and in the foot getting away, out of reach.

Unless conditions are quite moderate, it is safer not to unhook the sail until it is fully lowered. Get all the sail up along the weather rail so the water on the lee side won't take it overboard, then unhook, starting with the head, and, as the sail comes off the stay, pass it aft where there is more room to stow it and less spray and motion. In rough water particularly, the greatest danger is between the time the sail is lowered and the time it is gotten aft.

We usually have an unnecessary fear of getting sails in the water. Occasionally, due to lack of manpower, extremely bad conditions or excessive size, particularly of a spinnaker, the sail will get in the water. When this happens, don't let it act as a scoop. Never hold two corners without holding the part between. Don't get the clew of the genoa forward of the rigging until the foot is all on deck, clear of where it can get overboard.

Once a sail is overboard, start at the tack and work along the foot and/or the luff. The skin friction of the water rushing by a sail is relatively easy to overcome—easier, of course, if the boat is slowed down as much as possible.

Almost all sail drill is about as hard or as easy as you make it. If only the forces which often seem so hard to overcome can be made to work in the desired direction, you have a powerful ally. For example, you may have exhausted your vocabulary and even called for the cook in trying to get the inboard end of your spinnaker pole away from the mast preparatory to jibing or dousing the spinnaker. How much easier it will be to run dead to leeward momentarily, then slack the spinnaker sheet so that the sail just doesn't "break." If the lift and foreguy are slack and the guy reasonably square, the pole will have a tendency to pull away from the mast.

When it comes time to take in a parachute, again check the halyard first. Then break out whatever headsail will be used next. Then let the pole go forward against the stay and unhook the tack of the sail. Or if you have an outhaul, slack it right away clear. At the same time, the sheet should be hove in from amidships on the lee side till you get hold of the clew. Work along from the clew, gathering in the foot and then the luff of the sail.

It is important to have all cotter pins and rough projections in the rigging thoroughly taped as the sail will get against the rigging as you start to lower. Don't get the sail in too near the shrouds or it may wrap itself around them. In a hard breeze, when everything is wet, give yourself more time, as the wet sail is more apt to cling to the shrouds, which takes time to clear. Try to have a clear place to pile the sail as it comes down. It is slow work to extricate a jibsheet that is under the middle of the spinnaker.

In course racing, timing is perhaps the most important feature of sail changing. The variables are so numerous that strict rules are not practical. In general, plan so that 95 per cent of the changing work is done when you are off the wind or reaching. Under these conditions, men can work standing up and the helmsman's concentration is less important. Also, a couple of sails flogging around will not have much effect on speed. Then, if you are on the wind approaching a mark, after which you want a spinnaker, have things handy but sit tight till you reach the mark. If you get all rigged up and spinnaker hoisted ahead of time, you will probably have slowed the boat down a little. Also, the spinnaker may break out too soon. Thirdly, if at the last instant you have to tack, some of your preparations may have fouled the weather jibsheet, and it's just too bad.

When conditions are such that there is little choice between spinnaker and a genoa, take time to get everything straight, since delay costs almost nothing. But when you are going to be dead before it, and the spinnaker is to do most of the work, get it up and drawing, any old way, so that it will pull you along; you can clear up and make minor adjustments later.

Spinnaker jibing plays an important part in almost all downwind races. Thanks to the reversible pattern of the present spinnakers, plus the modern reversible or double-ended spinnaker poles, highly efficient jibes are now possible. A complete set of instructions, however, would be as awe-inspiring as a restaurant menu and they'd probably not have one thing you wanted.

To learn this art, next time you're out for a sail square off before the wind with mainsheet flat, set the spinnaker, fasten the lift and the foreguy to the middle of the pole and set the lift so that it holds the pole at a convenient working height. Leave the foreguy slack. Mark the after guy at the lead block when the pole is almost back to the shrouds. Lead the spinnaker sheet to the corresponding lead block on the opposite side and mark it the same distance from the end as the guy is marked. Set both sheet and guy to the marks, unhook the pole from the mast and hook into the sheet of the spinnaker. The sail should stay full as the pole takes a position a couple of feet forward of the mast, half on each side of the boat.

As you jibe the mainsail, push the spinnaker pole across the foredeck the *opposite way*. It shouldn't take much pressure if the boat is kept fairly dead off even after the mainsail is jibed. Then jibe back, sliding the spinnaker pole again opposite to the main boom. After you have done that, unhook the lee corner of the sail from the pole and hook the pole to the mast. Then start all over again.

The most difficult racing jibe will differ only as to later refinements. The mainsheet must be trimmed, runners handled and mainsheet slacked. And, as you may jibe from one reach to another reach, the spinnaker must be squared *to the marks* on sheet and guy before jibing, and after jibing must be retrimmed, letting the pole go forward and leading the sheet 'way aft if necessary.

In hard going, when reaching, the lift and foreguy should be shifted to the outer end of the pole after the jibe; otherwise, the pole may be broken. But the actual jibe is executed just exactly as it was in the simple case just described. Timing, coordination, practice, are essential—and don't forget to keep the lee runner clear of the spreaders.

52

When in Doubt, Carry Your Spinnaker

by RODERICK STEPHENS, Jr.

[1939]

IT'S A TALL ORDER, and may sound a bit wild, but the advice given in the title to this article will probably get you there quicker if you have a good parachute spinnaker and trim it about right. These spinnakers are not entirely inhuman. When you are thoroughly acquainted with them, they will seem much more rational and be easier to get along with.

But just what is a parachute spinnaker? Perhaps a second cousin of the single spinnaker. It hoists to the same place and sets on the end of your spinnaker pole, and is generally used going down wind. But, beyond this, it severs all family connections. Primarily, it is a very full sail, cut so that when set its surface approaches that of a portion of a sphere.

Due to the great draft cut into the sail, it sets to best advantage with the pole held up well above the deck. This gives the luff slack which permits it to reach out and use wind which would get by the old type of spinnaker. As a result of the inherent fullness, the body of the sail bulges 'way forward (or to leeward) of all head rigging. For that reason, the sheet is invariably carried around outside of all forward and lee rigging. This permits efficient use of great width, the sail being from 1.5 to over 3 times the length of the spinnaker pole in width.

The single spinnakers were seldom wider than 1.5 times the length of the spinnaker pole. They were not carried outside of the jibstays, so were kept narrow enough to set mostly to windward of them. The clew was held somewhere near the middle of the balloon jib, into which you hoped the spinnaker would spill a helpful amount of its partially used air. The pole would generally be guyed as far aft toward the shrouds as possible, and seldom could be carried advantageously further forward than 45° from the center line of the boat.

Inherent in the parachute is the "double" construction. Luff and leach are of the same length and shape, the prime virtue of this being that either lower corner of the sail may serve as tack (on the pole) or as clew (for the sheet). As this sail is clear outside and ahead of everything, in jibing it is necessary only to shift the pole from one side to the other.

A proper parachute will do its best work *without* help from other headsails, with the possible exception of a small balloon staysail, which can be made to help when reaching.

The question of *when* to set the parachute hinges almost entirely on *apparent wind*—the strength and direction of wind felt by your boat and is greatly affected by your course and speed. If it were always possible to get on the course and up to speed before having to decide about the spinnaker, then you'd only have to look at your wind pennant.

As it is often impossible to get the direction of the apparent wind by the above trial and observation method, it is often necessary to investigate on the chart. Draw a small line *AB* on the course you will sail, the length of the line equivalent to your best estimate of boat speed *with everything set*. From your point *A,* and to the same scale, draw the *actual* wind direction *AC,* the length of this line being equivalent to your best estimate of wind strength. *BC* will represent apparent wind—both in direction and velocity. This diagrammatic solution of the apparent wind is tremendously useful as you approach a mark in a race and want to be properly prepared for the next leg, or if you are late getting out to the start and want to be all ready once you get there.

If the apparent wind is abeam or further aft, it is time for the spinnaker. The exact wind angle where it will pay to set the spinnaker depends largely on the wind strength and partially on the cut and width of sail.

If the breeze is light (under four miles), you can get some help from a good spinnaker with the apparent wind (when the spinnaker is set and pulling) one-half point forward of the beam. At eight miles' wind strength, abeam is the limit. At 16 miles, probably one-half point abaft the beam, and so it goes. The main limiting factor is the boat's stability as opposed to the tendency of the large spinnaker to overpower her. Thus, if it is blowing hard, the wind will have to be well on the quarter for the spinnaker to pay. The strength of the sail, not to mention spinnaker poles and guys, etc., all work toward the same limits. Note by a diagram how much stronger the apparent wind will become as it comes more abeam, even though the strength of the actual wind is constant.

Perhaps more important than *when,* is *how* to carry the parachute. Happily there are a few simple generalities which answer most of the questions. First of all, keep the pole at right angles to the apparent wind. Thus, with the apparent wind abeam, the pole will be against the headstay; when the wind is dead aft, the pole should be about square off the center line or back to the rigging.

With the best pole angle so easily established, there is only one more pole problem. This relates to the pole's proper height, primarily of its outboard and secondarily of its inboard end. The outboard end of the pole must be controlled by a lift. No weight is kept on the luff of the sail; thus it can sweep out and increase its useful area and take its proper shape. Just keep the *tack* of the spinnaker (outboard end of pole) *at the same height as the clew* (where sheet is attached). To make this rule hold true you should use a sheet whose weight is commensurate with the wind strength. If you are drifting in a zephyr, use marline or flag halyard to let the clew rise all it will.

For the inboard end of the pole, remember to keep it so the pole is level. The higher the inboard end, the easier it is to keep the outboard end down, and *vice versa.* Level gives you the greatest effective length.

If you know when to carry the spinnaker and how to set the pole, there is but one more variable, the sheet. The position of the deck lead for the sheet is of little importance when the wind is 'way aft. Elimination of chafe is of cardinal importance, and convenience and simplicity of lead should be stressed.

As the wind comes more abeam, it is important to get the sheet aft as far as possible. If the counter of the boat is short or the boom is long, or both, trim to the end of the boom when the rules do not prohibit it. Otherwise, trim right out to the lee corner of the transom. It is this correct position of the sheet that makes possible such good reaching results with a parachute. The sail will be flattened out when the flattening is obviously most necessary. The clew will still be a good bit to leeward and a positive driving angle be maintained, even though the pole may be against the headstay, square off an apparent beam wind.

The principal advantage and reason for speed from a parachute spinnaker is that its curved edges can reach far beyond the theoretical confines of the imaginary triangle formed by the end of the spinnaker pole and the mast at the head and the deck.

As the leach is largely behind the mainsail, it can be seen that the luff is doing the work. The actual value of the parachute depends largely on how far out this luff can be made to go. It is held out only by the pressure of the air in the sail. The amount the luff can be made to extend depends on two vital factors: first, the cut of the sail and, second, the skill with which the sheet is handled. A badly cut sail is difficult to coax out or to keep out even with the greatest skill and perseverance on the part of the sheet man. Nor will the best parachute stay full and working without skillful help from the one who handles the sheet.

Let us assume that the sail is well cut, the pole square off the apparent wind and held so that tack and clew (with proper weight sheet) are both at equal height. Further, the sheet is led right aft as the apparent wind is just a point abaft the beam. By virtue of a most commendable burst of profanity and suggestions from all hands, the parachute has blissfully consented to bulge out. The problem is to keep it so.

Any time a decent parachute collapses it is for one of three reasons. The wind may be too much against the luff (course too high and/or sheet too slack). The wind may be too much against the leach (boat too wide and/or sheet too hard), or there may be no wind (AEolus, a competitor, or a tall building or lighthouse).

The trim of the guy and lift are clearly defined above and present no difficult problem. The boat's course has much bearing and should be modified (*before* the collapse) to maintain the wind from an angle in harmony with the spinnaker trim (so here you have a chance to give the skipper hell now and again).

But the "head goat" is the man on the sheet. He must have a neck which can assume and maintain a 75° angle from the spinal column, and hands that can hold *and pull* the sheet at any given second.

Then, as we reach along with parachute happily full, the first signs of collapse will show in the luff. Just as this *starts* to collapse, the sheet man gives a quick jerk—like the bass fisherman who has already lost three frogs—and, presto, the sail stays full. But *give back what you take* on the sheet or else, before you know it, you've pulled the whole sail around behind the mainsail, your competitors are fading into the distance and, when you try to cure the next collapse, you can't get any more, the clew being "two blocks." The damned spinnaker is no good, you think.

Even when the wind is absolutely steady and the sea smooth, keep that sheet going out, get the luff to reach out and claim new territory. Play it as you would coax a kite up into the air, but with your eyes glued to the luff; when the telltale reverse curve appears, give a jerk.

Thus the sheet man is king pin but the helmsman must be on the alert, keeping the fly (apparent wind) at an angle to suit the scope offered by any existing position of spinnaker pole or sheet lead. The men on the guys and lifts must retrim as often as the wind or course changes.

Last but not least, remember that it is the wind that keeps your parachute working. So, helmsman, steer so that your crew

can get some wind to keep in the spinnaker. Don't get off by
the lee; no trim of sail or pole can cure this. And, the lighter
the wind, the more it becomes necessary to sharpen up a little
to keep that life-giving pressure in the sail—even though the
change in course may later demand a jibe.

53

On Being a Good Racing Crew

by ROBERT N. BAVIER, Jr.

[1950]

THE UNSUNG HERO of many a winning yacht is the crew. The best skipper is licked in keen competition without a good crew and many an average helmsman can thank his "bilge boys" for putting him at the top of his class. By the very nature of the sport more yachtsmen serve as crews than as skippers, but a top notch crew can often get as much fun out of a race as a skipper. And if he's a really good crew member, one can land a berth in almost any boat of his choosing. Those who aspire to racing their own boat some day (and who doesn't?) can gain invaluable training from an expert skipper.

It is every skipper's dream to find a crew who will help with the labor of commissioning the boat and getting her in winning form. You don't *have* to do this to be a good sailing crew, but those who are around when the work is to be done not only have a better chance of landing a good berth, but also get more satisfaction from later successes by virtue of having contributed to them from the beginning.

Particularly in light, sensitive boats in which hiking is important, it is helpful if the crew is in good physical condition. When the German *Pimm* created such a sensation by her amazing speed in the 1937 Star World Championship, her skipper and her light, flexible rig were given the lion's share of the credit. And with good reason, but her crew, Joachim Weise, gave a real demonstration of what good hiking could be. For long periods he was able to hang almost completely outboard and below deck level. This increased stability, reduced windage and was in no small measure responsible for *Pimm's* speed. Only a man in top condition could have kept it up as Weise did. We can't all be athletes and all boats don't require such acrobatics, but we can and should see that our efficiency is not impaired by tender hands. This may seem a trivial matter, but I can remember one heavy weather race in early season when my hands and those of everyone else on board became raw from sheet handling. By the end of the race, sails were being trimmed with less care and the jib was seldom sheeted home properly. You may not wish to go to the extreme of pulling on an old rope tied to a tree in your back yard (though it has been done) but until your hands have hardened it is wise to bring along a pair of work gloves.

To increase personal efficiency still further, be sure to wear nonskid shoes and dress properly. Wear enough warm clothes and foul weather gear so that when the skipper wants you to lay out on the weather rail for the entire windward leg it won't seem like an eternity. Personal equipment should also include a *sharp* knife, a pair of pliers and, particularly if you are the spinnaker man, a supply of stopping twine. Climax stopping twine, which is uniformly rotted cotton, is the best I know of. It is large enough to tie easily yet always breaks reliably, and comes in weights suitable for sails of all sizes.

A good crew arrives on board long enough before the start to stop sails, bail and help scrub the bottom if necessary. He checks the halyards to make sure they are clear, sees that he knows where all gear is and that it is in readiness.

Once underway, the crew has a chance to practice trimming sails while tacking or jibing. Even in strong winds, in popular-sized boats, it is a simple matter to trim the jib flat enough after a tack, providing it is done at the right time. Timing is everything. By trimming too soon, before the tack is almost completed, you may back the jib and reduce headway. By trimming too late, it will be difficult to flatten it properly. Learn also to get your back into it when trimming and to brace properly.

Most skippers like to read the race circular themselves and all of them should. Even so, a wise crew does so too. Once in the vicinity of the committee boat, one crew member can check the starting signals and the course, becoming thoroughly familiar with the latter. Thereafter, he should make sure whether signals are changed at the last minute. The skipper is mighty busy at this time and it is small wonder that when last minute changes are made he sometimes misses them.

Once the race is underway, one of the crew's big jobs (particularly in small centerboarders) is to shift his weight to keep the boat on her best sailing lines. The skipper will have told him how much he wishes the boat to heel. In light airs it will then be the crew's job to shift slowly to leeward. In puffs he will move to windward to maintain the desired heeling angle, and in a strong breeze will hike out to windward to prevent excessive heeling. A crew that shifts his weight thus, without being directed, permits the skipper to concentrate on the tactics of the race. The crew must also so place himself as to maintain the boat on her best fore-and-aft lines. In a planing type boat, he must be particularly conscious of his position, moving aft to get the bow to lift and sometimes lunging forward as she starts to plane in order to coax her into a full-fledged plane. Some skippers of two-man boats divide the responsibility of maintaining balance, directing the crew to move only from side to side and shifting their own weight forward and aft, except on windward legs or close reaches when both will have to hike out to windward when it blows hard. In any event, a good crew knows the importance of shifting his weight and, knowing *how* it should be shifted, does so automatically without order from the skipper.

A good crew also anticipates the skipper's commands regarding sail trimming. On windward legs, the helmsman will usually order the final adjustments in sail trim, since he can best feel how the boat is going. But the crew trims first to what he considers is the right position. A really experienced crew may even play the sheets on the windward leg, easing out slightly in the light spots to give more drive, taking it back as the wind freshens and occasionally spilling wind by sudden slacking of the main in wicked puffs. More often, however, these changes are made as the skipper directs. In dinghies and many other two-man boats small enough to permit him to do so, the skipper usually holds the mainsheet in his hand, both on windward and leeward legs, so that he can play it. This lets the crew concentrate on hiking and also permits him to tend the jib, if the boat has one.

The crew's responsibility in sail trimming is greater on leeward legs. Then, except in boats of dinghy size, the usual custom is for the skipper to select his course and leave it up to the crew to trim and slack sheets as the wind shifts, or as the skipper changes course. The skipper usually announces when he is about to head up or bear off but otherwise, if he has a good crew, he will rely on him to keep the sails trimmed properly. The crew learns, by observation, and by asking the skipper while sailing to or from the race, just how much the sails should be trimmed for the conditions in hand. The man on the spinnaker sheet is especially important. He must keep the spinnaker eased as far as it will go without breaking and collapsing. Each collapse loses considerable distance, so it takes real skill and continuous attention to trim to best advantage. The crew who can do all this without direction leaves the skipper free to concentrate on tactics and helmsmanship.

In centerboard boats a good crew automatically raises the board on down-wind legs and lowers it prior to coming on the wind again.

One of the crew's main tests is his speed and ability at handling light sails, especially setting, dousing or jibing the spinnaker. The proper procedure for these operations has been discussed in detail in several books, or any experienced skipper can explain the process step by step. The crew should review, mentally, each step in the operation and think out all actions which each member must perform. Next, they must take time between races to practice, correcting errors and learning to work as a team. Soon it becomes automatic. If each crew member knows what his job is and understands each step to be taken, spinnaker handling becomes a pleasure.

It might seem that what we have already discussed gives the crew more than his share of responsibility. An experienced one, however, finds time to help in other ways. Being aware of the course, he looks for the next mark and, once it is located, warns the skipper against overstanding. He also keeps a weather eye open for wind shifts, stronger winds and the progress of competing boats. He tries to keep track of boats the skipper is particularly anxious to beat. The top crew knows the racing rules and warns of impending jams and of boats which have the right of way. Sometimes the skipper may fail to see them until too late, and a timely warning has averted many a foul. In boats having several crew members on board, only the most experienced one should take time off from sail trimming to act thus as advisor to the skipper. If every crew member did this, there would be the inevitable confusion of "too many chiefs and not enough Indians" and the actual handling of the boat and her sails would be neglected. A good crew man learns to work smoothly with other members of the crew and doesn't do things which another crew member can do better.

It is largely up to the skipper, however, to assign responsibility among his crew. He should let them all know which one will handle the jib, which the main, etc., and should assign each one a job for each standard maneuver. He should also designate one of the crew as another pair of eyes and advisor to him. Of course, any crew member who spots something which he feels has been overlooked and which will have a bearing on the race, should sing out. But even from the crew member who has been designated as advisor and lookout, too much talk can be distracting. A good crew member learns how much advice or information his skipper likes to receive and acts accordingly. He bears in mind that the final decision rests with the skipper, and after expressing an opinion and assuring himself that he has been heard, he doesn't press the point further. Above all, he talks only shop. Enthusiasm is fine but all talking in a race should pertain to the race and should help, not hinder, the success thereof. Otherwise, be quiet. And bear in mind that nothing burns up the average skipper more than optimistic chatter when things are going poorly or an overly apprehensive attitude when on top but being closely pressed.

This doesn't mean that the crew has to hide his own feelings about the race's progress, but they should be realistic and not based on fancy or wishful thinking. He should have a strong will to win and the ability to keep trying no matter how heavily the odds may seem to be stacked against success.

By taking a serious approach to the race and to his own job, the crew will have fun. That, after all, is why he is out there. And if the race is won, the good crew who has gone all out all the time gets the satisfaction which comes from knowing he was a vital member of the team which brought home the bacon. When his boat loses (as she must sometimes) he has the consolation which comes from having made a good try.

54

Consistency Wins in Series Racing

by C. STANLEY OGILVY

[1939]

THE DISTINCTION between the tactics of a single race and those of a series is not often fully recognized. In a race which is a single important fixture, the main object from the competitive standpoint is to win; second and third places don't amount to much. The theory of such a race is clearly to take any gamble that offers itself to get into first place. If, through some mischance, a good skipper finds five or six boats ahead of him, some of which he feels pretty sure are going to stay there, he usually decides that there isn't much use fighting it out for fifth or sixth; so he splits tacks or, if on a leeward leg, goes away by himself.

Even if the leading boats are on the "preferred" tack, the course which past experience has proved to be the favorable one, he must get away at any price and trust to luck that something may happen to benefit him. By sticking with the others, he cannot win; by going off alone, he may. Of course, the gamble may fail, in which case he comes in last. In this race, however, last is no worse than third or fifth, except, possibly, in its effect on the skipper's confidence. But to be apparently doomed to a place somewhere in the middle of the fleet, to take a flyer and to have it come off—by good luck, if you like, although it is always more than luck—is one of the ultimate thrills of yacht racing.

None of the above has anything to do with series strategy.

In a series, there is little or no premium on daily firsts; seconds and thirds are almost as good. With 20 boats in the race, a third place will improve any percentage under .900—and how many boats can boast a .900 at any time during a series? Yet many a skipper, not content to hold a hard-earned third place, has taken a chance, tried for first and failed, ending in a far worse position.

Consistency rather than brilliance wins every series. Although the winner may also have the largest number of daily firsts to his credit, this is by no means necessarily the case. All of us can recall race weeks in which some dark horse has created a sensation by winning the first two or three races, only to fall into obscurity later. It is surprising how often yesterday's winner finishes 12th today; gets, perhaps, a fourth tomorrow, fouls out the next day and winds up the series with another first. His erratic record is, of course, topped by that of the fellow who may have taken no first places but who has finished fairly well up day after day. In ordinary fleets, an average of third wins most series. The exceptions occur in fleets having two or three outstanding boats noticeably faster than the rest. Naturally, it does no good to average third if your most dangerous rival is consistently piling up firsts and seconds.

The accompanying table is made up of data taken from ten important series of the 1938 season, chosen at random. Records from widely scattered localities avoid any possible influence of local conditions. The results tabulated in the last column show that a comparatively poor daily average often wins a series, especially if the entry list is large.

The temptation to toss caution to the winds on the outside chance of winning one race has thrown many a potential series candidate out of the running. Probably you can recall having been through some experience like the following: You are in second place on the last leg, beating up to the finish. There are boats close behind you but what interests you far more is that the leader is not far ahead. That first place looks mighty good. The whole fleet is on the port tack, because under the shore there is usually a better breeze. The leader has been covering

TABLE OF WINNING AVERAGES IN TEN SERIES

Series (1938 unless otherwise stated)	Class or Type of Boat	Locality	No. Entries	No. Races	Name of Winning Boat and Skipper	Average Daily Place
Sears Bowl	Atlantic O.D.	Southport, Conn.	8	8	Pequot Y.C. Crew	3.2
California Midwinter Regatta (Feb. 1939)	6- Meters	Los Angeles, Cal.	9	5	*St. Francis*, V. Jervis	2.6
Intercollegiate Championship	Cape Cod Knockabouts	Wianno, Mass.	10	16	Harvard	3.6
Atlantic Coast Championship	Star	Riverside, Conn.	14	5	*Jubilee*, H. B. Atkin	3.8
Snipe Class Championship	Snipe	Lake Wawasee, Ind.	21	3	*Chasme*, Chas. Gabor	2.7
World's Championship	Star	San Diego, Cal.	22	5	*Pimm*, W. Von Hutschler	1.8
Class Season Championship	International O.D.	Long Island Sound	24	14	*Rascal*, Frank Campbell	3.5
Inland Lakes Regatta	Class E Scows	Lake Winnebago, Wis.	28	4	*Hurricane II*, W. E. Schons	4.0
Larchmont Race Week	Atlantic O.D.	Larchmont, N. Y.	42	6	*Ann*, Francis Page	5.5
Comet Class Championship	Comet	Lake Skaneateles, N. Y.	47	3	*Shu-Fly*, E. K. Merrill	3.7
					Average of averages	3.4

you carefully but now you tack, on a slightly more favorable
slant, and he lets you go. You fail to notice that he is working
farther into the same favorable slant, while you are gradually
being knocked off. You finally come back to the port tack just
as the leader and three other boats come over to the starboard
and, to your horror, you realize that those other three are now
ahead of you, too. It is against your racing principles to go
under their sterns so you go about again. But you are desperate
now and are tacking on all the wrong shifts; as you approach
the finish, two more boats appear from out of the blue and
cross the line ahead of you. As you wind up a rousing seventh,
the general gloom surrounding your ship is hardly lightened by
a member of your crew who takes this choice opportunity to
remind you that you were second not 20 minutes ago.

The moral, of course, is that it is just as important to cover
second, third or even fourth as it is to cover first. No one would
think of splitting tacks with the fleet while in first place; the
same should apply to any boat in the top group. Where the top
group ends and the fair-to-middling begins depends entirely on
the particular situation involved in each fleet and each series.
A general rule to follow in any midseason race of a long series
is: if finishing in your present position will lower your series
standing, use every means at your command to overtake the
fellow ahead; but if your present position will raise your series
standing, settle down to the job of holding that position. This
is a conservative method which will keep your standing on the
upgrade and should find you at the end of the season with a
most respectable score, perhaps the winning one.

There is only one time when the policy of "first or nothing,"
logical enough for a single regatta, is of any use in a series:
when a skipper is last and, consequently, has nothing to lose.
Even then, if he is only nominally last, as at the end of a badly
managed leeward leg with all the others bunched just ahead, it
may pay to work by them one by one rather than to take a wild
tack. But take the case of the skipper to whom the worst has
happened: he is over the line too soon and, by the time he gets
clear and starts again, the fleet is so far ahead that a stern

chase seems hopeless. His only chance is a wind hunt. The moral is: don't get into a position where it is impossible to re-cross the starting line *immediately* if recalled.

A skipper often finds himself rounding a mark about in the middle of the fleet, say in tenth place, with a windward leg ahead. There is nearly always a preferred tack and all the boats ahead are on it. An inexperienced skipper is inclined to take the other tack, merely for the sake of getting away from the leaders, but this usually amounts to handing them the race. For, in addition to whatever the disadvantage of the unfavorable tack, there is also the extreme difficulty of sailing a boat to her best advantage without a competitor near by. Even an expert is seldom willing to rely on his sense of the feel of the boat alone to tell him whether she is trimmed to perfection and balanced absolutely right. Only when others are racing alongside can he be sure he is getting the utmost out of his own boat.

What happens, then, to our hypothetical tenth boat if she is handled by an able skipper? He rounds the mark neatly, passing it close aboard at the end of the turn, and has his boat trimmed and organized for the windward leg *while rounding,* without a second's wasted time. By carrying out the maneuver efficiently, he may gain a length or two on some of his competitors and at the same time increase his chances of getting a free wind. Then he follows the crowd.

Before long, he has overhauled two boats which had reached well but could not hold their positions on the wind (every fleet has one or two such boats). A third competitor tacks to clear his wind; in doing so he is forced to give way to someone else and, finally, falls behind our skipper. Soon the going gets heavier; maybe somebody up ahead breaks down. "Can't quite see what the trouble is but it looks as if a halyard let go. . . . Glad we checked ours this morning. . . . Still breezing up. . . . Take the main in a hair and we'll catch number 27, he's not so good in a blow. . . . That's better, we're really moving now. . . . Ready about for the mark. . . . Look, a bad jam there! Blue boat hit the mark? No, white boat's withdrawing. . . . That makes us fifth. . . . Weather jib sheet, Bill, it's dragging over-

board." And so on, until pretty soon the race is over and our
boat has managed to pull a third or fourth out of the hat, just
by sticking to it and sailing carefully and hard. Ashore they say:
"The old so-and-so finished up in the money, as usual. How does
that bird do it? He was tenth around the first mark."

It is only by making the best of the bad breaks as well as the
good that a skipper can maintain a high average. If he can do
reasonably well on the bad days, the good days will take care
of themselves. Anyone can win a race given a good start and a
little luck along the way; the fellow who deserves the credit is
the one who pulls up from the ruck by sheer ability to make
his boat go faster than her competitors.

Because two or even three or four boats sometimes go into
the final race of a series practically tied on points, we often
think of that as the deciding race. The simple fact so often
overlooked is that every other race of the series was exactly as
decisive as this one. The series has already been won or lost
20 times over earlier in the season, in races which were sailed
carelessly because they did not seem so vital. The skipper who,
in a tough spot, says, "Tomorrow is another day—we'll do
better next time," is to be commended for his philosophy but
not for his racing strategy. One bad day can wreck a series, as
we all know through experience. The clever tactician gets his
boat in shape early in the season, enters the series with sails
and rigging well shaken down and knocks off a couple of firsts
during the races in which his rivals are still "tuning up." A high
standing built up early in the season is invaluable later on,
when the competition begins to tighten down.

A match race within a race doubtless has its place on the
last day of a series when two opponents are tied and the next
boat is far behind on points. But it is no uncommon thing to
see "dog fights" taking place between two boats during the early
part of a series. Is it worth while then to single out a pet rival,
covering or luffing when necessary to prevent her passing? The
answer is generally "no." Even though, since all races have
equal weight in the standings, it might at first glance seem

right to use the same methods in the first race as in the last, it is not difficult to see why this is not so.

In the first few races of almost any series, we simply don't know who is going to become our most dangerous competitor. We may think we know, but we are too often wrong. Regardless of reputations, every series has many potential winners before it starts. The only sound procedure is to sail your own race all through the early days of the series. If you let yourself be drawn into a tacking duel or luffing match, half the fleet may sail by, and somewhere in that group may be the ultimate winner of the series. Finishing in a respectable position behind one of the best boats is certainly preferable to beating that one and letting several other equally good ones through. The result of a single yacht race is usually even less predictable than that of most other sports, because of the greater number of variable factors involved. Who, then, can venture to predict the outcome of a whole series?

55

It's the Little Things That Count
in Yacht Racing

by C. STANLEY OGILVY

[1943]

THESE NOTES were written at an Army post a thousand miles
inland and a mile high; where brass once polished retains its shine
indefinitely, so great is the distance from the nearest salt water.
It would be difficult to find surroundings less conducive to
thoughts of yacht racing. Yet, the more adverse the circumstances, the more pleasant it is to call up memories of the sport,
and to discuss certain details which will be applicable when
next we swing away from the mooring.

Most racing discussions deal with rigging and tuning, tactical
maneuvers, the value of good sails well set, and the like. Here
we are going to take most of that for granted and deal only
with some of the apparently much less consequential "little
things," which are not nearly so unimportant as might be supposed. Many skippers are vaguely aware of the value of attending to details yet most of us never take the trouble to adopt
any system to guard against carelessness and its accompanying
misfortunes.

A stop watch seems to be an elementary requirement,
but . . . An International One Design on Long Island Sound,
sailed by one of the country's leading skippers, underwent an
embarrassing experience not long ago. There were three racing

timers aboard, theoretically enough for a small boat, but one was a chronic invalid, not to be trusted in a crisis. Somebody forgot to wind the second one, although part of his job before the start was complete charge of that watch. After running for a few minutes, it stopped and, in the tension of the last few minutes before any race, no one thought to wind and reset it on the preparatory gun because the third watch, worn by the skipper himself, was still functioning and was the one he ultimately depended on anyway. Everything might still have gone according to schedule but for one unhappy trifle: the skipper's watch was about two seconds fast when he checked it by the five-minute gun. He reset it accurately four minutes before the start, certainly an understandable but, as it turned out, a disastrous move. For the watch now read as if there were five minutes left when in reality there were only four, and what could be more natural than to forget to make the correction for the missing minute? The boat boomed across the line with a perfectly timed and executed start—exactly one minute late.

A good rule is to check all timers early enough so that they do not have to be touched after the 15- or, at latest, the 10-minute gun. At least one and preferably all of the timers should have a dial reading to 20 or 30 minutes. Particularly to be avoided are the five-minute non-repeating type, which have to be set on the preparatory gun. Five minutes before the start is no time to be fiddling with stop watches.

Someone may ask how the skipper mentioned above could have reset his timer four minutes before gunfire when the average committee has no four-minute signal. It's easy, if the weather is not too boisterous. All you have to do is hover around the committee boat within talking distance and listen: the timekeeper generally calls time every minute and frequently more often. Similarly, if you are checking watches on the gun of a class that starts before yours, it is a big help to be near enough to hear the ". . . four . . . three . . . two . . . one . . . FIRE!" which precedes the gun. By doing this, you will avoid any possible lag between the committee timer and the man who fires the gun, or between the gun and your own finger. Of course, this assumes that you race where several classes start in one regatta. If you are the first or only class, the best you can do is to catch the 10-minute gun accurately or else start your timers on shore by the Race Committee chronometer. This last is hard to do, because stop watches, which get such rough treatment in small boats, are rarely accurate enough to maintain time within a second for longer than about half an hour.

In every department of the race, but especially regarding start and course, it pays to make assurance doubly sure. Insist that every member of the crew read and understand the circular so that he has the course firmly in mind. If you are approaching a mark that looks like the right one, check before you round it; it may be a deceptively similar buoy near your own. You may be sure that the day you neglected to note from the instructions which way to round the outer mark, subconsciously figuring that you could follow the crowd, will be the one day that you'll get there first. A frantic search will reveal that your only circular blew overboard in the middle of that last jibe. So bring along all the circulars you can beg, borrow or steal from the club office, and have everyone study them.

There should be one man in the crew whom you can trust implicitly to act as an observer. He is the "eyes of the ship." His particular job is to keep you accurately informed, enpecially when sailing to windward, of the positions of your competitors, the relative speeds of the boats, the wind shifts that seem to be developing ahead (or astern), changes in the current, the whereabouts of the next mark—in short, all the hundred and one important matters that otherwise plague a skipper when he should be devoting his whole attention to sailing his boat. To be able to keep your eyes glued to the luff of the sail, or the foam at the lee rail, or whatever else it is your habit to sail by, with the satisfying knowledge that everything else is being competently taken care of, makes a perfectly astonishing difference in the speed of your boat. The difficulty, of course, is in obtaining a crewman with enough experience to be an observer. The ideal observer can even inform you of the proper tactical maneuvers to be made; but, if he is as good as that, he will pretty surely be racing a boat of his own.

It is depressingly easy to be late for the start or, if not actually late, to arrive at the starting area with too little time in hand. You should be there early enough to take a good look at the line and the first leg of the course, study the situation, and plan your campaign accordingly. Hair-raising last minute starts seldom pay. Everybody is so excited and disorganized that it takes half the first leg to get the boat and the crew down to business—and by that time the race is as good as lost.

If the regatta is at any distance from your home port, make every effort to sail there, weather permitting, rather than to pick up a tow. The extra hours afloat are just what you need to regain the feel of the boat. You will also have the time, during this leisurely sail to the line, to check all standing and running rigging, blocks, turnbuckles, and all the rest, being especially sure to turn in or tape all cotter pins. You will have another advantage over the fellow who does not sail to the race: during the morning, the wind may go through some significant changes which you are in an ideal position to observe. You will be familiar with the day's weather and able to predict or feel what is going to happen to the breeze during the race. Perhaps you may pass through the area in which the race will be sailed, giving you added knowledge of conditions on the course.

The importance of a well-trained and efficient crew is obvious. Be sure they are as well acquainted as you are with the boat's idiosyncrasies. They must know what *every* cleat is for, not only the principal ones. They must know where the winch handles go; where the spinnaker sheets hang; where to find the oil can or the sponge in a hurry. By the way, carry at least two sponges aboard if you use them at all; they go overboard with remarkable ease. The crew must also be good at keeping out of the way, and to this end should have assigned positions for each point of sailing. Insist that they wear some form of non-skid sneakers. And tell them to cut their finger nails before coming aboard. Constant contact with water separates the ends of the nails from the finger tips and softens them until they tear or break at the slightest provocation. Soft hands which blister after three good hauls on the mainsheet may be unavoidable at the beginning of the season, but the discomfort and annoyance of broken finger nails can easily be prevented.

In return for these considerations, you owe your crew some favors. Keep them happy. If someone is a confirmed cigarette addict, don't prohibit smoking for too long a stretch. Have enough slickers and sun hats aboard to supply those who forget to bring their own. An uncomfortable crew soon becomes irritable and sluggish. If it is discovered that there is no water aboard, everyone will instantly develop a burning thirst. Little things, psychological things, but they count.

Give yourself a break, too. Cater to your own particular fads. If you are a weight-saving addict, spare no pains to remove *all* extra weight from the boat. It will make you feel better and you'll therefore sail the boat faster, even though the weight might not make any real difference. If the tiller doesn't exactly suit you, change it for one that does. Some prefer a knob on the end; others wish they could saw the damned knob off. Some like them thick, some thin, some long, others short, some prefer mahogany, others ash—everyone has his own idea of how a tiller should look and feel. It is the one part of the boat with which the skipper is in constant contact, hour after hour and, if it is not just right, the permanent petty annoyance, though not consciously recognized, will none the less work a detriment to peace of mind, hence to performance.

The maintenance of a completely equipped racing machine implies frequent checking of everything. It is well to memorize a little list and reel it off to yourself before going aboard every race day. A typical small boat list might include sails, battens, circulars, stop watches, binoculars, sun glasses and drinking water. The point is to have a fixed, familiar list, so that it will not be possible to forget any one vital item. One of the best Star skippers in the East, who has a reputation for systematic thoroughness, discovered only half an hour before the start of a recent race that he had no battens aboard, simply because, unknown to him, his handy man had removed them from the boat for varnishing and then forgotten them. Even mainsails can be left at home in the excitement of a race day. It is sometimes possible to borrow from friendly competitors in such a crisis, but the delay involved in locating and fitting the spare equipment usually leaves so little time before the race that the start becomes a frenzied rush.

There are numerous other bits of gear that assume great importance under certain conditions—especially when they turn up missing. The bailing apparatus should be the right size and shape. If the boat is bailed with a can, have one aboard that fits the bilge so that a maximum quantity of water can be removed with the least lost motion. If you use a pump, keep it in functioning order. Some patented pumps seem to be out of commission most of the time; perhaps the best one to have on board is the old faithful galvanized plunger type. But, in any case, don't carry along a lot of broken-down plumbing.

Go over all the spare gear often, eliminating all unnecessary material. Don't allow the hardware locker to accumulate a mass of cast off junk that cannot possibly be used again. On the other hand, be sure you have one of each of the few items which common sense tells you ought to be carried. Pay particular attention to the sizes of spare shackles. On small boats, some of the frailer fittings are fastened with tiny shackles which are subject to breakage. When an accident occurs, a search usually uncovers no shackle small enough to pass through the hole in the fitting, and things have to be wired up. Minor breakdowns cannot always be avoided; quick and effective repairs save precious seconds.

If you sail by pennants or "flies," as is practically mandatory in light weather, have plenty of them on the shrouds and keep them fresh by renewing them every week or two. Cotton yarn is as good as useless for this purpose, and thread is almost invisible. Light weight torn (not cut) silk or rayon streamers do the best job. A telltale on each main shroud, one on each runner, and one on the permanent are not too many. Each will be useful on some point of sailing.

Finally, we come to a matter so fundamental that it can hardly be classed as a "little thing" and yet it seems to be taken far too much for granted: crossing the finish line the right way. Obvious, isn't it? Unless, as so often happens when least expected, the finish line is arranged in an unorthodox fashion. Perhaps it was so designed, or perhaps something went wrong and the stake boat wasn't moved in time, or an anchor dragged in a squall. Whatever the cause, somebody notices, as you approach the line, that the marker and committee boat are switched end for end. There is not much time left for consultation so you decide to "play it safe and cross it both ways," a maneuver resulting in as complicated a ring around the rosy as you would care to see, frequently throwing the committee into a state of utter confusion, to say nothing of the other boats, some of which are trying to do the same thing.

The best way to avoid this messy predicament is to make sure, before the race, exactly what the committee expects you to do at the finish. Some fleets sail special courses which regularly involve "backward" finish lines. If through some mishap the line is not shifted and there are no special rules, the committee is legally bound to honor only the finish which passes the marker on the same hand as all the other marks of the course —but committees have been known to deviate from this rule. If the worst happens and, because of uncertainty regarding how a freak finish will be handled, you feel you must cross the line both ways, there is one hint worth remembering. The decision (Appeal No. 13, July 28, 1941) of the North American Yacht Racing Union concerning passing marks on the proper hand makes it no longer necessary to "unwind yourself" in order to recross. Simply to sail straight across (either way), tack or jibe once and sail straight back now constitutes passing the marker first on the one hand and then on the other, and must count as a fair finish under anybody's decision.

56

Modern Team Racing Strategy

by WILLIAM S. COX

[1948]

WITH THE SPORT of yacht racing growing rapidly, more and more yachtsmen are being introduced to the most exciting type of racing—*team* racing. Quite often a team composed of supposedly superior skippers is beaten by a team of individually less able skippers, and the reason is usually because the beaten team used old-fashioned team tactics; while the winning team used modern team racing strategy.

Old-fashioned team tactics are primarily "man to man" tactics; whereby each skipper of a team pairs off with a predetermined opponent and endeavors to beat him around the course. Thus the team race degenerates immediately into a number of individual match races, and the only excuse for calling it a team race is the fact that each team emerges with a team score.

Modern team racing strategy calls for all members to work together in a concerted effort involving close cooperation among all hands, and with definite team strategy in mind. Team strategy actually begins before the preparatory gun, when the team captain sizes up the starting line and the first leg of the course, then instructs each teammate as to the kind of team start to make and where each member shall be at gunfire. The choice of a start usually boils down to one of the three types illustrated in the figures on the next page.

Shortly after the start, the next strategic decision comes up

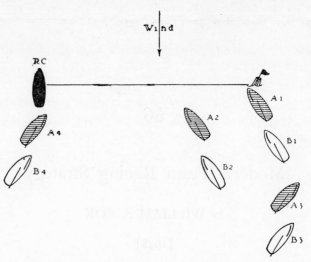

Match Race Start: Each boat picks a predetermined opponent and beats her across the line, regardless of gunfire.

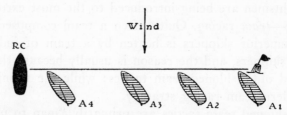

Geographic Start: All boats start evenly spaced, at predetermined positions along the line. This start is especially good when it is favorable to continue on the starboard tack.

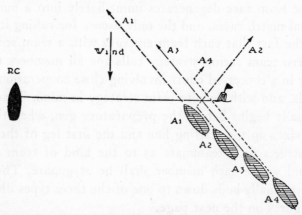

Follow the Leader Start: Especially good when local conditions favor coming about quickly onto the port tack. A_1 and A_3 block opponents from tacking, while A_2 and A_4 head for favorable water. A_3 permits A_2 to tack because they are teammates.

—whether the entire team should work together with defensive tactics or with offensive tactics. This decision is dictated by the positions of the boats, as to whether or not your team now has a winning combination. A simplified table of winning combinations is shown below, calculated for the usual team match of four boats to a side:

WINNING COMBINATIONS

If Your Team Has Positions	*To Win You Need at Least*
1st and 2nd	7th and 8th
1st and 3rd	6th and 8th
1st and 4th	5th and 8th or 6th and 7th
2nd and 3rd	4th and 8th or 5th and 7th
2nd and 4th	5th and 6th

This table should be carried by each member of your team so he will know quickly and accurately at all times exactly how

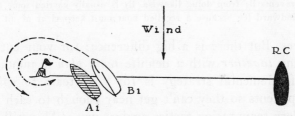

Intentional Recall: A₁ takes B₁ over early at leeway end of line, then restarts with B₁ in the "hopeless position." (Not to be tried around the windward starting mark!)

you stand, and to avoid possible mathematical error in adding points during the excitement of a race. The points are 8¼ for the winning boat, and 7, 6, 5, 4, 3, 2, 1, respectively, for the rest, the extra ¼ point for the winner making a tie impossible.

Let's suppose now that you are on Team A and that your side has the following positions: 1st, 3rd, 6th, and 8th. Schematically, reading from left to right, the positions of all eight boats would be:

A₁ B₁ A₂ B₂ B₃ A₃ B₄ A₄

A glance at the table of winning combinations tells each member of your team that you have a winning combination. Obviously, then, your team wants to employ defensive tactics, to maintain your winning combinations. But how?

The answer is quite simple, especially if the opposing skippers are exponents of old-fashioned team tactics, for your team begins at once to employ what looks like old-fashioned tactics

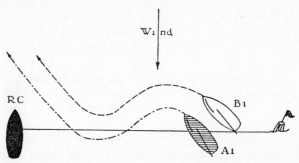

Kidnapping an Opponent: A_1 takes B_1 over the line early, restarts by dipping the line, yet prevents B_1 from doing likewise. B_1 is usually carried some distance up the windward leg because a recalled boat must keep clear of all others.

yourselves. But there is a big difference: for your entire team is working *together* with a definite *team plan* in mind.

The fundamental strategy is for your team to spread out your opponents so they can't get near enough to each other to use modern team-racing tactics against you. (This will be more fully explained later.) Accordingly, if on the windward leg, your team intentionally breaks up the race into four little match races:

$$(A_1 \quad B_1) \qquad (A_2 \quad B_2) \qquad (B_3 \quad A_3) \qquad (B_4 \quad A_4)$$

But that is not enough. Your team must make *sure* of your positions. So A_1 goes off with B_1 on one tack, while A_2 "invites" B_2 to take the opposite tack. Such an invitation can be extended by offering B_2 a peep of undisturbed wind on the desired tack, A_2 covering from a parallel position up to windward and forcing B_2 out to the lay line. When B_2 finally tacks for the mark, A_2 sits squarely on her wind the rest of the way. Meanwhile, A_1 has driven B_1 to the lay line in the opposite direction, with the result that, no matter which way the wind shifts, your team is assured of first place, and that precious ¼ point.

Back in the rear, A_3 and A_4 comprise an equally important part of the race, even though being beaten by their respective

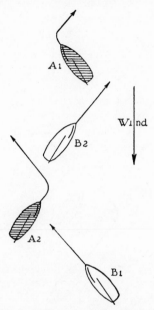

Swapping Partners: A_1 stops distant covering of B_1 in order to take B_2 off A_2. A_2 then covers B_1, thus giving Team A the upper hand in both pairings.

opponents, because either A_3 or A_4 can easily lose the race for your team if he doesn't cooperate in the general defensive strategy to maintain your winning combination. They can see that 1st and 3d are assured, as described above. It's up to them to make certain of 6th and 8th. Opponent B_4 must *not* be given a chance to finish ahead of A_3—or the race will be lost.

Accordingly, A_3 tries to sail the windward leg in reasonably fast time, while A_4 endeavors to make B_4 waste as much time as possible. A_4 can kill time with B_4 in several ways: (1) Go off on the unfavorable tack into rough water, head tide, poor wind conditions, etc. (2) Go about as often as possible in a series of short tacks. (3) Try occasional fake tacks and double-tacks.

In this way A₃ and A₄ assure victory for your team by putting so much distance between A₃ and B₄ that A₃ can never be "passed back" to finish behind B₄. A₄ has played the sacrificial

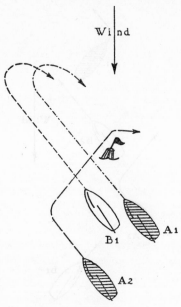

Riding Past a Mark on the Wind: A₁ rides B₁ well past the mark before tacking to round, enabling A₂ to pass B₁.

role—a bad last, intentionally. But A₄ deserves just as much credit from a team point of view as his clubmate who finished first. The entire team sailed a perfect race in making sure of maintaining a winning combination, once they had it.

The race outlined above illustrates the general principles of defensive team tactics. How to turn a losing combination into a winning combination, however, brings us to the principles of offensive team tactics.

In fleet racing, when one boat is attacking another single-handed from astern, the possible tactics are well known and somewhat limited in scope. But when two teammates work together against a single opponent—well, that's what makes team racing. These two-against-one combinations can be: (1) Two boats of the same side attacking an enemy from astern. (2) Two boats ahead of an enemy working together to hold him back or ride him off the course. (3) Two boats of the same side with a single enemy between them—the so-called sandwich position.

Proper choice of tactics depends partly on the team score and partly on the relative distances between boats. Occasionally

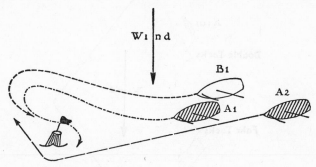

Riding Past a Mark Running Free: A_1 (who would have had to give room to B_1 at the buoy) luffs B_1 past the mark, then breaks the overlap while jibbing. A_2 goes into the lead.

there is just one obvious thing for a team to do. At other times there are two or more possibilities to choose from, in which case it is vital for your entire team to decide at once on the maneuver most likely to succeed. Your team captain can't quarterback this for you; the boats are too spread out. Yet your team as a whole must choose the right offensive maneuver. This comes only with study and experience.

To illustrate this problem of choosing the right maneuver, let's pretend that you are now on Team B, with the boats in the same order as before:

$$A_1 \quad B_1 \quad A_2 \quad B_2 \quad B_3 \quad A_3 \quad B_4 \quad A_4$$

Your team has a losing combination. What to do? Looking over the possibilities for two-against-one cooperation, you notice immediately the two "sandwich" formations bracketed herewith:

Sandwich I	Sandwich II

A_1 $(B_1$ A_2 $B_2)$ $(B_3$ A_3 $B_4)$ A_4

Only one "sandwich" need be resolved in your favor for you to win the race, 19 to 17¼. Should your team try to resolve both "sandwiches," or just one? If one, which?

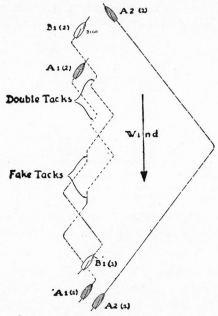

Intentional Slowdown: A_1 engages B_1 in a series of short tacks, fake tacks and double tacks to get clear. B_1 becomes so intent on covering A_1 that A_2 is forgotten. A_2 sails two long boards to pass B_1.

Let's analyze these "sandwiches" a little further. If B_3 and B_4 work together in "sandwich II" to shove A_3 to the bottom of the sandwich, there is real danger that A_4, unmolested in the meanwhile, may pass one of the B boats, which would be fatal.

Sandwich I, however, is made to order because a teammate (B_3) is the next boat, instead of an opponent. Sandwich I, therefore, holds the key to the race for your team. If B_1 can slow down A_2 just enough to let B_2 through, then your team will have 2nd, 3rd, 5th, and 7th, a winning combination.

It is important that this conclusion be reached simultaneously by all members of your team, for all must work together with the same fundamental strategy in mind. Accordingly, B_1 doubles back on her course and gets in position to bother A_2, so B_2 can attack A_2 with improved chances of getting through into 2nd place.

Meanwhile, having judged Sandwich II to be too risky, B_3 and B_4 cooperate with what is going on up ahead by shifting

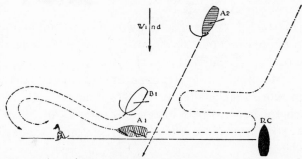

Guarding the Line: A_1, with spinnaker down and refusing to cross the line, lies in wait for B_1. With perfect timing, A_1 converges under B_1, then luffs B_1 sufficiently to let A_2 through. If A_1 should miss his timing, or if B_1 should swing sharply under A_1's stern, A_1 could still beat B_1 because of being only a few feet from the line.

to defensive tactics, in order to delay opponents A_3 and A_4 as much as possible, tack for tack, and the more the merrier. These time-killing maneuvers are important to your team to make sure of the winning combination of 2nd, 3rd, 5th, and 7th *after* Sandwich I is resolved in favor of your team:

$$A_1 \quad (B_2 \quad B_1 \quad A_2) \quad B_3 \quad A_3 \quad B_4 \quad A_4$$

If either B_3 or B_4 should not employ those time-killing maneuvers, one of the last two pairs (for instance, B_3 A_3) might easily finish ahead of all three boats of Sandwich I, in which case your team would be on the short end of 18 to $18\frac{1}{4}$, like this:

$$A_1 \quad B_3 \quad A_3 \quad (B_2 \quad B_1 \quad A_2) \quad B_4 \quad A_4$$

However, if enough time remained, your team could still make up for B_3's lack of cooperation by having B_2 and B_1 combine against A_2 to let B_4 come through. (This could only be accomplished safely if A_4 were not too close.) The race would then end in your favor, with the winning combination of 2nd, 4th, 5th and 6th:

$$A_1 \qquad B_3 \quad A_3 \qquad B_2 \quad B_1 \quad B_4 \quad A_2 \quad A_4$$

This finishing order bears practically no resemblance to the original positions A_1 B_1 A_2 B_2 B_3 A_3 B_4 A_4. Your Team B has sailed a masterful race, turning two losing combinations into two winning ones. Your only cause for regret was the performance of B_3, obviously the weak sister of your team, despite finishing first among your teammates! However, the rest of your team more than made up for B_3's boner.

So much for general principles and examples of offensive and defensive strategy. Now for some facts and suggestions in condensed form:

SCORING OF TEAM RACES: The best scoring system in each individual race is one point for every boat you beat, a point for finishing, and an extra ¼ point for the winner. For a *series* of team races there are two possible methods of scoring. (a) *Race by Race*. The winning team to be the first to win two races out of a possible three, three out of five, or four out of seven. Each race is scored separately. This method brings out the best in team racing. (b) *Total Points Carried Forward*. The number of races is specified in advance. Each team's points are added up, race by race, the team with the greater total at the end of the final race being the winner. This method should be discouraged because one fluky day, or a disablement or a disqualification, can easily decide the whole series.

TYPES OF TEAM RACES: (a) *Two two-boat teams*. Unsatisfactory because 1st place, with its extra ¼ point, will decide the race, 5¼ to 5, even though his teammate comes in last. (b) *Two three-boat teams*. The minimum for real team-racing tactics. The smallest winning margins are 11¼ to 10 or 11 to 10¼.

(c) *Two four-boat teams.* The best team race from every angle. The smallest winning margins are 18¼ to 18 and 19 to 17¼.

(d) *Three teams in one race.* This discourages true team tactics and is not real team racing. It would be better to hold a round-robin series with two teams meeting each other at a time.

TYPE OF BOAT: Any evenly-matched one-design class.

WINDWARD STARTS: Mandatory for the best team racing.

TYPE OF COURSE: Best of all is a right-triangle with the right angle at the windward mark. On the first round the triangle is completed; on the second round the 2nd mark is omitted (*i.e.,* a windward-leeward second round). Such a course provides every point of sailing—dead beat, beam reach, broad reach, and dead run, with a second windward leg for good measure.

TEAM CAPTAIN: Should have the final say in planning team starts, strategy, etc.

CO-CAPTAIN IN EACH BOAT: Strongly recommended, so the helmsman can concentrate on getting the most out of his boat while relying on the co-captain for a running account of what's happening and what to do for the good of the team.

MATHEMATICAL CONSIDERATIONS: In a match between two four-boat teams, calculation of the possible scoring combinations shows that (barring disablement or disqualification) there are 70 ways for a team to finish—35 ways of winning and, likewise, 35 ways of losing. Of the 35 ways to win, 28 of the 35 include 1st place. Thus the first boat to finish is theoretically on the winning side four times out of five. In practice, however, these odds do not quite hold because, after the leading boat finishes, the other team then has four boats to gang up on the remaining three. Under certain conditions this numerical advantage toward the end of a race may prove decisive.

If the first two boats to finish are of the same team, it is impossible for that team to lose, barring disablement or disqualification. This one-two finish is known as the "big double." If first place goes to your opponents, there are only seven ways out of 35 for your team to win, and six of these seven require both second and third places.

If a boat fouls out or is disabled, this makes your team lose the race (theoretically) four times out of five. In practice, the penalty is even more severe because your opponents then have a numerical advantage of four boats against your three. Last place causes your team to lose the race five times out of seven.

In view of these mathematical peculiarities it is most important for your team to avoid a withdrawal or disqualification, keep out of last place, and secure first place, in about that order.

If your team at any time needs two more points, you can win if only one of your boats passes an opponent because, when you gain a point, your opponents lose a point, a net gain of two for you.

When you and your teammates have a good working knowledge of modern team-racing strategy, you should be able to defeat teams that still use old-fashioned tactics and if you come up against another team that knows as much as you— well, that's the most fun of all!